P9-CEB-987

THE CONTEMPORARY DISCUSSION SERIES

THE MANY FACES OF RELIGION AND SOCIETY

The Many Faces of Religion and Society

EDITED BY
M. DARROL BRYANT
AND RITA H. MATARAGNON

A NEW ERA BOOK

PARAGON HOUSE PUBLISHERS
NEW YORK

Published in the United States by
Paragon House Publishers
2 Hammarskjold Plaza
New York, NY 10017

A New Ecumenical Research
    Association Book

"Civic Altruism and the Resacralization of
    the Political Order" by Richard L. Rubenstein
        © Richard L. Rubenstein, 1985

Library of Congress Cataloging in Publication Data
    Main entry under title:

    The Many faces of religion and society.

        (God, The Contemporary Discussion Series)
        includes index.
        1. Religion and sociology—Addresses, essays,
    lectures. I. Bryant, M. Darrol. II. Mataragnon,
    Rita H., 1947– . III. Series.
    BL60.M32 1984   291.1′71   84-26539
    ISBN 0-913757-20-9 (hardbound)
    ISBN 0-913757-21-7 (softbound)

Contents

INTRODUCTION

M. DARROL BRYANT
AND RITA H. MATARAGNON

The essays in this volume contribute to the growing discussion of the multiform relationships of religious faiths, institutions, ideas, and traditions to social life. When these topics are approached globally, it is not possible to speak in the singular about the relationship between religion and society. Rather, as these essays make clear, the relationships between religions and different societies are understood in different ways in different religions and different societies. This fact considerably complicates the task of the editors in writing an introduction to this volume, but it should also alert us to a very important feature of our current situation. At precisely the moment that we are recognizing the presence of different religions and societies on our planet we are also becoming more aware of our mutual interdependence and the fact that we increasingly share a common planetary future. Thus, the universal and the particular now come into a new configuration. This new configuration will be evident to the discriminating reader of these essays.

Although the essays in this volume range widely—from philosophical analyses of modern Western culture to Buddhist social philosphy—it is possible to set them against a common backdrop. They can all be seen in relation to a pervasive global situation. We are currently in the midst of a deep, widespread, and perhaps epochal transition. The scope of this transition is not limited to a few nations, it is global. In varying ways and to varying degrees, it touches all peoples, religions, societies, and cultures. Many believe it is a period of epochal transition. Located, as we are, within this period of transition, it is not yet possible to discern fully its shape, nor to fully know its consequences. But we are all aware—regardless of our judgments of the significance of this transition—that long-standing relationships between religion and society are undergoing enormous change. These essays reflect, in various ways, the impact of this time of transition.

This situation has given rise to a growing concern in the general public and renewed interest in scholarly circles to explore anew the theme of religion and society. Despite the often repeated assertion that religion would "wither away" in an increasingly technological civilization, religions persist and even reassert their presence—often in disconcerting ways. Why is this the case? What roles do different religions play in their respective social settings? Do all religions understand their social significance in the same way? Are there crucial contributions that religion can make to processes of social change? Can religiously inspired viewpoints help us to understand social dynamics and processes? These questions are explored in the essays in this volume and, we believe, some light is shed on them.

A distinctive feature of this collection is that the authors are not drawn from a single discipline, nor from a single philosophical perspective, nor even from a single continent. This may prove disconcerting, but it should be instructive. Although disciplinary, religious, philosophical, or geographical commonality might add a certain uniformity to the volume, it could also distort the reality of our global situation. Instead, the reader is invited to enter into different standpoints and to see particular issues from those positions. As difficult as this may seem, it should also enlarge our horizon for understanding the meaning and significance of this period of transition. This is precisely the experience of those who participated in the second New Ecumenical Research Association (New ERA) Conference on "God: The Contemporary Discussion," at which these papers were initially presented in a section that dealt with religion and society.

As scholars rooted in Buddhist, Christian, Hindu, and Jewish traditions and working out of social scientific, historical, philosophical, religious, and theological disciplines, the writers of these essays have selected their own focuses within this larger theme. The result we have before us is a number of different studies, all of which seek to illuminate particular issues, questions, or cases relevant to our time of transition. In this volume we have organized the essays around four themes that emerged from the essays themselves: religion and modernity: the social dimensions of religious traditions; religion and society; issues and cases; and religion and society: some future directions. Let us now briefly review the essays in each section, so the reader may have an initial orientation to what lies ahead.

In Part I, "Religion and Modernity," we have included the essays by Richard Rubenstein, a Jewish theologian and cultural analyst from the United States; Rita H. Mataragnon, a social psychologist from the Philippines; and Padmasiri de Silva, a Buddhist philosopher from Sri Lanka. These essays deal with distinct but interrelated aspects of the theme of religion and modernity. Professor Rubenstein offers a striking analysis of the impact of modernization on Western civilization and calls for the resacralization of the political order. Rubenstein thus dissents from secularization theorists in pointing to the necessity for societies, even modern and technological societies, to ground themselves in the sacred dimensions of life. Professor Mataragnon asks whether religion and modernization must move in opposite directions as some social scientists claim. She then examines the social scientific literature on this question to see if it has uncovered any significant correlations. Contrary to widespread belief that there is an obvious and significant correlation, she finds that the issue is still unresolved, that no significant correlations have been established. Professor de Silva examines Freudian psychotherapy—often a modern substitute for classic religious care of the soul—from a Buddhist perspective. Although he respects the contributions of Freud, de Silva raises crucial questions about the adequacy of the Freudian tradition to address the profound spiritual dimensions of the self's quest for enlightenment that are often latent in psychological disorders. De Silva suggests that this modern therapy might profit from an encounter with Buddhist analyses of the self.

In Part II, "Social Dimensions of Religious Traditions," we have included four essays that deal with three different religious traditions: Judaism, Buddhism, and Eastern Orthodox Christianity. Professor Manfred Vogel, a Jewish historian of religions, offers a phenomenological explication of the social dimension of faith in Judaism. His perhaps surprising conclusion is that a sovereign national state is necessary to the full realization of Judaism in its classic form. Only in this way, Vogel argues, can the horizontal or social dimensions of Judaism be realized. This view in Judaism stands in marked contrast with Gesche Tsepal's presentation of the meaning of liberation in Buddhism. A Tibetan Buddhist, Tsepal argues that in a Buddhist perspective suffering and social malaise are only overcome through an inward, spiritual liberation. Suffering arises not because of structural features of society, but because of an inward disorder that is overcome through religious discipline. Another angle of vision on Buddhism is provided in the essay by Professor Siddhi Butr-Indr. A philosopher and head of the Department of Human Relations at Chiang Mai in Thailand, Butr-Indr presents the humanitarian virtues of Buddhism that could, in his view, support universal brotherhood. And finally, in this section we have an essay by Dr. Constantine Tsirpanlis, a Greek Orthodox historian and theologian, which offers an exposition of the social and political dimensions of Orthodoxy. This strand of Christianity, argues Tsirpanlis, did not develop in a way that leads to the separation of church and state as a desirable goal. Instead, the thrust in Orthodoxy has been to attempt to suffuse the social and political orders with the power of transcendent love. Each of these essays, then, attempts to present the social dimension of a particular religious faith.

In Part III, "Religion and Society: Issues and Cases," the focus shifts to four studies that examine particular issues or cases that cast light on the relationship of religion and society in different cultural contexts. Professor Olusola Olukunle, a Nigerian professor of religious studies, examines the social uses and abuses of religion in developing, especially African, societies. The result is a sharp critique of the way in which religion has often served colonial and imperial interests rather than its own proper purposes. A parallel theme is explored in the essay by John St. John, but here in relation to English Christianity and society. Mr. St. John reviews the history of the relationship of faith to social issues in the English context and then calls for a new synthesis of political and religious consciousness to address the current social crisis. Dr. Gustavo Benavides, a Latin American student of religion who teaches in the United States, offers an important critical analysis of Latin American liberation theology. He views liberation theology as an attempt to deal with emerging sociopolitical realities in Latin American societies, but raises important questions about the adequacy of such responses. And in the final essay in this section, Professor Ninian Smart, a Scottish historian of religions who divides his time between the University of Lancaster and the University of California at Santa Barbara, examines the notion of liberation within Eastern and Western traditions. Professor Smart finds in these types of religious liberation an implicit critique of modern politics, which would have us believe that the whole of human destiny is linked to the life of modern national states. The religious types of liberation see the issue in broader terms. In these essays, then, we glimpse something of the complexity and variety that confronts us when we examine the relationships between religion and society.

In Part IV, "Religion and Society: Some Future Directions," we have included the essays by Helmut Fritzsche, a Lutheran theologian from East Germany; T. K. Oommen, a social scientist from Jawaharlal Nehru University in New Dehli; and M. Darrol Bryant, a Christian theologian teaching in Canada. Each of these essays proposes some new directions either for relating to developments within contemporary society (Fritzsche) or for understanding the relationships of religion to society (Oommen and Bryant). Professor Fritzsche argues that the modern focus on freedom as central to the social project has roots within the Judeo-Christian tradition. Nonetheless, modern societies turn in an increasingly secular direction. Christians, Fritzsche argues, should respect this turn even though they have a more complex notion of freedom than that current in secular societies. Speaking then from the context of a socialist society, he argues that Christian freedom embodies itself in *service* as the form freedom takes in our time. Another direction is proposed by T. K. Oommen, who calls for a new understanding of the divine, the human, and nature, in their mutual relationships. This, he argues, is necessary if we are to move beyond the antagonisms that too often characterize our present situation. For Oommen, the traditions of Hinduism offer important correctives to the overly dualistic tendencies of Western religions in relation to their social context. And finally, M. Darrol Bryant, a student of religion and culture, explores the thought of the little-known Christian social thinker Eugen Rosenstock-Huessy. Bryant finds that in Rosenstock-Huessy we have the beginnings of a fresh approach to discerning the life of the spirit in society. These more exploratory essays conclude the volume.

In these fourteen essays, then, many different aspects of the relationship between religion and society are explored. Using the insights of their particular disciplines and traditions, and acknowledging their distinctive commitments, each of the authors addresses the common issue of the place and role of religion in social life. Yet the content of each study is diverse since all writers deal with religions or societies they know best. Given all of these divergences, it is significant that a careful reading of this collection also reveals some point of convergence. All of the writers, with one exception, are agreed in their rejection of reductionism in their approaches to the study of religion and society. Religion, whatever its form, cannot be reduced to a function of some other sphere of culture. Reductionism has been a constant temptation in studies of the relationships between religion and society, but that temptation is resisted in these essays. In the most characteristic forms of reductionism, religion has been reduced to mere ideology or to a superstructure of underlying economic processes. But the writers, with one exception, though they come from differing religious traditions and disciplines, respect the integrity of religion as such. Religion is therefore regarded as having an integrity of its own whether that religion be Buddhism, Christianity, Hinduism, or Judaism. This respect for the integrity of religion is apparent even though most of the authors are sensitive to the impact of the social context on religious beliefs, practices, and institutions.

A second point of convergence shared by most of the writers in this volume is that religion will continue to play a vital role in the social life of humankind. This point too is often missing in contemporary literature, despite the abundant evidence provided by history and the sociology of religion for the continuing, albeit changing, role of religion in age after age. Although several of the writers call for new syntheses in religion, or for new directions, or for recoveries, they nonetheless acknowledge the crucial role that religion plays in social life. Thus, even though the fortunes of a particular religion in a particular place may wane, such fluctuations should not blind us to the spiritual and social vitality that is present within the religious traditions when we consider the matter from a global point of view. In saying this we are not affirming that every outburst of spiritual vitality and renewal is necessarily desirable, but simply that when we judge the state of religion it is best to consider the matter from a global perspective.

But when we explore the relationships of religion and society in a global perspective, we are not, as these essays make clear, in a territory that allows for easy generalizations. Instead, we find ourselves participating in the beginnings of a global conversation that requires us to acknowledge the partiality of our own views and the different assumptions and vantage points that others bring to the conversation. The differences between religions are real and have impressed themselves on the societies in which they have been significant; likewise, the differences between societies are significant and have made their impact upon the religions of the world. This multiform relationship between religion and society must, then, be respected if we are to deepen our understanding of the realities of our global situation. These essays will serve to instruct us in some of the currents and countercurrents that shape the impact that religious beliefs and practices have made—and continue to make— upon the world. They should also serve to instruct us in the requisite humility and sensitivity to multiformity that will be increasingly required of us all as we search for ways of living together on our common planet.

Part One
RELIGION AND MODERNITY

1

Civic Altruism and the Resacralization of the Political Order

RICHARD L. RUBENSTEIN

One of the most fundamental and intellectually fruitful distinctions made by Hegel in his political philosophy is that of state and society. Although Hegel's frequently misunderstood and misinterpreted doctrine of the state is exceedingly complex, for our purposes it is sufficient to note that his model for the state was the ancient polis. Hegel was under no illusion that the polis could be reconstituted in modern times, but there are certain characteristics of a state that are perennially indispensable to the maintenance of a genuine community, one of the most important being civic altruism. It was Hegel's opinion that, like the ancient polis, the ethical basis of a true state is solidarity rather than the quest for individual self-aggrandizement. Without the willingness of citizens to risk and sometimes give their lives for the security of the community, perhaps the most important act of civic altruism, no state could long endure. Hegel thus rejected the bourgeois conception of the state as the institution whose purpose is to render secure its citizens' pursuit of their individual self-interest. If any modern political institution can truly be regarded as a state as understood by Hegel, it would be characterized by universal altruism.[1]

According to Hegel, with the advent of the modern period, the public sphere began to differentiate itself into a class concerned with the management of public affairs and a class concerned "exclusively with their own affairs."[2] This class was the bourgeoisie, and it constituted the social basis of civil society, whose operative values Hegel saw as in profound tension with those of the state. Hegel acknowledged the extraordinary achievements and power of bourgeois society: "Civil society is the tremendous power which draws men into itself and claims from them that they work for it, owe everything to it, and do everything by its means."[3] Nevertheless, Hegel was under no illusions concerning the destructive egoism and individualism upon which civil society was ultimately based. As

3

citizens of the state, men relate to each other altruistically. As members of civil society, their relationships are, according to Hegel, motivated by universal egoism. Members of civil society have little choice but to treat their peers as a means to their own personal self-aggrandizement: ". . . individuals in their capacity as burghers in this state are private persons whose end is their own interest."[4] Put differently, in bourgeois civil society the private interests of the individual (or individual corporation) take precedence over the well-being of the commonwealth. Community threatens to explode as society comes to consist of a congery of self-regarding atoms whose interest in others is purely instrumental. There is absolutely nothing like the Confucian conception of the union of ethics and politics in bourgeois individualism.

Nevertheless, in spite of the tension between state and society, it was Hegel's conviction that the individualism of bourgeois society could be reconciled with the altruism of the political order, that the rights of man could be reconciled with the duties of the citizen. Unfortunately, at least in the West this conviction does not seem to have been validated by experience. To this day, the contradictory claims of state and society continue to beset modern men and women. Insofar as private individuals accord primacy to maximizing their personal interests, there appears to be little room for altruistic concern or involvement in the well-being of others, especially where large resources are at risk. On the contrary, socially irresponsible business behavior such as the following appears to be characteristic: dumping poisonous wastes as cheaply as possible with no concern for the health of the adjacent population; shutting down large-scale manufacturing operations, even when they are profitable, because they fail to yield a rate of return on investment deemed satisfactory;[5] and the manufacture of automobiles with fuel tanks known to be unsafe and possibly lethal because the estimated cost of legal judgments holding the company responsible for loss of life is calculated to be less than the cost of changing the fuel tank design.[6] These examples are meant to be illustrative rather than inclusive. Unfortunately, in the domain of business and commerce, cost-effectiveness rather than concern for the well-being of the community is normally the overriding imperative.

Because economic egoism in both its individual and corporate manifestations seems to be ultimately destructive of genuine community, one would imagine that it would be rejected by society out of hand. This was certainly the case before the beginning of the

4

modern period. In our times. however, such individualism has, more often than not, been interpreted by social theorists as in the long-range public interest. Sometimes the legitimation of individualism has been combined with faith in the benevolent effects of the self-regulating market economy, as in the thought of Adam Smith. In other legitimations civilization has been regarded as an evolutionary development whose viability depends on the ability of strong and gifted individuals to meet the test of survival in a mercilessly competitive struggle. I refer, of course, to Social Darwinism with its doctrine that survival of the fittest is nature's means of furthering the evolution of the species both within society and in the larger biological context.[7] Social Darwinism rejects altruism and elevates egoism to the status of a biological and social imperative. Given the perspective of Social Darwinism, those who fall by the wayside deserve their fate because they have failed nature's test. Social Darwinism naturalizes human society and uses the animal kingdom as the interpretative model for understanding human economic and social relationships, a view rejected by classic political theorists. Put differently, legitimation of self-aggrandizing individualism has been made possible by the naturalization and the radical desacralization of political values and institutions.

In no nation of the Western world has the elite of the business community consistently maintained a more important position in the leadership of public affairs than in the United States. This is undoubtedly partly due to the fact that even in the colonial period American civilization was fundamentally postfeudal. By the time of the founding of the Massachusetts Bay Colony, England was well on its way to becoming a predominantly bourgeois-capitalist society. Moreover, even in the seventeenth century, the ability to emigrate normally presupposed a degree of mobility available only to those who were emancipated from feudal obligations. Thus, the earliest emigrants to English North America were predominantly men and women whose livelihoods were dependent upon a market economy rather than the old subsistence economy of agrarian feudalism. This arrangement was obviously conducive to business leadership of the larger community.

Another factor making for the predominance of business leadership in America was the country's distinctive religious inheritance. Although the United States has been overwhelmingly Protestant since its inception, there was from the outset a profound difference between Protestantism in Europe and in the United States. In

Europe most people were members of the established church. In America the vast majority were dissenters, in spite of the establishment of the Anglican church in Virginia and the Congregational church in New England. The Congregational church was a dissenting church, as were the Presbyterians, Baptists, and Quakers. These four were the dominant American religious groups until the Revolutionary War.

In Europe it was generally assumed that every member of the community was automatically a member of the established church. In rural England, the parish was responsible for the rendering of assistance in times of distress. Those who were not members of the established church had no right to turn to the parish for sustenance when other means failed. In America the parish system did not last. Only Virginia and New England had it to begin with. What sociologists call "church-type religion" was not the predominant way religion was to develop in English-speaking North America. The early Puritan settlers regarded the church as the covenanted community of the select and the elect. The church in North America was inherently a church of outsiders who stood apart from the established church, and hence to a large extent from the established political order as well, except in New England.

As historian Oscar Handlin has observed, the dissenter had to rationalize his separateness.[8] In general he did this by emphasizing the elect character of his group and the decisive role it was destined to play in God's plan for the salvation of mankind. In addition to the element of dissent and the conviction of election, the hazardous ocean journey could be interpreted as a kind of baptismal experience in which the old European man was reborn as the new American Adam in the virginal and paradisiacal wilderness.

The dissenters' social location also tended to differ from that of the majority of their original compatriots. The emigrants tended to be townspeople, burghers, rather than peasants.[9] They were therefore predisposed to a certain element of rationality and system in the conduct of their affairs. As masterless men, they could not rely on a human external authority to impose order on their lives. Order was either self-imposed or disorder would rule, with predictable economic and social consequences.[10] The tendency toward rationality was also fostered by the fact that the townspeople were dependent upon a money economy long before the peasantry. Not surprisingly, the dissenters tended to value literacy far more than did the churches of the peasants and feudal lords.

6

Among the important consequences of the predominance of dissent in America was the fact that the laity achieved an importance in religious affairs in the New World that it did not have in the old. Convinced of their election, the dissenters stood in awe of no man-made office, whether it was that of the altar or the throne. God's elect were humanity's true aristocrats.

In the New World, the experience of election gave the businessman a sense of authority and dignity he had possessed in few other societies. In cultures as widely separated as ancient Greece, medieval Europe, and premodern Japan, there was a profound distrust of those engaged in commerce. Unlike the warrior, who was prepared to risk his life for the sake of his community, the merchant was distrusted because of his seemingly asocial pursuit of gain. The modern elevation of the businessman to primacy of status constitutes an extraordinary transvaluation of values. Nevertheless, it could not have occurred until the businessman's sense of his own status was radically transformed. No one is accorded high dignity who does not first perceive himself as worthy.

The Calvinist belief that prosperity in the pursuit of one's calling constituted a credible certification of election contributed decisively to the unprecedented sense of authority and dignity of the successful businessman. It must be remembered that before the bourgeois-capitalist era mere possession of wealth was normally insufficient to confer a sense of preeminent dignity and status on an individual. Since the dignity of other status groups, such as the clergy and nobility, had been religiously legitimated in premodern Europe, an effective claim to high status on the part of the commercial class had to be religiously legitimated as well. This was accomplished by the Calvinist doctrine of vocation and the experience of election. As Max Weber has pointed out, the Calvinist doctrine of double predestination left the individual bereft of a mediating institution capable of offering him credible assurance of election and salvation.[11] Because of the intolerable existential uncertainty this situation engendered, believers came to look for hints of election in the way an all-powerful, supramundane deity had guided them in the pursuit of their calling. Vocational success came to be the most credible sign that one had been elected to salvation. Within Calvinism the successful businessman came to enjoy a sense of divinely ordained status that gave him an authority and dignity in his own eyes the commercial classes had never before known. At the same time, the doctrine of double predestination carried with it a baleful evaluation of those who failed to prosper. Lack of prosperity was as credible a sign of eternal rejection by God as prosperity pointed to election. The successful businessman was assured of the primacy of his status and the dignity of his vocation; he was further assured that the indigent had been accounted worthless by the just and all-powerful deity. The new ethic was thus accompanied by a new harshness in the way the poor were regarded, a phenomenon amply documented by other scholars.[12]

A far-reaching consequence of the rise of lay authority within the church was the unprecedented elevation of the authority of a class that had never before enjoyed a comparable dignity. As the political order was desacralized and the connection between religion and public life severed, the bonds of community between persons tended to weaken. As religion became privatized, those who were convinced that they alone were elect citizens of the heavenly commonwealth, the only true commonwealth, saw little reason to create a genuinely altruistic commonwealth in the here and now. In the United States, the attenuation of communal bonds was aggravated by a lack of ethnic homogeneity in the general population.

As noted, a particularly striking example of the destruction of the bonds of community can be seen in the tendency of American-controlled multinational corporations to transfer operations to countries in which labor and other costs are significantly lower than in the United States with no concern for the unemployment such transfers cause at home. Until recently, corporations transferred manufacturing operations but left their office staffs intact. Currently, satellite technology makes it possible to transfer data- and word-processing operations from American urban centers, where office labor is relatively expensive, to the island nations of the Caribbean, where English-speaking office workers command far lower wages. The examples could continue, but the point is obvious. There are business enterprises prepared to accept the destruction of the economic base of whole communities in their native land if their operations can be rendered more profitable by moving elsewhere. This phenomenon has been worsened by the consolidation of large-scale enterprise. Corporate decisions concerning the closing or relocation of plants are made in distant offices by executives with no involvement in the life of the affected communities.[13]

The ascription of primacy to economic values is dangerous to a community in any age. In the age of the microprocessor revolution, it could prove to be an unprecedented disaster. According to a recent in-depth study in *Business Week* magazine, within the next two decades approximately 45 percent of all jobs in the United States, approximately forty-five million in number, will be displaced because of computerized automation.[14] A very significant number of those rendered workless in the current recession will never return to the jobs they lost. When one considers the worldwide implications of the microprocessor revolution; the demographic and social problems confronting the rapidly increasing populations of the developing nations; the rise of the nations of East Asia as successful industrial, technological, and economic competitors of the West, it becomes apparent that the unemployment crisis besetting the United States and other industrial nations is not merely a consequence of the current business downturn and will not be resolved by what will be characterized as an "economic recovery." On the contrary, each "recovery" since the 1960s has left the United States with a new definition of what constitutes an acceptable level of "normal unemployment."[15] Moreover, as "normal unemployment" continues to rise in the United States, millions of desperate Hispanics seek to enter the American labor market because of the even worse conditions facing them at home.

We could elaborate further on the nature of the economic and social problems confronting the United States and the Western world, but such elaboration is not necessary for our purposes. If this analysis has merit, it would appear that Hegel's distinction between the state and civil society as the respective domains of universal altruism and universal egoism has special relevance for our time, in spite of Hegel's misplaced optimism concerning the degree to which the realms could be reconciled. Unfortunately, if the realms cannot be reconciled, sooner or later we shall be confronted with large-scale social catastrophe. There are, for example, basically only two ways of solving the problem of unemployment: a jobs program in which the federal government becomes the guarantor of full employment, employing all whom private industry is unable to employ; and elimination of the unemployed by radical means. Indeed, one wonders whether there is any connection between the fact that unemployment has risen to its highest levels since the Great Depression and that responsible government officials are for the first time stating that the United States must be prepared to win a "protracted" nuclear war in which twenty million deaths would be considered a sustainable casualty rate.

Assuredly, there must be a better way to solve the growing

problem of unemployment than getting rid of the unemployed. We must, however, recognize how difficult it will be to implement any other solution. A government sponsored jobs program would have a profound effect on society. In all likelihood it would involve redistribution of the total national workload and possibly redistribution of resources as well. Such redistributive efforts have never been welcomed before and it is not likely that they will find easy acceptance even if the unemployment crisis becomes far worse than it is today.

Insofar as the United States retains a predominant bourgeois ideology, which accords primacy to economic over political values, redistribution will be resisted. As we have seen, the primacy of economic values has been religiously legitimated within American culture. Those who, at any level, regard their prosperity as certifying divine election are not likely to consent to share part of what they have for the poor, whom they believe God has in any event rejected.

The viability of a program involving redistribution is further weakened by the fact that most Americans do not see the political order as an end in itself, as did Aristotle, but as a means to private felicity. Most Americans would agree with John Locke: "The great and chief end of men uniting into commonwealths and putting themselves under government is the preservation of their property."[16] Locke's instrumental view of government accords with the Judeo-Christian view that the political order is justified only if it serves an end beyond itself. Although we cannot go into detail, there would appear to be a significant connection between the subordination of the political order to a divine plan in biblical religion and its subordination to the economic order in Locke and in bourgeois ideology. By contrast, the instrumental view of the political order does not accord with Aristotle's view: ". . . as all associations aim at some good, that one which is supreme will aim at the supreme good. That is the association which we call the Polis, and that type of association we call political."[17] Unlike Locke and Hobbes, Aristotle did not see the political order as an instrument of a higher good. It aims at the supreme good. Similarly, Hegel saw the state in noninstrumental terms. One of his most controversial statements held: "It is the way of God in the world, that there should be [literally, is] a state."[19] Although Hegel's statement has been taken as a glorification of state power, in reality Hegel was really interested in reminding us that it is the existence of a viable political order that makes both civilization and freedom possible. Hegel identified the state as "freedom universal and objective."[20] In civil society, self-realization implies lack of concern for the fate of one's peers, save as they serve one's interests. In a genuine political order, self-realization is mutual. It should, of course, be remembered that Hegel was fully cognizant of the shortcomings of actuality.

If Aristotle and Hegel are correct that the state aims at the highest good, there may be a limit to the degree to which the political order can be secularized, a limit we are rapidly approaching as the unemployment crisis worsens. In a purely secular order, there is simply no credible rationale for civic altruism. We are left with the economic egoism of civil society and universal mistrust and fear. Neither the purchase of handguns nor anticrime programs will halt the trend toward social atomization. In reality, there is no humane alternative to the rediscovery of civic altruism. Without it we are likely to be confronted with ever greater civic disorder punctuated by war and mass violence whose latent purpose can only be to eliminate physically those who have already been eliminated economically.

It is my conviction that some credible form of resacralization of the political order is indispensable. Given America's religious pluralism and the claims of so many of its denominations to possess exclusive religious truth, there is little likelihood that resacralization will be based upon unanimity of religious opinion. However, one of the most important lessons the civilizations of the Orient have to teach us may be that genuine coexistence of different religious traditions within a common community is altogether possible. Perhaps an even more important lesson is that the sacred need not necessarily be theistic in the way Western monotheistic exclusivism has been. In the West the dichotomy of sacred and secular has meant that without theism all relationships and obligations have been secularized. Having secularized our politics, the major political alternatives envisaged by Western intellectuals have been some form of free-enterprise capitalism, with its tendency toward economic egoism and social atomization, on the one hand, and some version of bureaucratically administered collectivism on the other. Regrettably, both secular alternatives can engender disastrous social consequences. We have noted some of the negative effects of economic egoism. Yet, as undesirable as the phenomenon may be, it still permits a measure of personal freedom that has wholly disappeared from secular, bureaucratically administered collectivism. Moreover, the horrors of Stalinism may not be accidental but intrinsic features of such collectivism. Where the only rationale for state behavior is the mythical future well-being of the group as a whole, there is, as we have learned, nothing to stop those in power from the most murderous demographic violence in the name of that ever-receding felicity. If technology produces the kind of social crisis we have outlined above, only a resacralization of human relations could offer a hopeful alternative to free-enterprise capitalism or bureaucratized collectivism.

It is ironic that at a time when so much attention is being paid by managers of American business enterprises to Japanese managerial methods, very little of the discussion has focused on Japanese religious and ethical teaching, although it is obvious that Japanese management techniques cannot be divorced from the fundamental ethos of Japanese society. There has been one significant exception, the publication of a mass market paperback edition of *A Book of Five Rings* by Miyamoto Musashi (1584–1645), a leading samurai of the Tokugawa period.[21] In his book Musashi notes the difference between the various Ways ("Michi" or "Do", or in Chinese "Tao"). According to Musashi, there is the Way of Confucius governing the Way of learning, the Way of salvation by the law of the Buddha, and the doctor's Way of healing. There is also Musashi's Way, the Way of the warrior, which he informs us is "the resolute acceptance of death."[22]

It would, however, be a mistake to see the Way of the warrior as one of either excessive morbidity or gratuitous longing for death. On the contrary, the real meaning of the Way of the warrior is the utterly selfless acceptance of the path of service in the performance of one's duty. The editor of *A Book of Five Rings* quotes Yamamoto Tsunenori, another seventeenth-century samurai, to clarify what Musashi meant by "resolute acceptance of death": "If you keep your spirit correct from morning to night, accustomed to the idea of death and resolved on death, and consider yourself a dead body, thus becoming one with the Way of the warrior, you can pass through life with no possibility of failure and perform your office properly."[23] Clearly, the Way of the warrior precludes egoistic self-preoccupation and concern for anything whatsoever but the discharge of one's duty. Paradoxically, the warrior who is resolute in his acceptance of death is far more likely to survive a continual round of life-and-death struggles than the self-preoccupied warrior.

Musashi knew whereof he wrote. By the age of thirty, he had killed over sixty opponents in duels. Yet, he was no brute. He had a profound feeling for art and poetry and was deeply religious. He understood his Way to be supremely honorable in his society and was utterly faithful to it. Put differently, for Musashi his Way was holy even unto death. He wrote *A Book of Five Rings* while living in a cave a few weeks before his death. We might note that for Musashi there is a Way for every meaningful human role.

It is not our purpose to enter into the complicated question of the extent to which the religious traditions of the Orient influenced Musashi, although it is clear that Confucian, Taoist, and Buddhist elements are present. We need only note that for Musashi the Way of the warrior was sacred without being theistic. This is apparent in the last book of *A Book of Five Rings*: "The Book of the Void." It is brief and deserves to be quoted extensively:

The Ni To Ichi Way of Strategy is recorded in this Book of the Void.

What is called the spirit of the void is where there is nothing. It is not included in man's knowledge. Of course the void is nothingness. By knowing that things exist, you can know that which does not exist. That is the void.

People in this world look at things mistakenly, and think that what they do not understand must be the void. This is not the true void. It is bewilderment.. . . .

. . . To attain the Way of strategy as a warrior you must study fully other martial arts and not deviate even a little from the Way of the warrior. With your spirit settled, accumulate practice day by day, and hour by hour. Polish the twofold spirit heart and mind, and sharpen the twofold gaze perception and sight. When your spirit is not the least clouded, when the clouds of bewilderment clear away, there is the true void. . . .

In the void is virtue, and no evil. Wisdom has existence, principle has existence, spirit is nothingness.[24]

It is interesting to note that Musashi wrote his meditation on the void within weeks of his death, an indication of the fundamental seriousness with which he wrote. There is irony in the way Musashi's work reached the American mass market. In their quest to understand Japan's managerial success, well-informed American corporate managers have discovered that *A Book of Five Rings* serves as a guide for contemporary Japanese business executives. The Way of the samurai has become the Way of the business executive. Having attempted to uncover the secret of Japanese managerial technique to enhance their own economic self-interest, American executives have come upon a guide that is thoroughly imbued with the spirit of nontheistic, mystical selflessness. If the American executives who read this book attempt to emulate their successful Japanese counterparts, they will be compelled to change more than their managerial techniques; they will have no choice but to change themselves and their fundamental values. There is no place for egoistic self-enhancement in Musashi's Way.

The intention of the American businessmen who have turned to works on Japan has been to find a technique with which to meet Japanese competition. Ironically, there is no technique to master. Like Musashi, they will have to learn to find and be faithful to their Way and they will have to learn, as did Musashi, that "in the void there is virtue and no evil." This will require a conversion, not from Christianity to Buddhism, Confucianism, or Taoism, but within themselves and their culture as Christians, for they can no more start wholly anew than can other civilized men. They must build on who they are and what they have been. For the first time, they have come into contact and competition with the East in a way in which everything is at risk. Of necessity, they will be changed by that contact.

Although I can offer no blueprint for the form the resacralization of politics could take in the West, it is possible to give expression to what resacralization could mean: put simply, to sacralize an institution or a domain of activity is to accord ultimacy to it. This was clearly understood by Musashi, who accorded ultimacy to the Way of the samurai. As he makes unmistakably clear, even life itself must be subordinated to the Way. One may object and say that to accord ultimacy to the political order is a form of idolatry. This certainly has been the perennial conviction of the Western religious tradition, a conviction that contributed greatly to the long-range secularization of Western politics. It can, however, be argued that the political order deserves ultimacy because it is that which makes possible the distinctively human form of existence as distinguished from that of animal existence. That is why the ruler and the warrior have historically been accorded greater respect than the merchant. It is the political order that enables men to create a physical and cultural space in which they can protect themselves from the ravages of both physical nature and the worst aspects of human nature, thereby forming the basis of civilization. We know what happens to men and women when the political order breaks down or becomes impotent.

Since the political order alone makes civilization possible, it alone must be regarded as self-validating and self-legitimating. That is why the institution of divine kingship so long commanded the loyalties of men in widely scattered cultures. This is also why Aristotle saw the polis as aiming at the highest good and why Hegel claimed, "It is the way of God in the world that there should be a state." Even the hermit who utterly flees the society of men is in his use of knowledge, his prayers, his memories, and his meditations the child of the political order. To resacralize the political order is merely to come to understand the true nature of the political order and to abandon the Way of the bourgeois for that of the citizen. Of special importance is the fact that if membership in the political order were regarded as the highest good, no citizen would be regarded as superfluous because he or she had been rendered vocationally redundant by technology. The first concern of the community would be to abort the drift toward wasted lives on the part of those whose jobs had, through no fault of their own, disappeared.

Briefly stated, the resacralization of politics would mean the end of economic egoism and the restoration of shared obligation within the community. Compare the samurai's selfless commitment to his Way with the concept given expression by Adam Smith—and currently enjoying renewed respectability—of why men perform their tasks: "It is not from the benevolence of the butcher, the brewer, or the baker that we expect our dinner, but from their regard to their own interest. We address ourselves, not to their humanity but to their self-love, and never talk to them of our necessities but of their advantages."[25] There is an optimistic component in Smith's thinking that his successors did not share. Implicit in his thinking was the view that the sum total of private selfishness could somehow yield the common good. Ironically, if American executives continue to act out of egoistic self-love, they will lose that which they prize most, their ability to win the contest of life in their chosen field of endeavor. They will be no match for those who are selflessly committed to their Way not out of self-interest but because of the ultimacy of that obligation. The resacralization of politics means at the very least a selfless commitment to the common good, an end to the privatism, self-indulgence, and self-preoccupation that so destructively besets contemporary society.

Conclusion

It is easier to discern the need for resacralization than to predict with confidence when and how it will come about. That is not my purpose in writing. I can do no more than analyze the increasingly problematic character of secularization and to point to what must eventually follow. America remains both a young and a rapidly changing country. Sooner or later the sacred will find its place in American life. When it does, it is my conviction that we will understand it as the same ultimate reality as the holy nothingness of the Western mystics, the *en sof* of the kabbalists, and Miyamoto Musashi's void.

═══ NOTES ═══

1. Shlomo Avineri, *Hegel's Theory of the Modern State* (Cambridge: Cambridge University Press, 1972), 134–35.

2. Georg W. F. Hegel, *Political Writings,* trans. T. M. Knox (New York: Garland Publishing, 1984), 202.

3. Georg W. F. Hegel, *Philosophy of Right,* trans. T. M. Knox (Oxford: Clarendon, 1942), addition to par. 238.

4. Hegel, *Philosophy of Right,* par. 187.

5. Carol Teich Adams, "The Flight of Jobs and Capital: Prospects for Grassroots Action," *Community and Capital in Conflict: Plant Closings and Job Loss,* ed. John C. Raines, Lenora E. Berson, and David McL. Gracie (Philadelphia: Temple University Press, 1982), 12–13; see also Barry Bluestone, "Deindustrialization and the Abandonment of Community," *Community and Capital in Conflict,* 38–61.

6. The company in question is the Ford Motor Company. The car with the defective gas tank was the Pinto. See "Ford Study: Death, Injury Cheaper than Fixing Cars," *Tallahassee Democrat,* October 14, 1979. This was a *Chicago Tribune* wire service dispatch.

7. Richard L. Rubenstein, *The Age of Triage: Fear and Hope in An Overcrowded World* (Boston: Beacon Press, 1983), 217–23.

8. Oscar Handlin, *The Uprooted,* 2d ed. (Boston: Little, Brown, 1973).

9. Richard H. Tawney, *Religion and the Rise of Capitalism* (London: J. Murray, 1926), 197ff.

10. Christopher Hill, *The World Turned Upside Down: Radical Ideas During the English Revolution* (London: Temple Smith, 1972), 39–56.

11. Max Weber, *The Protestant Ethic and the Spirit of Capitalism,* trans. Talcott Parsons (New York: Scribner, 1958), 110 ff.

12. Rubenstein, *The Age of Triage,* 56–103.

13. Adams, "The Flight of Jobs and Capital."

14. "The Speedup in Automation," *Business Week,* August 3, 1981.

15. For a visual representation of this phenomenon see the charts on "The State of the Economy," *New York Times,* October 29, 1982, p. 11. The charts on unemployment use data supplied by the Bureau of Labor Statistics.

16. John Locke, *Two Treatises of Government,* book 2, chap. 9, 124.

17. Aristotle, *The Politics,* book 1, chap. 1.

18. Hegel, *Philosophy of Right,* addition to par. 258.

19. Walter Kaufman, ed., *Hegel's Political Philosophy* (New York: Atherton Press, 1970), 279.

20. Hegel, *Philosophy of Right,* par. 33.

21. Miyamoto Musashi, *A Book of Five Rings,* trans. Victor Harris (Woodstock, N.Y.: Overlook Press, 1974).

22. Musashi, 38.

23. Yamamoto Tsuncnori, *Hidden Leaves* (Ha Gakure) cited in the notes to Musashi, *A Book of Five Rings,* 39.

24. Musashi, 95.

25. Adam Smith, *The Wealth of Nations* (Harmondsworth, Middlesex: Penguin, 1974), 119.

Modernization and Religion: Must They Move in Different Directions?
RITA H. MATARAGNON

The term *modernization* has been popularly used in the study of social change despite its lack of a consensual definition, conceptual clarity, and precision. The appeal of the term apparently lies in its capacity to evoke generalized, universalistic images of an evolutionary process moving from one set of attributes called traditional to another set of attributes called modern.

Although a distinction is properly made between modernization (a process or the product of a process) and modernity or modernism (a set of attributes), it is clear that the study of modernization would ultimately have to rely on the variable of modernity or modernism, which is the more tractable and measurable variable. "Changes in the proportion of people holding modern values, or changes in the extent to which individuals have gone modern constitute modernization."[1]

Indeed, one of the undisputed assumptions in modernization theory and research is that there are certain characteristics and behaviors that can be identified for the modern man, i.e., a class of attributes called modernity or modernism. The question is: does this class of attributes include a decreased interest in, or even disavowal of, religion? Do individuals in a modernizing society become less religious? Does modernization necessarily move in a direction away from religion?

Modernization and Religion: Ambiguity of Relationship

An investigator interested in establishing the relationship between modernization and religion soon discovers, to his surprise, a virtual absence of empirical evidence that directly relates modernization to religion or vice versa. Furthermore, an examination of the tangential contexts in which religion is mentioned in modernization studies suggests a serious ambiguity in the relationship between modernization and religion. It appears that the problem is not just a matter of the magnitude of relationship, but the nature of the relationship.

In several studies in which the components comprising a measure of modernity are listed, religion or religiosity is cited as one component. Typically, a measure of modernity is developed through item analysis: to identify salient characteristics, items that comprise the different components are initially scored in what is *felt* to be the modern direction and correlations are then computed between each item and the total score to determine which ones are more highly related to an overall measure of modernization.[2] Although in some cases respondents are employed to judge which response constitutes the modern direction of each item, the fact remains that subjective judgment is used to determine that religious behavior is more unmodern. Since the measurement of modernity becomes its operational definition, if the items on religion are significantly correlated with the total score and the items are adopted, an inverse relation between modernity and religion becomes automatic. The original basis, however, was intuitive.

To give a flavor of religious components in the modernity or modernism scale, the following are offered as examples. Kahl posited fourteen dimensions in which attitudes may change with modernization.[3] One of them was "low religiosity." Inkeles started with thirty-three themes, which included, "religious causality" and "religious-secular orientation." Although these themes did not comprise the final salient characteristics, several of the final chosen themes could be tangentially related to religiosity—faith in science and medicine rather than fatalism, subjective efficacy, or belief in man's control over the environment. Inkeles's final shortened scale of ten items included this one characteristic of the modern man: he is willing to acknowledge that a man can be good without being religious.[4] Schnaiberg included among his Modernism Items a short religiosity index in which items concerned type of marriage, frequency of prayer, and length of fasting.[5] Finally, Stephenson's culturally derived Modernism-Traditionism Scale included religion as one of the seven value areas. It must be noted that although the judgments about the direction of modernism for each item were derived from indigenous judges, the seven "value areas" were determined as bases for classification prior to judging. Using a Guttman scale, Stephenson also showed that among the seven value areas religion is the next-to-the-last area to be changed, i.e., it is not so vulnerable as opinions about innovation and education.[6]

It can be readily seen that scholars and laymen alike often intuitively see an inverse relationship between modernization and religion, or modernity and religiosity. This is especially evident in the tendency of many, though not all, investigators to include at least initially a component of religion or religiosity among the areas of attitudinal and value changes expected to be affected by modernization processes. It is also reflected on the part of scholars in their choice of the unreligious attitude or behavior as "the more modern one." Although in some careful studies the religiosity component does not come out as a critical factor, still the fact that certain areas are chosen and not others reveals underlying assumptions and value judgments about the end-state of modernization.

Although one does not get much insight from correlating modernity and religiosity if the latter were a subsumed component and therefore part of the definition of the former, this state of affairs, if uniform, would at least leave no doubt about the nature of the relationship between modernization and religion. However, the relationship is apparently more elusive than that. First, the studies that initially included religion as a component have yielded equivocal outcomes in their eventual enumeration of critical or salient components. In some, religion has weak, marginal significance, whereas in others it provides no contribution whatsoever to overall modernity.

Second, there is no explicit agreement that religion or religiosity is under the rubric of modernization or modernity rather than an external variable that affects or is affected by modernization. A number of studies have used religion, or changes in religious values, as an intervening variable to explain or interpret the effects of modernizing structures on behavioral changes. For instance, Coombs and Freedman concluded that changes in familial and religious values mediate between urbanization and family life.[7] As Fawcett has pointed out, prominent among the themes that relate modernization processes to fertility change are the effects of changes in cultural and religious values.[8]

The shifting back and forth of religion as a subsumed variable under modernity or as an external variable to be correlated with modernity partly reflects the theoretical imprecision of the modernization concept, something for which it has often been criticized. It is perhaps worth noting, though, that religion, whether subsumed under the modernity rubric or treated as an externally correlated variable, does not seem to have the same strength, consistency, and centrality other components of modernity show, such as openness to change and subjective efficacy. In fact, the latter two are never treated as external variables but always make up part of the definition.

Thus, the supposed inverse relation of religion to modernization can be said to be more intuitive than empirical. There is little direct evidence and little serious attention to a formal relationship between modernization and religion. References to a "relationship" are frequently assumed or inferred from other variables that are tangential to religion, such as fatalism, time orientation, and subjective efficacy.

Measurement Problems

Where religion/religiosity has been included as a component or external intervening variable, operational definitions and measurements of this variable have been wildly discrepant. The following are examples in Goldberg's study. Turkish women were asked, "How often do you pray? Do you fast during Ramadan?" The same questions were asked of the women about their husbands, along with "How often does he go to the mosque?" Mexican women were asked about themselves and their husbands: "How often do you (or does he) go to mass?" "How often do you take communion?" "How often do you pray outside of church?" "What type of religious instruction have you had?" "Have you ever gone to a religious school?"[9]

Consider the religiosity index of Schnaiberg, also used in a study of Turkish women, which had the following items: (1) Couple has had a civil marriage only; (2) Wife prays less than five times a day; (3) Wife does not fast for the entire period of Ramadan.[10] Another study by Bose, this time on Indian peasants, establishes a negative relationship between religious inclination and adoption of innovation just on the basis of one item about religion: "After death the soul is not destroyed but passes on to the next world."[11] Another single item for a whole component of religion, found in Stephenson's Modernism-Traditionism Scale, was: "The old Bible (the King James Version) is the only true word of God."[12] Still another study by Coombs and Freedman on Taiwanese women defined a religiosity index in terms of observance of ceremonies for ancestors.[13]

Although many investigators do not publish their questionnaires, the ones that have been published suggest an explanation for the status of the religion/religiosity variable in modernization research. Commonly the most traditional belief or the most conventional ritual is represented. The very broad and rich concept of religion, with its endless variations of personal beliefs and forms of observation and participation, is tragically oversimplified. Not only are there not enough items exploring cognitive ideas and overt behaviors, there are virtually no items on affect or feelings about the supernatural and on one's relationship with the supernatural. In general, there is a significant lack of content validity in the measure of religion/religiosity as a variable in modernization research. Notwithstanding, data based on one or two statements are often used in asserting relationships between religiosity and modernity.

Is religion merely the observance of religious ceremonies? Is it merely the subscription to the King James Bible as the Word of God? Is it having a religious wedding ceremony? These are traditional expressions of religiosity and are likely to be present in individuals who came from traditional families that expect them to toe the line with regard to basic practices. Religiosity measured in this simplistic manner is frequently correlated with familism. Furthermore, since the type of religiosity tapped involves the observance of highly traditional practices, it does not allow a fair test of personal religiosity, which could take more serious forms such as "spirituality," "faith," "strength of belief," "significance of God in one's life."

In this connection, it is important to point out the distinction between tradition and traditionalism. Religion is often associated with tradition. People talk of religion and tradition together, or in some cases even of religious traditions. But religion need not be traditional in its expression. "Tradition refers to the beliefs and practices handed down from the past; as we reinterpret our past, our traditions change. In contrast, traditionalism glorifies past beliefs and practices as immutable. Traditionalists see tradition as static; they urge that men do things only as they have been done before. Traditionalism, by virtue of its hostility to innovation, is clearly antithetical to the development of modernization; traditions, which are constantly subject to reinterpretation and modification, constitute no such barrier."[14]

Misplaced Polarities

In an oft-cited article, Gusfield raises the point that tradition and modernity are misplaced polarities in the study of social change.[15] The same thing could be said about religion and modernity. Gusfield presented seven fallacies in the assumption of the tradition-modernity polarity. These fallacies can be examined in the context of the religious tradition. Although several of these fallacies overlap with each other, (notably fallacies four, five, six, and seven), they will be presented one by one, as they were in Gusfield's analysis.

Fallacy one is that developing societies have been static societies. Religion, as it is present in any culture, has not always existed in its present form. Conquests of foreign powers and the growth of social and cultural movements have deeply influenced religious beliefs. In the same way it can be expected that modernizing influences will continue to influence religion but not destroy it.

Fallacy two is that traditional culture is a consistent body of norms and values. The distinction between popular or folk religion and the religion of the literate elite have coexisted in many cultures, making it difficult to characterize "the religion" in a given society. Individuals who subscribe to the same religion in one culture may show wide variation with regard to their specific religious beliefs and practices. There is room for both the traditional and the modern.

Fallacy three is that traditional society is a homogeneous social structure. Although Weber referred to "the Protestant ethic," the specific sects that carried the ethic were by no means typical of all Protestant groups. The Jews in Europe, the Muslims in West Africa, the Chinese in Southeast Asia, the Indians in East Africa—all are examples of groups whose marginality has spurred them toward entrepreneurial achievement. In India, the Parsees and Jains have been potent carriers of economic innovation and the development of large-scale industrial production. Asian religions, viewed by many Westerners as an obstacle to modernization, have in many cases proven to be capable of positive adaptation to social change.[16] What is characteristic of all these communities, according to McClelland, "is an intense religiously based feeling that they are superior to other people around them and that in one sense or another they hold the key to salvation."[17]

Fallacy four is that old traditions are replaced by new changes. "The acceptance of a new product, a new religion, a new mode of

23

decision-making does not necessarily lead to the disappearance of the older form."[18] Paganism and Catholicism have often been accommodated together in a new form of ritualism. Many modern schools teach science and religion side by side. Interaction results in fusion and mutual penetration. Far from being replaced, religion has been the guardian of culture and civilization across the centuries. It has built schools, hospitals, and community centers. It continues to be a repository of all that is best and enduring in a culture, a reflection of its *zeitgeist* and stage of development.

Fallacy five is that traditional and modern forms are always in conflict. The picture of a conflicted society undergoing development or of a tormented individual choosing between traditional and modern options does not seem to hold. The "traditional" society often contains sufficient diversity of content to allow it to accept some and refuse other components of modernization. Japan is unlike the West in the ways in which feudalism and industrialization have been fused to promote growth. A collectivist orientation and commitment to emperor and family also allowed it to reject the individualism of the West. In individuals, fusion as well as compartmentalization allow a sane adjustment to modernization. Modern forms of communication and transportation allow him better access to religious activities. Role inconsistencies are tolerated by compartmentalization. In the words of the famous informant who told the British anthropologist, "When I put on my shirt and go to the factory I put off my caste."[19] Inkeles and Smith's study on personal adjustment of urban and rural dwellers in each instance compares favorably on psychosomatic symptoms with control samples of the rural population. The notion of psychic stress in urban life is probably due not so much to an incorrect view of city life as to a mistaken image of relative security and emotional support in traditional village life.[20]

Fallacy six is that tradition and modernity are mutually exclusive systems. Religion ranks with the extended family as the institution most often identified as both an obstacle to economic development and a victim of the same. As has been pointed out under *Measurement Problems,* this is because religion has always been operationally defined as the traditional expression of religion. "Systematic evidence for this proposition is, however, much less ample than one might imagine."[21] The caste system in Indian life has been exaggerated as an impediment to economic growth through failure to consider its role in the division of labor and in caste mobility as an impetus to growth.

Fallacy seven is that modernizing processes weaken traditions. Modernized structures, especially mass media, allow the rapid dissemination and reinforcement of whatever are the predominant values of the society. People are discriminating about what is meaningful to them and what impinges on important aspects of their lives. Mass media can broadcast propaganda incessantly, but if friends and relatives preach different values, the mass media are not likely to win. "The persistence of belief in God in countries where atheist propaganda has gone on for decades is a case in point."[22]

The trickle effect of ideas from the accepted indigenous elite to the masses increases rapidly with modernization. Thus, Srinivas contends that, whereas higher social levels appear to be "Westernizing" their life-styles, lower and middle levels seek mobility by becoming more devotedly Hinduistic, following more Brahminical styles, and otherwise Sanskritizing their behavior: ". . . tradition may be changed, stretched, and modified, but a unified and nationalized society makes great use of the traditional in its search for a consensual base to political authority and economic development."[23]

Portes has in fact theorized that modernity, presumably because it leads to Western attitudes, can interfere with mass mobilization.[24] On the other hand, traditional structures can do the job better. Indirect support comes from a panel regression study, which concludes that indigenous modernizing institutions such as school or education registers a more substantial contribution to economic development, whereas exposure to exogenous modernizing institutions such as imported cinema actually hinders economic development. The authors argued that "the cinema impedes economic growth by transmitting and promoting Western values incompatible with the social ethos that must accompany programs of national economic development."[25] This is still more evidence that indigenous religion and modernization need not be polarized, but that one can in fact be the impetus for the other.

Symbols and Myths amid Changing Times

Modernization is a concept that evolved in the social sciences to depict a phenomenon of the twentieth century. Compared to religion, modernization is a relative new-comer; yet, at best, it allegedly threatens to undermine religion; at worst, to send it on the way of the brontosaurus. Equivocal empirical evidence so far does not warrant such apprehension. At this point, some perspective is needed.

People have always sought, and will always seek, meaning in their lives. This impulse is in recognition of man's mortality and the need to transcend it. Each age and culture provides its own symbols and myths, which form a structure of meaning from which people generate values by which to live. Myths here do not refer at all to falsehoods, but to lasting truths shared by a people.[26]

Whether modernization will solve more ills than those it unleashes is for future history to decide. In the meantime, however, it has to be reconciled to some of the symbols and myths that have for years provided a comfortable structure of meaning for individuals in a culture. Breakdown in cherished symbols and myths leave a people bereft of guideposts for coping and rules for living. Experimentation in different life-styles and the flourishing of new psychotherapies may be viewed as modern attempts to discover personal meaning. Modern interpretations and expressions of religion, modern forms of religion, and even modern religions also come to the rescue.

The challenge is to discover new forms of cultural symbols and myths. The rebirth of symbols and myths is creative, dynamic, and unending.

Generations have trod, have trod, have trod;
And all is seared with trade; bleared, smeared with toil;
And wears man's smudge and share man's smell: the soil
Is bare now, nor can foot feel, being shod.
And for all this, nature is never spent;
There lives the dearest freshness deep down things; . . . [27]

Such is the inexhaustible essence of religion and of things spiritual that defies the imperative of human societal transition.

NOTES

1. John B. Stephenson, "Is Everyone Going Modern? A Critique and a Sug-

gestion for Measuring Modernism," *American Journal of Sociology* 74 (1968): 265–75.

2. David H. Smith and Alex Inkeles, "The OM Scale: A Comparative and Socio-Psychological Measure of Individual Modernity," *Sociometry* 21 (1966): 353–77.

3. J. A. Kahl, *The Measurement of Modernism: A Study of Values in Brazil and Mexico* (Texas: University of Texas Press, 1968).

4. Alex Inkeles, "Making Men Modern: On the Causes and Consequences of Individual Change in Six Developing Countries," *American Journal of Sociology* 75 (1969): 208–25.

5. Allan Schnaiberg, "Measuring Modernism: Theoretical and Empirical Explorations," *American Journal of Sociology* 76 (1970): 399–425.

6. Stephenson, 265.

7. Lolagene C. Coombs and Ronald Freedman, "Some Roots of Preference: Roles, Activities and Familial Values," *Demography* 16 (1979): 359–76.

8. James T. Fawcett and Marc H. Bornstein, "Modernization, Individual Modernity, and Fertility," in *Psychological Perspectives on Population,* ed. James T. Fawcett (New York: Basic Books, 1973), 111.

9. David Goldberg, *Modernism* (The Netherlands: International Statistical Institute, 1974).

10. Allan Schnaiberg, 399–425.

11. Santi Priya Bose, "Peasant Values and Innovation in India," *American Journal of Sociology* 67 (1962): 522–60.

12. Stephenson.

13. Coombs and Freedman.

14. Myron Weiner, ed., *Modernization: The Dynamics of Growth* (New York: Basic Books, 1966).

15. Joseph R. Gusfield, "Tradition and Modernity: Misplaced Polarities in the Study of Social Change," *American Journal of Sociology* 72 (1967): 351–62.

16. Milton Singer, "The Modernization of Religious Beliefs," in Weiner, *Modernization,* 59–70.

17. David C. McClelland, "The Impulse to Modernization," in Weiner, *Modernization,* 29–42.

18. Gusfield, 354.

19. Singer, 68.

20. Alex Inkeles, and David H. Smith, "Personal Adjustment and Modernization," George De Vos, ed., *Responses to Change: Society, Culture and Personality* (New York: D. Van Nostrand Company, 1976), 214–33.

21. Alex Inkeles, "A Model of the Modern Man: Theoretical and Methodological Issues," Cyril E. Black, ed., *Comparative Modernization,* 320–48.

22. Ithiel de Sola Pool, "Communications and Development," Weiner, *Modernization,* 105–18.

23. Singer, 63.

24. A. Portes, "The Factorial Structure of Modernity: Empirical Replications and a Critique," *American Journal of Sociology* 79 (1973): 14–44.

25. Jacques Delacroix and Charles Rogin, "Modernizing Institutions, Mobilization and Third World Development: A Cross-National Study," *American Journal of Sociology* 84 (1978): 123–52.

26. Rollo May, "Psychology Today/The State of the Science," *Psychology Today* 16 (May 1982): 56–58.

27. Gerard Manley Hopkins, "God's Grandeur," *Poems of Gerard Manley Hopkins* (New York: Oxford University Press, 1970).

Mental Health and the Dilemmas of Freudian Psychotherapy: An Eastern Perspective

PADMASIRI DE SILVA

Sigmund Freud wrote a stimulating paper toward the latter part of his life entitled "Analysis Terminable and Interminable."[1] Apart from raising some significant queries regarding the question "Is there such a thing as a natural end to an analysis?" it also contains some significant conflicts and tensions regarding the main concerns of this essay: the "normal" and the "abnormal," and "sickness" and "health." I wish to refer to the issues of normal/abnormal and sickness/health as tensions rather than clear dualities, tensions that emerged due to Freud's ceaseless exploration of the human predicament on the one hand, and the cautious voice of science, which made him disclaim any moralistic purpose in his writings, on the other. There were also other types of conflicts. There was a technical demand on the termination of analysis: if continuous analysis is a time-consuming business, how do we accelerate the slow progress of analysis? Can we set a fixed time limit? Freud, however, expressed a willingness to spend a number of years with one patient; even the well-being of one human being, he felt, is a matter of "ultimate concern."[2] When the work "Analysis Terminable and Interminable" is placed against the wider background of Freud's other writings, it may be said that in Freud we see a kind of oscillation between a limited ideal of therapy and a more ambitious one, as well as optimistic and pessimistic conceptions of cure and therapeutic transformation.

Already in Freud's "Studies in Hysteria," we find the celebrated passage: "No doubt fate would it easier than I do to relieve you of your illness. But you will be able to convince yourself that much will be gained if we succeed in transforming your hysterical misery into common unhappiness."[3] On similar lines, in the work, "Analysis Terminable and Interminable," Freud comments: "Our aim will not be to rub off every peculiarity of human character for the sake of a schematic 'normality', nor yet to demand that the person who

29

has been 'thoroughly analysed' shall feel no passions and develop no internal conflicts. The business of analysis is to secure the best possible psychological conditions for the functions of the ego; with that it has discharged its task."[4]

From a very specific eastern perspective, I found another contrasting vision of the goals of therapy mentioned in "Analysis Terminable and Interminable" more interesting:

". . . but we reckon on the stimuli that he has received in his own analysis not ceasing when it ends and on the processes of remodelling the ego continuing spontaneously in the analysed subject and making use of all subsequent experiences in this newly acquired sense. This does in fact happen, and in so far as it happens it makes the analysed subject qualified to be an analyst himself."[5]

The path of continuous self-exploration that is mentioned here has attracted some contemporary writers, such as Anthony Storr, on the concept of "cure." He says quite clearly that psychoanalysis certainly offers something more than mere relief from symptoms, and as the patients often lose interest in the symptoms for which they wanted to be treated, they seek the process of analysis as an end in itself. Storr says that in this manner analysis is sought not so much as treatment but more as a way of life.[6] This is the sort of dimension in which analysis as both therapeutic transformation and growth of self-knowledge offers a point of convergence for an Eastern, and more particularly, a Buddhist perspective.

A possible objection to my approach is that Freud grappled with the neurotic and the abnormal and that we have no right to use these insights to understand the normal mind, and, even more, to bring them into the Buddhist context. Though Freud was primarily interested in the mentally sick, his psychology had a broad basis. In fact, Philip Rief, who deals at great length with the therapeutic dimensions of Freudian psychology, claims that both Freud's dictum that "we are all somewhat hysterical" and his claim that the difference between so-called normality and neurosis is only a matter of degree comprise a central Freudian position rather than a peripheral one. In fact, we also know that Freud dealt at a very deep and intensive level with what may be called the "pathology of normalcy," as found in his *Psychopathology of Every Day Life.*[7] Freud certainly went beyond the narrow confines of a therapy for mentally sick patients. As MacIntyre points out, "The scope in principle of Freudian explanation is all human behaviour: had it been less than this Freud would have been unable to draw the famous comparison between the effect of his own work and that of Copernicus."[8] Here again, "Analysis Terminable and Interminable" confirms this standpoint: "Every normal person, in fact, is only normal on the average. His ego approximates to that of the psychotic in some part or other and to a greater or lesser extent; and the degree of its remoteness from one end of the series and of its proximity to the other will furnish us with a provisional measure of what we have so indefinitely termed an 'alteration of the ego.'"[9]

After this brief glimpse into our special interest in Freud's study of the termination of analysis, in the rest of this essay, I will divide my discussion into three phases: first, I will present a summary of "Analysis Terminable and Interminable," then briefly discuss some parallels to and differences from the Buddhist concern with sickness and health, and next examine some of the Freudian dilemmas that stand in the way of a terminable analysis. I will try to make you understand this tangle from a Buddhist position. I will conclude with a few remarks that will relate this essay more closely to our theme of religion and society.

Before I conclude this introductory discussion, I should mention two special reasons for selecting this particular essay by Freud for detailed analysis. First, in spite of the conflicting strands of thought regarding the ideal of mental health, it is possible to agree with James Strachey that in this work the skeptical, pessimistic outlook dominates. This is especially so compared with the more optimistic outlook in works such as the *New Introductory Lectures,* which preceded it, and the *Outline of Psychoanalysis,* which followed it. But in a rather paradoxical manner, such pessimism seems to increase our interest in schemes of therapy that go beyond the accepted patterns of scientific psychology. Perhaps, as Charles Rycroft says, "psychoanalysis could be regarded as a semantic bridge between science and biology on the one hand and religion and humanities on the other."[10] The dilemmas of Freud call for a widening of the frame that we can use to plot the perennial conflicts inherent in the human situation.

The second reason, which I consider quite significant, is the insight that is available from Freud's own dilemmas regarding the crucial role of the ego in this interminable analysis. At this point, I wish to open up a line of inquiry from a Buddhist perspective and place it before you as an exercise in exploration. Apart from the complexities of psychoanalytic writings on the subject, there appears to exist a semantic thicket that has to be cleared. It is to the credit rather than discredit of Freud that he stumbled on this during the latter stages of his research and left it to future workers (including his daughter Anna Freud) to find an answer.

Analysis Terminable and Interminable: A Summary

Psychoanalytic therapy, which is designed to free people from neurotic symptoms, inhibitions, and abnormalities of character, is a time-consuming business. Attempts have been made to shorten the duration of analysis. Apart from the technical problem of how to accelerate the slow process of change, there is the "more deeply interesting question": is there such a thing as a natural end to analysis?

From a practical point of view, it is easy to answer the question: "An analysis is ended when the analyst and the patient cease to meet each other for the analytic session." Normally, such an end is reached when the patient is free from the symptoms he had and has overcome his anxieties, and the analyst feels that a certain amount of repressed material has been made conscious and intelligible and internal resistance has been conquered. At this point, "there is no need to fear a repetition of the pathological process concerned." The other meaning of the "end" of analysis is a kind of absolute normality, where all the patient's repressions have been resolved and gaps in the memory filled. Freud was not only skeptical about the more ambitious ideal of psychic normality, but he came across three factors that interfered with the decisive termination of analysis.

In the early days, Freud dealt with a large number of patients who wanted to be dealt with as quickly as possible. He later dealt with a smaller number of severe cases, where the therapeutic aim was no longer the same: "There was no question of shortening the treatment; the purpose was radically to exhaust all the possibilities of illness and to bring about a deep-going alteration of their personality."[11] Now, there were three factors that interfered with the decisive termination of an analysis: the influence of traumatic events, the constitutional strength of instincts, and the "alterations of the ego." As the attempt to deal with the traumatic factor had good results, the traumatic factor (as compared with the constitutional factor) was not a major obstacle. Thus here we are mainly concerned with the two other factors: the strength of instincts and the alterations of the ego.

The key question for Freud here is: "Is it possible by means of analytic therapy to dispose of a conflict between the instinct and the ego, or of a pathogenic instinctual demand upon the ego, permanently and definitively?"[12] The terms *permanently* and *definitively* do not mean that they cause the demand to disappear, but rather that there is a kind of "taming of the ego," where the instincts are brought into complete harmony with the ego.

Though the aim of analysis is thus to replace repressions that are insecure with reliable ego-syntonic control, this is not always achieved. In the defensive struggle, the ego gets dislocated and restricted. This unfavorable situation stands in the way of a permanent cure. The "constitutional strength of instincts" adds to the difficulties. Though attempts were made to maintain the autonomy of the ego in harmony with the demands of the instincts, Freud discovered that the ego is developed from the id, and at some point the topographical distinction between the ego and the id collapses. There are other obstructions to a permanent cure, such as the "adhesiveness of the libido" and the conflict between eros and destructiveness. These dilemmas, especially those springing from the ambiguous role of the ego in therapy, are of special interest for an Eastern perspective on the question and will be discussed in the subsequent sections.

At this point, it is necessary to appreciate that, following the logic of his own system, Freud honestly encountered these difficulties and stated them. It appears that the development of what may be called "ego psychology" has not done very much to ease the situation. It is possible that ego psychology is merely moving in a vicious circle. These are built-in difficulties in the Freudian ego concept, and unless the question is approached from a different angle, as for instance from an angle found in the Buddhist tradition, we may well come up against a wall and a conceptual thicket. Take the overburdened ego of the Freudian system: it is a part of consciousness and control, perception and motility; it is a drive (the self-preservation drive); it is a reservoir of libido; it is the cause of repression; it conforms to reality (identical to the reality principle); it is a reaction to the drive and it constitutes the basis of character; it carries out reality testing.[13] In the final analysis, Freud discovered that the ego is developed from the id. The poor ego is at the same time, "a precipitate of object losses" and the seat of sanity, order, and reason. It is not only that in a semantic sense it is an overworked concept, but that the inherent psychological ambiguities drive Freud into the real difficulties honestly voiced in "Analysis Terminable and Interminable." The inherent ambiguities in the "self and world" relation, "self and other" relation, as well as the self attempting to relate to itself are meticulously worked out in the Buddhist sutras.[14]

Analysis Terminable and Interminable: A Buddhist Perspective

There have been three attempts to view Freudian psychotherapy from a Buddhist perspective that are relevant for this discussion: Erich Fromm's *Zen Buddhism and Psychoanalysis,* from a neo-Freudian standpoint; David Levin's "Approaches to Psychotherapy," where a critique of Freud is presented from the standpoint of Tibetan Buddhism, with basic sympathies for a Jungian position; and my own *Buddhist and Freudian Psychology.*[15]

I have found Fromm's definition of well-being very much in line with the early Buddhist position: "Well-being is possible only to the degree to which one has overcome one's narcissism."[16] Fromm says that "well-being means, finally, to drop one's Ego, to give up greed, to cease chasing after the preservation and the aggrandizement of the Ego, to be and to experience one's self in the act of being, not having, preserving, coveting, using."[17] If the Buddhist is asked to recommend a general working norm of health and sanity, at least to be approximated in varying degrees, overcoming narcissism is one I prefer and find conducive in light of the Buddhist tradition. It may even be a point of convergence for a general religious perspective on therapy, and not merely for an Eastern position. In spite of the dilemmas of ego psychology, it is also a concept that makes sense to a Freudian, especially in the light of Freud's paper on narcissism. Fromm has not merely revitalized the Freudian concept of narcissism, but he takes it beyond this and brings it close to the doctrine of the Buddha. Fromm comments: "The awakened person of whom the Buddhist teaching speaks is the person who has overcome his narcissism, and who is therefore capable of being fully awake."[18]

Fromm says that, quite contrary to popular assumptions, Freud's system transcends the traditional Western concepts of "illness" and "cure." According to Fromm, Freud's system is concerned with the "salvation" of man rather than a mere therapy for the mentally sick:

Psychoanalysis is a characteristic expression of Western man's spiritual crisis, and an attempt to find a solution. This is explicitly so in the more recent developments of psychoanalysis, in "humanist" or "existentialist" analysis. But before I discuss my own humanist concept, I want to show that quite contrary to a widely held assumption, Freud's own system transcended the concept of "illness" and "cure" and was concerned with the "salvation" of man, rather than only with a therapy for mentally sick patients.[19]

For Fromm the liberation of the individual from neurotic symptoms is a task with a quasi-religious mission.

Some of these converging lines between psychotherapy and Buddhism have become relevant to the post-Freudian world, and more so in the world in which we live today. The patients who came to Freud in the early stages of his career were those who suffered from certain symptoms, such as a paralyzed arm or an obsessional symptom or a washing compulsion. The difference between these patients and those who went to the regular physician for treatment was that the cause of their symptoms was not organic but mental. But there was a common pattern of cure: once the symptom was removed, the patient was cured. The new kind of patient who came for treatment was not sick in the traditional sense and had no overt symptoms. These patients were not insane or considered sick by their relatives. Yet they complained about being depressed, not enjoying their work, and so forth. Though these people thought they suffered from certain symptoms, their apparent symptoms were perhaps socially recognized ways of grappling with their inner deadness and lack of vitality. Fromm describes the situation well: "The common suffering is the alienation from oneself, from one's fellow men, and from nature; the awareness that life runs out of one's hand like sand, and that one will die without having lived; that one lives in the midst of plenty and is yet joyless."[20]

In spite of these converging lines between Buddhist therapy and Fromm's "humanistic psychoanalysis," the Freudian system as such was subject to tensions between descriptive clinical diagnosis and the norms of therapeutic recommendation. The medically oriented psychologist talks in terms of "psychological maturity" and "ego strength," whereas in nonmedical contexts one speaks of the authenticity of moral concern and personal integrity. These dual worlds seem to separate in Freud's work due to a scientist's respect for the recognized idiom and the proper semantics of communication, but these worlds run into each other. As Freud said, "The aim of psychoanalysis is not to tell the person what is good or bad, or right or wrong in a specific context, but to 'give the patient's ego freedom to decide one way or another.' . . . The medical aim is thus in substance a spiritual aim. It is to help the individual become an agent and cease being a patient, it is to liberate not to indoctrinate."[21]

The Dilemmas of Ego Psychology and the Buddhist Theory of Motivation

According to the psychology of early Buddhism, the mind can be considered a dynamic continuum that extends over a number of births. As such, it is composed of a conscious as well as an unconscious mind in which is contained the residue of emotionally charged memories, going back not merely to childhood but to past lives. The mind is viewed in this way as a continuum subjected to the pressure of the threefold desires of sense gratification, egoistic pursuits, and self-annihilation, which have some strange affinities to the Freudian concepts of the libido, the ego instinct, and the death instinct. The drive for selfish pursuits, which is fed by the illusion of an indestructible ego, is the most relevant concept for the present study. The Buddha considers the ego the seat of anxiety and the attachment to a false sense of the ego nourished by unconscious proclivities as a base for the generation of tension and unrest. Although the ego-anxiety linkage offers an interesting point of intersection for Freudian and Buddhist therapies, the Freudian system is darkened by the ambiguities inherent in the ego concept as used by Freud.

I wish to make three specific points in the light of the Buddhist theory of motivation, very briefly outlined here: First, there are two significant uses of the term *ego* that have to be clearly distinguished. Sometimes it is used to describe an aspect of the personality that coordinates mental functions. It is also used in a completely different sense to convey a strong self-interest. Thus, in the latter sense, the word *egotistical* is used to refer to people with a "strong ego" in a negative sense. When Freud finds that the ego is rooted in the id and yet it has to control it, and that the ego derives it strength from the id, he creates a veritable tangle. As Freud remarks:

When we speak of an "archaic heritage" we are usually thinking only of the id, and we seem to assume that at the beginning of the individual's life no ego is as yet in existence. But we shall not overlook the fact that

36

id and ego are originally one; nor does it imply any mystical overvaluation of heredity if we think it credible that, even before the ego has come into existence, the lines of development, trends and reactions which it will later exhibit are already laid down for it."[22]

It is because of this impasse that we in the East, when we speak of personality growth, do not speak of strengthening, adding or accumulating. Rather our root metaphor is "let go" and "give up." These metaphors are now gaining entry into the humanistic psychotherapies.

This is the reason those like David Levin feel that, compared with the Buddhist approach of the analyst, the Freudian approach is coercive. What is necessary is an open, nondirective approach: "Freudian analysis is indeed reflective. But its way of reflecting is very different from the Buddhist's. The latter is like a clean mirror, or like the calm surface of a mountain lake; the former is more like an Expressionist portrait painted to reveal the sitter's true self."[23]

The dynamic psychology of Buddhism also provides a scheme of evaluating motives that are nonegotistical, nonaggressive, springing from detachment, compassion, knowledge, etc. The basic springs of human motivation are analyzed into three unwholesome roots—greed, hatred, and ignorance—and three wholesome roots—nongreed, nonhatred, and wisdom. There is no ambiguous ego structure or a flow of energy running both ways; the ways of parting for healthy and unhealthy actions are clearly laid down, and the tricks played by the ego concept, whether they be "conceptual" and semantic or experiential, are cautiously handled. They are not merely handled at an intellectual level, but also at the deeper levels of a "meditative" therapy, of tranquility meditation and insight meditation.

The second point that makes the termination of a successful analysis difficult according to Freud is the duality between Eros and destructiveness that generates conflicts. The Buddha's analysis sheds a great amount of light on the Freudian position—the inherent conflict between the two instincts. The drive for self-preservation and that for self-destruction, paradoxically, emerge from the same root of an ego illusion; they are like the two sides of the same coin. Buddha's psychological insight lay in pointing out that such apparently contradictory attitudes as narcissistic self-love and self-hatred or ambivalent attitudes such as the desire to live and to die stem from the same root. Suicide for example is paradoxically a strong form of self-love.

37

The enigmatic puzzle for Freud was "how can one who is infected with such an amount of self-love consent to his own destruction?" Freud came within the very doors of an interesting solution to unravel this puzzle, when he saw a link between "wounded narcissism" (injured self-love) and the state of depression described in "Mourning and Melancholia," but this was never integrated into his complete system as it could have been done.[24] In the Buddhist context, self-destruction would be "reactive" rather than "appetitive." But all the same, the two forms of craving, the craving for self-preservation or egoistic pursuits and the craving for self-annihilation are not "opposites"; they are merely the contrasting attitudes of a man who is subject to the illusion of a separate and indestructible ego.

The Buddha describes the vagaries of ego attachment with a graphic image: "just like a dog, brethren, tied up by a leash to a strong stake or pillar—if he goes, he goes up to that stake or pillar; if he stands, he stands close to that pillar or stake; if he lies down he lies close to that . . ." The pillar represents the "ego" (fivefold grasping group). Thus, if we take the "body" (which is one of the five grasping groups) as an example, whether we adorn the body, or like Narcissus fall in love with the reflection of one's own body in the pond, or we inflict torture on the body, we are like the dog tied to the pillar going round the same illusory pillar—the ego.

It is unfortunate that the first expounder of the concept of narcissism in psychoanalytic theory, Sigmund Freud, could not completely get out of the spell of the strong sexual overtones of his writings. It remained a mission for Erich Fromm to revitalize the Freudian notion of narcissism: "Narcissism is a passion the intensity of which in many individuals can only be compared with sexual desire and the desire to stay alive. In fact, many times it proves to be stronger than either. Even in the average individual in whom it does not reach such intensity, there remains a narcissistic core which appears almost indestructible."[25] It is true that the Buddhist doctrine of egolessness offers a clue to the besetting dilemmas of the narcissistic man, but Fromm feels that it is a dimension that fits in with all the great religions of the world, East or West.

Third, the constitutional strength of instincts and the "adhesiveness of the libido" are all accepted in the Buddhist concept in its recognition of the deep-rooted nature of craving. The Buddha does not exaggerate the role of sexuality as Freud does nor consider the duality between the life-and-death instinct as leading to a kind of interminable analysis. While accepting the strength of instincts, they can be tamed, redirected to sublimated goals, or even completely mastered. Although the ideal of harmonious living is sought by the householder, the recluse who has renounced the world seeks a path for the "elimination of all conflicts."

When Freud said that he was merely translating "hysterical misery into common unhappiness," he was underrating the potential of his own system. "Analysis Terminable and Interminable," though it is colored by a heavy tinge of pessimism, paradoxically contains within itself a deeper search for the roots of human happiness. I shall conclude this analysis with the observations of Robert H. Thouless, who wrote when searching for a wider mission for psycho-analysis:

One can speculate on the possibility of a future development of the therapy based on psycho-analysis to do more than this, to produce a radical mental reorientation that led to the complete disappearance of internal sources of unhappiness. If such a development of psycho-therapy did take place, one can predict that it is likely to demand more time and energy than those of the few hours per week taken up by psycho-analysis. It is more likely to be a lifelong activity as is that of those striving for the final achievement of the Buddhist saint.[26]

Instincts, Society, and Civilization: Summing Up

It is known that people have limited problems of adjustment, specific symptoms that disappear due to the impact of analysis, weakness of memory, oddities, compulsions, and so forth. Some of these and more of a similar type can certainly be handled within the limited goals of psychotherapy. But types of patients and patterns of sickness have changed; the nature, effectiveness, stature, and status of modern analytical therapy is being reexamined; new cross-cutting pathways across psychoanalysis and other disciplines have emerged. In this context, a second glance at "Analysis Terminable and Interminable" can be a rewarding venture. The work also provides a good meeting ground for therapeutic orientations and metaphors of "health" and "sickness" found in the East and the West, as well as for exploring well-being within society.

Freud had conflicting notions regarding the relationship between instincts and society. He very clearly believed that society was so constituted that men were subject to emotional disturbances. Culture and civilization led to the repression of instincts. Freud also saw a strong element of aggression integrated into the development of the superego, the voice of morality and religion. If society is so constituted that it aggravates man's anxieties, why not change society? Though he seems to have favored revolutionary changes he did not turn to such a task. He also has a limited vision of the more positive and creative role that social interaction could play in the development of love and understanding. As Reuben Fine has pointed out, Freud became curiously hesitant at this point and seems to even accept the idea that it is not society that is at fault but the instincts themselves.[27] Freud also saw a kind of ambivalence and circular dialectic built into the notion of instincts such that attempts to control or tame them appeared to be difficult. In the clinical context he advocates rational and conscious encounter as the panacea for these ills, but works such as *Civilization and its Discontents*[28] provide a more perennial note of discordance and for this reason makes the case for the close understanding of "Analysis Terminable and Interminable" even more important.

NOTES

1. Sigmund Freud, "Analysis Terminable and Interminable," *The Standard Edition of the Complete Psychological Works of Sigmund Freud,* ed. James Strachey (London: Hogarth Press, 1966), 23: 216–53.

2. See Erich Fromm, in *Zen Buddhism and Psychoanalysis,* ed. Erich Fromm and D. T. Suzuki (New York: Harper, 1960), "Zen Buddhism and Psychoanalysis," 77–142.

3. Sigmund Freud, "Studies in Hysteria," *The Standard Edition,* vol. 2: 305.

4. Freud, "Analysis Terminable and Interminable," 250.

5. Ibid., 249.

6. See Anthony Storr, "The Concept of Cure," *Psychoanalysis Observed,* ed. C. Rycroft (London: Constable, 1966), 53.

7. Freud, "The Psychopathology of Everyday Life," *The Standard Edition,* vol. 6: 278.

8. Alasdair C. MacIntyre, *The Unconscious: A Conceptual Study* (London: Routledge & Kegan Paul, 1958), 25.

9. Freud, "Analysis Terminable and Interminable," 235.

10. Charles Rycroft, "Causes and Meaning," *Psychoanalysis Observed,* ed. C. Rycroft (London: Constable, 1966), 21.

11. Freud, "Analysis Terminable and Interminable," 224.

12. Ibid., 224.

13. See Dieter Wyss, *Depth Psychology: A Critical History,* trans. Gerald Onn (London: George Allen & Unwin, 1966), 121.

14. A more fruitful connection between Buddhism and Freudian analysis might begin with Freud's paper, "On Narcissism: An Introduction," *The Standard Edition,* 14:73–102, which is a great contribution. See my discussion of the Freudian notion of "narcissism" in the light of the ego concept in early Buddhism, in Padmasiri de Silva, *Buddhist and Freudian Psychology* (Colombo, Sri Lanka: Lake House Investments, 1978), 127–32.

15. See Fromm's "Zen Buddhism and Psychoanalysis"; David Levin's "Approaches to Psychotherapy: Freud, Jung and Tibetan Buddhism," in *The Metaphors of Consciousness,* ed. R. S. Valle and R. Von Eckartsberg (New York: Plenum Press, 1981), 243–74.

16. Fromm, "Zen Buddhism and Psychoanalysis," 91.

17. Ibid., 92.

18. Erich Fromm, *The Heart of Man* (New York: Harper & Row, 1964), 88.

19. Fromm, "Zen Buddhism and Psychoanalysis," 80–81.

20. Ibid., 86.

21. Herbert Fingarette, *Self-Deception* (London: Routledge and Kegan Paul, 1969), 142.

22. Freud, "Analysis Terminable and Interminable," 240.

23. Levin, "Approaches to Psychotherapy," 255.

24. Sigmund Freud, "Mourning and Melancholia," *The Standard Edition,* 14: 243–58.

25. Fromm, *The Heart of Man,* 72.

26. Robert H. Thouless, "Foreward," *Buddhist and Freudian Psychology,* viii ix.

27. Reuben Fine, *The Development of Freud's Thought: From the Beginning* (New York: J. Aronson, 1962), 74.

28. Sigmund Freud, "Civilization and its Discontents," *The Standard Edition,* vol. 22: 143.

Part Two
SOCIAL DIMENSIONS OF RELIGIOUS TRADITIONS

The Social Dimension of the Faith of Judaism: Phenomenological and Historical Aspects

MANFRED H. VOGEL

The purpose of this essay is to examine the stance that Judaism takes with respect to the political dimension in life. We should note, therefore, at the very start that we are concerned here with the stance that Judaism takes rather than with the stance that Jews may or may not take toward the political dimension. It is important to note this, as it is by no means the case that the stance that Jews take is always and necessarily the same as the stance that Judaism dictates. The needs and requirements of the former are by no means always and necessarily identical with those of the latter. Indeed, the whole history of Judaism and of the Jewish people (and it is rather a long history) bears witness to the continuous tension between the two. What Jews as human beings wish and require is not necessarily what Judaism wishes and requires for them. Conversely, therefore, it also follows that what is good for the Jews is not necessarily good for Judaism, and vice versa, what is good for Judaism is not necessarily good for the Jews. This ironic discrepancy characterizes the situation throughout Jewish history, but it certainly comes to the fore and is most pronounced in the modern era in the context of the emancipation. There can be no denying that in this context the interests and needs of the emancipated Jew often collide head-on with the interests and needs of Judaism. Thus, what we may claim on behalf of Judaism may not at all be what the emancipated Jew would want to claim as his or her position. But be this as it may, our concern is with the position of Judaism and not with the position of Jewry, specifically, emancipated Jewry. We are not concerned with the historical, sociological, or psychological analysis of the attitude taken by a certain collectivty of people, but rather with the philosophical analysis of a certain *weltanschauung,* that is, a certain view of the world and man's place and vocation in it, that we call Judaism; or rather, as we would be inclined to say, we are concerned with a philosophical analysis of the structure of faith that constitutes Judaism.

We must realize, however, that Judaism in its historical manifestation, as, indeed, all other historical religions, encompasses a number of structures of faith. It is not monolithic; rather, it is a mixture of different structures of faith held together by shared symbols, rituals, and institutions. Thus, we should specify that our intention is to deal exclusively with the structures of faith that can be encountered in the prophetic strand of the Bible and in the nonmystical halackic strand of rabbinic Judaism and that we do not propose to deal here with those structures of faith that may manifest themselves, for example, in the priestly strand or the wisdom strand of the Bible or in the mystical or hasidic strand of rabbinic Judaism. Had we dealt with these latter strands the picture that would have emerged regarding our topic would have been quite different. Our choice to deal with the former strands, that is, the prophetic and nonmystical halackic strands, is not, however, completely arbitrary. For we would want to argue that these strands represent the mainstream expression in the historical manifestation of Judaism and, what is even more significant, they represent the *distinctive* expression of Judaism. (Indeed, no less significantly, though on a different level, a case can be made that it is by virtue of the structures of faith encountered in these strands that Judaism could survive through millennia of years of diaspora existence.) But whether or not one accepts the validity of these justifications, it is important for us to be clear about the parameters of our investigation, namely that when we refer to Judaism in this essay we have in mind the prophetic and nonmystical halachic strands of Judaism.

Lastly, as clarification, we should specify that the notion of "political dimension" involved in our discussion here is used in its broadest sense, namely, as the dimension that encompasses not only the political (now, in the narrower sense) relations, but also the social and economic relations; in short, the notion is used here to signify what we may call the "horizontal dimension" of life in its totality.

Thus, the task before us in this essay is to examine in what way (and if at all) the structure of faith of Judaism (specifically, of the prophetic and halachic strands) implicates involvement in the horizontal dimension of life. Is involvement in the horizontal dimension of life a necessary, essential, and inextricable aspect of the religious life or is it of no real consequence? And if the former, in what sense does it constitute the religious vocation for Judaism?

The Social Dimension of the Faith of Judaism

We can answer this central question in a very straightforward and unqualified way: our thesis is that the structure of faith of Judaism necessarily implicates, as an essential and inextricable act, its involvement within the horizontal dimension of life in all its aspects, i.e., social, economic, and political. Take away the possibility of involvement in the horizontal dimension of life, and the very structure of faith of Judaism (i.e., of prophetic and nonmystical halachic Judaism) disintegrates. The task before us now, of course, is to justify and explain this claim.

To justify this claim should not, in our judgment, be too difficult. For it can hardly be denied that biblical prophecy by its very essence is deeply involved in the horizontal dimension of life. Take away the critique of social injustice, of economic oppression, the involvement in international politics, and what is left of biblical prophecy? And isn't the distinctive and imposing feature of the halacha the fact that it encompasses a comprehensive civil, political, and criminal law in addition to the ritual law, thus encompassing the totality of the horizontal dimension of life? The point, I think, needs no further elaboration. Indeed, biblical and rabbinic scholarship has almost universally recognized and acknowledged this point. To quote at random only a few sources: "the justice of the prophets is social justice. They demand not only a pure heart but also just institutions. They are concerned for the improvement of society even more than for the welfare of the individual";[1] "the Hebrews were the first who rebelled against the injustice of the world . . . Israel demanded social justice";[2] "our social legislation is derived from the spirit of the prophets. Also in the future will the spirit of Israel remain the instigator and awakener of social reforms";[3] "the basis of Judaism is ethics";[4] "the idea of the inseparateness between religion and ethical life arose for the first time in Judaism . . . this idea of the unit of ethics and religion passes through the whole Bible . . . and this applies equally to rabbinic literature";[5] "in any reading of Judaism the ethical dimension is of supreme importance. Judaism has always taught that God wishes man to pursue justice . . . to make his contribution towards the emergence of a better social order. This is a constant theme in the Bible and in the Rabbinic literature."[6] Any further buttressing of this assertion is not really called for; what is called for, however, is an attempt to explicate why and how this is so. This is the intriguing and challenging task and we will try to accomplish it in the remainder of this essay.

We would submit that the key to the understanding of why the structure of faith in these strands of Judaism necessarily and essentially implicates the involvement within the horizontal dimension of life lies in the fact that the very structure of faith here formulates itself from the ethical perspective rather than from the ontological perspective. What do we mean by this? We mean that the fundamental predicament of man is not perceived here to lie in the "way man is constituted" but rather in the way in which he expresses and realizes himself within the possibilities and limitations of his given ontological constitution. The fact that man is constituted, to use Buberian terms, as an It-Thou being, as body and soul, as material and spiritual, as divine and earthly—as the bearer of the divine image and a being of nature, a member of the animal kingdom—is not perceived to constitute the fundamental predicament. There is nothing wrong with the way man was created; by and large, there is no pessimism or desperation about this—the judgment about creation is positive, that it was good. Rather, where the fundamental predicament, the problematic, is perceived to lie is in the balance that man, all too often, strikes between these two dimensions in the way he expresses and realizes himself. The problematic lies in the fact that man all too often realizes and expresses himself as a beast—albeit a sophisticated beast but therefore also, all too often, as a very mischievous beast—rather than as the bearer of the divine image. To use Buberian terms again, the predicament lies in the fact that man, all too often, acts and relates to others in the I-It rather than in the I-Thou context. Therefore, the salvation that is envisioned and yearned for does not involve the ontological transformation of man, the new creation of man as a "new being," but rather the steadfastness of man in striking and maintaining the proper balance between the two dimensions constituting his being—indeed it is a redemption rather than a salvation that is envisaged.

It should be clear that as such the perceived predicament and the envisaged redemption are centered here not on the way man is constituted, on his ontological makeup, but on his actions, on his relations with others. Consequently, the perspective involved here, that is, the perspective in terms of which the structure of faith formulates itself, is evidently an ethical perspective. For the evaluation of actions and relations, specifically of *man's* actions and relations, is precisely what constitutes the business of ethics.

But a structure of faith that formulates itself from the ethical perspective would necessarily implicate involvement in the horizontal dimension of life. For in being concerned with the proper balancing between the It and the Thou dimension in man's expression and realization of himself in his actions and relations, it must of necessity encompass the action and relations of man with respect to the world, specifically, to the human world, that is, to the human horizontal dimension of life. The horizontal dimension of life cannot be left out of the picture as inconsequential precisely because the perceived predicament and thus the envisioned redemption necessarily involve here (at least in part) man's actions and relations that impinge upon the horizontal dimension of life. Thus, man's actions and relations with respect to the horizontal dimension of life become an inextricable part in the forumulation of the two basic categories of the structure of faith, that is, of the category of the fundamental predicament and that of redemption.

But even more to the point (and this, indeed, is the very crux of the matter), the very actions and relations of man with respect to God and, conversely, God's actions and relations with respect to man must be "refracted," mediated, through the horizontal dimension of life. For we must not overlook or forget that the It dimension in man is not to be extirpated, which is tantamount to saying that man is to remain a this-worldly being.[7] But this, in turn, means that all actions involving man, thus including the actions and relations that express the Thou dimension, must inevitably be "refracted" through the It dimension. Thus, even man's action and relation with respect to God, which in terms of God being a pure Thou being (the eternal Thou) are to belong exclusively to the pure Thou dimension, must be "refracted" here through the It dimension, that is, through the horizontal dimension, because of the inextricable presence of the It dimension in the constitution of man. This, of course, means that the most fundamental and central aspect of the religious life, namely, the relation between man and the divine, must be mediated through the horizontal dimension. Indeed, in the prophetic and nonmystical halachic strands of Judaism the burden of the expression of the relationship of man to God, namely, the burden of the expression of faith and of worship, is not expressed in direct vertical relationships, but rather in indirect relationships, that is, in relationships that go through the horizontal dimensions, specifically, the human horizontal dimension (seeing that man is the only being in nature endowed with the Thou dimension).[8] Or to make the same point, but this time not with respect to the divine, it is indeed the case that in the structure of faith of the prophetic and nonmystical halachic strands of Judaism's God, who is constituted as a pure Thou and as transcending the world, is nonetheless represented as deeply and essentially involved in the relations of man to the world, again, specifically the social world of man. God, the pure Thou, the transcending God, is affected in the most real and profound sense by what man does or does not do with respect to the world, especially with respect to his fellow man.[9] Thus, in the prophetic and in the nonmystical halachic strands of Judaism, man can fully witness to God, in the last analysis, only through the world—he can fully establish his relationship to God only through the world, he can work for redemption and redemption that can be realized only through and in the world. Take away man's involvement in the horizontal dimension of life, and the whole structure of faith collapses. Thus, in the strands of Judaism represented here one cannot separate the vertical from the horizontal, the sacred from the profane, relegating the religious concern, that is, faith, exclusively to the former. The religious concern, that is, faith, which of course must ultimately come to rest in the vertical, is nonetheless inextricably intertwined within the horizontal.

But let us be clear about the precise meaning of the relationship that exists between faith and the horizontal dimension of life. Clearly, it is diametrically opposed to the model whereby faith, taken as the direct vertical relating of man to the divine, is completely (one is tempted to say hermetically) separated from the horizontal dimension (a model that may be found, for example, in some formulations of German Lutheranism). But let us note what may not at first sight appear so clear—that it also differs from the model whereby faith, still constituted as the direct vertical relating of man to the divine, is now connected with the horizontal dimension; where faith is brought to bear upon the horizontal dimension, for example, by molding and guiding it or by manifesting its fruit within it (a model that may be encountered, perhaps, in Calvinism or in Catholicism). For in Judaism the very constitution of faith is effected through the horizontal dimension. It is not that faith is constituted here independently as a direct vertical mode of relating, which is then brought into relation with the horizontal dimension of life; rather, faith is constituted here as an indirect mode of relating, which is refracted through the horizontal dimension of life. Without relating through the horizontal dimension of life there can be no faith. Perhaps we can put the matter thus: the relation of faith to the horizontal dimension of life is not established in the context of sanctification; it is established in the very context of justification.

But to return to our main line of argument, there is an all-important aspect that the formulation of the structure of faith from the ethical perspective further implicates for the prophetic and nonmystical halachic strands of Judaism. In implicating the involvement of religion in the horizontal dimension, it also implicates an inextricable bond between religion and the category of the ethnic-national entity. This is to say, it establishes religion as being primarily not the affair of the individual but rather the affair of the collectivity, specifically, of the ethnic-national entity. (It is not surprising, therefore, that the human pole in the divine-human relation, both when it is the active agent and when it is the receiving object in the relation, is represented primarily by the ethnic-national collectivity and not by the individual.)

The claim that religion must implicate the collectivity rather than the individual as the primary context of its expression can be seen in the consideration that, inasmuch as religion formulates itself from the ethical perspective, it impinges not on questions concerning the being of man, but rather on questions concerning the actions and relations of man. As such, it cannot impinge exclusively on the individual person, but must impinge on man and the object of his actions or on man and his partner in relation. Because of a number of considerations that cannot be elaborated on here, this partner, this "other" must be a fellow man. (Suffice it to say that inasmuch as the ethical perspective involved here represents an ethics that is grounded in accountability and responsibility, it must impinge on actions and relations that arise exclusively between man and his fellow man and not upon actions and relations that may arise between man and the inanimate objects of nature.) Thus, religion cannot impinge upon man in his monadic individuality; it must impinge upon both man and his fellow man. But a twosome, that is man and his fellow man, already constitute a collectivity, a human community.

The claim that the collectivity implicated here cannot be just any collectivity but must be specifically the ethnic-national collectivity can be seen from the consideration that only the ethnic-national collectivity can encompass the full gamut of relations constituting the horizontal dimension of life on which a religion formulating itself from the ethical perspective would optimally have to impinge.

All other subnational or extranational collectivities (as, for example, the family, the clan, or any of the social, cultural, professional, ideological, or political associations) can present only some of these relations, but never all of them. Thus, if the horizontal dimension of life is to be made available to religion in all its relations—the social, economic, and political—the collectivity that is to be implicated must be specifically the ethnic-national collectivity.

It must be clear, however, that the ethnic-national entity cannot really fulfill its function optimally with respect to religion, that is, it cannot make fully available to religion the horizontal dimension of life, unless it has sovereignty. The ethnic-national entity must have the power to shape, regulate, and determine the relations constituting the horizontal dimension of life. It must have the power to impose its wishes and judgments with respect to these relations. In other words, it must possess a horizontal dimension—a horizontal dimension must rightfully belong to it. It must be at its disposal freely to determine its destiny.

We have thus far argued, therefore, that the prophetic and non-mystical halachic strands for Judaism in formulating themselves from the ethical perspective implicate an indirect relating to the divine, a relating that is "refracted" through the horizontal dimension of life, thus involving Judaism in a very fundamental and essential way in the matrix of the horizontal dimension of life in all its aspects bar none. We have further argued that this implicates an inextricable bond between Judaism and an ethnic-national entity. And last, we have argued that for Judaism to optimally express and realize itself, the ethnic-national entity that is inextricably bound to it must possess sovereignty.

Indeed, in light of these considerations one can come to understand and evaluate the major transformations in Jewish history not only from the vantage point of the fortunes or suffering of Jewry, but from the vantage point of the needs and requirements of the structure of faith of Judaism. We can gain different insights into the strengths and weaknesses that will be judged now not from the vantage point of how they impinged on the well-being of Jewry, but rather from the vantage point of how they impinged on the viability of the structure of faith of Judaism.

Thus, from this vantage point, the essential strength and advantage of the biblical period lies in the fact that it provided sovereignty and consequently that it could place the horizontal dimension in all its relations at the disposal of Judaism. In such a context Judaism

could express itself fully and in this sense it was indeed the fulfillment of the promise. Indeed, the tradition knew this for its continuous yearning for restoration signified for it not only the liberation
from the physical sufferings of exile, but the renewal of the opportunity for Judaism to express itself *fully* (in its language: the renewal
of the opportunity to observe *all of God's* commandments). It is not
a coincidence that the tradition links its messianic hope to the
restoration, making the former contingent upon the latter.

On the other hand, the essential predicament and problematic
that diaspora existence presents must be seen to lie principally in the
fact that diaspora existence signifies the abrogation of sovereignty.
But more specifically, the problematic of the abrogation of sovereignty must be seen here to lie not so much in the scattering of the
Jews or in their dependence for their very physical survival on the
good graces of others, but in the fact that the abrogation of sovereignty threatened the availability to Judasim of the horizontal
dimension of life. For without a horizontal dimension at its disposal
Judaism could not survive.[10] Indeed, Judaism managed to survive in
diaspora existence only because it succeeded, partly due to for-
tuitous circumstances, to establish what has been called "a state
within a state," namely, only because it succeeded to create in
diaspora, and thus without sovereignty, a portable horizontal dimension that was at its disposal. True, this horizontal dimension
provided by "ghettoized" existence was limited and consequently
the expression of the structure of faith of Judaism in these circumstances could only be a truncated expression. Still, it evidently was
sufficient to allow for the survival of Judaism.

By this very same logic, however, when things are to be viewed
from the vantage point of the interests and requirements of the
structure of faith of Judaism, the crisis that the emancipation precipitates in modern Jewish life must be seen now to lie essentially in
the fact that the thrust of the emancipation is to abrogate this
limited horizontal dimension that Judaism managed to establish for
itself in the context of diaspora existence. For what the emancipation really signifies is the exit of Jewry from its ghettoized existence
and its entry into the life stream of the host nation, and the real crisis
that this represents when viewed from the vantage point of the
structure of faith of Judaism, is the loss of the horizontal dimension
to Judaism. For the horizontal dimension, albeit the limited, truncated horizontal dimension, that Judaism managed to constitute for
itself in the context of ghettoized existence could not be transferred

into the life stream of the host nation. This meant that to the extent Judaism did manage to accompany emancipated Jewry, albeit in a restricted and mitigated way, into the life stream of the host nation, it was nonetheless, in terms of its own structure, made impotent in the process. Thus, from the vantage point of the structure of faith of Judaism the real crisis that the emancipation precipitates for Judaism must be seen to lie in the fact that the emancipation abrogates the horizontal dimension that was at the disposal of Judaism and that consequently it necessarily emasculates Judaism and renders it impotent.[11]

Finally, the real significance of the reestablishment of the state of Israel (again, when viewed from the vantage point of the structure of faith of Judaism) must be seen to lie in the fact that it rescues for Judaism the horizontal dimension in terms of emancipated Jewry— and indeed it rescues the horizontal dimension no longer in a truncated form but in its full extention. For only in the context of the reestablished state of Israel can Jewry reenter the life stream of history, can Jewry be emancipated from its ghettoized existence, in a way that allows Judaism to accompany it fully and in a viable manner. If Judaism is to survive in the context of the emancipation, therefore, the reestablishment of the state of Israel becomes a condition sine qua non. For only in the context of the reestablished state can the horizontal dimension in terms of emancipated Jewry be placed at the disposal of Judaism. And indeed, because the horizontal dimension is provided here with sovereignty, it not only allows Judaism to survive, namely, to hold the fort and mark time (as the horizontal dimension in the context of ghettoized existence did), but it should allow Judaism once more to pursue its vocation in full force.

Thus, we have tried to argue that by its very structure of faith, seeing that it formulates itself from the ethical perspective, Judaism must express itself in the horizontal dimension. It must impinge upon the horizontal dimension in all its aspects. The availability, therefore, of the horizontal dimension is essential to Judaism. Without a horizontal dimension at its disposal, Judaism would disintegrate. *In no other religion* is this requirement—to be involved in the horizontal dimension, to impinge upon it in all its aspects—more central or essential than it is in Judaism. But we've also tried to argue that Judaism can impinge upon the horizontal dimension only if the horizontal dimension rightfully belongs to it, only if it possesses sovereignty over it. It can impinge upon the horizontal dimension only in its own "backyard," in its own "home." But this means that the most that Judaism can do in the context of diaspora existence is to constitute, if allowed, a limited horizontal dimension, as an enclave separated and isolated from the life stream of the host nation, upon which it can impinge. Evidently, it cannot impinge upon the horizontal dimension of the host nation. No host would allow it and rightly so.

But one may contend that although this argument may be valid with respect to host nations that are homogeneous, it would have to be greatly mitigated if the host nations had pluralistic societies. For shouldn't Judaism in these circumstances have a partial rightful claim on the horizontal dimension of life and shouldn't it therefore be allowed to impinge, at least in part, upon it? Thus, if the emancipation is to take place in the context of a pluralistic society, shouldn't the problematic that it precipitates for Judaism be greatly mitigated? There is no question that at first sight the pluralistic alternative appears very attractive. But after a closer look, we would submit, its attractiveness is greatly diminished. First, there are any number of very difficult practical problems that a pluralistic situation presents. How, for example, would such an arrangement work when there are several religions claiming the right to impinge upon the horizontal dimension? Would it work by finding the least offensive common denominator of these religions and allow only the common denominator to impinge upon the horizontal dimension; or would the horizontal dimension be partitioned among the various religions, allowing each to impinge on only part of it? Clearly, neither of these alternatives would be satisfactory to Judaism nor, I dare say, to any other religion. But as far as Judaism is concerned, there is even a more serious problem, not of mere practicality but of substance. To see this we must ask, what kind of pluralism are we talking about? Are we talking of a pluralism that is merely religious or are we talking of a pluralism that is actually ethnic? If it is the former, then Judaism, unlike other religions, may well be unable to avail itself of its opportunities. For, as we have seen above, Judaism is inextricably bound to a specific ethnic-national entity and it would perforce be excluded by virtue of this ethnic bond. Thus, for pluralism to present meaningful possibilities to Judaism in diaspora existence, one must envision a pluralism that is specifically ethnic. But given the way the world is, I'm not at all sure that such an ethnic pluralism is feasible. I certainly do not know of any instance of authentic pluralism that is stable and viable and that appears to be a permanent state of affairs (let alone any instance that would also incorporate Judaism as a full-fledged ethnic partner). [12]

Thus, we must conclude that as far as diaspora existence is concerned, Judaism, in the context of the emancipation, is not really in a position to impinge upon the horizontal dimension of life. (What *emancipated Jewry* does is, of course, quite a different story.) This is somewhat ironic because Judaism, perhaps more than any other religion, is a religion that by its very essence requires that it impinge upon the horizontal dimension of life. But then, this is part of the price that diaspora existence exacts.

NOTES

1. Julius Wellhausen, *Israelistische und Juedische Geschichte* (Berlin: Vereingung Wissenschafllicher Verloger, Walter de Gruyter Co., 1921), 114.

2. Ernest Renan, *Histoire du Peuple d'Israel,* 3 (Paris: Calmann-Lévy, 1889), vi–vii.

3. Herman Gunkel, *Deutsche Rundschau,* 2 (Berlin: Verlag von Gerbrüder Baetel, 1875), 231.

4. K. Kohler, *The Ethical Basis of Judaism,* (New York: The Young Men's Hebrew Association, 1887), 143.

5. Isidore Epstein, *Emunat Ha-Yahadut* (Jerusalem: Mossad Harave Kook, 1964), 18–19.

6. Louis Jacobs, *A Wish Theology* (New York: Behrman, 1973), 231.

7. See, for example, Martin Buber, *I and Thou* (Edinburgh: T. & T. Clark, 1958), vol. 11, 34.

8. See my essay, "The Distinctive Expression of the Category of Worship in Judaism," in *Bijdrachen,* 43, no. 1 (December 1982): 350–81.

9. For a striking description of this aspct of the divine in prophetic literature see Abraham J. Heschel, *The Prophets,* (New York: Harper & Row, 1969), vol. 2, chaps. 1, 3, 4.

10. Max Wiener, *Judische Religion in Zeitalter der Emanzipation* (Berlin: Philo Verlag, 1933).

11. For a fuller analysis of the problematic that the Emanicipation precipitates for

Judaism see my essay, "The Dilemma of Identity for the Emancipated Jew," reprinted in *New Theology*, no. 4, ed. Martin E. Marty and Dean G. Peerman.

12. For a further critique of the notion of pluralism as it impinges on the state of Judaism and Jewry in diaspora see my review article, "The Impact of the Emancipation on Continuity and Change in Judaism," in the *Journal of Religion*, 59, no. 4 (October 1979).

5

Liberation in Social Life: A Buddhist View

GESHE LOBSANG TSEPAL AND ACHARYA KARMA MONLAM

Namoguru Manjugoshaya (Homage to Manjugosha)

In this essay, I would like to throw some light on the possibility of liberation in social life based on the teachings of Buddha. Rationality will be the means through which this topic will be discussed. This seems appropriate since in this atomic age, science based on logical reasoning dominates all social activities. Here, seemingly, only logical reasoning has a part to play.

In our view, where the three baskets of the teachings of Buddha prevail, together with a noncontradictory understanding and practice of the three Disciplines, there abides the teachings (shasna) of Buddha, the Enlightened One. Where the sublime remedy (upaya) is accompanied by compassion, there is said to prevail the teachings of Mahayana. Moreover, there is provision within Mahayana to practice equally investigative and fixed meditations and for the practice of Sutra and Tantra in combination. Therefore the questions are: What is to be practiced? How is it to be practiced? And what can we achieve as result of such practice? It is also important to understand these practices in the right context.

Whoever desires to be happy by intellectual means has to search for the remedies that can liberate us from the sufferings of cyclic existence (samsara). Moreover, such a person must learn what the appropriate things are that can be observed for attaining liberation. The intellectual way of investigation must be based on the four Relying-on's. First, we must not rely on the person but on the dharma, the words or teachings. Second, we should not rely on the words alone but on their meanings. But in respect to the meanings of words, we must—and this is the third—rely on their *definitive* meaning rather than on their *interpretative* meaning. And fourthly, in the investigation of meaning we must not rely upon the mind, but on wisdom. In this context, to rely on or not to rely on means to confide in, to believe as true.

The first two ways—relying on dharma and meaning—are to be accepted while we acquire knowledge. That is, one should be fully concerned with the subject (even if it turns out that it does not show the correct way of liberation or is not helpful) and not about the person who is talking or teaching the subject at hand. One may be of any social status or have any type of personality. Likewise, when regarding the subject at hand, one should investigate and examine thoroughly the *meaning* of that subject, but not its expression. Then, when meditating or during the analysis of meanings, one should rely on and strive for the definitive meaning of the subject, that is, the correct understanding of that meaning. Interpretive meanings should only be regarded as complementary for understanding the definitive meaning.

While practicing for the accomplishment of liberation, one should not be satisfied with the knowledge of learning alone. Rather one should be seeking the deeper knowledge of actual experience through meditation. Thus one must rely on the fourth element: wisdom. (The necessity of relying wholly on wisdom is thoroughly explained by Acharya Asanga.)

The practice of the four Relying-on's enables a person to create a deep respect for the profound dharma, to practice the profound knowledge, to avoid misunderstanding the meanings of prophecy, and to obtain the wisdom-without-passion. As it is said in the *Sutra-Alangkara* by Arya Maitrinath: "One likes and practices, hears correctly from others and by inexpressible wisdom, one will not be betrayed."

In regard to Buddhism one who accepts the Triple Gem (Trirat-tana) as the ultimate refuge is said to be Buddhist. The way of accepting the Triple Gem is explained by Bodhipadhpradipam as arising from (1) understanding the virtuous qualities of the Triple Gem, (2) understanding their characteristics, and (3) by not accepting through the four means. The view that *going for refuge* is the watermark for differentiating a Buddhist from non-Buddhist is unanimously accepted by Acharya Shantideva, Atisha, and rJe Tsongkhapa. And it is a very important point.

Establishment of the Correct View

Here it seems important to briefly review some other views, that of nihilism, for instance. Nihilists assert in their philosophy: "Pleasure should be sought till death. After death there is nothing to enjoy as the body is turned into ashes and there is no question of rebirth. Therefore, there is neither life nor future incarnations." They assert that there is no previous birth because purush (soul) originates from the body, and the body itself is composed of the great elements. Thus there is no previous life. They also deny future rebirth on the grounds that at the time of death the body disappears into the four great elements and the soul likewise disappears. The analogies often cited are alcohol and its power of intoxication, the lamp and its light, and a wall and its paintings.

To refute such views, many logical, rational discussions have been furnished by Acharya Chandrakirti and also by Acharya Bhavaveveka in *Tarkajaval*. Here we will not go into detail on their arguments in order to save space and time. But nonetheless, the question arises: How can we prove the existence of previous lives and future births? What is the cause of the first moment of the mind of a new born common person? Its cause is a former mind. There is also the case with the present mind. Likewise, the last moment of the mind of a common man at the time of death causes the mind to continue and make chain connections for the future births because it is a mind with continuity of attachments. Thus the mind continues and causes reincarnation or the next life.

In this way, then, we can prove former and future life. We can also prove that one can gain enlightenment. Compassion and wisdom, which are the inevitable means of Buddhahood, can be practiced for many lifetimes, and such practices can develop to infinity. Moreover, such qualities of mind are steadfast and once gained remain. In each successive life, then, they come automatically without repeated effort. This creates a steadfastness in the mind. It is a quality in the nature of the mind that will not require repeated effort because, once created, compassion will remain on the mental continuum and no additional effort is needed to create it again.

To those who are of the view that there cannot be an enlightened person purified of all sins, we ask the following questions: (1) Do they believe so because they believe faults such as passions are permanent?; (2) Do they believe that if these faults are impermanent there is no remedy to overcome them?; (3) Do they believe that even if there is a remedy there is no one who understands it?; (4) Do they believe that there is no one who puts forth the effort to know it?; (5) Do they believe that though there might be someone who seeks to know it, there can't be anyone to teach that remedy?

Now let us repudiate these views one by one. First, passions cannot be permanent because they have causes behind them, that is, they can be destroyed by the removal or negation of their causes. Second, we are not without a remedy to remove these passions. Rather, as we focus our practice on the origin or cause of these faults, they will be completely uprooted. Third, the remedy can be understood because when the nature of the cause is known its overcoming can be understood. And fourth, it is also not the case that there is no one who would try to know the remedy. Rather, as a person arrives at the conclusion that he himself is suffering worldly sorrows and pains, he understands that it is the causes that make him suffer. And, by understanding the causes of suffering, we turn to annihilate that suffering by bringing the causes to an end. Finally, the assertion that there is no one to teach the remedy is also invalid, because when a person gains enlightenment, then he will show the way or method through his own experience to overcome suffering. This would be done without any selfish motive, but because of his compassion for suffering beings.

Such reasoning is in accordance with the logic of the teaching of Chandrakirtri. As he said, "As there is cause, it can be annihilated by practicing the antagonism of it." This means that by putting an end to causes, things such as suffering can be eliminated forever. Thus, we can deduce that the mind by its own nature is pure, clear, and faultless; but it is obscured by temporary clouds of faults.

Four Noble Truths

The essence of the path to be practiced for liberation consists of the sixteen features of the Four Noble Truths. Consequently, we would like to briefly introduce these elements. Since each of the Four Noble Truths has four features, there are sixteen elements in all.

(1) The four features of "True Suffering" are based on misunderstandings of being clean, happy, permanent and on the existence of an I or atman. (a) We are void of anything clean for there is no I or atman which is different from the suffering body itself. (b) This physical body, which is the real samsara, is not happiness because it is completely under the control of action (karma) and afflictions (klesha). (c) This body cannot be permanent because it is undergoing change at every single moment. (d) The causal body is without an I or atman, as there does not exist such an I or atman.

(2) The four features of "True Case" are: the cause, the all-

growing, the effectively encouraging growth, and the agent. (a) These are the roots of all sufferings, karma, and cyclic existence with passion, the true cause. (b) Likewise, karma and cyclic existence with passion is all-growing, because all kinds of pains and sorrows are caused by them over and over again. (c) Karma and cyclic existence effectively encourage the growth of suffering for they create very strong sufferings. (d) They are also the agents since the passion for cyclic existence is the spontaneous agent of sufferings.

(3) The four features of "True Cessation" are: cessation, calmness, complete satisfaction, and sure liberation (definite deliverance). These are the remedies of the four misunderstandings regarding cessation, namely, believing in the nonexistence of liberation, mistaking some passioned aspect for liberation, looking for liberation above the end of suffering, and believing that there cannot be definite deliverance. (a) The elimination of suffering forever through antagonistic methods is cessation. Here one is free of sufferings. (b) As it is devoid of all afflictions, it is calmness. (c) It is completely satisfying because it is the supreme stage of bliss and liberation. (d) Once this liberation is achieved there is no losing it, thus it is definite deliverance.

(4) The four features of "True Path" are: suitability, accomplishment, path, and definitely giving forth (definite emergence). (a) Wisdom, actually knowing the nonexistence of I or atman is the path because it leads to liberation. (b) This wisdom is suitable for it is the direct antidote of afflictions. (c) It is also accomplishment as it correctly knows the real state of mind. (d) It has the aspect of definitely giving forth because it brings forth the esteemed object.

Logic of Establishing the Nonexistence of I or Atman

The logic for establishing the nonexistence of I through understanding the main causes binding us to worldly existence is discussed in the Madhyamika Shastras, the texts of the central philosophy of Buddhism. This logic can be categorized into two groups, based on the person and phenomena. These two—the person and phenomena—are the main causes of cyclic existence (samsara). Thus, they should be the main subject of discussion when establishing the nonexistence of the two selves. It is said in Dan-nge-nam-jed: "attachment to the person, regarding which one thinks it is Me, the I and the phenomena on its continuum are the main binders, thus they are also the main subject of belief in the existence of Self. Therefore, the logics are also condensed for the repudiation of these two Selves."

The main logic for establishing the nonexistence of the phenomenal self is the logic of not originating through the four ends. Acharya Nagarjuna, while commenting on the theory of entering the sixth Bhumi (stage) by ten equal aspects, observed that the "equal aspect of nonoriginating is the most important." Thus, it is mentioned at the very beginning of the *Mula Madhyamikakarika*: "Neither from self nor from others . . ."

Likewise, Acharya Chandrakirti discussed nonorigination through the four ends in the *Madhyamika-avatāara*. Thus the main logical reason for establishing the nonexistence of the phenomenal self is reached by discussing nonorigination through four ends. This does not mean that there is self-origination. Now, let us discuss the logical reasons for establishing the nonorigination through four ends in their own perspectives. They are: (1) originating from self, (2) originating from other than self, (3) originating from both, and (4) originating without cause.

For example, a grown sprout need not grow again because it is already grown. A thing which has obtained its identity does not need to grow again. Otherwise, there is no end to growth and a grown thing would be required to grow again. It is also said in *Buddhapalita,* "Things do not grow or originate from themselves because there is no purpose and moreover, there will never be completion of growth, which is absolutely irrational." Something that has obtained itself need not grow again as there is no purpose for such growth. If a thing originates from such causes having self-definition then it must grow from everything, as everything has the same aspect of being other. Thus it is said in the twentieth chapter of the *Mula-Madhyamika-karika:* "If a different fruit grows from a different cause then there is no question of one and not the other being the cause of a thing. So, from the above two reasons it is clear that there can't be origination from both. Nothing occurs without any cause, otherwise, everything must grow from everything in all times".

The nonexistence of the self or person (purush-atman) can be established by examining the seven aspects of the example of a cart. A cart is composed of several elements and parts, which together are called a cart and serve the purpose of a cart. But each component part is not the cart. By assembling all the parts together into their right places, a cart comes into existence. It is the same case with the self or person. Thus it is said in the *Madhyamika-avataara* when discussing this example: "A cart can neither exist apart from its component parts, nor be the same as its parts, . . . nor is it only the composition, nor the shape so formed." This means that a cart does not exist in these seven aspects, but by depending on the parts we can be sure that there is a cart which can actually be used for certain purposes. It is the same with the self.

Furthermore, it would be a mistake to identify the self or person with the physical body. First, such an identification would be meaningless because the physical body is caused by causes. Second, such a self would be as many as there are parts of the physical body. Thirdly, if the physical body is the self then the self must be born and must also die together with the physical body. Here a question can arise: what is wrong in accepting the self as being born and dying? If it is just an etymological fact, there is nothing wrong with this view. But when birth or death of self means "independent by one's own self," it is mistaken in three ways. If the originating and ceasing of the self is independent and by its own self then (1) there can't be anyone who remembers his or her previous birth or life, (2) such efforts or collection of deeds (karma) would be of no importance, and (3) one can suffer or enjoy the fruit of a thing with which one has no relation whatsoever.

But we can't hold that the self is completely separate from the body. Otherwise, we can't accept the originating, ceasing, and lasting of the self as we know it. So, in the *Madhyamika-karika* it is said "If the self is completely separate from the physical composition, then there can't be the existent nature of the self."

Just as the composition of the aggregate can't be accepted as the self, neither can we assume that the shape of the aggregate is without any form. By this analysis, the self cannot be regarded as having an independent nature. Thus the self does not exist by itself. There is no self as such except in an etymological sense.

Various aspects of the nonexistence of the self are taught by the Enlightened One. These teachings are designed to suit intellectual powers of different individuals. They include the views of a permanent single, independent I, an independent, substantial self, the absolute that is void of subject and perception. All such phenomena exist in an etymological but not in an absolute sense. These matters are crucial to the principle of cause and effect as well as the overcoming of worldly bondage and the attainment of liberation. The former views are the steps of understanding the later ones and there is no contradiction in gradual practice.

We have thus briefly discussed how our basic bondage to cyclic existence can be recognized in order to be able to practice the methods of liberation. So, in short, those having ability should practice in accordance with the five texts by Arya Maitrinath, the six texts on central philosophy by Acharya Nagarjuna, and the graded course to enlightenment by Acharya Tsongkhapa.

Therefore, we have to practice wholeheartedly while we are in contact with such precious guidance for liberation in order to make this human life meaningful for oneself and others. By doing so we can lead a happy and benevolent social life and guide fellow beings toward a better future and ultimately gain liberation from all worldly chains. It is not necessary or essential to remain solitary or torture oneself to such extremes in the name of such practice for liberation.

As man is a social animal, he should seek happiness and liberation while being in society by conquering his own mind and eliminating all negative views and thoughts. Thus there is the possibility of liberation in social life.

MAY ALL SENTIENT BEINGS GAIN THE WISDOM OF PERFECTION.

The Social Philosophy of Dhammology

SIDDHI BUTR-INDR

A Thai Preface

According to the "domino theory," a country such as Thailand was internally vulnerable and would tend to fall in whatever direction her neighboring countries of Indochina moved. This view contains an assumption that can be shown to entail a logical fallacy: *ignoratio elenchi*. Moreover, this view failed to recognize the possibilities inherent in Thai culture itself. In this essay, I want to show a way that overcomes the domino theory. My essay is extracted and revised from a larger work in progress entitled "The Social Philosophy of Humanism." There I philosophically explore, after an introductory chapter, the topics of man and man, man and nature, man and culture, and the future of humanity. My purpose there, as here, is to develop a social philosophy from an Eastern, Buddhist perspective. It is formulated within the intellectual culture of Buddhist humanism. But I also seek to engage some Western views. Its final aim is to initiate or propose some form of a dialectical principle that, however limited, might contribute to the creation of new patterns of philosophizing that can serve the *social unification of man*.

My research method is to adapt the Four Noble Truths of the Buddhist tradition to a more contemporary style and situation. This is what must be done since, to my knowledge, the Four Noble Truths are well known and familiar to Eastern peoples, especially to those raised in Buddhist civilizations. My approach, then, proceeds step by step along this path. First, I point out the real, effective phenomena in human society today, the things we are actually experiencing. It is the experience of a world full of difficulties and suffering. Next, I try to explain what the root causes of this situation in the world are and why they remain. In this context, I show that the root cause of this misery can be traced to man's intellectual and spiritual illusions, especially to his dogmatic clinging to philosophical particularity.

Then, I argue that by human striving and endeavor there can be a positive cessation of the root causes that underlie social crises and suffering. The pragmatic truth of the human potential for well-being and human welfare sustains and supports the logical principles proposed. Thus the social philosophy outlined here is neither a dream in the air, nor a fallacious speculation, but a real existence. And in the last section of this essay, I suggest the means and ways that will lead to the extinction of social evils (the negative) and to the establishment of an ideal world (the positive). Central here is the universal cultivation and development of social conscience.

For about three decades now, we in Thailand have been subject to undue stress and strain caused, in part, by the imported philosophical systems of Western culture. These philosophical systems have manifested themselves in socioeconomic and political ideologies and movements. They show, in essence, two historically contradictory elements: dogmatic capitalism and dogmatic communism. Both stand for extremes. But in the Thai perspective these are relative or conditional goods. Democracy based on liberalism is conditionally good and socialism is also, to a degree, agreeable. Yet these elements can be dialectically analyzed and synthesized into "one" through their critical unification in terms of "the Middle Way of Life." This would free us from the extremist cultures these social philosophies—democracy and socialism—have given rise to in the West. This unified social philosophy would be "the social philosophy of humanism," whose essence is embedded in dhamma. If it were to be introduced in the Thai way of life it would surely overcome the domino theory and lead us toward a more promising future.

General Statement

The present age signifies an age of humanism in need.[1] Philosophical interest has shifted from the older interpretations of God, matter, and science to man. Man is a dhamma being. With the dhamma he goes beyond and lives free from the illusive bondage of categorical ideologies and particular systems: religious, philosophical, social, political, and economic. Universal brotherhood based on truth, righteousness, goodness, and peacefulness underlies the social philosophy of dhammology. The social philosophy of dhammology is blooming above the fashions of so-called capitalism, socialism, and even democratic socialism. Without the application of the dhamma to our situation it is impossible to achieve unification in human society.

Human life and society are essentially corporate. Any solution of present-day problems, which are complex in their components and vast in their scope and manifestations, must be a cooperative enterprise. This enterprise may be everlasting so long as humanity continues to inhabit the world.

The world, which has become ecumenically one, longs to be consciously one. No nation, however great, can now live in isolation. It cannot survive by seeking to have a life of its own. It needs to share what others are and have. The brotherhood of nations is important and necessary. It is important no matter how men in any particular society, or in any particular language—political, economic, or philosophical—come to express this idea. Developed countries are as much concerned about the brotherhood of nations as are the developing countries.

In the world today, we have pledged ourselves to international cooperation and to efforts to establish the peace. There is no isolation anymore, even though there remains a great deal of geographical, social, cultural, political, and religious differentiation. The humanist philosophy, with its spirit of cooperation, must be carried beyond the nation to the ecumenical community of mankind. We must employ a democratic way to reinforce such a spirit.

Everyplace is thus called to democracy. It is a social system and method by which we attempt to raise the living standard of people and to give opportunities to every man to develop and fulfill his personality. Democracy becomes a common denominator of social philosophy today. It is crucial in all of our dealings for the welfare and well-being of mankind. It is what is required for the utilization of the principles of wisdom, cooperation, harmony, and mutual respect, based on humanitarianism.[2]

All leaders of democratic societies admit that we should give all members of society the opportunity for a full and fruitful life.[3] This way of life requires us to move toward peaceful coexistence and cooperative living. It asks and urges us to strive patiently and persistently for mutual understanding and to explore every avenue to reach synthetic agreement through the principle of reciprocity.

Living reciprocally, we must have faith in the spirit of man—the spirit capable of suffering and compassion, of endurance and sacrifice, the spirit that has inspired human progress and prosperity. At the same time, we should admit the fallibility of man as a constant factor in human affairs. Yet we do not ask for submission, which is the product of despair, or appeasement, which is the result of demoralization.

We are well advised not to be governed by fixed ideas or ideologies. The basic issue is no longer the victory of this or that nation, of this or that group, of this or that social ideology. What is at issue is the survival or suicide of man. Ours is a time for decision, not despair. The choice is either extinction or human brotherhood. It cannot be left to the vagaries of chance. The test of a nation's right to survive today is measured not by the size of its armaments, but by the extent of its concern for humanity as a whole.

Man is a social and ethical being, with sentiments and emotions developed in the direction of other men. Human personality develops and takes shape in a social environment. The ethical situation leads not only to an intensification of his own inwardness, but also to a recognition of the same inwardness in others. Man is a religious being, craving and searching for cosmic and divine support for his life and activity, and desiring communion with the truth.

Man is a rational being, questioning himself, evaluating his thinking, verbalizing, acting, wondering if he is mistaking fancies for truths or truth for falsity, right for wrong and good for evil. He is a complex creature, leading an inward and outward life and craving stable support both ways. And above all, man is a dhamma being, always striving for the ecumenicalization of the truth, the right, and the good.

Man now wishes to come to face his fellow man more closely, to understand and appreciate him intimately, and to avoid conflicts that involve the entire planet. There is a growing realization in such a risky situation that we have only two alternatives before us: a recognition of the brotherhood of man or the annihilation of man. This necessity to understand and recognize each other—each other's point of view, each other's culture, values, religion, and philosophy—paves the way to establishing what we wish to call "unification in human society," according to the social philosophy of dhammology.

Dhamma and Social Unification

I agree with Professor Northrop when he writes that ours is a paradoxical world.[4] The achievements that are its glory threaten to destroy it. The nations with the highest standard of living, the greatest capacity to take care of their people economically, the broadest education, the highest grade of democratic culture, and the most enlightened enterprise in religious mission exhibit the least capacity to avoid mutual violence and destruction in war of various forms. It would seem that the more civilized we claim to become, the more incapable of maintaining civilization we are.

Probably a better answer to clarify the above situation would suggest that we lack and need the practice of dhamma. One of the main purposes of this thesis is to seek and make available to each culture the values of the others in their common essence, so that each can develop by incorporating all that is valuable in the rest. And the value of any culture can be appreciated only with reference to the value of human brotherhood.

According to the social principle of dhamma, man is the same everywhere and can assimilate the values of every culture and benefit from them. The welfare of humanity based on the conscience of brotherhood, which leads to a fuller and deeper life for man on earth, is much more important and urgent than the spread, by competition and contest, of one's own religion or philosophy for the defeat of all others.

Although we have old rivalries and conflicts of ideas, these must become synthetic moments of the advancing force of the dhamma ethos by which people of different cultures are united and bound into one march of humanity. On this faith depends the hope of the future of mankind. All leaders of humanity—the Buddha, Jesus, Muhammad, and others—realize, I believe, this ecumenical principle of oneness and sameness in humanity. Otherwise, it is nonsensical and useless for UNO and UNESCO to attempt to make available the values of all cultures to each other and to utilize these values.

The principle of dhamma and the social unification of mankind are very intimately related.[5] The possibility of the latter is based in the application of the former. The principle of dhamma formulates the middle way philosophy for mankind. It encourages and establishes unity, harmony, sameness, oneness, brotherhood, and peace in the human community, which becomes finally only one community.

According to the principle of dhamma, the delusion of and attachment to the mistaken conceptual principles of categories, species, accidents, and particularities lead people to become intoxicated by the differentiation of ideologies and systems: philosophical, religious, social, economic, political, etc. The truth is that the more we think and speak of different philosophies, religions, and social ideologies, the more splitmindedness will arise. Thus it is important to understand that all differences are only on the surface of the mind. If we have an enlightened understanding, then we will realize the essence of the truth, we will recognize the fallacies in these differentiations. Then terms such as *ultimate reality, God,* the *Buddha,* the *kingdom of God, nibbana, capitalism, socialism*—call them what you will—will appear as the same in their essence. And that essence is dhamma.

But, as we know, an ordinary man is under the impression that there are many different religions and philosophies and that they are all different to the extent of being hostile and opposed. Thus he considers Buddhism, Christianity, Islam, and so on as incompatible and even bitter enemies. Precisely because of views like this, there exist different religions and philosophies hostilely opposed to one another. If, however, a person has penetrated into the fundamental nature, essence, and purpose (dhamma) of religions and philosophies, he will regard them all as essentially similar. Therefore, the truth, the right, and the good (dhamma) constitute the heart of all religions and philosophies, even though their interpretations and expressions are different and diverse.

But particular religions, philosophies, and social systems are not essentially different. The label "Buddhist social philosophy," for instance, is attached only after the fact. This is also the case with other systems of social philosophy. All leaders of humanity are seeking to teach the truth, the right, and the good—the dhamma. Although we call ourselves Buddhists or Christians or Muslims, we have not yet attained the truth (dhamma) of Buddhism or Christianity or Islam. At this stage, we are simply aware of the shell, the outer covering, which makes us think our religion or philosophy is different from this or that other religion or philosophy. And we are probably inclined to look down upon other religions or philosophies, while praising and supporting our own. We tend to think of ourselves as a separate or superior group: outsiders are not part of our fellowship. They are wrong; only we are right. Such judgments show our ignorance and foolishness.

People who quarrel, who interfere with others, who violate others, or who lose patience with others lose their humanity. They are not really human beings due to the lack of certain qualities of loving-kindness and the like and are depraved. Thus, people who think and claim that other religions and philosophies are different from, inferior to, and incompatible with their own—attitudes that cause hostility, persecution, violence, and mutual destruction—are the most stupid and ignorant of people.

When religions and philosophies are regarded as in opposition and conflict with one another in their beliefs and practice the result is that people become enemies. Everyone concerned thinks: "We are right; they are wrong." This leads to quarreling, fighting, and destruction. Such people only display their foolish egoism. What they are quarreling about is only the outer, conventional form of things. This is due to their ignorance of the inner essence of dhamma. When people of dhammic intelligence and humanitarianism get together over essential matters concerning religions and philosophies, they recognize that they are all the same.

Though outwardly religions and philosophies seem to be contradictory, the person of dhamma knows that the inner spirit and purpose is the same in all cases. The inner essence is similar no matter how different the external forms. Consider the analogy of water: the essential nature of water, in Asia, America, or outer space, is always the same no matter how filthy it appears on the outside. The water is not dirty. It is the other elements and conditions mixed in with the water that are dirty. The essential nature of water is composed of two parts hydrogen and one part oxygen; this is the same everywhere.

Whenever there exists a quarrel, conflict, or violence, whether it is among the rich, the poor, capitalists, socialists, theists, or atheists, it may be likened to people drinking polluted water. In this case the pollutants are prideful bias and egoistic self-centeredness, and just as impure water must be distilled before it is consumed, so we must be purified by means of enculturation of the fourfold dhamma. This will give rise to the purified social consciences to be discussed below.

The problems that arise in a social group have their origin in the desire to satisfy selfish feelings that lead to mutual conflicts and break down human solidarity and unity. When we analyze closely the clashes between nations or between opposing blocs, we discover that there, too, both sides are slaves to their feelings of selfish interest. A war is not fought simply because of adherence to a doctrine or an ideal or anything of the sort. In point of fact, the motivation is the satisfaction of the feelings of craving, lust, hatred, fear, and so on. Each side sees itself making all sorts of gains, scooping up benefits for itself. Such a doctrine is just camouflage or, at best, a purely secondary motive. The most deep-seated cause of all strife is really subservience to feeling. To understand feeling is, then, to know an important root cause responsible for our falling slaves to mental defilements, to evil, to mutual violence, and to the suffering experienced by all humanity.

When dhamma is realized and reached, however, we will reach the central heart of all religious, philosophical, and social truths and come to recognize that Western, Eastern, American, Thai, Chinese, Muslim, capitalist, communist, and so on are all of one and the same humanity. We will finally come to enjoy the union of universal fraternity, which will lead to the complete cessation of suffering.

Development of Social Conscience

Social life is a matter of interorigination, interdependence, and interexistence. That implies a continual process of living according to the principle of what I call "reciprocal altruism."[6] This points further to the more deeply ethical-spiritual interpretation of human brotherhood that any conception of genuine social unity implies and requires certain virtues that produce social consciences culminating in "like-mindedness or one-heartedness" in the people and a certain recognition that their good (and interest) is a common one. It is on this philosophy that the social ideal of fraternity can be built up and worked out.

Men live together and are bound to each other, not by mere instincts and impulses, but by the rational application of certain moral and spiritual values. These values are enculturated, ultimately speaking, by a conscience that may be called "the human conscience of social bond." Accordingly, to establish, maintain, develop and strengthen the social bond and to live together happily and peacefully, people must be advised to cultivate a sense of "fraternity,"[7] to practice the virtues of loving-kindness, compassion, sympathetic joy, and impartiality toward each other and to learn to develop the idea of identity with all others. For, as one's own self is everywhere most dear to oneself, so it is with others; therefore, one who loves oneself should not inflict evil upon others.[8]

Loving-kindness (metta). The virtue of loving-kindness is one of the factors most beneficial both to spiritual development and to the development of a sound pacific relationship in society. With this virtue, people should neither allow their minds to become perverted with enmity nor utter any evil speech. The thought of loving-kindness should free us from hatred and harmfulness. We should show kindness and love toward persons. By starting with one person we should extend this virtue until it suffuses the whole world with the heart of loving-kindness. Loving-kindness would thus become far-reaching, widespread, immeasurable, without enmity and malevolence.[9] "As low-down theives might carve limb from limb with a double-handled saw, yet even then whoever sets his mind at enmity," said the Buddha, "he, for this reason, is not a doer of my teaching."[10]

A man of loving-kindness wishes others to be happy. That is clearly to his own advantage, since, at least, it makes them so much more pleasant to live with. Thus, it is by cultivating within oneself interest in the welfare and well-being of others and feeling their happiness as one's own that we realize loving-kindness. "Just as I want happiness and fear suffering and just as I want to live and not to die, so also others do. . . ." Loving-kindness will encourage one to be able to regard one's enemy without resentment but with the same friendliness as one regards one's own admired, dearly beloved companions.

One should extend loving-kindness toward all living beings equally without making any difference between oneself and others, or between one's own beloved, favorite, pleasant, and agreeable people and those who are neutral to oneself, and even one's enemy. We should always be thinking: "May all living beings be without enmity, without ill will, untroubled; may they keep the self well . . . may they all be safe with the disappearance of all fear and calamities; may they be satisfied with physical pleasure and may their hearts rejoice with all mental bliss."[11]

To remove the evil habit of anger or hatred and to replace it with the virtue of tolerance or patience, one develops the social conscience of loving kindness. One should not allow one's own thought of enmity and ill will to grow against others, even though they might do something wrong to oneself. On the contrary, one should keep one's mind in balance, think of the virtues possessed by others, and forgive faults done to oneself. The exercise of loving-kindness leads, finally, to the path of nonviolence (ahimsa). Ahimsa consists in delighting in the happiness of others, doing no harm to anyone, and cultivating sentiments of loving-kindness. One is meek and kind, compassionate and merciful, benevolent and useful to all living beings, laying aside all sorts of weapons. "Among human beings all should learn to be of one mind with nonviolence," said the Buddha. "They should not violate, destroy, and quarrel with one another as beasts always do."[12]

Compassion (karuna). The virtue of compassion characterizes the social conscience that expresses itself in a sense of participation with others in their time of troubles and difficulties, making one's head tremble and quiver at the sight and thought of suffering experienced by others. Compassion even arouses the desire to take upon oneself these things, to put an end to them and to strive to do something, to help and release others from them.

When a compassionate person sees or hears or even thinks of others who live in troubled circumstances, his heart becomes overwhelmed with compassion. The virtue of compassion has for its characteristic the activity of removing from other people those bad conditions of life that cause trouble; it has for its essence the inability to neglect others' sufferings; it has for its function the establishment of selflessness, and for its basis the sight of helplessness of others in such bad conditions. In a word, a compassionate person is unhappy at seeing others in trouble, he feels himself in solidarity with them and furthermore attempts to make them happy. He counts the harm and other bad conditions of others as his own. In this way he identifies himself with others who are in pain, depression, frustration, misery, calamity, lamentation, horror, and so on. Therefore, the social emotion of compassion signifies the virtue that is cultivated with a view, on the one hand, to uproot the ill will to harm others and decrease the evil habit of selfishness and, on the other hand, doing good to them, to make people sensitive to the troubles and difficulties of others to such an extent that they do not wish to increase them further, but to decrease and remove them.

In order to cultivate and develop the virtue of compassion one goes through a process similar to that of loving-kindness. Those toward whom compassion is to be expressed are those who are in trouble and difficulty. Those toward whom one feels compassion one strives to help and make free as much as possible from such situations. Psychologically speaking, compassion is closely allied to cruelty and the two may be easily mistaken for one another. They are the opposite sides of the same medal. Both the compassionate and the cruel are sensitive to the troubles and difficulties experienced by others and keen in observing them. But the sharp difference is that the former experience pain, while the latter derive pleasure from what they see, hear, or even recollect. That is, the compassionate person shares his heart and emotion with those who are in suffering; the cruel one keeps them away and even tries to make them suffer more.

Sympathetic Joy (mudita). The virtue that makes one glad and joyful when seeing or hearing of or even recollecting the success and happiness of others is called "mudita."[13] It has for its characteristic the state of (mutual) rejoicing, for its essence the absence of envying, for its function the suppression of disgust, and for its basis the cheerful acknowledgment of good fortune and prosperity achieved by others. From the above description we see that the virtue of sympathetic joy requires a deliberate effort to identify oneself with those who live successfully and happily and that it enables a person to feel a genuine joy at the happiness of others as much as at his own. It also enables one to share with others their joy of possession, their material or spiritual success, their promotions to positions of civil or national or other importance, or their receipt of titles and glories. It counteracts conceits of all kinds. Its growth and development checks craving's grip in the heart of man. A person, particularly one who is under the influence of jealousy, is advised to cultivate this social emotion of sympathetic joy. He should arouse within himself thoughts that foster this emotion and cultivate the habit of sincerely congratulating those who are released from troubles and difficulties and attain the fulfillment of their wishes. He should rejoice with them in their welfare, prosperity, and well-being. On seeing or hearing or even remembering others to be happy, cheerful, or joyous, the man of sympathetic joy thinks within himself: "Verily, how good, how excellent it is that this fellow lives happily." He treats all people, and even all living beings, with wholehearted gladness in the same manner as he does himself and his own beloved person. And, moreover, he prays that their good fortune, prosperity, and well-being may last long.

The virtue of sympathetic joy helps a man to learn how to appreciate, with a sincere heart, the prosperous conditions of others, to be heartily pleasant in his dealings with them, and to share their happiness even by making it resound in his own heart. It also furthers the sense of altruism and subdues the latent feelings of grudge or ill will against people in superior positions. By virtue of his ability to identify himself with others, the sympathetic man always welcomes with joy the happiness of his fellow man and never welcomes their miseries, and gets rid of what we might call mental isolation caused by selfishness. In the depth of their hearts, some people harbor a definite aversion to dwelling on the happiness of others, since egoism and jealousy are a strong and deep-seated, though rarely admitted, counterforce in their minds. All the time, we find men jealously comparing their lot with that of others and begrudging others their good fortune. Therefore, to remove this evil attitude and habit, the cultivation of the social spirit of sympathetic joy is introduced.

Impartiality (upekkha). This principle, in its literal sense, implies the virtue enabling one to keep one's own mind in a balanced state. [14] The virtue of impartiality (or even-mindedness) has the characteristic of evolving the mode of being balanced as regards beings; its essence is seeing the equality of beings; its manifestation is the suppression of aversion and bias. Turning to the kammic point of view relating to the practice of impartiality, we find that it implies the arousing of an equal attitude toward all living beings and makes one see them as equals in as far as there is a possibility, according to the law of kamma, for all of them to act and react freely and live in accordance with their own actions. In this respect, the virtue of impartiality points to two considerations. First, one is advised to realize that all beings are equal in all their aspects and conditions: as "beings," all are essentially the same under natural law. And second, one should consider the effect that the actions of beings have on themselves, the reason they act as they act and endure what they endure. Thus one realizes that one's action determines one's own fate and destiny, that whatever befalls one has been brought upon by oneself, and that only oneself can alter one's own fate and destiny. Consideration of the workings of this law of action leads us to understand that whatever is, is so because it must be, that everyone must manage one's own affairs, and that everyone must discharge one's own duties. In regard to the mode of mutual conduct in society, the modern discussion also uses the term "upekkha" to explain the virtue of impartiality in the sense of just, fair, or righteous treatment. In this regard, it is closely related to its other above-mentioned aspects and to the first three virtues already discussed. [15] Thus a person of impartial spirit does act differently toward those who are beloved, pleasant, or favorite and those who are otherwise, but he behaves toward others in accordance with the principle of dhamma. In his dealings with others he avoids the four ways of unfair treatment, based on either favoritism or personal preference, hatred, illusion, and fear. [16].

Given its deeper, spiritual implication, the virtue of upekkha relates to the principle of nonattachment (anupadana)—the thought of "I-ness" and of "mine-ness." The purpose of this is to teach us that acting in a nonegoistic way helps us to destroy impurities. Such a viewpoint results from not having an ego, not being attached to "myself," not conceiving relationships to anything in terms of "I" and "my," which exist only on a conventional level but not at the dhammic level of nonattachment.

With the presupposition of "I" and "my," people are driven to conflict, quarrels, violence, destruction, war, and away from achievement of world peace. Many people, moreover, have restless or agitated minds filled with the dark clouds of egoistic delusion. Consequently, they are wary, gloomy, and insecure. Eventually, they may suffer severe depression and nervous breakdown. Disorders of the mind, diseases of insecurity, anxiety, and neurosis result from clutching at and clinging to such things as fame and money, to being caught up in such matters as profit and loss, happiness and unhappiness, ease and disease, praise and blame. In such a situation, people are advised to practice the social virtue of nonattachment, which underlies the principle of impartiality. They should practice this virtue always thinking: "Do work of all kinds with a mind that is void, and then to the voidness give all of the fruits."[17]

NOTES

1. There are several forms of humanism: the naturalistic, the evolutionary and pragmatic, the communistic, the scientific, the theological, and the atheistic. For more details, see Siddhi Butr-Indr, *The Philosophy of Humanism* (Chiang Mai: Faculty of Humanities, Chiang Mai University, 1980), chap. 1.

2. For a more detailed explanation, see Siddhi Butr-Indr, *The Philosophy of Humanism,* 274–85.

3. For a more detailed explanation, see Siddhi Butr-Indr, *An Introduction to Sociopolitical Philosophy* (Bangkok: Phrae Pitya Publishing House, 1979), 211–19.

4. See Filmer S. Northrop, *The Meeting of East and West* (New York: Macmillan, 1946), 1.

5. In the original Pali language, the term *dhamma* (*dharma* in Sanskrit) is used to refer to all the intricate and involved things that make up what we call nature. In the main, according to Buddhadasa's interpretation, dhamma embraces nature itself, the law of nature, man's duty to act in accordance with the law of nature, and finally the benefits to be derived from acting in accordance with

the laws of nature. See *Buddha Toward the Truth,* ed. Donald K. Swearer (Philadelphia: Westminster, 1979), 60.

6. For more details, see Siddhi Butr-Indr, *The Social Philosophy of Buddhism* (Bangkok: Mohomakuta Rajvidayalaya Press, 1973), 130–34.

7. Ibid., 183 ff.

8. Ibid., 246, 256.

9. For more details, see ibid., 129 ff.

10. Ibid., 166 f.

11. Ibid., 244, 245, 342 ff.

12. Ibid., 211.

13. Ibid., 268.

14. Ibid., 246.

15. Ibid., 246. As a matter of fact, the climax of the first three virtues—of metta, karuna, and mudita—suggests that one should identify oneself with others. In this respect, one learns to treats oneself as righteous and is not given to the habit of partial, unjust treatment toward others.

16. Ibid., 1ff.; see also note 31, above.

17. Buddhadasa, 95. For further material, see T. W. Rhys Davids, ed., *Digha Nikaya,* 3 vols. (London: PTS, 1949); V. Fausboll, ed., *The Jataka,* 6 vols. (London: PTS, 1962); M. Leon Feer, ed., *Samyutta Nikaya,* 5 vols. (London: PTS, 1960); H. Oldenberg, ed., *Vinaya Pitaka,* 5 vols. (London: PTS, 1964); V. Trenckner and R. Chalmers, eds., *Majjhima Nikaya,* 5 vols. (London: PTS, 1960); and H. C. Warren, ed., *Visuddhimagga* (Cambridge: Harvard University Press, 1950).

REFERENCES

Butr-Indr, Siddhi. *The Social Philosophy of Buddhism.* Bangkok: Mahamakuta Rajvidayalaya Press, 1973.

———. *An Introduction to Socio-political Philosophy.* Bangkok: Phrae Pitya Publishing House, 1979.

———. *The Philosophy of Humanism.* Chiang Mai: Faculty of Humanities, Chiang Mai University, 1980.

Davids, T. W. Rhys, ed. *Digha Nikaya.* 3 vols. London: PTS, 1949, 1960.

Fausboll, V., ed. *The Jataka.* 6 vols. London: PTS, 1962.

Feer, M. Leon, ed. *Samyutta Nikaya.* 5 vols. London: PTS, 1960.

Northrop, F. S. C., *The Meeting of East and West*. New York: Macmillan, 1946.

Oldenberg, H., ed. *Vinaya Pitaka*. 5 vols. London: PTS, 1964.

Swearer, Donald K., ed. *Toward the Truth*. Philadelphia: Westminster, 1974.

Trenckner, V. and Chalmers, R., eds. *Majjhima Nikaya*. 5 vols. London: PTS, 1960.

Warren, H. C., ed. *Visuddhimagga*. Cambridge: Harvard University Press, 1950.

Social and Political Dimensions of Eastern Orthodoxy
CONSTANTINE N. TSIRPANLIS

What is the Orthodox understanding of the terms *politics* and *society?* The word *politics* in the Eastern Orthodox experience means not only the "art of governing a city or polis" (the *politiké techne* of Aristotle), but also the art (*politiké areté*) of developing right personal, social, and existential relations based on the Trinitarian interpersonal life and relations. Thus, politics is not just a useful compromise in social life, but a problem of truth, a problem that determines the meaning of human life and existence, the spiritual and cultural goals that transform time and matter and make perfect man's humanity as God's creation.

Accordingly, the Orthodox do not divide this world into "two kingdoms" or "two cities," in the fashion of Saint Augustine, since this world is also God's creation and as such cannot be separated into sacred and profane. This truth does not, however, ignore the fact that this ontological unity of God's creation was broken with man's fall, with his alienation and separation from his creator. Hence, restoration of personal and cosmic unity, harmony and peace, constitutes the main objective of a genuinely humanitarian political system. The antidote to the political pessimism of Augustine and Tertullian was of course Eusebius's theocratic "harmony" of the two authorities, divine and human, church and state. Thanks to a political system that stresses organic unity comparable to that of the soul and the body, and the close cooperation but not identity between church and state, with common spiritual values and goals, the famous Byzantine Empire prospered and survived for more than a thousand years, a unique event in world history. Certainly, the Byzantine pattern of church-state relations cannot be applied to our contemporary political systems in all aspects. However, our politicians and church leaders must be willing to learn important lessons from Byzantine political philosophy and church history.

The Orthodox church, considering herself witness of God's kingdom and of a continuous spiritual event of God's incarnation,[1] a continuous catharsis of man throughout the centuries, rather than a legalistic or hierocratic institution, does not exclude from her loving care sinful kings and politicians, heretics and criminals. She does not have enemies as human persons. Her only enemy is sin per se, not human beings. Eastern Orthodox humanism is rooted in and based on the truth of the human person as a God-centered social and loving being, contrary to Western humanism, which is anthropocentric or self-centered, and as such doomed to despair.

The Orthodox church as the "assembly of sinners" (the expression of Saint Ephrem of Syria) and as eucharistic *koinonia* (Christ's society and communion of love) views herself as a community of love, of "saints" who strive to restore themselves from the temptations of fallen nature—narcissism and self-love—within the world, but not according to the world's standards. Nevertheless, the entire world in the eyes and experience of Eastern Orthodoxy is sacrament. The term *sacrament* is not a didactic reduction of the Word, a *verbum visible,* as Augustine put it. The Greek word *mystery,* used by Eastern Christians for the Eucharist, has two connotations: being initiated into the heavenly choir surrounding the presence of God, and an act of love between God and his universe through the mediation of man in Christ. The two are linked. Initiation implies participation, and true participation is love, a mutual *perichoresis* in which God and the universe embrace and penetrate each other. In a sense, this is why marriage is a sacrament or mystery: not because through it grace is given, but because the marriage relationship at its best is the reflection and sacrament of this mutual self-giving, this mutual embracing and interpenetration of God and the universe of love.

This union with God and with each other in Christ is also the true meaning of the Eucharist. This eucharistic union, in which we are one with the whole creation in our responsive self-offering to God, is the mystery that fulfills human existence. And this mysterious reality is depicted in our initial offering (of bread and wine) in the Eucharist, an offering not merely of two things, but also of our whole world, our whole life in all its dimensions.

In the first chapters of Genesis, we find a clear statement of this sacramental character of the world. God made the world and then man; and he gave the world to man to *eat* and *drink.* The world was God's gift to us, existing not for its own sake, but in order to be transformed, to become life, and so to be offered back as man's gift to God. Hence, in our relation to nature we have to walk the precarious path and live in the difficult rhythm between *mystery* and *mastery*. It is not technology and theology or science and theology that need to be reconciled. It is, rather, these two attitudes—mastery of nature and mystery of worship—which have to be held in balance. Our mastery of the universe is like the mastery of our bodies; it is not that we may have it for our own use, but that we may give nature, as our extended body, into the hands of the loving God in the great mystery of the eucharistic self-offering. This is the mystery of the cross. Christ gave himself, with humanity and nature, to God in self-denying love, and thereby saved humanity and nature. It is in that eternal act of sacrifice and love that we too are called to participate. Technology is a way of humanizing the world of matter in time-space, and thereby of extending the human body to envelop the whole universe. But that humanizing and extension, if it is to be salvific, must find its proper culmination in man's offering of himself and the universe to God in love. A secular technology of mastery of nature for oneself is the "original" sin of refusing our mediatory position between God and the universe, dethroning God, and claiming mastery for the sake of indulging our own cupidity, avarice, and greed.

The Roman Catholics as well as the Orthodox are criticized by the Protestants for laying too much stress on the priest's difference from ordinary men, on the supernatural character of his function. This criticism has much truth in it. But as an Orthodox theologian of Russian descent puts it:

In such matters, we should perhaps understand the "supernatural" as being the natural in an extraordinary degree. Man was created as a priest: the world was created as the matter of a sacrament. But sin came, breaking this unity; this was no mere issue of broken rules alone, but rather the loss of a vision, the abandonment of a sacrament. Fallen man saw the world as one thing, secular and profane, and religion as some-thing entirely separate, private, remote and "spiritual." The sacramental sense of the world was lost. Man forgot the priesthood which was the purpose of meaning of his life. He came to see himself as a dying organism in a cold, alien universe.[2]

Christ as the new Adam, the perfect man, restored that priest-hood, the simple original act that man failed to perform, and with it matter and nature were restored in its original unity with humanity.

This point is stressed in the prayers and experience of the eucharistic liturgy and it is declared by Saint Paul in Romans 8. God includes the whole universe in his creation as well as in redemption in Christ. This does not remove all distinctions between humanity and the rest of creation. Humanity has a special vocation as the priest of creation, as the mediator through whom God manifests himself to creation and redeems it. But this does not make humanity totally discontinuous with creation, since a priest has to be an integral part of the people he represents. Christ has become part of creation, and in his created body he lifted up the creation to God; humankind must participate in this eternal priesthood of Christ. This participation becomes possible in the liturgy, which is not only a message of Christ's incarnation, death, and resurrection, but is especially a taste of God's kingdom, a participation in his glorified body and blood through the real presence of the Holy Spirit, a living reality that belongs both to history and to eschatology. For Orthodox Christians, liturgy does not simply mean a specific cultic act, but a definite life-style (the work of people), which, while certainly rooted and focused in the eucharistic liturgy, *also embraces the whole life of the person.* For the Orthodox faithful, liturgy in this sense means "bringing the heavenly into the earthly, in the way that John Chrysostom suggested when he heard the singing of the heavenly choirs and the harmonies of an eternal song in the very midst of the things of time. But at the same time liturgy is the elevation of the earthly into the heavenly places, the fulfillment of every immanent creaturely *telos* (goal) and its transfiguration by grace."[3]

As a representative Greek Orthodox bishop and theologian expressively wrote:

The Liturgy is not an escape from life, but a continuous transformation of life according to the prototype Jesus Christ, through the power of the Spirit. . . . Each of the faithful is called upon to continue a personal "liturgy" on the secret altar of his own heart, to realize a living proclamation of the good news "for the whole world." Without this continuation the Liturgy remains incomplete. Since the eucharistic event we are incorporated in Him who came to serve the world and to be sacrificed for it, we have to express in concrete diakonia, in community life, our new being in Christ, the Servant of all. The sacrifice of the Eucharist must be extended in personal sacrifices for the people in need, the brothers for whom Christ died. Since the Liturgy is the participation in the great event of liberation from the demonic powers, then the continuation of Liturgy in life means a continuous liberation from the powers of the evil that are working inside us, a continual reorientation and openness to insights and efforts aimed at liberating human persons from all demonic structures of injustice, exploitation, agony, loneliness, and at creating real communion of persons in love.[4]

The Orthodox Emphasis on Eucharistic Ecclesiology

It is not accidental that in recent years Orthodox theologians have placed strong emphasis in Orthodox ecclesiology on the eucharistic understanding of the church. There are two main reasons. First, there is a strong trend today toward changing the church into a mere sociopolitical institution or into an ally of the established government. Therefore, many Orthodox theologians, laymen as well as clergymen, constantly urge the churches to persevere trustingly in their appointed role as "bond-servants to God," for only by so doing can they maintain their freedom over against ideologies and political systems, which the church cannot under any circumstances or for any considerations of expediency enter into coalition or even identify herself with, but of which she must always remain the prophetic "crisis." Second, there is the modern misunderstanding of the nature and mission of the church, which was originally understood and experienced as Christian *diakonia,* witness and promotion of God's kingdom on earth, and as a contribution to the creation of a fellowship of solidarity, in the sense of a metamorphosis of "natural" orders and the outlook of a society composed of individuals into a *koinonia* of persons. Of course, this remains a constant task of the church, but one that is supremely urgent today when modern conceptions and conditions of life are forcing appalling *paramorphoses* (deformations) on human society, *paramorphoses* that aim at obliterating the very fact that man has been created in the image of God (moral and intellectual freedom). Precisely this fact lays upon us an inescapable obligation to defend the human dignity of the person in all its aspects. Consequently, *cultura agri* (living conditions), *cultura animi* (sanctification, *theosis*), and *cultura Dei* (Eucharist, doxology) are inseparably connected. The Orthodox emphasis is placed on the individual and his spiritual powers to act in a morally right way. The state cannot be venerated or respected except as an agency representing the will and interests of the people, and hence individuals are obligated to give to society what it needs to perform its mission so that human beings can live in an atmosphere that guarantees the free exercise of man's spiritual powers. The primary witness of the church as a eucharistic community living the Trinitarian life on earth is to generate and sustain the specificity and uniqueness of persons to the end that persons-in-relation do not sunder the community, nor does the community suppress or destroy the specificity and uniqueness of each member. Such a relationship of mutuality in love and freedom eliminates the need to compete with each other or to affirm oneself by suppressing the other. It excludes domination, repression, or exploitation and seeks to conserve the dignity and freedom of all persons. It also means that we must respect and foster cultural, racial, political, economic, or other group identities, making sure, however, that no group identity becomes closed or absolutized.

The Christian attitude, according to the Orthodox experience, is never that of the abstract idea of the good, is not defined through a system of impersonal relations; it is always an interiority, a conversion, a call for the love that God has for us in Jesus Christ, an obedience that renews us, so that God may reveal himself through us to our neighbor as the lover. Even Orthodox monasticism, in its genuine spirit, is a strong witness—*martyria* and *martyrion* (martyrdom)—for the kingdom of God on earth, since the kingdom has been promised to the poor.[5] Making oneself actually poor for the love of and as a sign of that kingdom, which is our *only* wealth, becomes an undisputed criterion of perfection and of evangelical authenticity. Further, this means that the church should totally identify herself with the outcasts, with those who suffer and are persecuted because of their devotion to God's justice and love. This is also the reason an effective lack of an assumed or a voluntary poverty among Christians will make them lose the consciousness of their pilgrimage on earth. The gospel will then lose its savor. This *martyria*, or witness, recalls the remark of the Epistle to Diognetos of the second century: "they spend their lives on earth, but they are citizens of heaven." And that is possibly the special gift of Orthodoxy. "Let the dead bury their dead" is spoken to the living to remind them of the resurrection of the dead and to orient history beyond its boundaries. In the words of Paul Evdokimov:

The traditional Priesthood contemplates in Christ the perfect bishop and the perfect layman and knows that in Christ there is neither Jew nor Greek, neither man nor woman, neither bishop nor layman, for each finds there his fulness and his overflow (Col. 3:9–11). The body is

86

well organized, hierarchically without any confusion about equality. No layman exceeds a bishop, but the bishop can exceed himself in his sanctity: "we are not the masters of your faith, we are the *servants* of your joy" (the joy of final liberation). The only real power of a bishop is that he presides in love, with the gift of tenderness and of enlightened charity. His only power persuasion is martyrdom.[6]

One also notes that in Dostoyevski's eyes, the czar in his sacred vocation of noble revolutionary exceeds himself, and that Russian socialism is fulfilled in the universal church on earth.

What Sociopolitical System Does the Orthodox Church Support?

It is true that the Orthodox church as a whole has not presented the world with the sight of a limitless wealth. Orthodoxy has remained the church of the poor, of peasants, of artisans, of a large number of poor bishops and badly paid priests. However, since the church of the West has sided with the rich, the whole of Christendom has become the object of social criticism. This is a striking example of the solidarity of the Christian churches in evil as well as in good.

However, it is equally true that, first, the church must not identify herself with any of the structures of temporal existence, even if they are structures of liberation. She vigilantly maintains her freedom to enter into freely chosen relationships with any structure, in faithfulness to her own true identity. In the very interest of identification with the poor and the oppressed, she cannot as a church tie herself completely to any given structure. Second, the churches' highest priority is the renewal of their own Trinitarian-eucharistic life, in order that the church may truly fulfill her vocation as sign and sacrament of the kingdom. This means setting her own house in order, eliminating counter-Trinitarian elements in her own structures, and renewing the teaching and sacramental ministry. Third, in the very process of such renewal of her own life, she will be renewing and freeing her own members to become creative agents of transformation in society through their own God-given vocations. If members of the church, individually or as groups, felt called to engage in liberation struggles or fights against tyranny, it will be the churches' task to extend her special and discerning pastoral care to such people. The church witness is necessarily political since it is made within the city and thus disturbs some authority. An absolutely apolitical church is completely inconceivable; it necessarily is *in patria*. Did the Lord not render an eminently political judgment when he called Herod "fox"?[7] The church must always carry on the prophetic function of Christ, otherwise she ceases to be the people of God. Furthermore, social and political revolts in the history of Eastern Orthodoxy are not few, and they were supported by the church as long as they were motivated and controlled by the spirit of love of freedom, recovery of human dignity and rights, and the purpose of God's providence, which is "to *unify* by faith and spiritual charity those whom vice has sundered in various ways."[8] It should be pointed out also that the Orthodox church has consistently opposed all forms of racism. Typical of this opposition is an encyclical of the ecumenical patriarch Metrophanes III to the Orthodox Christians of Crete in 1568. At that time, Crete was still under Venetian rule. A quarrel between the Cretan Jews and Venice over the payment of certain debts provoked the Venetians to adopt anti-Semitic measures. The wave of anti-Semitism seems to have been initiated by the Latin patriarch of Venice, Laurentius Justinian. The Jews had appealed to the ecumenical patriarchate, complaining that even Orthodox Christians had taken part in hostilities toward the Jews. Whereupon the patriarch wrote that those who unjustly treat the Jews in any way are excommunicated and condemned, since injustice and defamation were wrong whoever the victim was, and no one who committed such wrong could possibly regard himself as innocent on the pretext that he had only wronged someone of another faith and not one of the faithful. For even our Lord Jesus Christ tells us in the gospel not to bully or blackmail anyone, "making no distinction and not permitting Christians to deal unjustly with people of other faiths."[9] At the very time Gobineau and Chamberlin were stirring up Europe with racist heresies, the Synod of Constantinople (1872) officially condemned contemporary racism with its nationalistic overtones (*ethnophyletismos*). This was, if not the first, certainly one of the first official pronouncements of the Christian church on this subject.

But let me go back to earlier centuries, to the Greek Fathers of the fourth and fifth centuries—Basil the Great, Gregory the Theologian, and John Chrysostom. Their message is the message of the power of their experience of God: "For the Kingdom of God does not consist in talk but in power."[10] In their experience, the Christian world becomes an actually lived social reality. The Basiliad of the great Cappadocian saint and doctor, which was the first Christian hospital for the sick, a social work of a certain breadth, is called a "new city" by Saint Gregory of Nazianzus.[11] Saint John Chrysostom considered just sharing of goods in the city of Antioch, which would abolish misery; the church sought to influence Byzantine legislation; monasteries freed all Christian slaves; judges periodically visited prisons to inspect personally the improvement of the prisoners condemned by them. The universal doctrine of the church in the East as well as in the West is that "the rich withhold the goods of the poor, even if this wealth is honestly acquired or legally inherited."[12] The church Fathers did not glorify poverty as such, nor did they condemn riches. Nor did they cherish any illusions. Saint Neilos writes, "the religious person is not the person who distributes alms to many, but one who treats no one unjustly."[13] Likewise Saint Augustine says, "you give bread to the hungry, but it would have been better that no one be hungry and that you do not give to anybody." This is not only the yeast of a social revolution, but the hope that a day will come in which the church will cease speaking of Christ, and show him forth, reveal him, become herself Christ by sharing his love for the whole of humankind.[14] Staretz Zossimus (in notes for *The Brothers Karamazov*) makes a very daring remark: "love men in their sin, love even their sins, for this is the love of God." "To love" in this case means to understand and have compassion.

NOTES

1. Cf. Gregory the Theologian, "IV Theological Oration 21," *Christology of the Later Fathers,* ed. E. R. Hardy (Philadelphia: Library of Christian Classics, Westminster Press, 1954), 193.

2. Alexander Schmemann, *Church, World, Mission* (New York: Saint Vladimir's Seminary Press, 1979), 223.

3. A. Papaderos, "Liturgical Diaconia," *An Orthodox Approach to Diaconia* (Geneva: World Council of Churches, 1980), 22.

4. A. Yannoulatos, *Martyria-Mission,* ed. I. Bria (Geneva: World Council of Churches, 1980), 66–67.

5. Luke 6:20.

6. P. Evdokimov, "Eschatological Transcendence," *Orthodoxy-Life and Freedom,* ed. A. J. Philippou (Oxford: Studion Publications, 1973), 45.

7. Luke 3:32.

8. Cf. Saint Maximus Confessor, *Capita de caritate,* English trans. with introduction by P. Sherwood (Westminster, Md.: Newman Press, 1955), vol. 4, no. 17, 194. Also see my study, "Aspects of Maximian Theology of Politics, History, and the Kingdom of God," *The Patristic and Byzantine Review,* no. 1 (1982): 1–21.

9. Luke 3:14.

10. 1 Cor. 4:20.

11. Saint Gregory of Nazianzus, "Oration" 43.63: *Nicene and Post Nicene Fathers of the Christian Church,* vol. 7, 416.

12. Saint John Chrysostom, *Patrologia Graeca* 61: 84. Cf. Homily 20 in 2 Cor.

13. Saint Neilos, *Patrologia Graeca* 79: 1249.

14. John 3: 16–17.

Part Three
RELIGION AND SOCIETY: ISSUES AND CASES

8

Social Uses and Abuses of Religion in Developing Countries

O. OLUKUNLE

Many have written on the crucial importance of religion in society, and no effort has been spared to show us that human beings are by nature religious. Writing about the Yoruba of western Nigeria, Idowu tells us that "the religion of the Yoruba permeates their lives so much that it expresses itself in multifarious ways. It forms the themes of songs, makes topics for minstrelsy, finds vehicles in myths, folktales, proverbs and sayings, and is the basis of philosophy."[1] I doubt if anyone can deny the positive use to which religion has been put and is still being put in establishing and maintaining the sanity of society. Yet few things have been subject to as much abuse as religion, which was meant to serve a salutary purpose in society. This is the point I wish to make in this short essay. My approach will be largely historical, with a few excursions into contemporary developments. I believe that we communicate with God by means of religion and try to convert others or reinforce their faith by means of religious language. Religion, then, becomes very germaine in any intelligible discussion on God. Most of the examples I use are from Africa, not only because it is the continent with the highest number of developing countries, but also because it is the terrain I know best. The fact that I am a Christian and that Christianity is virtually everywhere makes it the religion that will receive most of my attention.

For the purpose of this essay, I define *use* as proper application of something toward an end. By inference, an abuse would be an improper application of something toward a negative or even a positive end. Some things are basically good and serve a good purpose. Think, for example, of oxygen, which is absolutely necessary for the continuation of human life on this planet. On the other hand, some things are, I believe, basically evil. The example that comes readily to mind is a cancerous cell, which can only infect other cells of the body. However, some things that were initially meant to serve good purposes have ended up serving negative ends too. When Alfred Nobel invented dynamite, he meant it to be used by miners to help in blasting hard rocks, thereby making the job less tiring. As we all know, it has been misapplied since then. One can see religion in the same light. It was meant to create a unique link between God and humanity and between human beings. It was to remind man of the existence of the infinite, to help in regulating the relationship between men and in promoting peace. However, religion has been used and abused to promote wars, as in the Islamic Jihad and the Christian Crusades. My point is that men can adapt good things for negative ends if they so desire. Religion is no exception.

I am not the most traveled person, but of all the countries I have visited it strikes me that religion has a greater impact on the lives of individuals in developing countries than in other countries. I will offer an explanation of this later, but let me now provide an example. In 1972, I was a graduate student in the industrial city of Birmingham in the British Midlands and I used to ride the bus past a church. When I went back to Birmingham in 1976, that church had become an electronic warehouse. I imagine that the congregation had gradually thinned out, the parish priest gave up, and the building was sold. By contrast, during this same period at least fifty new church buildings, most of them branches of established churches, were put up in Ibadan, Nigeria. Most people in developing countries take religion quite seriously. Its influence can be seen everywhere. It influenced elections in Nicaragua and it was the rallying point the Ayatollah used against the shah of Iran. (What has been done with power since the Ayatollah took control from the shah is entirely another matter.)

Although I am suspicious of definitions, since they are seldom sufficiently encompassing, I will try to indicate what I mean here by a developing country. A developing country is commonly understood as one that is economically and technologically lagging behind Europe, North America, and Eastern Europe. It is characterized as having a low per capita income. However, according to Walter Rodney, "development in human society is a many-sided process. At the level of the individual, it implies increased skill and capacity, greater freedom, creativity, self-discipline, responsibility and material well-being. Some of these are virtually moral categories and are difficult to evaluate—depending as they do on the age in which one lives, one's class of origins, and one's personal code of what is right and what is wrong."[2] The word *developing* as used by Western scholars, especially economists, refers almost entirely to that narrow issue of economic sufficiency. I take the view that human development goes beyond economic well-being. Coming from Nigeria—one of the countries classified as developing—I am suspicious of the use of this word, which is often a euphemism for underdeveloped. Both terms are used to refer to practically all the countries of Africa, Latin America, and Asia with the exception of Japan. Japan is now often considered to be one of the Western European countries, as if economic well-being obliterates geographical separation. My objection to the use of the word *developing* is twofold. First, it is a term coined and applied by the same developed countries that colonized and still inhibit the development of the so-called developing countries. Colonization, in case anyone is in doubt, had a devastating effect on the colonized. It involved years of physical and enforced rule. This was often followed, in the years after "independence," by even more fears of mental bondage. This was often a pseudoindependence since, although the colonialists officially yielded political rule, they still held the reins of economic power, using surrogates from the formerly colonized countries and multinationals from their own countries to maintain control. My second objection arises from the fact that the concept of development seems to rest unduly on technological and economic considerations. Thus, a country with sophisticated technology, high-income earnings, and a large balance of payments (never mind if most of the money comes from the developing countries) may be said to be developed. But are they developed when the resources of the developed countries East and West have enough weapons to wipe out the whole world ten times over? Civilization or development is regarded as an improvement on earlier stages, but it would appear that our present development is like terminal cancer. The world is walking on such a dangerous nuclear tightrope that we are not sure it will exist into another century. Such a disaster will not arise because God has decided to end this creation; it would, rather, be because we have become too "developed" to learn to live with others in peace. In any case, I think that a so-called developed civilization in which the family—the basic unit of the society—has all but collapsed, in which money has overtaken man, in which the spiritual has been overtaken by the material, in which lethal weapons mean power, and in which God has become a mere footnote is probably heading for destruction. Nevertheless, when I use the term *developing* I use it in the sense of its inventors so that my readers will know which part of the world I am referring to. But, at the same time, I am suggesting that our understanding of development should be expanded to include the values one embraces.

It is possible that many of my readers do not know what it means to come from a developing country. Consequently I will try to describe this situation. My intention is not to create a sense of guilt (even though the developing countries did not create the situation), but to state the way things are in the hope that things will not continue to be as polarized and as one-sided as they are in a world supposedly created by a good God.[3] Being born into almost any of the developing countries of Africa, Latin America, and Asia is an ordeal. The first challenge is to survive at all. Although there are a few exceptions, most people are born into poverty. To be born into poverty is to be born with many disadvantages conferred on you by national and international circumstances over which you have no control whatsoever. It is like going into the boxing ring with both hands tied. You will be beaten before the bout begins. Most developing countries are permanently in recession. Consequently, when the world complains of recession, one must realize that the developing countries are already in desperation.

Of course, not all the people in developing countries are poor. Indeed, the economic and political situations are such that some are so rich, they cannot see the poor. Thus, what we have is not two groups, the haves and have-nots, but two extreme groups of have-mores and have-nevers. Such is the situation in a "democrazy" as opposed to a proper democracy. There is little doubt that most of the people are poor and have little hope of getting rich. Many therefore turn to religion, often in its most aggressive mode, so as not to lose out in eternity. Religious responses in developing countries are totally different from those in Europe. A peasant cannot afford the luxury of reading the writings of Paul Tillich when he has no money to buy new hoes to till his farm. Niebuhr would be meaningful only after you and your neighbor have enough to eat and there is no suspicion that one would rob the other's poultry or goats at night. Poverty has always contributed greatly to the abuse of religion in developing countries. Most of the people who died with the Reverend Jim Jones in Guyana were poor people who found solace in a man posing as a messiah who met their daily needs. His was a religious movement gone berserk. Its Muslim equivalent—the Maitasine group in Nigeria—claimed over three thousand lives in December 1980. Poor and disinherited people do not fear death because they have nothing to lose apart from their poverty. Our discussion of the use and abuse of religion may be easier once we bear these considerations in mind.

When we speak of the *use* in this context we mean the positive ends served by religion, whereas *abuse* means the negative ends. There is sometimes an overlap, where use and abuse defy clear-cut separation.

From the coast to the hinterland in practically all developing countries, the greatest use of religion was in the spread of Western education, without which the administration of the colony could not be carried out since most of the colonialists were victims of tropical diseases. Educated local people were to man the schools, hospitals, offices, and churches of the future. Thus, religion contributed in no small measure to the initial development of the developing countries. Writing about the relevance of the Christian religious missions to education, Ayandele noted that "they adopted a two-fold attitude to the society. On the one hand they sought to effect a moral and social regeneration through their churches and schools. On the other they exerted themselves to prevent the demoralization of the society by the white man's 'fire-water' liquor."[4] There is no doubt that the use of religion to introduce formal Western education and medical facilities is a credit no one can deny.

As mentioned above, poverty is rampant in developing countries, and religion, perhaps playing the role of an opiate, as Marx noted, has helped to stabilize or tranquilize many people who otherwise may have committed suicide out of sheer despair. As long as there is hope for a better tomorrow and a secure eternity, society is bound to be relatively stable. According to O'dea, "People suffering from extreme deprivation and people suffering from anomie (some groups may be experiencing both) display a considerable responsiveness to religions which preach a message of salvation—that is, which present the world as a place of toil suffering and offer some means of deliverance from it. Christianity is a religion of this kind. It offers the believer salvation through participation in Christ's victory over evil and death."[5] Although such use must not be overstressed, neither can it be denied. The house of God is one place where no one will physically turn you back because you are poor. Religion helps to keep the family together and sustain the cherished extended family system. Since the whole family usually worships at the same shrine, church, or mosque, religion remains a useful symbol of cohesion. Finally, religion may help to keep people united in times of trouble or stress. As Susan Budd noted, "the statistics of religious attendance suggest that those whose lives are relatively uncertain, risky or uncontrollable are often more religious. The greater religiosity of women can be explained in this way."[6] This sustenance in times of stress may even be nationwide. The people of Iran were united essentially by Islam to overthrow the shah. Poland is the most recent example in which religion holds the people together. Long after martial law was imposed and trade unions and demonstrations banned, the church remains the rallying point and focus of national unity that no one can ban.

I am not a particularly religious person and so I have no business defending religion when it has been abused or misused in developing countries, but charity demands that one should add that in many cases of abuse it has been by default or accident.

An obvious instance of perhaps accidental abuse of religion in developing countries arises in almost all cases when the introduced religion, especially Christianity, came before the colonialists. Since missionaries, traders, and colonialists came from the same country, they were classed together. In fact, the missionary was seen by some as the bait the colonialists used to make the indigenous people succumb to foreign domination. This linkage was confirmed by the fact that in Nigeria the soldiers helped the missionaries if they ever got into trouble. As Ayandele put it rather succinctly, "allied with, and in many cases inseparable from the British secular arm, at least until the beginning of the twentieth century, missionary enterprise resulted politically in the suppression of Nigerian chiefs by Christian white officials."[7] The missionaries demanded and received British protection and in return turned the territory they covered over to British administration. Nigerians have not forgotten this ambidexterity on the part of the missionaries. Consequently, they began to doubt the good intentions missionaries claimed to have. To mislead people in this way in the name of religion is to abuse religion. And as Ayandele noted elsewhere, "missionary propaganda in Nigeria was not just a religious invasion. In effect it was associated with a political invasion as well. In the background was the secular arm of Britain, to be invoked when practicable."[8] It is a sad commentary on religion that it inadvertently heralded the colonialists. There is an old story that when the colonialists came, they had the Bible in their hand and told the people to close their eyes for prayers. At the end of the "prayer," the colonialists had connived with the missionaries and succeeded in taking the peoples' land in exchange for their own Bible.

Another abuse of religion arises when it is used to propagate and enforce an alien culture. Western culture has always masqueraded as superior to other cultures, and the propagators of religion were expert in this. History books are replete with examples of the arrogance of British officials and missionaries in Africa and India. Initially, they were believed because they cleverly tied their position to religion and gave their work biblical sanctity. We may consider only two examples here. Polygamy was widely practiced in Africa. In part this was because the population was mainly agricultural. It was widely held that a chief must have more than one wife since he must not eat food cooked by any woman other than his wife. He must be polygamous in case one wife took ill or died. If a man was a successful farmer, he needed a large family to help him work on his farm, especially if he could not pay for laborers and agriculture was not mechanized. Thus a man married more than one wife not to satisfy any lust, but to meet a need. In this way everything worked out well. There were no unmarried girls to constitute a potential prostitute population, there was collective discipline in the extended family and so there was hardly any delinquent youth, and it was rare to find homosexuals. In its introduction into developing countries, Christianity was used as synonymous with European culture. Nowhere does the Bible categorically condemn polygamy, but Europeans read this into their religion. As Beetham observed:

"The ruling of the first missionaries was almost universally that polygamous men should at their conversion to the Christian faith put away all but one wife; otherwise they could not receive the sacraments of baptism and holy communion. There were some who did not think it right to break the existing marriage relationships and who therefore sought to retain such a man within the fellowship of Sunday worship and Bible study, but withhold the sacraments, though doing so with a feeling that the church's practice was at odds with the spirit of the Lord."[9]

Some men, in obedience to European (not biblical) order, disbanded their harems and drove away their children. Such children grew up to become social problems and some of them who became prominent men and women never forgave their fathers and resented Christianity, which had disinherited them and displaced their mothers.

The second example has to do with dressing. For some strange reason the earliest missionaries insisted that those who received communion must attend in European dress. Some at first consented, but most resented this requirement since it was mere cultural domination.

Another instance of abuse is religious intolerance, which is rather pronounced in developing countries. Practically all the religions that one can think of advocate peace and brotherhood, but almost all of them are intolerant of other religions and therefore contradict the teachings of their founders. Intolerance takes several forms, but usually comes in the form of the abuse based on numerical superiority. Thus, in one or two states in India in which the Sikhs are in the majority, they keep harassing the Hindus and Muslims. Muslims, on the other hand, oppress the Baha'is in Iran. The Unification movement undergoes systematic and official persecution in some countries. African traditional religion went through and survived this type of persecution at the hands of Christianity and Islam; time seems to have been on its side, however, for it survived several onslaughts. Abraham remarked that "an introduced religion depends for the depth of its success on the extent to which it can overcome or accommodate elements in the society into which it is introduced."[10] By considering itself superior, Christianity definitely abused the hospitality accorded it by African traditional religion. Most Africans, for example, gladly welcomed Christianity not because they felt it was superior, but because they believed a man had a right to worship the way he chooses.

Religious abuse in developing countries may be found in hero worship, which now has very serious political repercussions. In African traditional religion some of the gods were deified ancestors who by their might and valor saved their people from destruction and suffering. Fadipe tells us that, "as an example of the culture hero subsequently raised to the dignity of an *orisa*[11] and worshipped in the community may be mentioned *Obalogun* of the *Ijesa* people who, tradition claims, saved the country from the warlike intentions of the Nupe."[12] I suspect that many leaders of developing countries, especially in Africa, sought to transfer this status to themselves. Employing the same religious pattern, they saw themselves as gods who saved their people from colonial rule and, as gods, they must be deified. Thus they sit tight in office long after their popularity has waned and postpone and rig elections for fear of losing. They thereby encourage the military to forcibly effect a change. Part of the political instability in Africa today is traceable to this self-identification of the ruler with one of the gods, which can be linked with the determination to remain in office at all cost. This is an indirect abuse of religious tradition.

Abuse of religion also comes when the moral position of religion is seriously questioned and deeds do not match words. Christianity came to Africa as a "superior" religion and with a "superior" culture and one would have thought with "superior" morality. Taylor declared that "this finished system was presented to simple peoples sanctioned by the authority and endowed with the surviving culture of the civilised world. It offered them mightier, superior and nobler knowledge, and a better ordering of life than they had known. The manner and authority of its presentation hastened its acceptance."[13] However, this "manner and authority of its presentation" did not quite fall into place with the actions of the propagators in subsequent years. Africans saw their continent arbitrarily partitioned in Berlin in 1885 as if it was a no-man's-land, they saw a nonissue begin the First World War among people who said they were civilizing others, and they were forced to fight in the Second World War, which they knew nothing about. They fought for the freedom of those who held them in bondage and did not for all that easily win their own freedom. South of the Zambezi, they listened to some missionaries use the Bible to justify the apartheid government, and they quite rightly questioned Christian morality. This, in a way, led to the foundation of the Pentecostal churches, which were protesting against a European Christianity that rallied the people but did not meet their aspirations. Beetham put it correctly when he said: "What remains crystal clear is that the Christian gospel is rejected by many Africans today because those of European race in Africa and outside, claim the name of Christ but do not do the works; their practice of racial segregation and acquiescence in unequal opportunities for the races being in fact a denial of fellowship in Christ."[14] The use of religion to rally people and unite them can also be abused to promote personal status as, in my opinion, the Ayatollah Khomeini is now doing in Iran. Certainly he cannot pretend that the war he is waging against Iraq, another Islamic nation, is for the sake of Islam. That would be a colossal contradiction.

Religion also seems to have encouraged the further stratification of an already stratified society. Instead of making people of one body, it tended to simply reinforce the stratification already in

society. Religion often fails to rise above society and quite uncon-
sciously takes on some of society's values, values that are not
necessarily positive. O'dea observed that "founded religions tend at
first to repudiate, at least implicitly, the stratification differences of
society, but that after a time they come more or less to accept these
local institutions. Important people in society consequently come to
be looked upon as important in the religious group as well."[15]
Somehow everyone would like to be thought of as important both
in the religious group and in the larger society. The result is a rat
race to get to the top by all means even if such means are neither
godly nor humane.

It was noted above that one of the salutary functions of religion in
society is the solace it gives its adherents. The optimism that makes
one look to the future and indeed to eternity with certainty is
definitely very refreshing. It deadens all rebellious desires and sustains the peace of the society. However, this may have its own
drawbacks. Carry patience too far and it becomes cowardice. Un-
fulfilled hopes in which hundreds of tomorrows fritter away and
stretch into unrealized dreams make one become a time bomb of
frustration. One more sermon of appeasement, one more word
about waiting in hope, and one more disappointment, and everything could blow up. This is why I think that when the blacks rebel
against oppression in South Africa and willingly face the gun rather
than continue to suffer, the church that has kept them waiting for so
long has no plausible answers to their questions. This is not because
the church created the problem, but because it has, until recently,
allowed itself to be used, albeit indirectly, to perpetuate injustice. As
Beetham pointedly noted:

For its members, the Church is a divinely founded fellowship within
which the Holy Spirit acts despite the human frailty of members of the
fellowship. There is for them an unknown spiritual dimension in any
equation the historian seeks to formulate. This does not exonerate us
from the attempt to assess the points of weakness and of strength of the
Church as it emerged from the colonial era; on the contrary it demands
the utmost honesty for, as the history of the Church repeatedly shows,
judgement has to begin with God's own household.[16]

To conclude, I might say that intolerance is perhaps the worst
form of abuse of religion. Ironically, intolerance is the pet child of
most of the so-called orthodox and established religions of the
world. They are often so jittery and intolerant of others that they

would do anything to maintain the status quo. They forget, however, that persecution simply helps in the spread of a new religion. Tertullian noted that "the blood of the martyrs is the seed of the church."[17] Nonetheless, intolerance is an abuse of genuine religion. There are many cases of intolerance in the world: the persecution of the Baha'is in Iran, the harassment of other Muslims by the Maitasine group in Nigeria, the Unificationists in America, and many others who labor under the intolerance that arises from the abuse of religion. Abuse in these cases arises from confusing religion with civil issues, or appending religious intolerance to issues that are not genuinely religious, or seeking to apply a religious cover to other issues so as to give them respectability and make them appear acceptable. When we consider the relationship of religion to society, we should not forget that, although religion has often contributed positively to society, there are examples of its abuse all over the world and these examples can be easily multiplied in developing countries.

NOTES

1. E. B. Idowu, *Olodumare: God in Yoruba Belief* (London: Longmans Green & Co., 1962), 5.

2. Walter Rodney, *How Europe Underdeveloped Africa* (Dar-es-Salam: Tanzania Publishing House, 1972), 9.

3. As for example in Gottfried W. Leibniz's expression of this idea in "The Best Possible World."

4. E. A. Ayandele, *The Missionary Impact on Modern Nigeria* (London: Longmans Green & Co., 1966), 284.

5. Thomas F. O'dea, *The Sociology of Religion* (Englewood Cliffs, N.J.: Prentice-Hall, 1966), 57.

6. Susan Budd, *Sociologists and Religion* (London: Collier Macmillan, 1973), 35.

7. Ibid., 5.

8. Ibid., 8.

9. T. A. Beetham, *Christianity and the New Africa* (London: Pall Mail Press, 1967), 37.

10. W. E. Abraham, *The Mind of Africa* (London: Weidenfeld and Nicholson, 1967), 37.

11. *Orisa* is the generic name for gods.

12. N. A. Fadipe, *The Sociology of the Yoruba* (Ibadan: Ibadan University Press, 1970), 261.

13. Henry O. Taylor, *The Medieval Mind,* 4th ed. (Cambridge, Mass.: Harvard University Press, 1959), vol. 1, 170–71.

14. Beetham, 88.

15. O'dea, *The Sociology of Religion,* 74.

16. Beetham, 24.

17. Henry Chadwick, *The Early Church* (Middlesex: Penguin Books, 1967), 29.

God and Mammon: Responses in English Christianity

JOHN ST. JOHN

Religion connects with social reality by means of various and often conflicting matrices of ethical values. These are not necessarily the same as, or even extrapolations from, the moral systems prescribed by virtually all faiths or the individual (e.g., the Judeo-Christian Ten Commandments or the Right Living of Buddhism). It is not as simple as that. When it comes to social ethics—to groups of people, to social classes, let alone nations and races—a different set of considerations and processes seems to operate; this is also true of the normally honest individual's relationship with society (e.g., the subtle, usually hypocritical difference between "legal avoidance" and "evasion" of personal taxation). In the words of Paul Tillich: "Any attempt to identify the problems of personal ethics and social ethics (as does legalistic pacifism, for example) ignores the reality of power in the social realm, and so confuses the organizational centredness of an historical group with the personal centredness of a person . . . [it] requires the development of a philosophy of power."[1]

Although this essay is limited to a consideration of social rather than personal ethics, inevitably the two are intertwined. I am also limiting myself in the main to the ethical development and values of Christianity in Western Europe, particularly in Britain—although even this one small nation covers such an immense slice of complex experience as to make it all but impossible to avoid oversimplification. Furthermore, I shall for the most part narrow the focus to Christianity's attitude to money, to the taking of interest and profits, to wealth and poverty, to what may be termed "commerce"—although, again, the penumbra of other social and personal ethical attitudes will always be present. As Britain was the cradle of the industrial revolution, its history provides certain insights into the shifts and conflicts between various sets of coherent ethical attitudes and responsibilities, all within the confines of a single faith that springs from the same divine inspiration, as recorded in an agreed text, the Bible.

My data are inevitably selective, but are intended to be representative, as well as illuminating, and not atypical. I have arranged these data under broad categories whose contents may overlap, but which do provide a framework within which to depict four contrasting varieties of religious response. In compiling the first category, I have leaned shamelessly on the work of R. H. Tawney (1880–1962), professor of economic history, University of London.

The Reflection and Justification of Contemporary Socioeconomic Structures

In *On the Seven Deadly Sins,* John Wycliffe (c. 1320–84) declared that anyone who makes money out of an upswing in the market must by definition be wicked—how otherwise could he have been poor one day and rich the next? In the medieval church the taking of "pure" interest—at a fixed rate in return for a loan without risk to the lender—was denounced unanimously as avarice or usury. It was in order for a man to seek a livelihood considered reasonable for his station in life, but to seek more was quite wrong. Payment "may properly be demanded by the craftsmen who make the goods, or by the merchants who transport them, for both labour in their vocation and serve the common need. The unpardonable sin is that of the speculator or the middleman, who snatches private gain by the exploitation of public necessities."[2] Profits could in certain circumstances be treated as a particular case of wages, provided the gains were not in excess of what society considered to be reasonable remuneration for the trader's labor; on the other hand, as Aquinas argued, if the trader is motivated merely by his own pecuniary gain without any respect for the public interest, he is guilty of converting a means into an end and his occupation "is justly condemned, since, regarded in itself, it serves the lust of gain."[3]

Medieval society was held together by elaborate balances of obligations. There were great differences in wealth and status, but on the whole everyone knew his station, knew where he fitted in; feudal landowners, merchants, traders, artisans, peasants, laborers—and of course the ecclesiastical establishments, including the influential monasteries and convents. It was the church that laid down all-embracing standards for human institutions and conduct. Its economic ethic reflected the realities of medieval agriculture, industry and trade. Its teaching and those of the Schoolmen expounded the belief that the existing social edifice and its economic rules reflected an underlying moral purpose. Self-interest was subordinate to the achievement of salvation. The usurer's conduct was in conflict with both human and divine law. He ran the risk of being refused confession, absolution, and Christian burial. The church's doctrine of money, interest, and commerce dominated the lawmakers and the courts, secular as well as ecclesiastic.

As in all societies, practice by no means always matched precept. The fiat against usury was seldom enforced in connection with the financial transactions of the king, the big feudal barons, or even the bishops and abbots. The papacy itself usually overlooked the immorality of the great European banking houses on which it relied, even helping them to collect their debts from others by threat of excommunication. Despite, however, frequent departures from the accepted code of commercial ethics at all levels, despite the growth of a European system of trade and banking houses that operated essentially according to a very different (and historically premature) code, "the most fundamental difference between mediaeval and modern economic thought consists, indeed, in the fact that, whereas the latter normally refers to economic expediency, however it may be interpreted, for the justification of any particular action, policy, or system of organization, the former starts from the position that there is a moral authority to which considerations of economic expediency must be subordinated."[4]

How is it that the church and the outwardly Christian society of Britain—also, by and large, of Western Europe—instead of looking upon the receipt of pure interest and anything approaching a dividend or debenture interest, let alone naked usury, as a serious sin, were able to change to the present situation in which the church (or most of it) and the bulk of Western society considers all forms of "making your money work for you" or what the tax collector calls "unearned income" as not only legitimate but also respectable, even praiseworthy? Does religion admit it was once wrong?

To seek the answers, even in terms of Britain alone, requires an analysis of political, economic, and religious history over some five centuries. It was a period that embraced the Reformation and the break with Rome (completed in 1534); the Civil War and the beheading of a king (1649); the Industrial Revolution; the discovery and colonization of America and about one-fifth of the earth's land surface; and much else. It would be simplistic and, for the most part, grossly inaccurate to equate the volte-face in moral outlook with the rise of Protestantism in its several forms, but there are certainly links and it can at least be ventured that the conflict between economic interests—between the semifeudal, mercantilist past and the thrusting, new-style capitalism—were often played out in religious language and in disputes over theological doctrines, ecclesiastic courts, monastic power and properties, and even ritual. Even so, religion and the economy were seldom in step, with the latter forging ahead and the former both refusing, for long periods, to recognize the need to catch up and at the same time acting as an intermittently effective social brake whose application at best did something to mitigate the most rampant expressions of the new type of exploitation.

Luther, the first giant architect of Protestantism, denounced the traffic in interest in even stronger terms than the orthodox economists. "The devil invented it, and the Pope, by giving his sanction to it, has done untold evil throughout the world."[5] In England under Elizabeth I (reigned 1558–1603) there was a growth of capitalistic enterprise and foreign trade, of speculation and a money market. The new commercial classes allied themselves most strongly with Puritanism, and it was Calvin, their seminal inspiration, who first "accepted the main institutions of a commercial civilization, and supplied a creed to the classes which were to dominate the future."[6] Although this new, permissive attitude toward interest rates was hedged with qualifications, Calvin assumes "credit to be a normal and inevitable incident in the life of society . . . [he] argues that the payment of interest for capital is as reasonable as the payment of rent for land, and throws on the conscience of the individual the obligation of seeing that it does not exceed the amount dictated by natural justice. . . . On such a view all extortion is to be avoided by Christians. But capital and credit are indispensable; the financier is not a pariah, but a useful member of society."[7]

In its earlier stages, alongside the commercial permissiveness, went a constraining social policy. Although there were still plenty of remnants of what in effect were outdated moral teachings on commerce, essentially the way had been opened to the development over the next two hundred years of full-blown, virtually unrestricted capitalism, the system in which private enterprise is energized primariy by the search for profits. In the decades following the restoration of the monarchy (1660), economic individualism in a variety of guises steadily took over from stricter forms of Puritanism. Religion, at least in some of its more influential manifestations, provided the justification, the sanctification, that an economy based increasingly on money for its own sake needed. It now "insisted, in short, that money-making, if not free from spiritual dangers, was not a danger and nothing else, but that it could be, and ought to be, carried on for the greater glory of God[8] . . . [economic] enterprise itself is the discharge of a duty inspired by God."[9] The Calvinist Doctrine of the Elect provided the reassurance that success in commerce is the outward sign of divine approval.

The fusion of commerce and religious ideals now opened the gates in the eighteenth century to free enterprise and in the nineteenth century to the full flowering of a laissez-faire economy and of the "Protestant work ethic." The new emphasis in religion, its less attractive, sanctimonious attitudes notwithstanding, released the outburst of financial and industrial energy that was to make possible modern industrial society. The nonconformist virtues of upright and sober living, of devotion to hard work, a high sense of personal duty, were of value to the businessman in the next world as well as in this one.

The new spirit of individualism and liberty for the commercial entrepreneur received further justification from the equally new skills of "political arithmetic" or economics. As the Christian moralists replaced the condemnation of usury with the condonation of profit making, they in fact abdicated a large section of their territory. Their usurpers were "scientists" who had no concern with right or wrong, but only with impersonal forces and laws of commerce. With the eventual arrival of Adam Smith and Ricardo, objectivity proscribed the hampering quiddities of religious commercial ethics. Business now really was business.

It would require much deeper research and analysis to provide a complete answer to the question posed earlier as to how it is that Western Christianity managed to reverse its attitude toward the morality of moneymaking. Two variations of the same question automatically follow. Was the church's moral teaching allowed to slither toward the transposition of evil into good or did it adapt itself gracefully and legitimately to suit the requirements of an ever-changing industrial/commercial economy? Did it express the passive reflection of those changes or did it mold them according to its own principles?

The answer to each question probably lies between the two extremes, although it will vary from decade to decade, from place to place. The church's teaching has both mirrored and helped shape the socioeconomic structures in which it operates, but it is also very skilled—one might say *too* skilled—at adapting its teaching to provide the morality required of it to lubricate the economic wheels. It is difficult to avoid the conclusion that most of what has passed for moral guidance has been to justify and buttress the establishment and to indoctrinate the have-nots rather than the haves. On the other hand, adaptation is not necessarily sinful nor need it mean "chickening out." Cannibalism is presumably considered to be perfectly moral in a cannibalistic society, although anthropologists have discovered that in any society there are taboos on various types of conduct. The church's role has likewise been to establish taboos and sets of values that enable the society of the day to function with reasonable smoothness.

Despite its behavioral norm of justifying and underpinning the prevailing establishment, the church has, as already mentioned, tended frequently to oppose it, not so much because it hoped to change its morality as because the church clung to the morality of an earlier period; its prophetic witness, embedded in the Scriptures, put it at odds with capitalist forms of exploitation. Eventually it had, however, to come to terms with the fundamental changes in the economy that occurred in the seventeenth century. Similarly, in the twentieth century its clergy, with a few exceptions, failed at first to recognize the forces of social reform that emerged with the large industrial trade unions and the political expression of the working classes in the young Labour Party. In Britain today all the Christian faiths, and in particular the Church of England, still have to be on guard against a complacent social antiquarianism, which has a musty odor reminiscent of her thousands of almost empty, ancient buildings.

The Alleviation of Suffering and Poverty

The search for biblical texts with which either to attack or condone moneymaking is unsatisfactory. Denunciation of usury, particularly in the case of the poor and either in money or kind, can be discovered in Exodus 22:25, Deuteronomy 23:19–20, and Leviticus 25:36–7, as well as in several of the prophets and psalms (15:5). The few occasions when Jesus touches on it can easily be misinterpreted: thus, the expulsion of the money changers from the Temple (Mark 11:15) can be seen either as an attack on profit making or merely as removing an inappropriate activity from a holy place; even "You cannot serve God and mammon" (Luke 16:13), coming soon after the, to my mind, ambiguous parable of the unjust steward, has to be set against the parable of the talents (Matt. 25:14–30), in which the servant who had buried his talent seems to have been admonished severely and cast into the outer darkness because he did not invest the money at the bank at interest.

Conditions two thousand years ago in that tiny, remote province of the Roman Empire were in any case so different from those of our own day that it is surely impossible to draw useful parallels with contemporary values. As with so many of the parables and sayings of Jesus, these examples can be taken at more than one level and the important meaning may be transcendental. But when it came to the poor, Jesus was unequivocal. He was on their side. The small-town carpenter was one of them. He was also against the rich. It was Lazarus, not Dives, who was "carried by angels to Abraham's bosom" (Luke 16:22). "If you would be perfect, go, sell what you possess and give to the poor, and you will have treasure in heaven . . ." (Matt. 19:21). It was "easier for a camel to go through the eye of a needle than for a rich man to enter the kingdom of God" (Matt. 19:24). Whether or not needle refers to a narrow gateway in Jerusalem, the message is ambiguous.

Down the centuries the Christian churches have taken this teaching very seriously. They have been pioneers in succoring the poor by means of alms, clothing, food, and accommodation—just as they have been pioneers in education and nursing the sick. On the other hand, their attitude toward poverty has changed dramatically, in parallel, it can be maintained, to changes in economic practices and beliefs. In medieval times the relief of the poor was one of the obligations built into society's structure. For those who possessed property, the refusal of alms to obvious cases of need was a mortal sin; many of the monasteries and nunneries were highly organized sources of relief. Quite apart from practical charity, poverty in itself was envisaged by many to be a virtue. The cult of saintly poverty reached its medieval climax with Saint Francis, although his followers were persecuted by the immensely wealthy papacy under John XXII.

There was of course no shortage of other rich prelates, but by and large the medieval church's acceptance of and obligation to the poor were unquestioned. With the ascendance of the Protestants, religious attitudes began to alter. The Puritans, for example, looked upon poverty not as a misfortune deserving pity, but as the result of moral failing. This of course was the obverse to the belief that riches were the outward sign of the upright life, of God's blessing. Increasingly, poverty was considered the result not of any economic cause, but of individual idleness. Society owed the poor nothing. Vagrants, including their children, could no longer expect automatic charity and, if unlucky, were caught by savage parliamentary acts that offered them a choice between harsh compulsory labor and a whipping. As Tawney comments wryly, "A society which reverences the attainment of riches as the supreme felicity will naturally be disposed to regard the poor as damned in the next world, if only to justify itself for making their life a hell in this."[10]

This attitude toward the poor continued through the eighteenth century and most of the nineteenth, softened only by help for the "deserving" as opposed to the "undeserving" poor. With the concentration of working people in the hastily built slums of Britain's new industrial towns of the Midlands and the north, poverty and squalor were matched by the horror of grossly long working days in factories and child slavery in mines and workshops. The condition of the poor did lead eventually to a profusion of charities of all kinds, before and during Victoria's long reign (1837–1901), in which the churches played the dominant part. But many of the old Puritan attitudes still prevailed, particularly in the influential movement within the Church of England known as Evangelicalism (founded in the 1780s), which laid heavy emphasis on man's sinfulness. Good works were necessary, but only faith could bring salvation.

It would be unjust not to credit the Evangelicals with their active concern for the disadvantaged groups such as the insane, and with their rigorous campaigns against slavery and the slave trade, against the employment of child chimney sweeps, and in favor of other reforms. Different religious groups and individuals also did devoted work: for example, the Ragged Schools movement, strongly linked with Sunday schools; the YMCA; the homes for children started by Dr. Barnado, who believed he was "under the direct leading of God in the work that he did for waifs and that without God he would never have done it. It cannot be doubted that the Christian drive of the Victorians included a drive to save and to better the poor and the sick. Christianity was integral to the ideals and the work of countless reformers."[11]

Without a Christian outlook and the widespread fashion of churchgoing, especially among the upper and middle classes, the extensive charitable work of the Victorians and of later generations would undoubtedly have been greatly diminished. It brought benefits to the well-to-do as well as to the poor. In addition to easing your conscience, the extent and nature of your charitable activities was a symbol of status and a sound investment in salvation. It also helped to dampen discontent in a century of social turbulence that had seen the Chartist agitation, the 1848 insurrections, and the horror of the Paris Commune (1871). In a laissez-faire economy the dispensing of charity was not, however, without its critics, because it interfered with the workings of a free market in labor, which, ideally, should go where it was needed, whereas charity was thought to keep the poor in areas where earnings were depressed. Worse, it sapped a man's will to improve his lot by his own efforts (see Samuel Smiles's best-seller *Self Help,* published in 1859 and directed particularly at the working man.)

Charity was no doubt often abused. The parochial clergy, particularly in the slum districts of large cities, were pestered by claims for help, many of them bogus. This led, under the influence of the Evangelicals, to the reinforcement of the conclusion that indiscriminate relief must at all costs be avoided; it should be reserved for the "deserving," thrifty poor. The "undeserving" should be left to the mercies of the deliberately harsh and inadequate Poor Law. To enforce such principles, the Charity Organization Society was founded and this led to the better coordination of the profusion of charitable bodies and to the investigation of individual cases. Although churchmen and religious lay workers played the leading part in this and other forms of systemization of charitable work, "the activities which developed from this newly gained knowledge and experience were in fact stages in the development of the collectivist State . . . systematic philanthropy was necessarily a step away from a system based on the ordinary personal service, which anyone can render, towards the creation of a scientifically organized State whose services could only be staffed by professionals."[12] Gradually and erratically, charitable services were being taken over by public, often local, authorities.

During the twentieth century much charitable work in Britain has been turned into social work; instituted largely after World War II, the so-called "welfare state" was originally designed to provide "cradle to grave" social services, including a universal medical service, as a *right,* subject only to relatively light inquiries into present circumstances. A great part of religion's social dimension has therefore been diminished and secularized. Nevertheless, with the poor and suffering there is certain always to be scope for Christianity's social dimension. Its belief that the other person matters, its central doctrine of love, should insure that this responsibility is not forgotten, although it may take new forms.

It was crystallized in the orotund words of Bishop Frank Weston, addressing an Anglo-Catholic Congress (1923): "You cannot worship Jesus in the Tabernacle if you do not pity Jesus in the slum. . . . It is folly, it is madness, to suppose that you can worship Jesus in the Sacraments and Jesus on the Throne of Glory when you are sweating Him in the bodies and souls of His children. . . . Go out and look for Jesus in the ragged, in the naked, and in the oppressed and sweated, in those who have lost hope, in those who are struggling to make good. Look for Jesus. And when you see Him, gird yourselves with his towel and try to wash His feet."[13]

Intercession and Concentration on the Individual Soul Rather than on Social Reality

The most obvious response of a Christian to the social dimension is through intercessory prayer. This is equally the case with a Christian who devotes all his energies to succoring the poor and distressed or to advocating radical measures to replace existing socioeconomic structures, as it is with the Christian who believes that no response other than prayer is called for. Those who hold the view that social reform and/or political activity of any kind are no concern of religion (whether or not they involve themselves in charitable work) can find quotations in the New Testament that appear to support them: "My kingship is not of this world" (John 18:36); "Then render to Caesar the things that are Caesar's, and to God the things that are God's" (Luke 20:25).

Some schools of theology have attached little importance to the social commitments of the church, if they have not rejected the need for them altogether. Today, as formerly, in many churches the stress is on the salvation of the soul rather than on social or political involvement, on individual (particularly sexual) morality rather than on social morals and justice. As Paul Tillich puts it: "It is regrettable that Christianity has often concealed its unwillingness to do justice, or to fight for it, by setting off instead of battling for the removal of social injustice."[14] It can be argued that this approach and extreme religious prudery are associated with authoritarian, right-wing politics. Radically minded Christians are certainly critical of it, declaring that "prayer and contemplation, in established religion, become purely private practices within a social order which they never question nor threaten. That order is simply a neutral backcloth for the practice of religion. Religion has become privatized, a phenomenon which some Christians actually welcome. Not only that, the private religions have become a multimillion dollar industry. They are part of capitalism's success story— religions as commodities, religions which in no way threaten or disturb social stability."[15]

Meditation, Christian or otherwise, which in recent years has attracted so many, might be thought an obvious target for this kind of criticism and, indeed, this may often be justified because naive meditation can lead to a denial of social reality; on the other hand, meditation, like prayer, can also lead to the reinforcement of the inner strength needed to cope with it, whether by means of charitable work or sociopolitical involvement. Those closed religious orders that eschew good works fall into a special category and can generate insights and spiritual power with which to energize religious social commitment.

A more vulnerable target is offered by those sentimental forms of pietism that cling to the gentle, comforting, reassuring aspects of the doctrine of Christian love and that would find the message in Saint John of the Cross's *The Dark Night of the Soul* totally alien. Spirituality, if it is not to be bogus, needs to be tempered by suffering, by encounter with the raw harshness of reality, with evil. But even the positive by-products of suffering can be twisted. Resignation of one's soul into the hands of God has always been a central and valid concept of Christianity, but, in the past especially, this too has been only too easily interpreted as a justification for ignoring social realities; for urging people to put up with poor wages and slum housing in this life so that they will merit rewards in the next one.

Of course, prayer and seeking a relationship with a personal God provide Christianity with its essence. There have always, however, been voices that have warned of the danger of allowing this central concern to lead to forgetfulness about others. Love of God and love of one's brothers and sisters, they say, should be inseparable. The fourteenth-century mystic John Ruysbroeck warned that "we find nowadays many silly men who would be so interior and so detached, that they will not be active or helpful in any way of which their neighbours are in need. Know, such men are neither hidden friends nor yet true servants of God but are wholly false and disloyal . . ."[16] In 1916 the sponsors of a National Mission of Repentance and Hope in Britain proclaimed that "there is a real difference between a converted nation and a nation of converted individuals. All the citizens of a nation might be individually converted, and yet the public life be conducted on principles other than Christian." Maurice Reckitt, after quoting this, comments: "the social order was in the intention of God a spiritual reality and an essential sphere of grace, with purposes which required to be understood and laws which needed to be obeyed. And since this was so, social righteousness could never be assumed to arise automatically out of the consecrated intentions of individuals."[17] It was another Anglican priest, Geoffrey Studdert Kennedy, who wrote: "Nobody worries about Christ so long as He can be kept shut up in churches; He is quite safe there, but there is always trouble if you try to let Him out."[18]

The Advocacy of Social Reform and Change

The church in Britain has never possessed the characteristics of a seamless garment. The widespread peasant uprisings in the fourteenth century, for example, were supported by the poorer parish priests and, in particular, by John Ball, who preached in favor of a primitive communism with a strong Christian character. This was also the time of John Wycliffe and the Lollards, who produced the first complete English translation of the Bible (1382), who attacked the rich upper echelons of the clergy and declared that in all society the right to wealth and authority should depend on the righteousness of the individual. From the sixteenth century onward the Protestant noncomformists showed a remarkable tendency to generate breakaway sects, which led to the proliferation into Baptists, Presbyterians, Quakers, Congregationalists, Unitarians, Methodists—so that it was said by an eighteenth-century Frenchman that "England has ninety religions but only one sauce!" Although these divisions were primarily religious, they frequently cloaked conflicts over social questions and differences in class status: thus the revolts of the Levellers and the Diggers against the dominant Presbyterians during Cromwell's Commonwealth had a religious as well as a political/class flavor; likewise the Primitive Methodists, who in 1810 broke away from the increasingly conservative main body, were identified with the humbler, working-class membership.

But for the most part the churches, as we have seen, have remained closely identified with the establishment of which they, and in particular the Church of England, have always formed an integral part. The gibe that the "Anglican church is the Tory (right-wing) party on its knees" has until very recently been essentially true. As the state church with the monarch at its head, with a bench of bishops in the House of Lords, and its huge network of parish churches and "livings," it has always been privileged. Until World War I many of its clergy were themselves wealthy, if not always quite on a par with the squire.

However devoted were many of its ministers, however valuable their service, it was inescapably a rich man's Church. It was endowed with great wealth, much of which had come into the personal possession of those who had held high office in it, and in the middle of the [nineteenth] century from time to time the large estates left by those who had been its bishops were noted in the press. Its priests tended to be recruited from one class in society, and to have been prepared for their work by an education which in normal circumstances was out of the reach of a poor man . . . this necessarily cut the Church off from a large section of society . . .[19]

In the large towns especially, the Anglican church, in comparison with many of the nonconformist chapels, was out of touch with the majority of the population.

Despite this separation there were, as already noted, quite a few professing Christians with power and influence who were concerned about the widespread poverty and degradation. The moral force of Christianity found itself at times in collision with an industrial and commercial system buttressed by the iron laws of political economy, which "forbade the exercise of wealth as the only desirable, indeed the only possible objective for corporate human endeavor."[20] Nevertheless, Victorian Britain, outwardly at any rate, continued as a Christian, God-fearing land. The later decades of the nineteenth century saw the emergence of what has been called the nonconformist conscience. "Its existence helped to condition public attitudes to moral issues, such as temperance, or prostitution, or Sunday observance, or Bulgarian massacres, or concentration camps in South Africa, or oppression in the Congo. It brought the strong conscience of the middle classes to bear upon national questions, sometimes in an emotional way, but seldom in a way which politicians could afford to disregard."[21]

Writers as different as Dickens, Ruskin, and Carlyle exposed and attacked the Victorian social order, including the churches. Their denunciations antagonized many of the senior clergy, but there were others who agreed. These included the Christian Socialists organized in groups such as the Guild of Saint Matthew and the Christian Socialist Union. Led by the Reverend F. D. Maurice and the writers Charles Kingsley and Thomas Hughes, they hoped for the peaceful replacement of the capitalist system by industrial cooperatives. Their movement remained very small, but they did present a coherent challenge to the worst economic practices and exploitation. Moreover, its influence endured and undoubtedly led to the early stages of British socialism taking on a Christian rather than a Marxist character.

Following the Great Depression of 1929–31, the churches could no longer be counted on as unquestioning defenders of economic orthodoxy or of the established social structure. Archbishop William Temple (of York and Canterbury) exemplified, despite great opposition in his own ranks, the church's deepening social conscience. For years he was actively concerned with issues such as chronic unemployment or the need for penal reform and abolition of the death penalty. Because of the doctrine of the Incarnation, he described Christianity as being the most materialistic of all religions. Always he took his stand on Christian principles, believing passionately that the church as the agent of God's purpose possessed a right and a duty to "interfere" in social and industrial problems.

In more recent times, in all the British churches, including the Evangelical wing, the stress on social/institutional/corporate sin has been more firmly established. In the main they have continued to reflect the broad stream of mild social reform, though individual clergy have adopted more radical responses. To a large extent this has echoed policies framed originally by secular groups and parties. On two problems in particular both the churches themselves and their adherents seem to have discovered an unfamiliar militancy; first, in the fight against apartheid legislation in South Africa (the Anglican communion remains a strong influence in most Commonwealth, ex-colonial countries) and against racial discrimination at home; second, in the campaigns for nuclear disarmament.

Theologically and liturgically, the Anglican church is extraordinarily tolerant. But one wonders how many of its incumbents and congregations would agree with the Reverend Kenneth Leech, one of its more openly radical priests, when he wrote recently that "the subversive character of Christian spirituality derives from the subversive character of Christ himself. . . . He was a threat to the established order of his day, to the *status quo* in Church and state, to established religion. The Kingdom of God dislocated the stable order and it does so still."[22]

The Alliance of the Supranatural with the Secular

It has been indicated that religion has steadily been edged out of the domains of commercial morality by economics, and of the relief of poverty and spiritual misfortune by social work sponsored by the state or local authorities. Similarly, other domains of religion have, in varying degrees, been surrendered to psychiatry and psychotherapy, to evolutionary biology, to astronomy and cosmology, to academic sociology and philosophy. The secularization of all departments of life has accelerated.

It can scarcely be denied that the purely or predominantly secular domains have stupendous achievements to their credit. The non-religious do not find it difficult to argue that it has been precisely the liberation from antiquated religious concepts and restrictions that has made many of the advances possible. Theists can of course reply that society, to the extent that its institutions work for mankind's benefit, is merely "living off the fat" of religious morality, that secular individuals are, without realizing it, performing Christ's work. The argument soon becomes sterile, particularly when it is realized that the secular/religious division is usually blurred; scientists, economists, social workers, doctors, even psychiatrists may as individuals hold religious beliefs. In any case, there seem to be far more agnostics (including "religious agnostics") than there are atheists in all their purity. There are even Christians who declare that their religion is, in the best sense of the word, materialist.

Once one turns to society's ethical failures, and in particular to global-scale failures that threaten to annihilate us, purely secular ethics—or, if it is preferred, humanist ethics—appear to be far less adequate. Without embarking on an investigation of Kant's theory of practical reason or of whether there exist in man and also in society innate moral insights, it is difficult to avoid the conclusion that sociopolitical action by itself is failing. Communist societies have their own moral, social codes and they can be very rigid and strict, but without supranatural reinforcement morality is only too apt to be swallowed up by expediency. Any means can be justified to serve an end. The ends themselves, however praiseworthy at first, are soon fouled by the means. La Rochefoucauld remarked that "hypocrisy is homage paid by vice to virtue." Statesmen in nominally Christian societies are noted for their hypocrisy; in non-religious cultures they do not need to bother.

No one, I am sure, would suggest that the churches consistently propose correct or acceptable ethical formulas, or that their adherents faithfully abide by their teaching. Quite apart from what seems to be their built-in tendency to be identified with the secular establishment, religious beliefs in themselves seem nowadays to be in danger of being secularized. The churches are too ready to settle for what are no more than sanctified forms of humanism. "Today many contemporary priesthoods have turned to secularized value systems in a search for popularity and credibility. The switch to rationalism cannot generate the charisma that accrues only to those whose inner practices give strength to the heart rather than to the thinking mind. . . . In the modern West the extensive secularization of religion has largely destroyed the relation between individual spirituality and the systems of belief to which it used to belong."[23]

The adulteration, in particular of its unique essence, by a series of defensive withdrawals in the face of the successes—and even the failures—of secularism needs to be resisted. Leszek Kolakowski, an exiled professor of the history of philosophy from Warsaw, has written recently: "A religious worship reduced to its secular utility and oblivious of its original function can survive for a time, no doubt, yet sooner or later its emptiness is bound to be exposed, the irrelevance of its form to its content will become apparent, its ambiguous life sustained by credit from a non-existent bank will come to end and the forgotten links with the Sacred will be resumed in another place, by other forms of religiosity."[24]

Perhaps the correct conclusion is that religion should never cease making its special arational or supranatural prophetic contribution to society, and yet at the same time it should endeavor to increase its influence in, rather than regain control of, the secular domains that regulate society.

NOTES

1. Paul Tillich, *Morality and Beyond* (London: Routledge and Kegan Paul, 1964), 45.

2. Richard H. Tawney, *Religion and the Rise of Capitalism,* (London: Pelican Books, 1938), 48, Holland Memorial lecture, 1922.

3. Ibid., 47.

4. Ibid., 52.

5. Ibid., 104.

6. Ibid., 103.

7. Ibid., 116.

8. Ibid., 238.

9. Ibid., 245.

10. Ibid., 265.

11. Owen Chadwick, "The Established Church under Attack," *The Victorian Crisis of Faith* (London: SPCK, 1970), 91.

12. G. Kitson Clark, *Churchmen and the Condition of England, 1832–1885* (London: Methuen, 1971), 274.

13. *Anglo-Catholic Congress Report,* 185–86.

14. Paul Tillich, 39.

15. Kenneth Leech, 50–51.

16. John Ruysbroeck, *The Sparkling Stone,* vii, quoted in *Ruysbroeck* by Evelyn Underhill (London: Bell, 1915), 117.

17. Maurice B. Reckitt, *Maurice to Temple: A Century of the Social Movement in the Church of England* (London: Faber, 1947), 160.

18. Geoffrey Studdert Kennedy, *The Word and the Work* (London: Longmans Green, 1925), 66.

19. G. Kitson Clark, 320.

20. Ibid., 290.

21. Owen Chadwick, 95.

22. Kenneth Leech, 51.

23. John H. Crook, *The Evolution of Human Consciousness* (Oxford: Clarendon, 1980), 359.

24. Leszek Kolakowski, *Religion* (London: Fontana, 1982), 235–36.

The Discourse of Liberation Theology in Perspective
GUSTAVO BENAVIDES

. . . da selbst der *kritische* Theologe *Theologe* bleibt. Karl Marx, "Zur Kritik der Nationalökonomie"

The publication in 1971 of Gustavo Gutiérrez's *Teología de la liberación,*[1] constituted a major event in the discourse of Christian theology. Gutiérrez's work, as well as the writings by Assmann, Segundo, Galilea, and other theologians,[2] have been considered the first significant contribution of Latin America to the interpretation of the Christian message.[3] The academic success of the theology of liberation means that the theological articulation of the Christian faith is no longer the private domain of European theologians; it means that Christianity—not just as faith or practice, but as theology, that is, as a second-degree elaboration, as "discourse"—has outgrown the relatively narrow frontiers of the Northern Hemisphere. After the publication of Gutiérrez's *Teología de la liberación,* the theological enterprise has, for better or worse, begun to be articulated from a new perspective determined by the specific economic and social characteristics of the so-called Third World.

From a strictly theological point of view, nothing could be more welcome than this expansion of the theological world. Now, from being a mission territory, the Third World has become a space in which the Word is spoken, this time with a theological accent. My aim in this essay is not, however, a celebratory one. This is not a religious essay, but rather an essay about religion: the distinction, often forgotten, is, in spite of theologians, a valid one. Therefore, I will not try to elaborate, theologically, on the theology of liberation, nor will I criticize it by proposing an alternative theology. The first task is already well under way, as the recent publications by Gutiérrez, Assmann, Boff, Dussel, Galilea, Segundo, and others show. As for the other, a theological critique would presuppose a series of assumptions that I am unable to make.

Instead, my purpose in this essay is to place the discourse of the theology of liberation, particularly the work of Gustavo Gutiérrez, in a perspective that may help to clarify its role within contemporary Catholicism. In this context, it should be emphasized that Christian theology is not being taken as an autonomous corpus of beliefs—the response to God's primordial manifestation in history. Rather, Christian theology will be considered a reflection on the system of values that constitutes the core of a given culture;[4] a system of values that depends on, and reinforces, the structure of a society in a dialectical way.[5] Thus, Christian theology acts as a "superstructural" element, that is, as an "ideology," whereas Christianity—or the idea of Christendom—acts as one of the key components of the very structure of any society that considers itself "Christian." The same can be said, *mutatis mutandis,* of Islamic or Buddhist theologies (insofar as Buddhism may be said to have a "theology").

The theology of liberation must be seen, then, as sharing with other theologies the uneasy position of being an ideological construction that must nevertheless claim historical autonomy. In the case of theology of liberation, the situation is particularly complex, since Gutiérrez stresses both the historical foundations of his enterprise and, because of its being *theo*logical, its autonomy. In the opening lines of the first chapter of *Teología de la liberación,* he writes that theological reflection arises (*surges*) spontaneously in the believer, that is, in those who have received the gift of God's Word.[6] Later on, theological reflection is defined as a "critical reflection" (*reflexión crítica*) that "by definition does not want to be a mere Christian justification *a posteriori.*"[7] However, in a book entitled *Teología desde el reverso de la historia,* Gutiérrez writes:

... theological reflection is bound to historical processes, it is part of historical blocks [*bloques históricos*] without which it cannot be understood. Theology, like all thought, must be placed in a historical context. Theologies do not follow one another as a chain of thoughts in the air; they are answers—and can and must also be questions—to vast historical processes. Theological discourse is an effort by concrete persons who believe and think their faith in definite conditions; who produce actions and interpretations which play a role in social confrontations. The theologian does not find himself in a historical limbo; his reflection is placed in, arises from, its material foundations; he speaks from a specific situation.[8]

The fundamental ambiguity of Gutiérrez's position is due to the impossible task he has set for himself: to maintain the transhistorical foundation of his faith, while at the same time trying to situate that faith in the concreteness of contemporary Latin America. Theological reflection, like any ideological discourse, is, as Gutiérrez recognizes, bound to social processes, and it is only within these social contexts that theological reflection is to be understood. Inasmuch as this is the case, there are limits that even the most radical theology must respect, if this theology is to be considered "orthodox." No theology, however radical, is free to question the structural values of a society without losing its legitimacy in the process. When a particularly heterodox system is produced by a social group, the new ideology—or rather "utopia" in Mannheim's sense[9]—faces several alternatives. If the new system is perceived as being too extreme, its members may face physical annihilation (consider, for instance, the fate suffered by Mazdak and his followers),[10] or may be forced to commit collective suicide (as in the case of the followers of Jim Jones in Jonestown). Another alternative is the "domestication" of the new heresy, its accommodation into the prevalent ideology. In this case, the originally "dysfunctional"[11] teachings are manipulated in such a way that they can be integrated into the ongoing discourse (the assimilation of Buddha into the cycle of the *avatāras* of Visnu is just one example of the remarkable ability of Hinduism to assimilate and neutralize extraneous ideologies).[12] A third alternative left to orthodoxy is the "spiritualization" of the new movement. In this event, the socially unacceptable—and socially concrete—proposals of the new group are diluted and projected onto a spiritual realm where they are no longer dangerous. Thus, for example, millenarian movements[13] become interiorized, spiritual, mystical.[14]

The alternatives mentioned above certainly do not exhaust the options left to the orthodox forces or to the heterodox ones. One may also consider situations in which the members of a heterodox movement engage in "antinomian" practices, while at the same time maintaining (or not) a public façade of irreproachable orthodoxy.[15] Finally, one must consider the possibility of a more radical solution: the breaking away of the new group, the establishment of a political structure that legitimizes, and is legitimized by, the new ideology. It is in this context that we have to examine the alternatives left to the theology of liberation, as well as, in general, to those groups within the Catholic church that have adopted a radical position in regard to the economic conditions prevalent in Latin America. The first of the options mentioned above—physical annihilation—was exercised against the Colombian priest Camilo Torres after he had joined a guerrilla group.[16] More recently, in El Salvador, and elsewhere in Latin America, priests have been murdered by right-wing groups, usually with the support of the government. The domestication of the theology of liberation—in this case, its "spiritualization"—is already well under way, as the attempts by Alfonso López Trujillo, Galat, and Kloppenburg show.[17] López Trujillo, for example, attacks the theologians of liberation for assuming a Marxist model, including the notion of class struggle, and proposes instead, as a paradigm for social reconciliation, the spiritual reconciliation in Christ of Jews and gentiles.[18] In similar terms, Kloppenburg stresses the need for contemplation, which he finds lacking in the socially and politically oriented writings of Gutiérrez.[19] The more radical solution, that is, the establishment of a new society, appears as the only option left to the new theologians. The difficulties involved in such an enterprise, however, would almost certainly lead to the demise of those thus engaged.

It would seem, then, that the entire discourse of the theology of liberation will either have to become more radical, and sever itself from the authority of the established Catholic hierarchy, or it will have to accommodate itself as a more or less tolerated radical ("dysfunctional") wing within the theological establishment. This last solution would imply not only a change in the thought of the theology of liberation, but also a rearrangement of the position of the church. In considering these options, it is first necessary to examine what is taken to be, on the one hand, the "content," the "message" of the theology of liberation, and, on the other, the type of reasoning, the particular language and vocabulary, employed by Gutiérrez in his *Teología de la liberación*. In doing this we are not presupposing the existence of pure theological content as opposed to style or form of thinking. On the contrary, it is by becoming aware of the inseparability of form and content in theological, as well as in other, more extreme forms of discourse (such as the mystical),[20] that we are able to grasp the intricate connection between goals and means—in this case, the goals and means of the theology of liberation. An artificial distinction between form and content is as insidious as the parallel distinction between the realm of the political and that of the religious (or the artistic) and must be considered an ideological construction whose aim is the fragmentation and depolitization of social life. Regarding, then, the "content" of the theology of liberation, it should be kept in mind that the following exposition is not intended to be regarded as independent from the subsequent discussion of the "language" of liberation theology.

As developed in the work of Gutiérrez, the theology of liberation is a radical interpretation of the Christian revelation, one that does not accept the traditional distinction between sacred and profane realism, between sacred and profane histories.[21] For Gutiérrez, salvation is not to be regarded as an otherworldly affair, nor as a purely spiritual process, but as an integral one, comprising the spiritual, social, and political aspects of life. Theology, then, is not considered a self-contained discipline, but rather a critical reflection that takes into account the social and economic conditions that had made this act of reflection itself possible.[22] In the Latin American context, theology, as historical praxis, has to be aware of the situation of underdevelopment and dependence in which the continent lives. In his book *Teología de la liberación,* Gutiérrez deals extensively with the problem of economic development, criticizing those theories that propose mere "developmental" solutions (*desarrollismo*), instead of a structural change in the economic system.[23] The discussion of economic problems, which may appear quite out of place in a theological work, is fundamental because the integral view of man proposed by the theology of liberation considers that salvation is not something "beyond the world" (*ultramundano*); salvation, on the contrary—"communion of men with God, and communion of men with one another"—is something that takes place, in a real and concrete form, already in this world. In consequence, sin is no longer viewed merely as an obstacle for an otherworldly salvation, but, insofar as sin is a break with God, it is regarded as a historical reality, as a break of the communion among men.[24] The crucial Christian concepts of creation and salvation are interpreted by Gutiérrez as being almost indistinguishable: "The creation is presented in the Bible not as a stage previous to salvation, but as inserted in the salvific process." Furthermore, the act of creation is seen as tied—"almost to the point of identity"—to the liberation of Israel from slavery in Egypt,[25] a liberation that is a "political act," and "the beginnings of the construction of a just and fraternal society."[26] Finally, the God of Israel is the God of history, of political liberation, a view that makes the distinction between religious and political liberation untenable.

In response to the examples adduced by Gutiérrez, it must be said that the use of historical events, such as the history of the Israelites or the death of Jesus (or his possible connections with the Zealots), as paradigms for legitimizing concrete historical options centuries later is, despite any claims to the contrary, a procedure that de-concretizes the current political and economic situations. When, in the chapter entitled "Liberation and Salvation," Gutiérrez writes that "the liberation from Egypt is a political act," and states further that "the early chapters of Exodus describe the situation of oppression in which the Jewish people lived in Egypt,"[27] he is undoubtedly right; similarly, one can agree with the statement, cited earlier, about the liberation from Egypt being not only a political act, but also—ideally—the beginnings of a just and fraternal society. However, when Gutiérrez uses these events as transhistorical models for the interpretation of contemporary revolutionary movements in Latin America, he deprives the modern situations of their historical urgency. This "sacralization" of social struggle may be theologically necessary in order to counteract the conservative religious legitimation of unjust social structures. The mechanism of religious legitimation, characteristic of "archaic" cultures—romanticized by Eliade,[28] and studied in depth by Topitsch[29]—is reversed by Gutiérrez, who now proposes a religious legitimation of social change. In doing so, Gutiérrez is, nevertheless, still imprisoned by mythical thought—by a revolutionary *illud tempus* that may prove to be the undoing of any concrete application of the theology of liberation.

And yet, in the context in which Gutiérrez's theological enterprise is carried out, it would seem impossible not to make use of this mythical reasoning. In a universe lived, or conceived, religiously, certain modes of thought seem to inevitably take over and impose themselves. In this sense, it is perhaps unfair—as well as naive—to ask theologians to give up being theologians. On the other hand, it is also possible that the only way to successfully carry out political change of a radical type, and to maintain it, is through the skillful use—or manipulation—of the symbolic universe shared by the members of a culture. After all, if a society legitimizes itself through a religious ideology, the only avenue left to those who want to change that society is the utilization of the utopian counterpart of the prevalent ideology.[30] However, it should be kept in mind that there is a limit beyond which symbols, or ideologies, may not be manipulated; in other words, it is not always clear whether it is we who are using the symbols for our own purposes, or whether the ideology constituted by those symbols manages to perpetuate itself by allowing a certain degree of change—of illusory change—in its own discourse. Another danger consists in what could be called a case of *l'apprenti sorcier:* a utopian movement that, having acquired "functional autonomy," becomes independent from logical constraints and ends up by destroying itself.

As an example of the self-perpetuation of typically religious modes of discourse, we can examine Gutiérrez's understanding of "God's freedom" and "God's love for the poor." According to Gutiérrez, God's preference for the poor is not due to the goodness of the poor, but rather, this preference is grounded simply in the poor's poverty. Free choice, which does not take into account "the moral and personal dispositions of the poor,"[31] reveals, according to Gutiérrez, the gratuitousness (*gratuidad*) of God's love. In an interview published in 1980, he says, "A God who loves the poor because the poor deserve it, is a perfectly comprehensible God. However, to accept that God loves the poor simply because they are in a situation of oppression and exploitation, shocks us, and reveals to us the absolute gratuitousness of God's love, beyond any anthropomorphism."[32] Such a way of reasoning, admirable as it is in its commitment, can be understood as an "empty formula" in Topitsch's sense,[33] and can be easily reversed. Thus, a conservative theologian (from the *Opus Dei,* for example) may argue that God's absolute freedom allows him to gratuitously love the rich, not only without regard for the rich's goodness or evilness, but even because of the rich's evilness. As we can see, arguments involving "God's absolute freedom" or "God's absolute love" or those stressing the incognoscibility of God, are empty statements that can be interpreted to account for any state of affairs whatsoever. The history of Christianity, and indeed of all religions, is full of paradoxical and tautological statements, one of whose functions seems to be the validation of any possible factual or logical state of affairs. To say that God's love is absolutely gratuitous is to abandon the realm of meaningful discourse and to reach the limits of the process of communication: the meaningless poles of tautology and contradiction.[34] As a paradox, God becomes a *coincidentia oppositorum*—that in which good and evil, poor and rich, exploiter and exploited, master and slave, are reconciled.[35] As a tautology, God's love is a case of love for love's sake: a limitless and, therefore, meaningless love.[36] In any case, tautologies and contradictions, fascinating as they are from a logical—or "metaphysical"—point of view, are, because of their logical promiscuity, immensely vulnerable to ideological manipulation.

I am aware that Gustavo Gutiérrez would vehemently dispute the conclusions arrived at above, and I should therefore stress that I am not by any means questioning Father Gutiérrez's social commitment and religious convictions (which for him are indeed inseparable). My purpose in this essay is not to raise doubts about the personal convictions of those engaged in the elaboration of a theology of liberation, but to point out the difficulties and dangers involved in interpreting theologically problems as grave and urgent as poverty, exploitation, economic and cultural dependence, violence, and liberation. No matter how deeply felt one's personal convictions may be, it is always possible that in spite of oneself, one's choice of discourse (in case "choice" is possible at all) may determine to a great extent the efficacy of the actions brought about by those convictions.

In the case of the theology of liberation—while acknowledging the inevitability of having to use religious categories in the context of societies that are part of Christendom—the very fact of its being a theology, a discourse about "God," may prove to be the cause of its eventual spiritualization, domestication, and ultimate assimilation by the church. Therefore, the political interpretation of the Bible undertaken by the theology of liberation must be itself interpreted politically. We cannot but agree with Fredric Jameson when he writes that the political perspective is not a supplementary method, but rather "the absolute horizon of all reading and all interpretation,"[37] that is, in the context of the history of the Catholic church in Latin America.[38]

In this context, then, the theology of liberation may be seen as the continuation of the denunciatory efforts of Bartolomé de las Casas, the sixteenth-century Spanish missionary who plays such an important role as one of Gutiérrez's spiritual ancestors (another important one is the Peruvian Marxist Jose Carlos Mariátegui),[39] as well as of the millenarian atmosphere, which was an important component of the discovery and conquest of America.[40] The continuation of las Casas's missionary spirit is apparent in one of Gutiérrez's works, in which he mentions that las Casas sees the crucified Christ as being crucified again in each exploited Indian.[41] However, las Casas's theological perception—or theological interpretation—of the exploitation brought about by the system of *encomiendas* gives the impression of being less a humanistic than a theological act and can be seen as the theological response to Juan Ginés de Sepúlveda's theological legitimation of the political regime imposed by the newly arrived Christians. Eventually, the denunciations of las Casas were assimilated—and neutralized—by the church, whose function had to encompass both the legitimation of the social order and the "humanization" of the ongoing process of conquest. Four centuries later, the movement known as theology of liberation seems to be fulfilling the same basic role: in the larger perspective of Latin American history—from the Spanish conquest to the current situation of hopeless underdevelopment—the radical social awareness which these theologians have forced on socially unconcerned Christians, as well as on the hierarchy, could be seen as an effort, from within the church, to prepare the ground—the ideological, the political ground—for an eventual accommodation between the church and any possible development in Latin America. The fact that a large percentage of the total Catholic population of the world lives both as Catholic and as underdeveloped makes it imperative that the church—if it is to survive at all—try to account, theologically, for any coming radical social changes. This certainly does not mean that the movement known as liberation theology is the only response that the church is prepared to offer to new political developments[42]; on the contrary, it means that the theology of liberation is but one attempt to articulate in theological terms a social, economic, and ultimately political view arising from a world that regards itself as "Christian," with the ultimate—and quite understandable—aim of securing the survival of Christianity, that is, the survival of the church.

NOTES

1. Gustavo Gutiérrez, *Teología de la Liberación* (Lima: Centro de Estudios y Publicaciones (CEP), 1971). There is an English translation, *Theology of Liberation* (Maryknoll, N.Y.: Orbis, 1973); all translations are my own.

2. For a general background see Roberto Oliveros, *Liberación y Teología, Génesis y Crecimiento de una Reflexión* (Lima: CEP, 1980); Equipo Seladoc, *Panorama de la Teología Latinoamericana,* (Salamanca, Ediciones Sígueme, 1975) (includes articles by Boff, Gutiérrez, Míquez, Dusseel, Comblin, Assmann, etc.); Juan Luis Segundo, *Liberation of Theology* (Maryknoll, N.Y.: Orbis, 1976); Arturo

Blatezky, *Sprache des Glaubens in Lateinamerika. Eine Studie zu Selbstverständnis und Methode der "Theologie der Befreiung"* (Frankfurt: Peter Lang, 1978).

3. See *Challenge of Liberation Theology: A First World Response,* ed. Brian Mahan and L. D. Richesin (Maryknoll, N.Y.: Orbis, 1981); Jose Míguez Bonino, *Revolutionary Theology Comes of Age* (London: SPCK, 1975); Robert McAfee Brown, *Theology in a New Key* (Philadelphia: Westminster, 1978); Robert McAfee Brown, *Gustavo Gutiérrez* (Atlanta: John Knox, 1981).

4. Cf. Clifford Geertz, "Religion as a Cultural System," *Anthropological Approaches to the Study of Religion,* ed. Michael Banton (London: Tavistock, 1966), 1–46; Jacques Waardenburg, "The Language of Religion and the Study of Religions as Sign Systems, *Science of Religion, Studies in Methodology,* ed. Lauri Honko (The Hague: Mouton, 1979), 441–57.

5. On the relationship between "structure" and "superstructure" see Marvin Harris, *Cultural Materialism* (New York: Random House, 1979), 70–75; Fredric Jameson, *The Political Unconscious* (Ithaca, N.Y.: Cornell University Press, 1981), 17–102; Raymond Williams, *Marxism and Literature* (Oxford: Oxford University Press, 1977), 55–71 (on ideology); 75–114 (on base and superstructure, determination, and hegemony).

6. Gutiérrez, *Teología de la Liberación,* 15.

7. Ibid., 179–80.

8. Gutiérrez, *Teología Desde el Reverso de la Historia,* 1st ed. (Lima: CEP, 1977); reprint, *La Fuerza Histórica de los Pobres* (Lima: CEP, 1979) 303–94, see esp. 390. The same fundamental ambiguity regarding the position of Christianity—and Christian theology—in an ideologically determined world can be found in Juan Luis Segundo, *Liberation of Theology,* p. 86; Segundo writes: "It must be admitted that the more we divest our minds of ideological trappings, the more we will free the message of Jesus from its ideological wrappings and get closer to its deeper, perduring truth." This statement, whose truth is far from self-evident (to a Buddhist or a Muslim, for example), is merely a repetition of the old doctrine about the soul being Christian by nature; on the other hand, Segundo writes on p. 122: "Faith, then, is not a universal, atemporal, pithy body of content summing up divine revelation once the latter has been divested of ideologies. On the contrary, it is maturity by way of ideologies, the possibility of fully and conscientiously carrying out the ideological task on which the real-life liberation of human beings depends." In other words, Christianity, like any other religion, is an ideology. The contradiction underlying the positions of Gutiérrez and Segundo could be resolved only if the theologians of liberation were prepared to consider Christianity as a provisional set of values, which because of the specific historical situation of Latin America (and only of Latin America), appears as capable of serving as a vehicle for radical social change. But even if they were to do so, it would still be difficult to imagine how it would be possible to provide a theological foundation for the liberation of the 'non-Christian' parts of the underdeveloped world, since this foundation is constituted by the mythologies of the Old and New Testaments. It would seem, then, that the theology of liberation is concerned only with providing religious legitimacy to move-

ments advocating radical social change in Christian societies, with the ultimate—and quite understandable—aim of securing the survival of Christianity.

9. Karl Mannheim, *Ideology and Utopia* (New York: Harcourt, n.d.); the German
edition, *Ideologie und Utopie,* was published in 1929; the revised English
translation was first published in 1936.

10. On Mazdak see Otakar Klíma, *Mazdak. Geschichte einer sozialen Bewegung im
sassanidischen Persien* (Prague: Ceskoslovenské Akademie Ved, 1957); Geo
Widengren, *Die Religionen Irans* (Stuttgart: Kohlhammer, 1965), 308–10.

11. On the dysfunctional aspect of religion see Robert Merton, *Social Theory and
Social Structure* (New York: Free Press, 1968), 82ff.

12. Cf. Jan Gonda, *Viṣṇuism and Śivaism* (London: Athlone Press, 1970), 122.

13. Cf. Mannheim, *Ideology and Utopia,* 237ff.; see also *Millenial Dreams in Action,*
ed. Sylvia Thrupp (New York: Schocken, 1970).

14. This does not necessarily mean that mystical movements, or "mysticism" in
general, are inherently passive or reactionary. See *The Mystical and Political
Dimension of the Christian Faith,* ed., Claude Geffré and Gustavo Gutiérrez
(New York: Herder and Herder, 1974); Matthew Fox, O. P., "Meister Eckhart
and Karl Marx: The Mystic as Political Theologian," *Understanding Mysticism,*
ed. Richard Woods, O. P. (New York: Doubleday, 1980) 541–63; Herbert
Grundmann, "Die geschichtlichen Grundlagen der deutschen Mystik,"
Deutsche Vierteljahrsschrift für Literaturwissenschaft und Geistesgeschichte 12 (1934):
400–29, reprinted in *Altdeutsche und Altniederländische Mystik,* ed. Kurt Ruh
(Darmstadt, Wissenschaftliche Buchgesellschaft, 1964), 72–99.

15. A classical example of antinomianism can be found in the movement founded
by Sabbatai Sevi; see Gershom Scholem, *Sabbatai Sevi, The Mystical Messiah*
(Princeton, N.J.: Princeton University Press, 1973); on the more extreme
antinomianism of the Frankist movement see Scholem, "La métamorphose du
messianisme hérétique des Sabbatiens en nihilisme religieux au 18 siecle," in
Heresies et Societes dans l'Europe Pre-industrielle (Paris: Mouton, 1968), 381–93
(and the discussion on 394—95); Scholem, "Der Nihilismus als religioses
Phanomen," *Eranos* 43, 1974, 1–50.

16. The writings of Camilo Torres are available in English translation in
Revolutionary Priest, The Complete Writings and Messages of Camilo Torres, ed.
John Gervassi (New York: Random House, 1971); on the Colombian political
situation at the time see Daniel Levine, *Religion and Politics in Latin America.
The Catholic Church in Venezuela and Colombia* (Princeton, N.J.: Princeton
University Press, 1981), 41ff.

17. cf. Oliveros, *Liberación y Teología,* 306ff.

18. Oliveros, 327–28; on López Trujillo see also Levine, *Religion and Politics,* 182.

19. Oliveros, 330.

20. The distinction between "form" and "content," or rather, between "experience" and "interpretation" can be found, for example, in Ninian Smart,
"Interpretation and Mystical Experience," *Religious Studies* 1 (1965): 75–87;
see, however, Bruce Garside, "Language and the Interpretation of Mystical
Experience," *International Journal for Philosophy of Religion* 3 (1972): 93–102;

and the articles contained in *Mysticism and Philosophical Analysis,* ed. Steven T. Katz (New York: Oxford University Press, 1978).

21. Cf. Gutiérrez, *Teología de la Liberación,* 186, 189ff.

22. Ibid., 28.

23. Cf. Gutiérrez, *Teología de la Liberación,* 35ff.

24. Ibid., 187ff.

25. Ibid., 191–94.

26. Ibid., 196.

27. Ibid., 194.

28. See, among other works, Mircea Eliade, *Traité d'histoire des Religions,* (Paris: Payot, 1970), first published in 1949; there is an English translation, *Patterns in Comparative Religion; Le sacré et le profane* (Paris, Gallimard, 1965), with an English translation, *The Sacred and the Profane; The Quest. History and Meaning in Religion,* (Chicago: University of Chicago Press, 1969). On Eliade's ideological position see Furio Jesi, *Cultura di Destra* (Milano: Garzanti, 1979), 38–50 and *Il Mito* (Milano: ISEDI, 1973), 66–69.

29. See Ernst Topitsch, *Vom Ursprung und Ende der Metaphysik* (Vienna: Springer, 1958).

30. On the dialectical interaction between ideology and utopia see Jameson, *The Political Unconscious,* 281–99, esp. 285, where Jameson deals with the utopian aspects of religion and Marxism; on this subject see also Jameson, *Marxism and Form* (Princeton, N.J.: Princeton University Press, 1971), 116–59 (on Ernst Bloch), esp. 117–18 and 157–58. For "gnostic" and neoplatonic elements in Marxism see Ernst Topitsch, "Marxismus und Gnosis," and "Entfremdung und Ideologie. Zur Entmythologisierung des Marxismus," in Topitsch, *Sozialphilosophie zwischen Ideologie und Wissenschaft* (Neuwied: Luchterhand, 1971) 3d ed., 261–327; Leszek Kolakowski, *Main Currents of Marxism* (Oxford: Oxford University Press, 1978), vol. 1, 9–80.

31. Luis Peirano, "Entrevista con Gustavo Gutiérrez," *Qué Hacer* (March, 1980), 110–11; see also Gutiérrez, *La Fuerza Historica de los Pobres* (Lima: CEP, 1979), 260ff. Gutiérrez discusses this problem in the context of the "Puebla Document."

32. Peirano, "Entrevista," 110–11.

33. Cf. Topitsch, *Vom Ursprung und Ende der Metaphysik,* 204–05 and passim: Topitsch, ed., "Uber Leerformel. Zur Pragmatik des Sprachgebrauches in Philosophie und politischer Theorie," *Probleme der Wissenschaftstheorie. Festchrift für Victor Kraft,* ed. E. Topitsch (Vienna: Springer, 1960), 233–64; Gert Degenkolbe, "Über logische Struktur und gesellschaftliche Funktionen von Leerformeln," *Kölner Zeitschrift für Soziologie und Sozialphilosophie,* 17 (1965), 327–38.

34. In Wittgenstein's sense; see *Tractatus logico-philosophicus* 4.46, 4.461, 4.4611, 4.462, 4.463, 4.464, 4.465, 5.142, 5.143.

35. The concept of "coincidentia oppositorum" plays an important role in the philosophy of Nicholas of Cusa (see n. 36). For a phenomenology of religion

with the notion of "coincidentia" at its core, see Vicente Hernández Catalá, *La Expresión de lo Divino en las Religiones no Cristianas* (Madrid: B.A.C., 1972). The ideological uses to which the idea of an ultimate reconciliation of opposites lends itself are obvious; these dangers are usually not examined in the "phenomenological" studies of religion or mysticism current today.

36. See, although in a different context, the preliminary observations found in Gustavo Benavides, "Tautology as Philosophy in Nicolaus Cusanus and Nāgārjuna," *Buddhist and Western Philosophy,* ed. Nathan Katz (Delhi: Sterling, 1981), 30–53.

37. Cf. Jameson, *The Political Unconscious,* 17.

38. See J. Lloyd Mecham, *Church and State in Latin America* (Chapel Hill: University of North Carolina Press, 1966), rev. ed.; Hans-Jürgen Prien, *Die Geschichte des Christentums in Lateinamerika* (Göttingen: Vandenhoeck & Ruprecht, 1978).

39. On Mariategui, see Alberto Flores-Galindo, *La Agonía de Mariátegui* (Lima: DESCO, 1981). John Baines, *Revolution in Peru: Mariategui and the Myth* (Tuscaloosa, Ala.: University of Alabama Press, 1972).

40. Cf. Marjorie Reeves, *Joachim of Fiore and the Prophetic Future* (New York: Harper & Row, 1977), 126–35, esp. 128–29, where Reeves discusses Columbus's *Libro de las Profecías;* Prien, *Die Geschichte des Christentums in Lateinamerika,* 143ff.

41. Cf. Gutiérrez, *La Fuerza Histórica de los Pobres,* 361, 370–71.

42. Recently, for example, the conservative *Opus Dei*—whose influence among the middle and upper classes should not be underestimated—has been granted special status by the pope; this promotion is part of the anti-liberal policies pursued by the Vatican, and of a general ideological position not very different from that of the Reagan administration; on these issues see the recent publications by Ana María Ezcurra: *La Ofensiva Neoconservadora. Iglesias de USA y Lucha Ideólogica Hacia América Latina* (Madrid: IEPALA, 1982); *Agresión Ideológica Contra la Revolución Sandinista* (Mexico: Nuevomar, 1983). English translation: *Ideological Aggression Against the Sandinista Revolution* (New York: New York CIRCUS Publications, 1984); *El Vaticano y la Administración Reagan* (Mexico: Nuevomar, 1984). In the different political context of the United States, we are witnessing a similar phenomenon: on the one hand, there is the hesitant, contradictory involvement of the Catholic hierarchy in the antinuclear movement and, on the other hand, the development among Catholic publicists such as Michael Novak of a "theology of the corporation" and of a theological legitimation of nuclear deterrence. See Michael Novak, *Toward a Theology of the Corporation* (Washington, D.C.: American Enterprise Institute, 1981), 37–42, esp. 40 ("Birth and Mortality," a rather peculiar theological darwinism); Michael Novak and John W. Cooper, eds., *The Corporation, A Theological Inquiry* (Washington, D.C.: AEI, 1981), 203–24, esp. 209–10. On the issue of a "just" nuclear war see Michael Novak, *Moral Clarity in the Nuclear Age* (Nashville, Tenn.: Thomas Nelson, 1983) with a foreword by Billy Graham and an introduction by William F. Buckley, Jr.; in this frightening little book, Novak uses as epigraphs Isaiah 2:4 (swords into plowshares), Joel 3:10 (plowshares into swords), Psalm 144 ("Blessed be the Lord, my rock, who trains my hands for war"); see also p. 90 where he laments the loss of "noble military causes."

11

Types of Religious Liberation: An Implicit Critique of Modern Politics

NINIAN SMART

Introduction

Much of contemporary life is taken up with the twin pursuits of freedom and happiness. The religious traditions of the world also in their own ways are concerned with these goals. But they provide a perspective from which to criticize secular aspirations for them. For what, in the ultimate analysis—or should we say "in the light of the ultimate"—is happiness? And in what consists true freedom? Thus for the Christian, Christ's freedom is something that goes beyond a merely commonsense absence of restraints; for the Buddhist true welfare or happiness (sukha) is in part consequent upon the recognition of the illfare and unhappiness that otherwise characterizes all sentient life. However, though the main religious traditions converge at certain points, there are also not inconsiderable differences. In the first part of this essay I wish to lay forth some of the chief varieties of belief in liberation or salvation; in the second part I will reflect briefly on them and consider how far they can be seen as complementary.

Types of Liberation

Since the main religions have a conception of the ultimate as somehow transcending "this world," however that may be analyzed, it is natural that liberation or freedom should be seen as becoming close to or realizing one's unity with, or attaining, the ultimate and thereby throwing off the restraints of this world. Liberation thus is seen as something transcendent itself or closely tied to what is transcendent. There is therefore, ineluctably, an otherworldly element in liberation. But as we shall see, this need not mean that we should not see salvation or liberation as having an important this-worldly component.

To flesh out my point: consider the following ways of seeing the state of salvation. It is the final departure of the soul (jiva), in the Jain tradition, from the karmic round of rebirth and its lodging motionless and omniscient at the summit of the universe. It is likewise, in Sāmkhya and Yoga, a state of isolation and absence of pain beyond the round of rebirth. In Theravāda Buddhism, there is no soul, but somehow in the disappearance of individuality there is attained the state of nibbāna in which and from which there cannot be any more rebirth. In Advaita Vedānta, liberation involves realization of one's essential identity with Brahman and the cessation of the karmic round. In theistic Vedānta on the other hand, through transcendence of the round of reincarnation (a common factor in the mainstream Indian traditions), salvation is pictured as everlasting life in heaven close to God. Incidentally, heavens are, of course, present in the Buddhist and other nontheistic traditions, but are thought of as places of nonpermanent residence, and since permanence is often seen as the mark of true and ultimate value, such heavens turn out to be no more than pleasant consequences of virtue, not ultimate goals to be striven for. Theoretically, this is the way it is seen in Pure Land Buddhism, that great efflorescence of Buddhist bhakti: but since in the Pure Land so many fervent spiritual hopes are centered, the goal of final nirvana beyond even the Pure Land itself fades—so that phenomenologically this variety of Buddhism approximates the Hindu theisms as much as the nontheistic schools. So far we come across two main motifs with variations: disappearance from rebirth into a static, blissful (or at least pain-free) state; and ascent to a permanent heavenly state close to God. The Advaita variant is in a sense intermediate: one is God, the Divine Being, and as such is liberated, save that you typically do not know it. In the first case, this-worldly individuality is lost. In Samkhya and Yoga and Jainism, liberated souls are "base," "nude," unclothed in bodily and psychological modes. In Buddhism, there is no real question of personality surviving since nirvana is delineated with a whole battery of appropriate negations. In Advaita, too, the worldly individual disappears, since the true self, which is discovered existentially to be divine, is not mine or yours, but unindividually universal. Similar remarks can be made about those Mahāyāna developments where the Buddha nature, as a kind of quasi-self, is spoken of. It is ultimately empty (sūnya) and suchness, and in no way is embedded as a swarm of individual Buddha natures in different living beings.

It is useful here to make a distinction. In Sāmkhya and Dvaita Vedanta, for instance, there are many individual souls. But in Sāmkhya they are "standardized" so to speak—they are individuals but without individuality. Liberation means continuing individuation, but there, as they say, "once you've seen one you've seen them all." On the other hand, there is a Dvaita, a sense of individual uniqueness, and this is also the usual interpretation of the Christian doctrine of the resurrection of the body. So it may be useful to distinguish between a pluralism of individuals or souls on the one hand and the notion of the individuality or uniqueness of each soul on the other. For short I will call the first the doctrine of *numerous* individuals or souls and the second the doctrine of *personal* individuals or souls.

In the major Western traditions of Christianity, Judaism, and Islam, reincarnation of course had not had much prominence, so the whole nexus of ideas surrounding karma, samsāra, and liberation does not apply. Rather, notions of heaven predominate (and hell, etc.) Also the concept of the resurrection of the body has entered into mainstream Western theism. This latter notion has as part of its cash value the notion that what is sacred is the whole personality, as embodied. Perhaps for most purposes this is the whole of its cash value, since both traditionally and today the resurrection of the body has often been seen as mysterious, as involving God's creating new bodies perhaps not of earthly stuff. So by consequence the difference between this idea and that of a personal soul becomes diminished. The problem of the soul idea is its abstractness and lack of clear relation to personhood; the problem of the resurrection idea is its overconcreteness and propensity to degenerate into speculations about material reconstitution, for example, of ashes.

So far we can perceive various patterns of belief concerning liberation. First, there is the doctrine of numerous individuals who have transcended the round of rebirth. Second, there is the doctrine of liberated personal souls somehow related to God. Third, there is realization of unity with the ultimate in which both the idea of numerous souls and that of personal souls disappears (Advaita and Sūnyavada in Mahāyāna Buddhism).

We should also mention the conception of ancestors. Though not primarily a notion of salvation or liberation, it does have a role in our thinking about an afterlife. Ancestors typically are important in extending the community; the latter is seen not merely as constituted by the living, but extends to those who have passed into the invisible world, but an invisible world still close to us. Thus the cult of ancestors—giving them offerings, say—is just an extension of the veneration given to the old and the wise. It reminds us that sometimes freedom or liberation or salvation can also be viewed as a collective matter. This can be so in a narrower or a wider way.

More narrowly the focus may be primarily on a given people, such as Israel. The people may look forward to "last things" in which God will, perhaps through some charismatic leader or messiah, restore the people and settle them in peace forever. Secular ideologies such as nationalism and Marxism can echo this concept. Indeed, it is worth noting that in modern times "freedom" very often is thought of in terms of a collective national or social liberation. (But freedom also has to do with individual rights, and collective and individual liberties can collide.)

The broader way in which a collectivity of liberation may be conceived is universalism—that is, the doctrine that all eventually will be saved and that since no one can be finally happy while others suffer, individual and collective bliss becomes notionally simultaneous. This idea occurs in some Christian theologies and in the bodhisattva ideal in Mahāyāna Buddhism. For the bodhisattva puts off his own liberation until all are liberated.

We may observe that only one type of liberation is strongly personalistic. Neither nontheistic systems that hold that there are numerous individuals or souls nor those that believe in a monistic unity of all souls conceive of liberation as personal. It is by contrast characteristic of Dvaita in the Hindu tradition and theisms that emphasize heavenly liberation after some kind of judgment and reconstitution of the individual that have a place for salvation of the person. Yet of course it is a paradox: for though I may thus be guaranteed my ego, yet that self now is seen as truly happy when dependent on God. As it is said, "whose service is perfect freedom."

So you can, it seems, have perfect happiness as a person in a state of dependence or perfect freedom if you are prepared to give up your individuality. Happy slavery or unconscious freedom—is this the choice?

But the contrast between the nonpersonal and personal (which are also theistic ideas) is not as strong as it at first seems. For the nonpersonal systems also hold to the concept of the person who is "living liberated" or jivanmukta. Such a one has attained assurance of release while alive and indeed is already liberated. His body and mind of course continue to operate, but there will be no rebirth when death arrives. As the usual image has it, he is like a potter's wheel continuing to spin after the potter has taken his hand off.

This notion of living liberation or jivanmukta means that we have the idea of an individual who will indeed lose his particularity at death (becoming either unutterable as in Buddhism or a standard soul as elsewhere in nontheistic Indian traditions); but on the other hand he is objectively a person. So he is a liberated person, or saint. I stress personhood twice here to drive home the point that here we have a living model of personal liberation, which does not in principle differ ontologically from that of the saved person beyond the grave in the theistic traditions—except only there is no relationship to God. But there is relationship to others in the community here and now. Also, of course, in theistic traditions there is sometimes the idea of living salvation, as when the believer has assurance that he is saved, because of some direct experience of God's grace, for example.

So far we have looked at ideas of liberation and salvation without asking the question "from what?" Here there is, of course, a variety of beliefs to consider. It is typical, however, of the Indian tradition that the most typical answer is at one level duhkha or illfare, suffering, pain (different translations are common but the first of these is what I favor). Deeper down we find that illfare arises in the last resort from ignorance, lack of insight. But monism does not see the problem simply in these terms because the doctrine itself implies that the multiple world of appearances is an illusion. So ontologically the world we transcend is unreal. Elsewhere it is real, but unsatisfactory. In gnosticism there was often the more radical idea that the world is evil. But it is only possible really to think of the world in this way if there is an evil creator of it (demiurge); for evil is an attribute that applys to the effects of an evil actor. Otherwise the world can be painful or illusory. On the whole, modern religious traditions have moved far from the concept of an evil God or even of a Satan. On the other hand, if there is but one God then the evil in the world is his responsibility unless you ascribe it to some primeval catastrophe, and this is where the Christian doctrine of the Fall comes in, and with it the idea that it is sin we need saving from, not ignorance.

Sin has come to have two components: one is that of alienation or estrangement or, in more traditional terms, unholiness in the sense of falling short of the holiness of God; and the other is moral evil and disobedience toward God. If we are to put matters positively, then the aim of those who would wish to be liberated from sin would be gaining holiness and communion with God on the one hand, and moral goodness on the other. But the very essence of a religion of the holy is a sense of duality between God and worshiper—that is, ontological difference—even when the sense of alienation is overcome. So salvation is not seen as merging or actually becoming God, but rather as being in the closest possible relationship to God. It is this sense of relationship, even in the life beyond, that no doubt accounts for the personalism of theistic salvation. Conversely, because liberation in the nontheistic traditions means isolation or unutterability, it is in *this* world, where relationships still exist, that we have the liberated person.

The holy or numinous character of God means that liberation can, strictly speaking, only come through his agency. For as the one God he possesses ultimately all the holiness there is—nothing beside him is holy. (If in Hindu devotional religion there seem to be gods and goddesses besides the Lord, they are, in the end, parts of him, refractions so to speak—which is why we may call such a system of myth and cult refracted theism.) Holiness flows from God, thus the ·idea of grace and of the transfer of merit. Even if we do things that are not admirable and are out of accord with his will, he can forgive us and count them as nothing. In such a way, though being good is in a sense a means to salvation, it is ultimately not so—for only grace is a means thereto. The moral endeavor is swallowed up in a wider and deeper sense of meaning.

On the other hand, in nontheistic systems, where there is scarcely any call to think of grace (except where bhakti and devotional religion begins to make itself felt, as with the growth of the bodhisattva ideal), moral action becomes an important ingredient in the path to liberation. It becomes much more directly a means of salvation.

But it is morality still in a context, and this supplies three motifs that typically affect the way goodness is considered. These are karma, tapas, and dhyāna—or in English, reincarnational effects, austerity, and contemplation. Belief in rebirth means that morality often becomes a mode—*the* mode sometimes—of acquiring merit and so of gaining a better life next time. Such a life may be in a heaven, but even here the worm of impermanence and potential suffering persists, for no heaven can provide ultimate freedom. So karma theory stretches the effects of moral striving. As for asceticism, in the Indian tradition especially there are deep impulses toward self-mortification as a means of neutralizing the effects of deeds, and we have as the ultimate symbol of this the great nude Jaina statues where creepers growing up the legs of a saint show how impervious he is to the environment, how indifferent to worldly things. Self-starvation becomes the perfect death. To the ascetic outlook belongs a view of the world not so much as illusion, as painful, or as sinful, but as entangling. Freedom must mean cutting off all those impulses that get you more deeply entangled.

But it is contemplation that possesses the greatest present-day interest. For it is characteristic of the Yoga traditions of India, of which Buddhism is in many ways the greatest, that they see the acquisition of a special type of higher consciousness as being the key to liberation. This higher consciousness is empty and pure, and yet it also brings knowledge. For the world seen now *sub specie eternitatis* has a different look, and the analysis that is part of the context of self-training is perceived existentially. So the world view of the yogi thus has confirmation in higher experience, and liberation also involves some kind of jñāne or vivcká or prajñā—in Greek, gnosis, a kind of what I call for fun "gnowing."

Such contemplative mysticism is not, of course, absent from theistic traditions, but there it has a different context and significance. For one thing, higher consciousness is seen as union with but not identity with the ultimate; and it is itself considered a product of grace. Moreover, since mysticism is not the predominant form of life in theism, where worship and sacraments are more pervasive, it has less centrality as a means of liberation than in the nontheistic religions.

We have seen some polarities and contrasts. Thus there is the sense of personal, heavenly salvation versus nonpersonal liberation in nirvana. There is individual versus collective liberation. There is liberation from sin and from ignorance and entanglement. There is the world as real and the world as illusion. There is grace as means of salvation versus austerity, morality, and contemplation. I wish now to reflect about some of these typical patterns in the more secular context that is becoming so pervasive in today's world.

Reflections on Traditional Concepts and Their Contemporary Relevance

Contemporary Western culture is dominated by utilitarianism, namely the doctrine that social policy should be aimed at maximizing happiness and minimizing suffering. We are descendants of Adam Smith and John Stuart Mill. There is much to commend in modern economics, and in social democracy there is an attempt to adjust and curtail the workings of "the market" in order to alleviate the suffering of the poor and needy. At the same time the most vital political force in modern times is nationalism, and this has sometimes run contrary to the individualism inherent in utilitarianism. Moreover, Marxism, with its collectivist thinking—especially as vulgarly understood by the ruling classes of Marxist countries—reinforces nationalism in practice, for it has proved a potent instrument of liberation from colonial and neocolonial bonds, which have largely been to the old capitalist nations of the north.

These reflections might seem far removed from the varieties of salvation I have been analyzing in this essay. But this is not so, for a number of reasons. First, the individualist ethos of liberal capitalism creates two problems, one of what may be called *external* identity, and the other of *internal* identity. As social persons we find identity in belonging to a group. For each person there may be an overlapping set of groups, but the most important is what may be called, in a somewhat Tillichian phrase, "the group of ultimate concern." In a nationalist era it is often the nation that functions thus, as that which demands if necessary your life in its service, and a large slice of your earnings and expenditure as a toll. Betrayal of the nation attracts the deepest opprobrium, as treason. But though national and ethnic identity may be built into the individual through his upbringing it need not be overriding. Its ultimacy may be questioned.

This is so in both theistic and nontheistic religion. Although one may be sympathetic to struggles for liberation (by Basques, Zimbabweans, Palestinians, etc.), the universal religions cannot see this political liberation as ultimate, for there is a higher community, of Christians or Muslims or Buddhists. Even where a faith is tied to a particular ethnic group (as appears to be the case with Judaism, except that the *ethnie* is both a matter of descent and of religious affiliation so that the religion defines the *ethnie* and not conversely), it may have a universal meaning, so that the group is a "light to the Gentiles" or an example to other nations. This means that though the group may be ultimate, its wider life is seen in a universal context.

Moreover, as well as widening our gaze horizontally to all humans as the ultimate group or even all living beings, the religions also expand it vertically, to the transcendent. And this becomes relevant to the problem of individual internal identity. It is by worship, in the case of theistic faiths, that you connect yourself to the transcendent, and by self-discipline and inner contemplation that you can aim for a "living liberation" as the ultimate ideal. This of course is relevant to the utilitarian program. For in both cases religions offer something beyond the usual this-worldly ideas of happiness or of suffering. Higher welfare need not of course be world negating, but they are what can be called world deepening and world transforming. They deepen the world, as in Buddhism, by inviting us to "see through" common sense. They can deepen it in theistic religions by creating a vision of the world as everywhere, even in its darkness, manifesting the Divine Being.

In all this, traditional religion becomes a critic of modern secular ideologies. It criticizes the flat happiness of materialist individualism; it criticizes the flat collectivism of Marxism; and it criticizes the narrowness of nationalism.

Yet the spirit of our secular age is pervasive. After all, how many people can believe, without effort or special commitment, in life after death or in rebirth? There is not much point in criticizing the ideologies of our time if it is from a radically foreign point of view. In certain important respects the old images of heaven and judgment and rebirth have to be taken now as regulative pictures. Let me briefly explain my meaning here.

One of the central problems, perhaps *the* central problem of philosophical theology, is how we conceive the junctures between the transcendent (whether God or nirvana or Brahman) and this world. I can understand the experience of realizing one's essential identity with Brahman; but how does this experience cause rebirth, a this-worldly phenomenon, to cease? I can understand how God supports and pervades the whole cosmos; but the manner of his becoming Christ eludes clear understanding. Again, how is it that there is a liberation, nirvana, and yet nirvana has no cause? In a sense, all questions of survival are such "juncture" questions: for if I survive only as a bull in the Argentine or as any kind of this-worldly being, how is that ultimate salvation? It is mere prolongation of life. So the images of redemption and the liberated state can hardly be clearly explicated. Rather, they help to point us to the ground of any hope and freedom, and that is the existence, as being or state, of that blessed transcendence to which the religions in varying directions point. In essence, then, the religions provide criticism of the secular because they have a transcendental outreach. This in turn means in human terms that a deeper experience of the world is found than in flat utilitarianism. Such depth experience helps us to see the world transformed.

This makes a difference to the significance of liberation theology, as distinguished from secular ideologies of liberation. The essential reason for seeing the material bases of human poverty and exploitation is that exploitation itself is an attack on human dignity, and that dignity is guaranteed by the divine spark or Buddha nature in each one of us. The worth of men and women relates not to class or ethnic group, but to their relation to the beyond and indeed reflection of what is transcendent.

The ideas of individual "disappearance" into the state beyond (in the style of Buddhism and other Yoga traditions) and of communion with God are complementary, for they point to two sides of religion and human life—a side that is full of images, worship, and outer cosmic vision, and a side that is empty of images, is contemplative, and seeks an inner light. We cannot know what liberation in the beyond is like, but we can here and now see its incarnated representatives. Thus the concept of liberation or redemption provides for transformed persons, who themselves are critics in their lives of the flatness and cruelty around us that follow from human nature and sometimes callous ideologies.

This is not to say Mill and Marx have not contributed to our world, but only when we see that material change and prosperity is essentially related to dignity do we see it in perspective. As I have said, the theories of salvation in the religions provide a deeper such perspective, even if we cannot say much about heaven or nirvana.

Part Four

RELIGION AND SOCIETY: SOME FUTURE DIRECTIONS

12

Freedom and Responsibility in a Secular World: A Christian View

HELMUT FRITZSCHE

The ideas of freedom and responsibility are fundamental to modern Western civilization and culture. This is especially the case in relation to humanity born in Europe, with its deep background in Christianity. We are accustomed to regarding human progress by the measures of personal, social, political, and spiritual liberty and responsibility. And I think it is right to do so. Freedom is one of the deepest values of humanity. But liberty without a deep sense of human responsibility is only another word for arbitrariness, despotism, or chaos.

At present we are faced with a deep crisis in relation to the ideas of freedom and responsibility. What does personal freedom mean for people in poverty or who are unemployed? Or for those torn by anxiety or oppressed? What does freedom mean for the wealthy who enjoy a high material living standard yet lack spiritual resources? What does responsibility mean for people without an adequate education? Facing the problems of our world—the anxiety of a threatening third world war, the arms race, oppression, and exploitation—the words *freedom* and *responsibility* run the danger of becoming a veil that more covers the lack of freedom than leads men to further liberation from actual oppression.

What does it really mean to be free, to be the artisans of our own destiny? What about personal and social self-determination? What are the connections between freedom and responsibility? What is the meaning of the liberation of peoples? Humanity's future depends on answers to these questions. It would be presumptuous to assume that Christianity and the other religions in the world could solve the problems of freedom and responsibility by themselves. But in the present dialogue of religions, cultures, and world views (weltanschauungen), especially in the struggle of ideas, lies an important claim on Christianity, because modern freedom and responsibility are ideas with a deep Christian background.

The modern ideas of liberty and responsibility—anticipated both in Greek humanism and the Christian announcement of salvation—were formed in the European Enlightenment and are therefore a product of secularization. Christianity and other religions should not try to roll back this process of secularization. On the contrary, they should seek to fulfill it. In the secularization process the human consciousness of freedom attains a new stage: man takes hold of the reins of his own destiny. In the process of secularization man has begun to enter maturity.

There is a close dialectical relationship between secularization and Christianity. Christian faith is one of the most important roots of the modern world's technical, industrial, and political power: these constitute, as it were, a commentary on the famous words of the Bible: ". . . be fruitful and multiply, and fill the earth and subdue it" (Gen. 1:28). On the other hand, the modern secularized world is a claim to humanity becoming as responsible as we should be before God.

In order to meet the present ambiguities in our understandings of freedom and responsibility, we must first understand the development of these ideas in the Bible and the history of Christianity. Against this background I will develop my own position. In the main, I will argue that freedom and responsibility are the central themes of a new experience of God in our age, one characterized by the ambiguities of humanity, power, and civilization in the age of progress.

The idea of freedom, especially the close connection between freedom and responsibility, is central to the Bible. In the Old Testament, prophets and priests are convinced that Yahweh has liberated his people from slavery in Egypt and will guide them to a freer life in an intimate community with God himself and without pressure from enemies, war, and miseries (Jer. 2). They were also convinced that catastrophes in history, like the deportation to Babylon, were God's punishment for sin. Prophets and priests emphasized that above all honors God gives to his people is the holy obligation to obey the high moral demands exemplified in the Ten Commandments. In the Old Testament freedom and responsibility are linked together and history is the point where human responsibility and God's grace or punishment meet each other.

In the New Testament the nexus of freedom and responsibility is even more important. Early Christianity worshiped Jesus Christ as God's son, who was crucified for human sin. His resurrection was understood as a victory over human failure and the beginning of a new age: men and women returning to God and grateful for God's salvation were thus free to love everybody. This new quality of freedom and responsibility is grounded in the power of Holy Spirit, which makes believers free from egoism and worldly anxiety and gives the believer a new attitude of trust and charity like that seen in Jesus Christ. Both the spirit of freedom and the awareness of responsibility are thus understood as gifts from God that transform the human heart.

An important stage in the historical development of the Christian understanding of freedom and responsibility was achieved in Martin Luther and especially his work *Christian Liberty*. Here we read the famous words: "The Christian is a free lord over everything and subject to no-one" and "A Christian is a servant of everything and subject to everyone." In this twofold formula, Luther emphasized that the true Christian attitude is grounded in faith since the one who believes in God's grace and doesn't trust in his own efforts is really free from egoism and anxiety and subservience. On the other hand, the believer lives responsible before God, free to serve the needs of all men in an attitude of charity.

Unlike the sixteenth century, we in Europe—and I think in America too—are now living in a secularized world. The central factor that characterizes a secular society is the separation between the state, social organizations, and education on the one hand, and religion, spirituality, and the churches on the other hand. For the secular mind, the world, its laws, its coming into being, and its prospects are viewed in wholly worldly terms without acknowledging God as creator and preserver. This scientific and humanistic view of the world is all-embracing. Modern man seeks the causes for our situation and its remedy in nature and history; he rejects the notion of transcendent causes beyond the realms of nature and history.

These convictions of human autonomy constitute a new stage in the awareness of human freedom and responsibility. Religion thus becomes a private matter. Everything in personal, social, and historical life, especially progress toward a more free and just society and the overcoming of human suffering, misfortune, hunger, war, and anxiety, depends on human activities or their failures.

Nevertheless, there is a deep continuity between the modern secular world and the spirit of Christianity. It was faith in God as creator and preserver of the world that gave wings to the discovery of the laws of nature and human responsibility for using them. Faith in God as creator and in the world as God's creation was the spiritual background for the idea of the perfectability of the world. And faith in Jesus Christ as Lord and brother of all men was the most important spiritual background for the awareness that human needs entail the moral claim to help address and overcome those needs. In every needy and suffering person one meets Jesus himself according to his words in Matthew 25:40: "Truly, I say to you, as you did it to one of the least of these my brethren, you did it to me."

The secularized mentality and the awareness of human responsibility for this world are two sides of the same matter. Here, however, we encounter the ambiguity of progress in dominating nature and the continuation of human evolution. Facing the future of mankind we encounter two possibilities: the destruction of the earth and the demolition of humanity; and the building up of a peaceful, just, and wealthy world for everybody and all peoples. In this situation Christianity and all religions are called upon by the secular world to make a significant contribution to understanding freedom and responsibility. Indeed, it isn't only the secular world, but God as creator, preserver, and savior who claims a new and deeper awareness of human responsibility for the fate of our earth.

The basic theological contribution that Christianity can offer to our time addresses itself to the ambiguity of human progress. The call to progress is a claim of God. But the challenge to Christianity in the secular modern world is to find a way to articulate a new experience with God. That new experience with God is centered in the practice of a partnership between God and humanity that acknowledges a greater degree of human responsibility for this world. In Christian terms I would say that it is necessary to become more and more aware of the fact that God disclosed himself in the *unmighty* Jesus as a sign that he will entrust his creation and himself into the hands of men and women.

Against this background, then, I will outline the contribution I envisage Christianity might give to understanding and promoting freedom and responsibility in the secular world. For this purpose I distinguish four aspects or levels of the Christian understanding and practice of freedom and responsibility.

First, basic to a Christian understanding of freedom and responsibility is the religious conviction that freedom arises from the communion of man with God. Thus freedom is not man's possession, but a gift from God. Freedom is not an object you can point to, but a relationship between God and human beings. Freedom is a historical gift from God that allows us to seek liberation for humanity.

In this view liberty is internal, a religious and spiritual freedom within, which depends on God and the impact of God's salvation in Jesus Christ. The practice of internal freedom is that which gives us every day a new liberation from anxiety and other kinds of worldly care. Internal freedom is a fountain for a more and more enhanced sense of responsibility before God. The Christian God is a personal one and to be with him in faith is the Christian's internal liberty.

The second level of freedom and responsibility embraces the political sphere. Here freedom means achieving a just human society. Such a society enables human beings to acquire ever increasing degrees of self-determination and self-fulfillment. The political basis for the idea of a more just and human society, both establishing and stimulating freedom, is the realization of human rights. These rights were formulated in the United Nations' General Declaration on Human Rights, December 10, 1948, the International Convention on Civil Rights, December 16, 1966, and the International Convention on Economic, Social and Cultural Rights, December 16, 1966. These human rights respect every person's individuality within the universal community of humankind. The individual's civil, economic, social, and cultural rights are not, and should not be, separated.

The modern world should be viewed as one interdependent social process toward a more just society. But there are very different stages of development in particular regions of the world today. Social progress is not only to be regarded as the development to a higher level of material well-being. In addition we must see that development means social justice, growing participation in education, cultural goods, and social planning and decision making. All these things belong together. The development of the productive forces of scientific and technological advances plays an important part in the process but must be accompanied by social progress as well.

In the political sphere, freedom is neither a possession nor a historical condition, but a development in a permanent process of liberation from oppression and alienation. The struggle for sociopolitical liberation and the realization of human rights has to be different in the diverse regions of the world. For example, in most countries of the Third World, elimination of the alienating conditions of life and the abolition of the social roots of poverty are the main goals. But the solution of these problems must be linked with the efforts to create a more just system of international trade. In the industrialized, market-economy societies, unemployment, despite the high level of the means of production and labor-saving innovations in technology in industrial production, is a basic problem that must be addressed. In my own socialist country, we must further develop the economic base and the social achievements thus far attained in order to attain a humane society.

It would be impossible to deal with all aspects of sociopolitical freedom and liberation. We are interested in discerning and holding together the different levels of reality, especially those of Christian faith and political activity. According to the Bible, the ultimate root of the poverty and injustice in which men live is sin. Sin is man's selfish turning in upon himself, a breach of the relationship with God. Salvation is God's own matter. The promised coming of Christ's kingdom must not be confused with the building up of a just society in the earthly realm. The establishment of a more just human society is an endeavor that exists in its own rights. It is based on a rational analysis of reality and is carried out through the means of social and political power. The political sphere has its own proper integrity. We have to respect the autonomy of the temporal sphere. But from a Christian standpoint it is also true that social development cannot be separated from the coming of Christ's kingdom, which promises liberation from alienation to all people. Social structures are not sinful in themselves. Social structures arise in connection with the development of the forces of production and many social and cultural factors. Social structures may become sinful if they favor selfishness. Then the time has come for changing such structures. Indeed, it may be a sin not to change what favors injustice. But new social structures must be based on political reason.

These few remarks regarding the internal and the political view of our problem lead to the next level in the meaning of liberation: the cooperation of God and man in history.

The third dimension of freedom is the historical dimension. Hegel, the first philosopher to offer an all-embracing view of human development, argues that the history of the world is the progressive unfolding of freedom. The historical process thus appears as the genesis of consciousness and as the gradual liberation of man.

It was a mistake of Hegel and many influenced by him—for

example, Teilhard de Chardin in our century, and Schleiermacher almost two centuries ago—to assume that the human process of liberation was only the triumphal procession of civilization to freedom based on the development of science, technology, culture, philosophy, and religion. Indeed, we have seen the two World Wars, Auschwitz, and the continuing conflict of the last years. We now know that it is possible that we may end all civilized life in a nuclear catastrophe. The majority of humankind is living in alienating poverty. The progress of technology jeopardizes the natural base of our life and exploits the necessary resources for the future of humankind. Nevertheless it is true that man has become the very subject of history in a world ever more interdependent.

The emergence of human responsibility for life includes a deep and dangerous ambiguity. The notion of humankind as the subject of history is more a challenge to create a new consciousness of all humanity's growing responsibility than it is a triumphal statement of fact. History is a challenge to create a man who will conquer selfishness and be willing to live according to the natural zeal for love and friendship with others. It is primarily a challenge to make peace. History is also a challenge to conquer those social and political conditions that favor selfishness and create poverty. Accordingly, the social sciences must develop a deep awareness of human responsibility for the future in an unjust world.

Regarding the reality of history, we maintain that although there is no easy identification of the history of God's salvation and human history, there is a close relationship between the temporal process and the growth of Christ's kingdom. But progress and the growth of the kingdom are not to be identified. The points that the Christian view adds to secular considerations of history are *sin* and *salvation*. We cannot deny the role of sin in the historical development of humanity. But we also believe in the impact of the salvific spirit of the triune God who accomplishes his work not without but through man.

The point of convergence between the Christian view and secular historical philosophies is the *new man:* man becoming free from all alienation and free for self-determination. For Christians, the new man must be in the likeness of Christ. We must not disregard the deep ambiguity of all human progress based on human efforts. To attack the root causes of ambiguity in human development and to transform social structures that favor selfishness—these are the historical missions of humankind in our day. The mission of Christians in our time is to serve the building up of the earthly city motivated by hope in the coming of the kingdom. After two thousand years of Christian proclamation and worship in Europe and in many parts of the world, we have no reason for a Christian haughtiness. It is true that Christendom has created a deep awareness of freedom and liberation. To accept God's grace in keeping his promise of salvation means that Christians and churches must serve the process of liberation by working together with others, Christians and non-Christians, in building up an earthly city characterized by more solidarity, justice, freedom, and peace.

The fourth dimension of freedom concerns the utopian dimension. The fullness of liberation, communion with God and with all humanity, is a goal that takes us beyond human history. Christians also hope for a new creation. Man must dream of a new life in a better future, but he has to know he is dreaming and he has to work in order to bring the dream into the reality of human history.

The utopian dimension is, on the one hand, a liberating call to hope. Now the world of peace is still a utopia, but we need utopianism in order to transcend the present situation and move toward a spiritual liberation, to that real world of peace we all demand to live in. Perhaps dreaming of a better future was one of the roots of the development of an awareness of freedom. Spiritually, becoming free is based on transcending the given present situation.

On the other hand, utopian views tend to a dangerous radicalism against a necessary historical realism. Martin Luther's realistic thinking in his time probably contributed more to social consciousness and progress toward a more just society than Thomas Muentzer's dream of God's kingdom. The rejection of exploitation that concerned Thomas Muentzer is indeed found in the Bible. For example, Leviticus 25:23 emphasizes that God is the only owner of the land given to his people. But you cannot directly transfer biblical viewpoints into social reality. Utopias can only be realized in accordance with the development of the means of production and other social and cultural conditions. Thus we have to maintain the dialectic between the utopian aspect and political reality. Nevertheless, as Moltmann observes, utopias make us free to hope in the future.

Furthermore, utopia is indeed a horizon of faith. But this must be distinguished from personal faith, which we discussed earlier. God is close to man in faith and spirituality at every point of history. In the moment of faith, man is in eternity. This idea of mysticism, emphasized by Schleiermacher, may not be confused with hope for historical progress based on God's salvation. But both are branches of the one faith in God's salvation by Christ.

All four levels or dimensions of freedom discussed here have the same goal: liberation from misery and enslavement. But they have different contents. To become free from emptiness, to conquer the alienation from oneself by faith and Christian spirituality is not the same as liberation from social injustice and alienation from man's enslavement to poverty and economic misery. But he who becomes free from selfishness by faith also becomes free for charity and hope, which motivates one to be engaged in social life. Historical progress aims at an ever increasing liberation of man. But history is never the simple fullness of God's promise to man to become his unalienated partner in a renewal of creation. He who hopes for God's promise will be a utopian, but he will also be a realist who knows the difference between the present time under the conditions of sin and the future of a renewed creation.

These four levels of freedom embrace all branches of humanity and all peoples. But they also respect the different dimensions of each level. God is closer to man in faith than he is to men and women in social history. And finally God's promise concerns all peoples, Christians and non-Christians. All men and religions are challenged to social progress, but there are different ways to more justice and more peace and freedom in the different parts of the world according to the different stages of development.

Nevertheless, Christianity and all religions are called upon to make their contribution to our understanding of freedom and responsibility. In conclusion, then, I would like to summarize what are, in my view, the ten principles that should inform Christians as they act in a secularized world.

Christian Freedom Is God's Freedom for All People.

Christian freedom involves faith, hope, spirituality, and service. It is based on the liberation that is a gift of God in Christ to all peoples. There is only one freedom for all human beings. Christians do not have a special freedom for themselves, but they do have a special theological understanding of freedom and are called to witness to God's freedom for humanity and to serve human freedom in imitation of Christ.

Christian Freedom in Its Unique Universality Is Singular.

Freedom in the Christian view embraces creation and salvation, social and individual life, and eternal and temporal reality. It is both otherworldly and intrahistorical. Freedom is always more than is realized in a given moment in time. Freedom remains, ultimately, of God. Churches and religions bear witness to God's liberation, which is greater than all human experiences of liberation.

Although, in my view, all religions and philosophies contain elements of truth concerning freedom, the singularity of freedom as understood by Christians is the basis for Christians to cooperate with others on all levels. But the Christian witness to freedom is inauthentic if it fails to confess our many failures in the history of Christianity to serve freedom.

One Aspect of Christian Freedom Is Inward Religious Disengagement from the World.

To be free from the world is to be free from the attitude of alienation from God, neighbor, and oneself. Faith in God's grace means to love God more than the world, which liberates the Christian from the attitude of stress in relation to the restlessness and troubles of this life. Inward disengagement from the world is necessary because the world is a *corpus mixtum,* God's good created nature and man's sin are mixed together. Disengagement from the world is not the way of salvation, but a good inward discipline for an engaged style of living. Here I agree with Frederick Sontag: "The transformation that Christianity seeks to induce in us is one that does not remove its believers from the world but transforms them in the world."

Christian Freedom Creates a Deep Spirituality that Unites Temporality and Eternity in Human Experience.

Christians affirm the impact of the spiritual presence of the triune God. We use the term spirituality to indicate the dominion of the Holy Spirit, which guides individuals and communities to the way to become servants in the creation of the new man. At the very root of our personal and community religious life lies the gift of the triune God's self-communication. Far from being a call to passivity, this gift demands a vital, vigilant attitude. The practice of spirituality does not eliminate tension and conflict, but sees in them the beginning of liberation from selfishness to service of God. Central to spirituality are the traditional practices of sacramental communion with Christ and his forgiveness, living brotherhood in a community, individual and common prayer, and the spiritual practice of meditation and contemplation. These are old branches of Christianity that are now being recovered under the impact of the East. Spirituality leads not only to service, but also to the emergence of the new man. Nevertheless, spirituality remains an experience of eternal life under the conditions of an earthly existence.

Christian Freedom Obliges Us to Solidarity with Other Religions insofar as They Take a Share in the Process of Liberation.

Given the scandalous involvement of Christian missions in the imperialistic policies of European states in the last centuries, Christians have no right to require conversion as the presupposition for solidarity. Although we believe in Christ, the light for all men, we meet other religions in dialogue presupposing the work of the spirit of the triune God in other religions. We join other religions in all efforts for liberation on both the religious and nonreligious levels of reality.

Christian Freedom Obliges Christians and Churches to Solidarity with All Efforts for a More Just Human Society.

The coming of the kingdom and liberating historical events are not identical, but liberation from sin embraces the social, political, and cultural spheres. Social exploitation, social misery, and political oppression are the reasons Christians must join the efforts to create a more just society.

Christian Freedom Stands Opposed to Socioreligious Messianism.

Jesus was not a zealot. He did not identify the social or political struggle with the coming of God's kingdom. His struggle for more love and justice was a universal one. All identifications of nationalism and religious faith are to be overcome for the sake of God's freedom for all men.

Christian Freedom Challenges Christians to Seek the Fulfillment of Secularization by Service to Liberation.

In the Christian view the very root of secularization is God's gift. God promises and grants that human beings may become the subjects of their own destiny. The proper realization of this self-determination is freedom in service to the liberation of humanity from all subjective and objective selfishness, haughtiness, and servility. Given the ambiguities in all human efforts and works, the separation of church and state is the better social basis for the free life of religions. The acknowledgment of the autonomy of social and political life was a spiritual liberation for Christians and churches in most European countries. But Christians must resist the temptation to retreat into an antiworldly, introspective attitude.

Christian Freedom Motivates Christians to Transcend the Given Situation in Hope for the Renewal of Creation.

Christian hope embraced the new being and intrahistorical new beginnings because Christian faith trusts in the permanent creation of new structured conditions for human beings sharing in God's own history.

Christian Freedom Requires Christians, Churches, Religions, and All Men to Seek Peace and to Create a World Where Nobody Need Fear.

God's own history, a history in which we all share, has reached a point where the self-destruction of humankind by a nuclear war has become a real possibility. It is a new stage in human history. God leaves his self-fulfillment in the hands of human beings. To destroy human existence is to offend God's existence. Since God has become man, humanity and human beings are God's living temple.

To stop the development and production of new systems of nuclear weapons, to stop the arms race by arms control, to support new serious negotiations concerning disarmament are some of the most important actual demands of Christian freedom today.

REFERENCES

Barth, Karl. *Das Geschenk der Freiheit*. Zollikon–Zurich: Evangelischer Verlag AG, 1953.

Fritzsche, Helmut. *Freiheit und Verantwortung in Liebe und Ehe*. Berlin: Evangelische Verlagsanstalt, 1983.

Gutiérrez, Gustavo. *A Theology of Liberation*. New York: Orbis Books, 1980.

Kasemann, Ernst. *Der Ruf der Freiheit*. Tübingen: J. C. B. Mohr, 1968.

Moltmann, Jürgen. "Die Revolution der Freiheit." In *Perspektiven der Theologie*. Munich: Kaiser Verlag, 1968.

Sontag, Frederick. *Love Beyond Pain*. New York: Paulist Press, 1977.

Tillich, Paul. *Systematic Theology*. vol. 3. Chicago: University of Chicago Press, 1963.

13

God, Humanity, and Nature:
The Dialectics of Interaction
T. K. OOMMEN

It is necessary to note at the beginning of this essay the sense in which the notion of God is employed in this essay. If God is understood as a force or principle that moves, motivates, and guides man and as an entity on which man puts great reliance and hope, one can then speak of both a theistic and a nontheistic conceptualization of God. Whereas theism locates the ultimate spiritual reality "beyond man," nontheistic gods are located within man. Embedded in these notions are varieties of relationships between God and humanity, nature and God, humanity and nature. In what follows I propose to explore the implications of the conceptualizations of God for the future of man and society.

There is an amazing similarity in conceptualizations of God and society in the contemporary West. The essential feature of this conceptualization is dichotomization or polarization. Dichotomous constructions of human societies, starting with *gemeinschaft* and *gesellschaft,* have become commonplace in Western social sciences. Parallel to this are human efforts to model relationships to God, to gods, or to supernatural forces on the existing social relationships of society. Thus, religion is influenced by its social milieu. The attitude of respect man holds for the sacred becomes but an intensification of the kind of respect found in other social relationships. The point is well formulated by Ludwig Feuerbach: the conception of God is anthropological. "Religion is man's earliest . . . indirect form of self-knowledge . . . God is the highest subjectivity of man abstracted from himself."[1]

Conventional sociologists, in their attempt to conceptualize God-society relationships, attribute "functional specificity" to God: he has been disengaged from all aspects of life save the differentiated structure of religion, the this-worldly institutional interpenetration between God and society that persists in less "modern" societies of the East where God is not relegated to the religious realm, but rather presides over all aspects of life: economic, political, and cultural. This endows God with a holistic position in human life as against the compartmentalized position God has been assigned in modern Western societies. To experience God according to this conceptualization, man has to enter the realm of the sacred or holy; it is a charismatic experience. Thus, though God is retained in society and his presence in society is explicitly recognized, he has been "localized" in one of society's segments: the this-worldly institutional instrument, religion.

The Marxian perspective characterizes God as the creation of man, particularly the vested interests that want to maintain the status quo. These vested interests use God, it is argued, as an instrument to resist basic social changes, and religion, which is but the opium of the masses, is manipulated by the bourgeoisie to maintain the capitalist system, which suits its needs and interests. The Marxian approach explicitly acknowledges the primacy of man as the creator and relegates God to the position of a creature, contrary to theistic positions wherein God is the acknowledged creator and man God's creature. However, common to all the Western conceptualizations—social, scientific, and theological—is the dichotomization between God and society. It is my contention that unless we transcend this central tendency in Western thought— opposition and epistemological dualism—we cannot adequately perceive the interpenetration of the two. The basic problem here is the ill-conceived polarity between matter and spirit, knowledge and belief, sacred and secular, God and society. The logic here is one of reciprocal opposition. Hence it leads to one displacing the other, of what I call the zero-sum game. But the empirical reality forcefully points to the coexistence and intermeshing of these apparently (but not actually) inimical elements. Many may be tempted to dismiss this complex empirical reality as a transitional aberration in the long chain of social evolution. But we recognize it as a reality in itself with distinct properties. Although we do not deny that the evolutionary process and human innovation will inevitably influence man's conception of God, it is unlikely that gods will disappear, even theistic gods. Viewed thus, neither the current social scientific theories nor the theological conceptions of the West seem to be adequate to grapple with the "real, living God."

The polarization in conceptualization that we have referred to above is, however, characteristic only of modern Western man. To quote Frankfort et al: "The ancients, like the modern savages, saw man always as part of society, and society as imbedded in nature and dependent upon cosmic forces. For then nature and man did not stand in opposition and did not, therefore, have to be apprehended by different modes of cognition. . . . The fundamental differences between the attitudes of modern and ancient man as regards the surrounding world is this: for modern, scientific man the phenomenal world is primarily an 'It'; for ancient—and also for primitive— man it is a 'Thou'."[2]

Notwithstanding the fact that monotheistic religions, particularly Christianity, have contributed to dualistic conceptualizations in modern times, the biblical understanding of the relationship between God, humanity, and nature does not seem to support it. As the World Council of Churches' Conference on Faith, Science, and the Future put it:

In contrast to all dualistic or spiritualistic pictures of hope, humanity and the non-human creation thus remain intimately bound together in an open-ended history: the promise of fulfillment applies to the whole creation . . . human beings have . . . a duty towards the non-human creation: human beings who bear God's Spirit are the sign of the great promise of freedom for all creation.[3] . . . Humanity is temporally the last link in God's creation and, therefore, a part of nature not apart from it . . . what authority they possess, they possess within creation and not over it; further that authority is a gift of God and one for which men and women will be called to account by God.[4]

Man can be viewed as a maker (*homo faber*) and a cultivator, but the first is often overemphasized to the neglect of the second. However, "As God's creature, humanity is above all a receiver. In modern times, to the detriment of all creation, this dimension of our relation to God and nature has been hidden by the one-sided emphasis on *homo faber*. To counter this, it must be emphasized that even in making and cultivating, humanity is a receiver."[5]

This perspective seems to correct some of the distortions that have crept into the Christian understanding of the relationship between humanity and nature. But the relationship between God and humanity is still characterized by a dualistic conceptualization: God is the giver and man is the receiver. This has two implications for man: intellectual and moral. First, it denies, in effect, the creative talents of man; it inhibits his creative potentialities. If man's "creativity" is a gift of God, insofar as he is a mere receiver, he need not make the effort he is capable of. But God expects man to work hard and to put to use his ability to the fullest extent, lest what has been originally bestowed on him should be withdrawn (Matt. 25:14–30). To ensure man's authentic participation, his efforts should be explicitly recognized and of course rewarded. Second, to be eternally relegated to the position of a receiver is morally degrading. What imparts dignity is giving and contributing, not simply receiving and taking. The inadequate recognition given to man may frustrate him and may consequently render him aggressive, particularly when man tastes his power independent of God. It seems to me that this is precisely what happened during the last couple of centuries. Armed with the powers of science and technology, man arrogated himself to be God. Perhaps he was trying to "liberate" himself from the subservient position of a receiver.

It is this changed context that necessitates a new conceptualization of the God–humanity relationship from that of a giver–receiver to that of coworkers, partners, and participants. This should not be construed as an effort to claim, much less to establish, equality between God and man. I consider that an untenable proposition because equality is possible only between entities of similar qualities, which is clearly not the case here. My point is an endeavor to establish an authentic fellowship between God and man, which should be essentially participatory. Thus, man should impart a sense of self-responsibility. In turn, an authentic fellowship should be established between humanity and nature. Here again, the character of entities involved differs and hence the type of relationship would also be qualitatively different.

In the first part of this essay I tried to highlight the epistemological dualism characteristic of contemporary Western thought and how it fails to illumine our understanding of the interpenetration of God, humanity, and nature. It remains our task to investigate the substantive aspect of the issue, namely, the social forces at work that molded man's perception and understanding of the relationship between the three entities.

In the past, when man was constrained to live and work under the limitations of natural conditions, he viewed anything that surpassed his strength as mysterious. Perhaps the only option open to him was to subject himself to those forces that he could not control: to worship the multitude of objects—mountains, rivers, sun, etc.— all of which were deemed gods. This in turn has given rise to the belief that divinity infuses the natural world. To quote Toynbee, "In the pantheistic view, divinity is immanent in the universe and is transfused throughout the universe. In the monotheistic view, divinity is withdrawn from the universe and is made external to it; that is to say, divinity is made transcendent."[6]

The implications of this externalization of divinity from the universe for social transformation is far-reaching. As Ikeda puts it:

The difference between monotheism and pantheism is very telling in human civilization. Under conditions imposed by monotheistic faith, a great need to relate everything to an absolute being defines society and civilization and promotes the development of an all-pervasive uniformity. Because this makes the acceptance of alien elements difficult, when confronted with something foreign and new, a monotheistic society must undergo a win-or-lose, all-or-nothing transition. For this reason, changes in the historical current of the West have often been basic and far-reaching. In pantheistic societies, on the other hand, the value of alien ideas and things is recognized. The society is tolerant toward them; consequently, they can be introduced without the necessity of fundamental social alterations. No matter what new elements enter, the society remains basically unchanged.[7]

With the passage of time, man came to organize human society in large and efficiently constructed communities. At this stage, the worship of collective human power—primordial collectivities including nation-states—overshadowed the worship of natural forces. The gods who originally symbolized the nonhuman natural forces were now conscripted to serve as symbols of human institutions. But the implications of infusing human institutions with divinity, the sacralization of society, differed in different societies. For the followers of exclusive-minded monotheistic religions, the coexistence of more than one religion or language, in one society or nation-state is difficult to comprehend. On the other hand, in societies where polytheism or pantheism exist, religious or linguistic pluralism has been the normal state of affairs. This means not only the coexistence of religion and magic, science and religion, nationalism and communalism, without much conflict and tension, but also the central tendency in these societies has been one of coexistence and reconciliation.

Man's ability to coerce and exploit nature was limited so long as he used only animate energy. But with the unlimited inanimate energy that he could generate through the application of science and technology, men thought they had the license to exploit nonhuman nature, which is but a gift to him by God. And Western man's tendency to exploit nature was not inhibited by the pantheistic belief that nonhuman nature is sacred and that it has a dignity, like man himself, which ought to be respected. Thus the modern West has substituted the post-Christian faith in science for its ancestral Christianity; it discarded theism but retained the misconstrued belief, derived from monotheism, that it has the right to exploit nonhuman nature. This selective retention of a distorted religious faith along with the power of science has serious implications for humanity's present and indeed future. If under the previous Christian dispensation Western man believed himself to be God's tenant divinely licensed to cultivate and nurture nature on the proviso that he worshiped God and acknowledged his proprietary rights, by the seventeenth century man cut off God's head and expropriated the universe. Drunk with the power he acquired through science and technology, Western man refused to remain as God's tenant on earth, but claimed that he was a free holder, an absolute owner. The religion of science, like nationalism, has now become a global phenomenon.

The next major development in human history was that of crystallization of secular ideologies. If capitalism was believed to be an explicit offshoot of Christianity, at least some of its sects and denominations,[8] communism is, in fact, a Christian heresy. But unlike previous heresies it has insisted on a particular Christian precept that the Christian establishment has neglected. To quote Toynbee: "The mythology of Communism is Jewish and Christian mythology translated into a non-theistic vocabulary. The unique and omnipotent god Yahweh has been translated into historical necessity; the chosen people have been translated into the Proletariat, which is predestined by historical necessity to triumph; the Millennium has been translated into the eventual fading away of the state. Communism has also inherited from Christianity the belief in a mission to convert all mankind."[9]

The new religions—science, nationalism, communism—as distinguished from old theistic religions—Christianity, Hinduism, Islam—vary in that the old ones strive to control human activity and suppress human greed. In their conceptualizations, man was a tool in the hands of God. The new gods are tools in the hands of man. The new gods seem to have given birth to, or at least have been explicitly used for, the fulfillment of that greed. However, all the gods, both theistic and nontheistic, share one thing: absolutization. The understanding and hope of the "believers" is that their gods, independently and unequivocally, hold the key to the ultimate solution of problems.

It seems to me that what we need is a new conceptualization about God: not a god who views man simply as his tool or a man who presumes to use the gods of his creation as his tools for his selfish advantages. What is feasible is a conceptualization in which God and man are viewed as partners. Further, we need to accept a system of laws universal to all forms of life. Such a system of laws should emphasize the harmony and unity of humanity with nonhuman nature also. From the current dichotomous constructions of the West we must move on to a trichotomy. The trinity involved here is God-man-nature, not necessarily in a hierarchical ordering, but in a mutually harmonious and nurturing relationship. It is incredible that modern Western thought did not attempt this task since the Trinitarian doctrine embedded in Christian theology "presents the relationships between God, humanity and nature as a differentiated unity."[10]

In the spiritual Trinity of Christianity, one, the son, had a human incarnation in Christ. This human incarnation of Christ facilitated the process of developing a concrete, historical, empathy-building relationship between God, humanity, and nature. This experientially crucial dimension, which is essentially a communication channel, a rapport-building enterprise between God, humanity, and nature, did not seem to have adequately registered in the cognitive map of Western Christian theology. In contrast, Eastern Christian theology has "taught 'union participation' not only between God and humanity in Christ but also between humanity and nature."[11] And this syncretism seems to be the inevitable corollary of the social milieu in which Christian faith is practiced, societies in which polytheistic and pantheistic religions have originated and coexist with monotheism.

I would like to point out here that the combination of modern scientific "progress" and a distortion of Judaic monotheism has been largely instrumental in the man-nature disengagement. At the core of modern scientific civilization lies the conception that man and nature are two oppositional entities and that for the sake of human progress it is necessary to conquer nature. The scientific method has been the chief instrument of realizing this conquest. The Judaic monotheistic belief that the spiritual presence in and behind the universe is a single, transcendent, humanlike God reinforced the further belief that nothing else in the universe is divine.

This God is not only the creator of man and nature, but is also endowed with the power and right to dispose of what he had created. And God placed the whole of his nonhuman creation at the disposal of his human creatures to use it for his benefit. God blessed man and said, in effect, "Have many children so that your descendants will live all over the earth and bring it under their *control.* I am putting you *in charge* of the fish, the birds, and all the wild animals" (Gen. 1:28–29). The convenient focusing of attention on one aspect of the story of creation has led to distortions. For example, according to Genesis 23:10, God has entrusted the land to his covenant people as a *loan:* it is not their possession. Further, every seventh year the land should be left fallow (the year for revitalization of the land) and every fifty years the land should be equitably redistributed (Lev. 25).

Before man developed the ability to control nature, nature's fury was believed to be capable of destroying man and his nonhuman environment. The story of the flood symbolizes the potentiality of natural forces to threaten mankind. But Noah's ark contained not only man, but representatives of nonhuman species. Yahweh comes to the rescue of man, as well as nonhuman creatures. In spite of this, on the one hand, man sees the relationship between himself and nature as an I-It relationship. On the other hand, believing himself to be closest to God of all creatures, he thinks it is natural that he subjugate all other species and put them into his service. Thus, once man developed the ability to control nature through science and technology, not only did he divest the natural environment of its former aura of divinity, but he even stripped God of his divinity. Indeed, modern Western man has no compunction about destroying the human environment.

It is important to remind ourselves here that the roots of this ideology were first formulated in Palestine as early as the ninth century B.C., but it was put into practice in Europe only after twenty-five centuries, that is in the seventeenth century A.D., when Western science emerged. Jesus taught that economic greed was incompatible with service to God. He averred: "You cannot serve both God and money" (Matt. 6:24). He advised the people: "Do not store up riches for yourselves here on earth, where moths and rust destroy, and robbers break in and steal" (Matt. 6:19). Jesus condemned the accumulation of capital, technology, and the glorification of economically remunerative work. It may be stressed here that Jesus lived in Palestine, when it was predominantly an agrarian society, wherein human living was in harmony with the nonhuman environment. Although accumulation of capital and conspicuous consumption were rare in his social environment, Jesus perceived and denounced the greed that is innate in human nature irrespective of time and place. Jesus glorified the nonmaterialistic attitude of birds and wild flowers and held this up as an example for human disciples to emulate. Yet distortions crept into the Christian conceptualization of the man–nature relationship, which combined with the advancement in science and technology to conspire against the harmony between man and his environment. This rendered the evolving and sustaining of an ecologically balanced and just society nearly impossible.

Recent thinking on this theme, however, has recognized the problematic involved. I cannot do better than quote a World Council of Churches document:

The cultural context has radically changed since biblical times. In the biblical period humanity was confronted with an overpowering nature. The command to rule the animals and to subdue the earth delivered people from fear and from the temptation to divinize or demonize nature, and encourage them to overcome suffering and to build culture. The power relations have since been reversed by science and technology. A desacralized nature is in the power of humanity which is now able to destroy its own species and perhaps even all life on the earth. Our own technological inventions and our social processes are threatening to get the upper hand to become as over-powering as nature once was. What needs to be emphasized today, therefore, is the *relatedness* between God and his creation rather than their *separateness*. The dignity of nature as creation needs to be bound up with our responsibility for the preservation of life.[12]

It is against this background that I plead for a new conceptualization about God. Notwithstanding all the spectacular achievements of man through science and technology, it is clear that he is infinitely inferior to the nonhuman natural world in several respects. At the same time, it is also certain that man's superiority is clearly discernible in several contexts. For future material development the Western monotheistic attitude is valuable. But for protecting the autonomy of all groups of people and for putting a stop to pollution and destruction of the natural environment, the Eastern approach is more viable. What is needed, then, is a religion, a conceptualization about God that can go beyond the differences of the East and West and bind the whole of humankind into a unified body. Such a religion will save the Occident from its present crisis and the Orient from its current hardships.[13]

The theological understanding and conceptualization about God, the gods, or the divine are invariably anchored in religious texts. The characteristic skepticism theologians have of scientific tools and empirical methods renders their analyses incomplete if one wants to understand God from the perspective of ordinary believers. In theological analysis we encounter only the abstract, universal, invisible, and transcendental God. In contrast, social scientists focus on the concrete, the local, the visible and the pragmatic God, which they can understand through scientific tools, often ignoring the fact that their subject matter in this context is not easily amenable to empirical analysis. Their effort is to understand God contextually, in terms of the social milieu in which it is located. If theologians strive for a top-down understanding of God, the social scientists insist on a bottom-up analysis. Although both these perspectives are valuable in themselves since they illuminate different aspects of reality, they are inadequate taken independently. The "universal gods" of theologians are not those experienced by people; the "specific gods" studied by social scientists are often vulgarizations of the sophisticated notion of God. And yet there is considerable interaction between the local and the universal gods; they mutually influence and, not infrequently, reinforce one another.

Even in a pluralistic society in which a diversity of gods are recognized and worshiped by the differing folk traditions, the elite tradition often recognizes only one God. On the other hand, notwithstanding the multiplicity of gods worshiped in the variety of folk traditions in a given society, there is invariably a tacit recognition of a sakti, a force or energy that is reckoned as ultimate reality. Therefore, the "disjuncture" between the monist God of the elite and the plurality of gods of the folk, is often a tension of form and not necessarily of substance. The significant question for us to investigate, however, is the basis of the differing conceptualizations of theologians and social scientists.

Broadly speaking, the two leading sources of conceptualizations about God are religious doctrines and societal characteristics. Ideally, we can postulate a continuum in each of these contexts, moving from unity and uniformity of religious doctrine to the multiplicity and diversity of religious doctrines. Similarly, we can arrange societies on a continuum from relative homogeneity to extreme heterogeneity. Variations in religious doctrines obtain not only among different religions that radically differ in their conceptualizations of God (monotheism, polytheism, pantheism), but even among different sects and denominations in the same religious tradition.

Similarly, the elements that contribute to societal heterogeneity are not only primordial identities—religion, languages, region, caste, tribe—but also variations in terms of sociopolitical ideologies—capitalism, socialism, communism, secularism—and the level of economic development and scientific and technological advancement. With this understanding, we can postulate four ideal-typical but empirically plausible societal situations that would influence conceptualization about God. These ideal types are shown in the following diagram:

Diagram 1: Sources and Nature of Conceptualization About God

Religious Doctrine(s)	Type of Society	Nature of Conceptualization About God
1. Homogeneous	Homogeneous	Consensual; single God
2. Homogeneous	Heterogeneous	Substance may be uniform but forms may vary
3. Heterogeneous	Homogeneous	Substance may vary, even if forms are uniform
4. Heterogeneous	Heterogeneous	Both substance and forms vary; plurality of Gods

The concrete societies of the contemporary world, with frayed edges and loose textures and constantly exposed to alien influences, afford only a few examples of type 1. Most of the societies in the world today would fall into either type 2 or 3. Indeed, there are a few cases of type 4, the classical one being that of India.

In all probability, protest against and rejection of old gods and accommodation of new gods will constantly take place, particularly in heterogeneous and complex societies. But whether or not this process will generate conflicts between gods who compete for loyalty from their existing or potential clients will depend on the overall ethos of the society, which in turn is largely conditioned by the nature of dominant religion of a given society. If the dominant religion is one that conceptualizes the sacred and the secular, the transcendental and the mundane in monistic and oppositional terms, the possibility of the coexistence of a multiplicity of conceptions about God is remote. On the other hand, if the dominant religion conceives the sacred and the secular, the divine and mundane, in terms of a continuum and as present in a variety of contexts, interpenetrating all aspects of life, the possibility is that differing conceptions of God will be accommodated with relative ease. Such a societal situation will not call for the displacement of one God by another, rather it would facilitate the coexistence of a multiplicity of gods. The process of redefiniton or reconceptualization of gods may take place either through the emergence of sectarianism or denominationalism within the same religion or through the acceptance of altogether new conceptions of God through the process of embracing new religions, either through conversion or by founding new ones.

Perhaps it is useful at this stage to briefly indicate how varieties of religious protests mold social conceptions of God. We may identify five such empirical possibilities as shown in Diagram 2.[14]

Diagram 2: Types of Protests and Social Conceptions of God

Style of Protest	Mechanisms of Articulation	Conceptions of God
1. Reform	Monasticism	Institutionally insulated
2. Retreatism	Mysticism	Individualized
3. Rebellion	Sectarian Secession	Oppositional
4. Innovation	Sectarian Secession	Communal insulation and oppositional
5. Revolution	Secession from one religion to another	New communal God, expansionist

It is not suggested here that all these styles of protest, mechanisms of articulation, and concomitant conceptions of gods will be found in any given society or at a given historical phase. What is, however, significant is that the styles and mechanisms of protest are likely to mold conceptions about the gods. If so, it is clear that for an adequate understanding of differing conceptions of God we should focus our attention simultaneously on the nature of religious doctrines and the historicity of our social milieu.

NOTES

1. Ludwig Feuerbach, *The Essence of Christianity,* trans. George Eliot (New York: Harper & Bros., 1957), 30.

2. Henri Frankfort, Mrs. H. Frankfort, J. A. Wilson, and T. Jacobsen, *Before Philosophy* (Middlesex: Penguin, 1949).

3. Paul Abrecht, ed., *Faith and Science in an Unjust World* (Geneva: World Council of Churches, 1980), 31; a report of the World Council of Churches' Conference on Faith, Science, and the Future, vol. 2, "Reports and Recommendations."

4. Ibid., 161.

5. Ibid., 34.

6. Arnold Toynbee and Daisaku Ikeda, *Choose Life: A Dialogue,* ed. R. L. Gage (London: Oxford University Press, 1976), 298.

7. Ibid., 297–98.

8. See Max Weber, *The Protestant Ethic and the Spirit of Capitalism* (Glencoe, Ill.: The Free Press, 1960).

9. Toynbee and Ikeda, 295.

10. Abrecht, 29.

11. Ibid., 29.

12. Ibid., 33.

13. Toynbee and Ikeda.

14. Compare Thomas F. O'dea, *The Sociology of Religion* (New Delhi: Prentice-Hall of India, 1969).

14

Toward a Grammar of the Spirit in Society: The Contribution of Rosenstock-Huessy

M. DARROL BRYANT

As we move into the planetary era in the history of humankind, it becomes increasingly imperative for the religions of humankind to disclose their respective contributions to our common but multiform social future. Unlike earlier ages, when the adherents of different faiths and the bearers of different traditions lived in relative isolation from one another, the believer increasingly today—and more so in the future—will live in the presence of other believers and the multiplicity of religious traditions. This emergent situation will place new demands on us all. As one who does not share the widespread conviction among Western intellectuals of a "religionless future," nor the belief that secularization means the end of religion, it seems crucial that the insights and wealth of our respective traditions be brought to bear on our common social horizon.[1] Thus one of the great questions that confronts us at the end of the second millennium of the Christian era is this: what contribution, if any, can faith make to our common, but multiform, social future?

Here my focus is on religion and society and the connection between the life of the spirit and society. Ever since the industrial revolution, there has been increased attention among Christian thinkers on the issue of the life of humankind in time, to social reality.[2] What does this shift from doctrine to society portend? In my view it reflects a growing awareness that we must find our way toward a viable social future in which we can discern anew the transforming presence of God amidst the seeming chaos of our multiform life in time. Moreover, it portends a quest—as every question does—for something still dimly glimpsed, but nonetheless passionately sought: social peace. For the Christian thinker, despite the seemingly endless debates among rival positions, God and the life of humankind *in time* are intimately and inextricably linked. Thus the life of the spirit may be discerned in the life of society.

But where do we turn in our efforts to understand the multiform relationships between the life of the spirit and society? Are there religiously inspired efforts that point us in fruitful directions? It seems to me that there are figures in our respective traditions who are addressing themselves to these issues, figures whose actions are luminous or whose perspectives are full of promise. I think here of the efforts of Gandhi earlier in this century and of the current actions of Dom Helder Camara in Brazil and Mother Theresa in India, or the intellectual creativity of Sri Aurobindo and Martin Buber. All of these persons act and speak in ways that transcend the boundaries, religious and otherwise, that often separate us from one another. At this stage of the emergent planetary discussion it strikes me as crucial that we strive to make the resources of our particular traditions better known to one another. To this end I will focus here on the work of the little-known Christian social thinker Eugen Rosenstock-Huessy (1888–1973).[3] His work has been immensely instructive to me and is, in my view, an example of a promising new direction from within the Christian tradition for those seeking to understand something of the connection between the life of the spirit and society.[4]

For Rosenstock-Huessy the events of our century disclosed the necessity for a grammar of society that could contribute to the creation of social peace. Unfortunately, in his view, the emergent social sciences had been bewitched by the methods of the natural sciences and the focus on the movement of objects in space. However, the social sciences required a new orientation, one that would focus on the *intergenerational life of humankind in time*.[5] Moreover, the tumult of our century requires new approaches that move beyond the reigning antitheses of modernity: subjective *or* objective, faith *or* science, materialist *or* idealist, determinist *or* indeterminist. But where does one turn to find a way beyond these reigning antitheses, a way that could lead to an encounter with the fullness of humankind's life in the spirit and in time?

For Rosenstock-Huessy, the inspiration for the project that was to occupy the whole of his life was drawn from the Christian faith. As he wrote in terms drawn from the Christian traditions, "Today we are living through the agonies of transition to the third epoch. We have yet to establish Man, the great singular of humanity, in one household, over the plurality of races, classes and age groups. This will be the center of struggle in the future. . . . The theme of future history will be not territorial or political but social: it will be the story of man's creation. The next thousand years may be expected, consequently, to concentrate on the third article, namely to wrestle with the task of revealing God in society."[6]

Faith as Orientation: Toward a Social Grammar

Rosenstock-Huessy was profoundly shaken by the events of the First World War. It meant, he believed, that one could not continue with "business as usual." Instead, we entered a new and more open situation where we had to relearn the dynamics of social life that lead to social peace. For Rosenstock-Huessy, the initial scent of the way beyond the dominant antitheses was to be found in faith that he understood in terms of *orientation*. Faith was not so much a set of doctrinal beliefs, but the way human life is oriented toward the future. In his words, "faith, properly speaking, is always belief in some future, a world to come."[7] Thus it is the power to move us beyond and ahead. It stands on the front line of the future as the antidote to decadence. This existential and temporal understanding of faith reveals Rosenstock-Huessy's dissent from those accounts of humankind's life in time that ground themselves in a belief in the autonomy of reason. It also points to a way ahead that acknowledges the spiritual foundations of social life.

When Rosenstock-Huessy grounds his grammar of humankind's life in time in faith it is not for the sake of placing his grammar beyond criticism, but rather to make explicit its own presuppositions. Moreover, the truth of an understanding of society is measured by its capacity to illuminate our lived experience in time, not by reference to a presumed standard of objectivity. On the other hand, Rosenstock-Huessy's approach to society not only stands over against conventional social theory, it also stands over against other explicitly Christian understandings of society in that it does not appeal to either doctrinal or ethical criteria for its justification. Rather, in speaking about the Christian faith, Rosenstock-Huessy argues that Christian dogma is "not an intellectual formula but a record and promise of life."[8] Thus, his path seeks to overcome the conflict between faith and science that has been so pervasive in the post-Enlightenment West.

The distinctive understanding of faith in relation to the creation of an adequate understanding of the life of society in time is reflected in Rosenstock-Huessy's discussion of the Christian creeds. As he writes, "Its three articles guarantee our trust in the unity of creation from the beginning (God the Father made all things in heaven and on earth), our liberty to die to our old selves (given us by God's Son, who implanted the Divine itself in human life by living as a man, and dying, yet rising again), and the inspiration of the Holy Spirit which enables us to commune with posterity and start fellowship here and now."[9] Here one can see the effort Rosenstock-Huessy is making to open Christian faith out to an account of the underlying spiritual dynamics that inform our life in society. He makes this even more explicit when he contends that

. . . the third article of the Creed is the specifically Christian one: from now on the Holy Spirit makes man a partner in his own creation. In the beginning God had said, "Let us make man in our image" (Genesis 1:26). In this light, the Church Fathers interpreted human history as a process of making Man like God. They called it "anthropurgy": as metallurgy refines metal from its ore, anthropurgy wins the true stuff of Man out of his coarse physical substance. Christ, in the center of history, enables us to participate consciously in this man-making process and to study its laws.[10]

Thus, although Rosenstock-Huessy's social grammar is inspired by Christian faith, his project is not a conventional religious one. For him the fundamental issue is not the knowing of God in himself, nor conformity to a received doctrinal tradition, nor the elaboration of abstract ethical norms, but rather it is to understand the life of humanity in time, the making and remaking of the human race. Hence the Christian faith opens out into the life of society in time, the world in which we daily find ourselves. It is here that the Spirit is present as our partner in our own making and remaking.

Faith, then, provided Rosenstock-Huessy with an orientation, not a solution, to the project that lay before him. The project was an understanding of the life of humankind in time, and the solution to that lay in a turning to the very processes and dynamics of social life, not in recourse to doctrine. In other words, it is the actual life of human beings in society that is the subject of social research and investigation. But that actual life is, in his view, one that is grounded in God, and humankind thus finds itself within a divine imperative—the making of humanity—and not as Enlightenment social theories argue, in relation to itself. Humanity is defined by response, not by autonomy. His rejection of the Enlightenment doctrine of "autonomy" as a modern conceit is parallel to his rejection of Christian approaches of the life of society grounded in ethics, or doctrine. Rosenstock-Huessy is seeking to articulate a grammar of social life that can disclose that the very processes of social life already bear witness to the life and presence of the spirit. Thus for Rosenstock-Huessy—unlike many others—the issue is not one of trying to overlay the processes of social life with a religious framework. Nor is he seeking to argue, as do many Latin American liberation theologians, for the identification of a certain stand of political development with the purposes of God. Instead, he is engaged in "the search for the omnipresence of God in the most contradictory patterns of human society."[11]

Rather than speaking of his project as "social theory," he prefers the term *social grammar*. The reason for this is that in a "grammar" we have performed a distinctive task, namely, the recognition and articulation of "multiformity within unity."[12] This is crucial since, in Rosenstock-Huessy's view, social thinkers have been too much burdened by the search for a single determinate cause in terms of which all social processes are understood. One sees this, for example, in Marxian theories, which make everything a reflection of economics. Instead, Rosenstock-Huessy argues for the necessity of basic terms that respect the multiform character of social life. Thus we need a grammar of social life that raises to the level of consciousness the very processes that are in fact taking place in our social exchange and interaction. Second, Rosenstock-Huessy described his work as a grammar because it is intimately linked to speech and language as central to all social processes. Speech is "the lifeblood of society,"[13] yet social thinkers tend to overlook this most obvious feature of our life together. As creatures of time, we are continually speaking to one another as we reason, pass laws, tell stories, sing, instruct our children, express our hurts, champion our causes, lament our failings. It is these manifold activities that Rosenstock-Huessy focuses on in his social grammar. In this social grammar, he writes, "a science is sought by which we may diagnose the power, vitality, unanimity and propriety of the lifeblood of society, of speech, language, literature . . . our method represents remedial linguistics, testing the powers of peace and war."[14] Moreover, he contends that "the grammatical method is the way in which man becomes conscious of his place in history (backward), world (outward), society (inward), and destiny (forward). The grammatical method is, then, an additional development of speech itself; for, speech having given man this direction and orientation about his place in the universe through the ages, what is needed today is an additional consciousness of this power of direction and orientation."[15] What is central to this social grammar—and implicit in the citation—is what Rosenstock-Huessy calls the "Cross of Reality." It is to this foundational insight and model that we now turn.

The Cross of Reality: The Crucible of the Creature

When we turn to the actual life of human beings, one of the fundamental features of creaturely life that discloses itself is that it is life lived in *space and time*. However, that space and time further discloses itself as multiform, not uniform. Thus Rosenstock-Huessy notes:

Now and here, we are living in a twofold time and a twofold space. As living beings, we are responsible for the conservation of the accomplishments of the past, the fulfillment of the future, the unanimity of the inner, the efficiency of the external front of life. In order to live, any organism must face backward, forward, inward and outward. . . . The now and here of all of us, means that we are living in a two fold space and a twofold time. And the term twofold is literally true. . . . Forward, backward, inward, outward lie the dynamic frontiers of life, capable of intensification, enlargement, expansion and exposed to shrinking and decay as well.[16]

These two axes of time and space, then, constitute the crucible of creaturely life, both personally and socially. Thus Rosenstock-Huessy came to argue that reality itself—not the abstract reality of physics, but the full-bodied reality of human life—is cruciform. Our existence is a perpetual suffering and wrestling with conflicting forces, paradoxes, contradictions within and without. By them we are stretched and torn in opposite directions, but through them comes renewal. And these opposing directions are summed up by four that define the great space and time axes of all men's life on earth, forming a Cross of Reality.[17]

This Cross of Reality, this crucible of creaturely life, can be presented schematically in the following diagram:

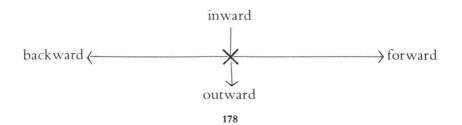

The creature and society live at the intersection of these four fronts of life. Here we live and die—and are renewed.

The Cross of Reality, as the *name* of our condition in time and space as creatures, is fundamental to Rosenstock-Huessy's social thinking. It is his denial of both reductionism and abstractionism. It serves to bring into focus those manifold forces that everyday assail our life and, at the same time, it clarifies the imperatives inherent in our situation. Moreover, wrote Rosenstock-Huessy, "since the four fronts differ in quality and direction they are *ultimate and irreducible dimensions of human existence,* but the mind with its imperious urge to relate and unify everything is tempted to over-simplify life and deny the Cross of Reality by reducing the four to one."[18] But it was this temptation that Rosenstock-Huessy resisted and the consequence is a grammar of the spirit infinitely richer than those that have dominated contemporary discussions. In the light of the Cross of Reality a major revolution in our social thinking is required.

This cruciform understanding of reality reveals, upon analysis, the spatial "conflict of inner and outer processes" and the temporal "conflict between responsibilities toward the past and the future."[19] These axes are not extrinsic to the creature, but pass through the very heart of our being. We are creatures of the cross. "Therefore," wrote Rosenstock-Huessy, "life is perpetual decision: when to continue the past and when to change, and where to draw the line between the inner circle we speak to and the outer objects we merely speak of and try to manipulate."[20] In the absence of a cruciform understanding of the reality of creaturely life, we tend to see only one or another front, one or another dimension of life. The consequence is a distortion of the situation of the creature, which then skews our thinking and our responses.

In our social life, the cruciform character of life results in a certain division of social labor. As Rosenstock-Huessy notes, "society compensates for our individual inadequacies by division of labor."[21] He continues:

Teaching, ceremony and ritual preserve our continuity with the past, and teachers, priests and lawyers serve on this front for all of us. We build up social unanimity by playing, singing, talking together, sharing our moods and aspirations and on this inner front poets, artists, and musicians are typical representatives. We win our living and protect our lives by learning to control natural forces and manipulating them for our ends in farming, industry and war; scientists, engineers, and soldiers typify the millions who fight for us on the outer front. Lastly, religious and political leaders, prophets and statesmen are responsible for initiating change and drawing society into its future.[22]

Thus, society itself takes on a certain cruciform reality in order to respond to the multiple claims upon its life. The virtue of Rosenstock-Huessy's insight here is that the division of labor is not just an economic phenomenon, but touches the very fabric of our life together in a society: the functions of different groups within society contribute to the welfare of the whole society. This perspective also contains a way of analyzing social distortion and social breakdown. For example, without the presence in society of those whose lives are given over to the fulfillment of the social task of nourishing social unanimity, the evil of inner disunity emerges. Contemporary society, "dominated for several centuries by natural science and its applications, suffers most of all from obsession with the outward front," and this obsession has "led to a distortion that threatens our future."[23] Hence, in Rosenstock-Huessy's view, "social health depends on preserving a delicate mobile balance between forward and backward, inward and outward."[24]

When the Cross of Reality is placed at the heart of one's social grammar the result is a multiform understanding of social life and the multiform character of speech. Against one-dimensional understandings of society and speaking, Rosenstock-Huessy asserts that "whenever we speak, we assert our being alive because we occupy a center from which the eye looks backward, forward, inward and outward. To speak, means to be placed in the center of the cross of reality."[25] However, we do not speak in a single mode, but rather in the mode appropriate to the front to which we are most attentive at a given moment. This results, says Rosenstock-Huessy, in a fourfold understanding of speech: projective (forward), subjective (inward), trajective (backward), and objective (outward).[26] Here again the creature finds himself called upon to differentiate his speaking so that it is appropriate to the dimension of our cruciform reality addressed. Moreover, the maintenance of these different modes of speech is at the heart of social well-being. In Rosenstock-Huessy's words:

Men reason, men pass laws, men tell stories, men sing. The external world is reasoned out, the future is ruled, the past is told, the unanimity of the inner circle is expressed in song. . . . The energies of social life are compressed into words. The circulation of articulated speech is the lifeblood of society. *Through speech, society sustains its time and space axes.* These time and space axes give direction and orientation to all members of society. Without articulated speech, man has neither direction nor orientation in time or space.[27]

Thus the Cross of Reality when correlated with a fourfold understanding of speech gives rise to a grammar of social analysis and points the way to social renewal. We are, in this sense, creatures of speech, or in Christian terms, the Word.

In making the point about the centrality of speech to social life, Rosenstock-Huessy turns to our actual life in time and space rather than to philosophical reflection upon speech as has become common in the contemporary interest in the philosophy of language. Contra the search of the early Wittgenstein for an ideal language, or the later Wittgenstein for the disease of ordinary speech, or Cassier's "symbol-making," or Heidegger's view of language as the "house of being," Rosenstock-Huessy turns his attention to speaking and listening as the key to social living and dying. Speech is the matrix of our life together.

Rosenstock-Huessy believed that the cruciform method he developed allowed for "the diagnosis of the complete soul" as well as the "healthy society."[28] Unlike the social thinkers who followed the lead of the natural sciences into a preoccupation with external space, Rosenstock-Huessy sought to turn our attention to the reality of human life on the cruciform of space and time. Here in the responses of human beings and societies to the imperatives that arise in the unfolding of events the fate of humankind is lost and won. Rather than searching for timeless abstractions, Rosenstock-Huessy sought to teach us the value of timing and timelessness. Rather than a philosophy of language, Rosenstock-Huessy sought to sharpen our ability to hear the spoken word since "all we can learn is to listen better and better," and heed the life-sustaining, renewing, and inspiring word we speak on the Cross of Reality.[29]

The Grammar of Social Life and Death

Earlier we indicated that Rosenstock-Huessy's social grammar acknowledges that the social thinker is a participant in, rather than an observer of, the social life of humankind. Thus the social thinker is compelled, as are other members of society, "to pass judgment on the trend of affairs in society. Is it decaying? Is it disintegrating? Is it going to last? Is it going to live?"[30] Thus, Rosenstock-Huessy claimed that "behind every one thinkable problem of our social sciences we can trace this major preoccupation of distinguishing between the living and the dead elements of the social pattern. The danger of death is the first cause of any knowledge about society."[31] Given Rosenstock-Huessy's cruciform analysis of the life of society, there emerges a set of characteristic social dangers and evils that face society on each front. Every society is faced with the perpetual problem of orchestrating the multiform imperatives of each front into a healthy whole in which each front is given its due. But this social peace is difficult to attain, indeed it is the perpetual challenge to every society.

"What is wrong with society?" asks Rosenstock-Huessy.[32] When we grasp the dynamics present within the Cross of Reality, then we can see that society is continually seeking to create inner unanimity, outer efficiency, respect for the past, and faith in the future. But each of these fronts of life is threatened by the evils of anarchy or the lack of inner unanimity or common aspiration, war or the inability to efficiently organize external space, revolution or being over-whelmed by the future and doing violence to the past for which we feel no sense of gratitude, and decadence or the inability of the older generation to inspire the new generation by giving it a heritage. These threats to social life on each front can be presented schematically as follows:

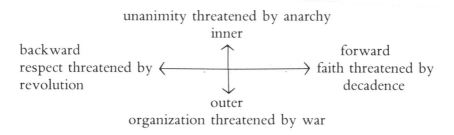

In terms of Rosenstock-Huessy's social grammar, the time axis involves the intergenerational life of society. Thus the issue is the capacity of the older generation to inspire the new generation such that there can be change without violence. At the same time, it is crucial that the past provide a heritage that does not stifle the need to let the new come into the life of society. Revolution is thus the result of the failure of peaceful intergenerational change such that the future is brought in with violence. On the other hand, the future may run roughshod over the past, including the "liquidation" of the past when there is no healthy respect for the achievements of past generations. Faith in the future and respect for the past require each other in order that the life of society in time can be sustained. Society finds itself continually confronted with the question of what from the past we need to let go of and what we need to conserve and what from the future we need to say yes to and what we need to resist.

Likewise, anarchy and war are "symptomatic of the evils of the order of society in space."[33] What Rosenstock-Huessy is pointing to here is the need to establish—or better create—a certain rhythm and connection between the inner life of the members of society and the outward organization of its space. When that inner unanimity breaks down, when everyone is preoccupied with "making his pile, grabbing more than his share"[34] then society cannot function as one body politic and rise to meet the challenges of organizing its life in space. Thus there is a reciprocal relationship between the inner and the outer just as there is between the future and the past.

Moreover, Rosenstock-Huessy notes that we "sustain the time and space axes of our civilization by speaking."[35] We, citizens and social thinkers alike, "take our place in the center of civilization, confronted as we are with its four aspects, its future, its past, its inner solidarity, its external struggle. And in this delicate and dangerous exposure to the four fronts of life, to the inner, the outer, the backward, and the forward front, our words must strike a balance; language distributes and organizes the universe, in every moment, anew. It is we who decide what belongs to the past and what shall be part of the future."[36]

Central to the process of articulating what is necessary to the achievement of social peace is the triumph over the social forms of death, the social evils that threaten social well-being. These triumphs over death are never, in his view, once-and-for-all events. Rather, they are daily events in our life in society. For Rosenstock-Huessy such a social grammar is rooted in the conviction that "God becomes known to us in all the powers that triumph over death."[37] Thus the survival of society is itself testimony of the presence of that divine spirit in our midst. "If," he wrote, "the Divine becomes known in our lives as the power of conquering death, it is something that can only happen to us in this or that particular moment of time; it is known as an *event*, never as an essence or a thing. And it can happen to us only in the midst of living."[38]

This dynamic and cruciform grammar of social life seeks, then, to heighten our awareness of the very processes of social life. It is a grammar grounded in the actual experience of human beings in society, though many of the basic insights are inspired by Christian faith. It is Christianity, in his view, that has seen most clearly the seemingly paradoxical relationship between death and life, namely, that "death" often precedes life. In the death and resurrection of Jesus Christ the great reversal takes place, but this is something we also know in our social and daily life. Often the way to the future involves our "dying" to old habits, enduring a great crisis, letting go of idols and in myriad ways seeing a new life emerge from suffering and spiritual "death." What is striking is the way that Rosenstock-Huessy wrests insights from faith that are illuminating for our life in society and time. For Rosenstock-Huessy the daily life of society depends on the *spiritual virtues* of faith and love, since it is finally these spiritual powers that are "stronger than death."[39] Thus our spiritual life and social well-being are ultimately linked to one another.

Death as a biological reality for the life of individuals and generations is also a central problem for society. Here the issue is the way to link intergenerational life within society so that society may achieve continuity despite death. Again we are confronted in this situation, argues Rosenstock-Huessy, by the centrality of the spirit to social life. What links generations together across the abyss of death is the spirit as loyalty to prior achievements, faith in those who come after us, and bonds of love that sustain us in the present. Through these spiritual powers we are threaded into intergenerational life. Rosenstock-Huessy remarks:

In society, in our historical community, we move as men born through the living Word into our times and places, into our future destiny. We have the singular privilege of contributing to the everlasting survival of acquired faculties which we embrace and to contribute to the everlasting relegation to hell of those acquired faculties which we wish to see extirpated. Thus, Creation is taking place under our very noses. And nobody can stay neutral in this spiritual war between bequeathing the good qualities to the future through faith or giving up from despair the task of weeding out the diabolical qualities.[40]

On our Cross of Reality we too take up the task of making and remaking society. It is this "life of the spirit" that constitutes the creation of "our true time, our full membership in history."[41]

Rosenstock-Huessy's attention to what he called "the full-bodied reality of human life" led him to a grammar of social life that was not predicated on the arbitrary distinction and separation of what we have come to call the "spiritual" and the "secular." Rather, his investigations led him to recognize the presence of the spirit in the daily life of human beings and society. The wholeness of life within our multiform reality cries out for a grammar of social life that accords with our lived experience on the Cross of Reality. In this effort to find a social grammar, Rosenstock-Huessy is, in my view, a pioneer of great importance.

Conclusion

At the outset of this essay, I pointed to the emergent necessity of opening the wealth of our respective religious traditions to our common, but multiform, future. Rosenstock-Huessy's social grammar is, in my view, one such pioneering effort in this direction. His work is, as we have seen, deeply indebted to the Christian faith from which he draws his inspiration and many of his basic terms. However, he certainly hoped, in doing that, not to create obstacles to grasping the grammar of social life he was attempting to articulate. Whether he was successful in this must be left to the judgment of others. But it needs also to be pointed out that Rosenstock-Huessy was aware—though this was not central to his own work—of the necessity of incorporating the inspiration of other traditions into the social grammar he was proposing. As he affirmed in *The Christian Future*, written in the late thirties and early forties, "Today Orient and Occident are shaken by a cataclysm which shows the insufficiency of both in isolation. A new penetration of the Cross is required which shall draw together the hearts of men in East and West by showing that each has some essential ingredient of life which the other needs."[42] He then went on to offer a cruciform analysis of "how Orient and Occident both have given us a pair of re-founders or re-directors of human nature—Buddha and Laotse, Abraham and Jesus—who together have created man's full freedom on all fronts of the Cross of Reality."[43] While he acknowledged the sketchy character of what he was attempting, it does point to the openness of his grammar. At the same time, the basically Christian sources of his inspiration and efforts must be acknowledged. At this point we are left more with a question than an answer: can we find our way to a grammar of social life that incorporates what Rosenstock-Huessy called "the oneness and interdependence of all mankind?"[44]

Although this question must remain open, it does seem to me that in the social grammar Rosenstock-Huessy articulates—and that I have here, albeit sketchily, outlined—is an important contribution to a dialogue and conversation that will only intensify in the future. The current and many-layered crises that societies both East and West, North and South, are undergoing make clear that the social boats that normally ferry each generation from birth to death are in danger of being swamped. As we move toward the end of this century we are all called to renewed efforts to rediscover and create anew patterns of life together that can sustain the future of humankind on the Cross of Reality—and that recognize the spiritual dynamics that make for social peace.

NOTES

1. Such views are not only widespread among intellectuals influenced by the Enlightenment view of religion as superstition, or the Marxian view of religion as an opiate, or the Freudian view of religion as illusion, but have also made considerable inroads among Christian theologians, particularly those known as the "secular theologians." Such views were especially popular in North American theological circles in the 1960s, but seem to have waned considerably more recently. For a collection of essays on this theme see *New Theology No. 5,* ed. M. Marty and Dean Peerman (New York: Macmillan, 1968).

2. Here I am thinking of the movements—for example, the Social Gospel movement in North America and the European and British movements for Religious Socialism—that arose in response to the industrial revolution. One aspect of this shift is the renewed interest among Christian thinkers in history. For a collection of readings on this topic see *God, History, and Historians, Modern Christian Views of History,* ed. C. T. McIntire (New York: Oxford University Press, 1977).

3. Since Rosenstock-Huessy is so little known and since his work is so intimately related to his own efforts to find his way through the agonies of our century, it may be helpful to briefly review his life. Eugen Rosenstock-Huessy was born into an emancipated, educated Jewish family in Berlin, Germany, in 1888. From an early age he revealed a fascination with languages and speech and even translated some Egyptian poetry into German for his sister's birthday when he was in his early teens. While still in his teens he entered the Christian church. He was a precocious student and completed doctoral studies at the University of Heidelberg in his early twenties. From 1912 to 1914—until the

outbreak of the war—he taught the history of law at Leipzig. The course of his life, however, was to be profoundly altered by the First World War. These events shook him, as they did many of his contemporaries, to the core. During the war he was an officer in the German army, serving at the front near Verdun. Later he was to call this period of his life a decisive turning point. For Rosenstock-Huessy, the meaning of the war was clear: the great institutions of European civilization—the church, the state, and the university—had failed in their task to preserve the peace. Consequently, after the war he turned down offers to work in these institutions and went instead to work in an automobile manufacturing plant. But already, in his correspondence with Franz Rosenzweig, a close friend who was to become a leading Jewish theologian, he had begun to outline a speech method that was to lie at the heart of his life and work over the next half century.

In 1914, Rosenstock-Huessy married a Swiss, Margrit Huessy, and following a Swiss custom added his wife's surname to his own. When their first and only child, Hans, was on his way, Rosenstock-Huessy returned to university life, becoming a professor of law at the University of Breslau. But his passions and efforts were still very much connected with issues associated with the Academy of Labor he had founded at Frankfurt. After the war and into the twenties he was associated with the Patmos circle—a group that included Franz Rosenzweig, Hans Eberhardt, and Martin Buber among others—and the journal *Die Creature,* which further developed his speech thinking and "grammatical method." When his Roman Catholic friend Joseph Wittig was excommunicated, he collaborated with Wittig in writing *Das Alter der Kirche.* And at the end of the twenties, he organized voluntary work service camps in Silesia that brought workers, farmers, and students together in an effort to recreate social relationships devastated by the war and its effects.

With great prescience, Rosenstock-Huessy anticipated and wrote about the emergence of a Hitler-like figure in German society. Thus, despite the fact that his great work, *Die Europaischen Revolutionen,* had been published in 1931 and did much to establish his reputation—it was later to be rewritten and published in the United States in 1938 as *Out of Revolution, Autobiography of Western Man*—he immediately resigned his post at Breslau when Hitler came to power. He then emigrated to the United States. After three years at Harvard, he joined the faculty at Dartmouth College, where he taught social philosophy until his retirement. While in the United States, Rosenstock-Huessy continued to write, publishing *The Christian Future, Or the Modern Mind Outrun* (1945), a much expanded *Soziologie* (1956–58), *Die Sprache De Menschengeschlechts* (1963), and *Speech and Reality* and *I Am an Impure Thinker* (1970). The last volume, *I Am an Impure Thinker,* well describes Rosenstock-Huessy, since he had no respect for the disciplinary boundaries that characterized intellectual life in the modern university. For Rosenstock-Huessy, it was the life of humankind in time that lay at the center of his attention, it was the sciences fixed on objectivity and space that needed to be challenged so that the temporal character of social life could emerge.

For two studies of Rosenstock-Huessy see Harold Stahmer, *"Speak That I May See Thee!" the Religious Significance of Language* (New York: Macmillan, 1968) and the more popular exposition of his thought in Clinton C. Gardner,

Letters to the Third Millennium (Norwich, Vt.: Argo Books, 1981). See also the unpublished doctoral dissertation by Bruce Boston, "'I Respond Although I Will Be Changed' The Life and Historical Thought of Eugen Rosenstock-Huessy" 1973, Princeton University, Princeton, N.J. The introduction to *The Christian Future, or Modern Mind Outrun* (New York: Harper & Row, 1966), reprint, by Harold Stahmer provides a fuller exposition of the leading events in Rosenstock-Huessy's life and an account of his work. The works of Rosenstock-Huessy cited in my account are available through Argo Books, Norwich, Vermont.

4. See my earlier analysis of *Out of Revolution: Autobiography of Western Man* entitled "Revolution and World Pluralism" in *The Ecumenist* 10, no. 3 (1972).

5. For Rosenstock-Huessy, the objective is but one of four modes of speech necessary to social life. See E. Rosenstock-Huessy, *Speech and Reality* (Norwich, Vt.: Argo, 1970), esp. 45–66. See also the important essay "Farewell to Descartes," in *Out of Revolution: Autobiography of Western Man* (Norwich, Vt.: Argo, 1969) reprint, 740–58.

6. Rosenstock-Huessy, *The Christian Future,* 115–16.

7. Ibid., 173.

8. Ibid., 98.

9. Ibid.

10. Ibid., 108.

11. Rosenstock-Huessy, *Speech and Reality,* 42.

12. Ibid., 9.

13. Ibid., 16.

14. Ibid., 17.

15. Ibid., 18.

16. Ibid., 17–18.

17. Rosenstock-Huessy, *The Christian Future,* 166.

18. Ibid., 169. It is important to stress the antireductionism of his position and at the same time to note that he seeks to give full voice to each of the four fronts of life. The temptation to reduce the four to one seems to be rooted in the tendency to oversimplify, but the real question is whether or not Rosenstock-Huessy's account of the four is adequate.

19. Rosenstock-Huessy, *Speech and Reality,* 54. His point here is that we often experience conflict between these two fronts, not that rhythm between them is impossible. The term rhythm is important here in order to emphasize the dynamic relationship between inner and outer.

20. Rosenstock-Huessy, *The Christian Future,* 168.

21. Ibid., 169.

22. Ibid.

23. Ibid., 170. Note that he speaks of an *obsession* with the outward front and thus his point is a certain distortion in modern civilization rather than a rejection of the dominant scientific methods as such.

24. Ibid., 168.

25. Rosenstock-Huessy, *Speech and Reality*, 52.

26. Ibid., 189. For a fuller discussion of these modes of speech see esp. 45–66 and 155–89.

27. Ibid., 16.

28. Rosenstock-Huessy, *The Christian Future*, 172.

29. Rosenstock-Huessy, *Out of Revolution*, 710.

30. Rosenstock-Huessy, *Speech and Reality*, 21.

31. Ibid., 21.

32. Ibid., 11.

33. Ibid., 15.

34. Ibid., 12.

35. Ibid., 19.

36. Ibid.

37. Rosenstock-Huessy, *The Christian Future*, 92. For a fuller discussion of this central theme see 92–131 and the material in *Speech and Reality*, 11ff.

38. Ibid., 94.

39. Rosenstock-Huessy, *I Am an Impure Thinker* (Norwich, Vt.: Argo, 1970), 69.

40. Ibid., 70–71.

41. Rosenstock-Huessy, *Biography-Biography* (New York: private printing, 1959), 24.

42. Rosenstock-Huessy, *The Christian Future*, 174. Every thinker develops his thought in relation to different sets of questions and issues. Rosenstock-Huessy's work was certainly centered in the Western tradition, and he once remarked that his work was devoted to refuting Nietzsche's claim that "God is dead."

43. Ibid., 174.

44. Ibid., 176.

Contributors

Gustavo Benavides Lecturer, Department of Religion, La Salle College, Philadelphia, Pennsylvania

M. Darrol Bryant Associate Professor of Religion and Culture, Renison College, University of Waterloo, Waterloo, Ontario, Canada

Siddhi Butr-Indr Head of the Department of Philosophy & Religion, Professor of Social Philosophy, Director of Graduate Studies in Philosophy, Chiang Mai University, Chiang Mai, Thailand

Padmasiri de Silva Chairman, Department of Philosophy, University of Peradeniya, Peradeniya, Sri Lanka

Helmut Fritzsche Dean of the Faculty for Theology, Wilhem-Pieck-Universitat, Rostock, East Germany

Rita H. Mataragnon Chairperson and Associate Professor, Department of Psychology, Ateneo de Manila University, Manila, Philippines; Population Council post-doctoral fellow in population psychology at the University of North Carolina, Chapel Hill, North Carolina

Acharya Karma Monlam Representative of His Holiness the Dalai Lama, India

Olusola A. Olukunle Lecturer, Department of Religious Studies, University of Ibadan, Ibadan, Nigeria

T. K. Oommen Centre for the Study of Social Systems, Jawaharlal Nehru University, New Delhi, India

Richard L. Rubenstein Robert O. Lawton Distinguished Professor of Religion, Florida State University, Tallahassee, Florida; President, The Washington Institute for Values in Public Policy, Washington, D.C.

Ninian Smart Professor of Religious Studies, University of California at Santa Barbara and University of Lancaster, United Kingdom

John St. John author and editorial consultant, London, United Kingdom

Geshe Lobsang Tsepal Lecturer, Namgyal Monastic Institution, Representative of His Holiness the Dalai Lama, India

Constantine N. Tsirpanlis Professor, Church History and Patristics, Unification Theological Seminary, Barrytown, New York

Manfred H. Vogel Professor, Department of Religion, Northwestern University, Evanston, Illinois

Index

Abraham, 185
Abraham, W.E., 100
absolution, 107
Advaita Vedanta, 136, 137
Africa, x, 23, 93, 95, 96, 99–101
afterlife, 21, 137
agnosticism, 119
agrarian societies, 5, 99, 106, 167–168, 179
alienation, 35, 81, 139–140, 151, 152, 153, 155, 156
altruism, 3–4, 5, 9, 11, 73, 76
ancestors, 22, 137–38
Anglican church, 6, 110, 112, 116–117
Anglo-Catholicism, 114
anthropurgy, 176
anti-Semitism, 88
Antioch, 89
anxiety, 36, 40, 78, 147, 149, 151
apartheid, 101, 118
Aquinas, Thomas, 106
Aristotle, 10–11, 15, 81
arms race, 147, 158
Asanga, Acharya, 59
asceticism, 140–41
Asia, 9, 95, 96
Assman, Hugo, 122
atheism, 25, 72, 119
Atman, 61–62, 63
attachment, 37–38, 60, 63, 70
Augustine, Saint, 81, 82, 89
Aurobindo, Sri, 174
Auschwitz, 153
Ayandele, E.A., 97, 98

Bahais, 100, 103
Ball, John, 116
baptism, 99

Baptist church, 6, 116
Basil the Great, 88
Beetham, T.A., 99, 101, 102
bhakti, 136, 140
Bhavaveveka, Acharya, 60
Bible, 21–22, 46–47, 82, 99, 101, 106, 110–11, 126, 154, 162, 168
   New Testament, 114, 138–50
birth, 60, 64
bliss, 62, 74, 138
Bhodipadhradipam, 59
Bodhisattva, 130, 138, 140
Boff, Leonardo, 122
Bose, Santi Priya, 21
bourgeoisie, 3–5, 7, 9–10, 15, 108, 117, 161
Brahmin, 26, 136, 143
Brazil, 174
brotherhood, 67, 69, 70, 73, 100, 157
Buber, Martin, 48–49, 174
Buddha, 58, 64, 70, 71, 74, 124, 185
Buddha nature, 136, 144
Buddhapalita, 63
Buddhism, viii, ix, xii, 14, 123, 135, 142
   liberation and, 58–65, 135–39, 141–42, 144
   psychology and, 30–39
   social philosophy, vii, ix–x, 12–13, 58, 61–62, 66–67, 68, 71–78, 105
Buddhist saints, 39
Buddhist sutras, 34, 58
Budd, Susan, 98
Byzantine empire, 81, 89

Calvin, Jean, 108
Calvinism, 7–8, 50, 108–9
Camera, Dom Helder, 174

Index

Index

Keep Your Kids Safe on the Internet

Simon Johnson

McGraw-Hill/Osborne

New York   Chicago   San Francisco
Lisbon   London   Madrid   Mexico City
Milan   New Delhi   San Juan
Seoul   Singapore   Sydney   Toronto

The **McGraw·Hill** Companies

McGraw-Hill/Osborne
2100 Powell Street, 10th Floor
Emeryville, California 94608
U.S.A

To arrange bulk purchase discounts for sales promotions, premiums, or fund-raisers, please contact **McGraw-Hill**/Osborne at the above address.

Keep Your Kids Safe on the Internet

1234567890 CUS CUS 01987654

ISBN 0-07-225741-5

Publisher .... *Brandon A. Nordin*
Vice President & Associate Publisher...... *Scott Rogers*
Acquisitions Editor .... *Megg Morin*
Project Editor .... *Carolyn Welch*
Acquisitions Coordinator .... *Agatha Kim*
Copy Editor .... *Bart Reed*
Proofreader .... *Beatrice Wikander*
Book Design .... *Scott Jackson, Jean Butterfield*
Illustrator .... *Kathleen Edwards*
Cover Design .... *William Voss*

This book was composed with Corel VENTURA™ Publisher.

"The book is easy to read and remarkable for its simple explanations. Simon Johnson demystifies the Internet for parents and enables them to understand how children are using the tool today, its possible dangers, and some safeguards that can be taken. Simon employs his professional IT security knowledge and experience to equip the reader with a sound understanding of the Internet and how to get the most out of it. This book should provide tips for parents on the issues posed by a challenging cyber world in which we live."

—Mrs. Carmee Lim, Chairman,
Parents Advisory Group for the Internet,
Singapore.
http://www.pagi.org.sg/

"Simon Johnson provides concise, clear explanations with good analogies, practical examples and no technobabble…Information on the combination of software necessary to protect young users will prove very beneficial to parents who want their youngsters to take advantage of the riches of the Internet without being exposed to its dangers."

—Marcellina Mian, President,
The International Society for Prevention of Child Abuse and Neglect

"Child sexual assault is preventable, but unfortunately our awareness comes too late for many children. This book expands our awareness and empowers parents to protect their kids online."

—Chris O'Connor, Executive Director,
kIDs.ap (Innocence In Danger – Asia/Pacific).
http://www.kidsap.org

About the Author...

Simon Johnson is a leading expert on children's safety on the Internet. He created and maintains the website www.keepyourkidssafe.net and has a professional background in IT Security spanning a decade.

Simon co-founded one of Australia's first IT security companies, Shake Communications, in 1997, and SecuritySearch.Net, an IT Security portal, in 1998. Simon maintained the SecuritySearch.Net Vulnerabilities Database (VDB), the first commercial database of security vulnerabilities. It provided corporations worldwide with the information they needed to fix security flaws in their computer systems, before hackers exploited them.

Prior to Shake Communications, Simon co-founded Internet Service Providers Pty Ltd in 1996, one of Australia's first ISPs, with points of presence in every state. He has also worked for a number of large corporations and government departments as a Security Advisor.

In 2002, shortly before the birth of his first child, Simon left the corporate world to pursue something more meaningful. He realized that he was receiving an average of 500 inappropriate, spam e-mail messages a day. While fixing his spam problem, he thought how he would hate to see his daughter encounter these messages. He searched for software, books, and reviews on the topic of protecting children online, but encountered only outdated or useless information—there was simply nothing available that was current and covered all the major risks. He decided to use the skills he acquired in corporate IT Security to evaluate software products and start www.keepyourkidssafe.net, a website to help all parents keep their children safe online.

Simon first started using the Internet in 1989 and holds a Bachelor of Computing (Information Systems) from Monash University, where he studied Information Security and Cryptography.

Dedication
For Amelie

Credits

Contents

Acknowledgments

I would like to thank my beautiful wife and soul mate, Anna, for translating my ramblings into something people can actually understand. Her support throughout the writing of this book has been tremendous. Without her, there would be no book. Thanks to my baby girl, Amelie Grace, for sleeping in the afternoon (most of the time), enabling me to work on this book. Having such a lovely baby was my inspiration to keep on writing day after day.

Thanks also go to my family, who supported me, asked questions, and shared their Internet experiences. They also provided me with valuable babysitting time so I could clear my head and spend some quality time with Anna. Thanks to Laurel, Peter, Bernie, Tony, Scott, David, Tiana, William, Amy, Isabella, Garry, Gayle, Denise, Kristin, Dan, and Fiona. Thanks to bets and everyone on #family_chat on IRC.

Special thanks go to the "moms advisory board," including Noel Applebaum, Lori Bulloch, Linda Jager, Linnea Lundgren, Ellen Nessen, and Wendy Rinaldi. Their feedback gave me a "mom's perspective."

Thanks to everyone at McGraw-Hill/Osborne, including Roger Stewart, Scott Rogers, Kate Viotto, Bettina Faltermeier, Audrey Tunick, Kathleen Edwards, Scott Jackson, Lee Healy, Dodie Shoemaker, Agatha Kim, Kate Loch, and Kim Seibokas. What you hold in your hand is the result of their hard work. I'd also like to thank Carolyn Welch, Bart Reed, and Madhu Prasher. Just when I thought everything was perfect, they brought it to the next level.

A very big thanks to my editor, Megg Morin, at McGraw-Hill Osborne. Megg saw the potential in my initial proposal and has worked tirelessly to help me develop and enhance the book. Her moral and professional support, hard work, and dedication have made the difference between a good book and a great book. I can't thank her enough.

I'd also like to thank Bill Gladstone and David Fugate from Waterside Productions, Inc. I couldn't have asked for a better agency.

Finally, I want to thank you, the reader, for buying this book. I'd love to hear from you, so please don't hesitate to send an e-mail to simon@keepyourkidssafe.com and let me know what you think.

Foreword

The Internet has dramatically changed the world we live in. The Internet has also created an entirely new world, a global community in which anyone who logs on can pose as anyone or do just about anything they desire. Internet use has grown exponentially since the late 1990s, and it has essentially defined a new way of sharing information and interacting with others throughout the world.

Kids and teens today will be global citizens for the rest of their lives. They view the Internet in a much different way than adults. The Internet provides a medium that allows kids and teens to believe that the communications they have online are with their peers, when in many instances the person on the other end is really an adult. Even though children and young people may be aware of the dangers inherent in communicating online, they continue to make decisions about engaging in online behaviors as if these were one-time situations.

Parents provide their children with a computer and Internet access. Many have the perception that the computer is a tool that helps make their kids smarter, helps them keep in touch with their friends, and keeps them off the streets and out of trouble. While there is no disputing the advantages this technology affords, the misconception that nothing harmful can happen from using the Internet is still prevalent despite recent cases of child abduction, online identity theft, and lawsuits from downloading music, movies, and other types of intellectual property.

Today's youth have grown up with the Internet as an integral part of society, and many are much more Internet savvy than their parents. A 2003-2004 i-SAFE America study indicates that 30.1 percent of students surveyed felt that their parents' Internet skills were either weak or very weak. Likewise, 53.9 percent of parents felt that their children were proficient or experts in using computers.

Results of these recent studies document notable disparities between parents and young people in their computer knowledge and proficiency. This difference is further heightened when noting that young children and teens are online constantly. According to a National Telecommunications & Information Administration report, 90 percent of American youth between the ages of 5 and 17, or 48 million kids and teens, use the Internet. Of nearly 4,400 students surveyed in a 2002-2003 study, four out of five (81.1 percent) spent at least one hour a week on the Internet, and parental estimates showed that three in ten children (29.8 percent) spent more than six hours a week on the Internet.

Unfortunately, this proliferation of Internet use among kids and teens, a large and highly vulnerable segment of the American population, has exposed a very dark side of the World Wide Web. The anonymity of the Internet and the ease in creating different identities has opened up an entire new avenue for online predators, identity thieves, hackers, and other devious individuals. Since kids and teens are typically unaware of the tricks and techniques these predators use to deceive their victims, and since most use the Internet as an everyday part of their lives, young people are at risk to a higher degree than other Internet users.

Regardless of how the information is provided (via a web-based or active learning approach), parents and their children need to be on the same page through constant open and honest communication. Communication is the key.

I would like to extend sincere congratulations to Simon Johnson for producing such a wonderful guide for parents.

Teri L. Schroeder, Chief Executive Officer
i-SAFE America, Inc., http://www.isafe.org
July 2004

Introduction

I didn't write this book to scare you. Nor did I write it to persuade you not to let your child use the Internet. The Internet benefits your child too much to warrant it being banned. I wrote this book to arm you with knowledge and tools you can use to ensure, as much as possible, that your child has a positive Internet experience while being protected from the Internet's dangers.

I wrote this book for parents with little or no knowledge of computers or the Internet. However, even the most experienced computer whiz or Internet guru will get something useful from this book. It is a product of my 14 years of Internet use, a decade of computer security experience, and my recent experience as a parent. I have given the same advice and recommendations to friends and relatives. I have also implemented similar security measures to protect employees of small and large companies and government departments.

Before we get started, I'd like to briefly explain my reasoning behind the nature and order of the content of this book. First, you will notice that I mainly talk about the threat of pedophiles on the Internet. I have done this because I believe that pedophiles do pose the biggest danger to your child—both in terms of prevalence and the potential damage they can cause. Apart from pedophiles, inappropriate content such as pornography can also harm and, in some cases, psychologically damage your children, so I discuss this threat in some detail as well. Although companies that spy on your Internet usage and profile your children are a serious threat, too, I don't believe they cause the same level of psychological and physical damage as pedophiles and pornography, so I don't talk about this threat to the same degree.

By now you may be wondering why you should let your child use the Internet at all! Chapter 1 contains my answer, as well as a brief explanation of what the Internet is and which features of the Internet your children are most likely to use.

In case you had any doubts about the seriousness of the risks presented by the Internet to your child, Chapter 2 is my wakeup call to you. It lists the major risks to children on the Internet, including statistics and cases of pedophiles using the Internet to target and abuse children.

Chapter 3 explains how children become exposed to a range of Internet dangers, and it contains my recommendations for how to avoid and reduce the risk of your children becoming so exposed.

Many of the recommendations described in Chapter 3 involve implementing certain software programs. In Chapters 4 through 8, I include comprehensive assessments, comparisons, and recommendations of which software programs are most effective for safeguarding children using the Internet.

In Chapter 9, I explain how you can put your overall defense together. Following that is an appendix on Spyware and Adware.

Some final points: First, there is no silver bullet for protecting your children on the Internet. I can't guarantee that by doing everything in this book you will fully protect your children from Internet predators, any more than I can guarantee that by locking your doors and windows, installing an alarm, and keeping watch over your home, you will prevent a burglar from breaking into your house. But, as with proper locks, a good alarm, and regular monitoring in relation to your home, the measures in this book are critical for protecting your children on the Internet. Doing nothing is not an option if you care about their welfare.

Second, a less important point is my use of "he" as the pronoun in reference to pedophiles, predators, and other criminals in this book.[1] This is simply because the majority of them are male.[2]

I sincerely hope that this book helps to restore the Internet as a place for your children to have fun, learn, and enjoy genuine friendships.

---

1. NCIS, 2003. "United Kingdom Threat Assessment of Serious and Organised Crime 2003." http://www.ncis.co.uk/ukta/2003/threat09.asp. August 23, 2003.

2. Kergus, Agnès, 2001. "Paedophilia and the sexual abuse of children." Innocence In Danger. http://www.innocenceindanger.org/innocence/faq_paedophilia.html#7. August 23, 2003.

PART I

Real Threats to Your Children
on the Internet and What You
Can Do about Them

CHAPTER 1

What Is the Internet?

In this chapter, I explain what the Internet is and how it came about, why it is such a wonderful and valuable resource for your children, and what they are likely to do on the Internet. You'll learn about websites, e-mail, instant messaging, peer-to-peer (P2P) file sharing, chat rooms, newsgroups, message boards, and Internet phone. By the end of the chapter, you'll have a solid understanding of how these things work and how and why your children benefit from using them.

What Is the Internet?

The Internet comprises millions of computers that are all connected together like a big spider's web. Some computers host information (such as a website), whereas others give people like you and me the ability to access that information. In January 2004, a survey revealed that there were 233,101,481 computers connected to the Internet.[1]

Who Created the Internet?

The Internet dates back to 1969 when the U.S. Department of Defense created the Advanced Research Projects Agency, known as ARPA. ARPA's task was to create a decentralized network of computers that could remain connected in the event of a nuclear strike during the Cold War. This network was called ARPANET. A number of other computer networks were also hooked into ARPANET in later years; this network grew to what we now know as the Internet. The following timeline shows the major milestones in the history of the Internet:

- **1969**   ARPANET was built.

- **1971**   Ray Tomlinson invents a program to send e-mail across a network.[2]

- **1979**   Usenet (newsgroups) created.

- **1984**   DNS (Domain Name System) introduced.

- **1984**   The number of Internet hosts goes over 1,000.

- **1988**   Internet Relay Chat (IRC) developed by Jarkko Oikarinen.

○ **1989**   Australia is connected to the Internet via AARNET.

○ **1991**   World Wide Web (WWW or "Web") invented by
Tim Berners-Lee and Robert Caillau.

○ **1993**   Mosaic (the first web browser) was created by
Marc Andreessen.

○ **1995**   Audio broadcast over the Internet in real time
using RealAudio.

Why Can't I Just Ban the Internet Altogether?

If I received a dollar each time someone asked me this, I'd be a millionaire!
If I didn't know about the Internet and this book, I'd probably ask the same
question. There are many reasons why "banning the Internet" is a very bad
idea. For one thing, you will disadvantage your children in terms of their
education because they will not have access to the resources that other students
have, and they will consequently be left behind. In any case, your children
are likely to access the Internet at friends' houses, local Internet cafés, and
places without proper protection. This substantially increases the risk of
them viewing inappropriate material, as well as falling victim to Internet
predators. It's better that they use the Internet at home, where you can keep
an eye on them, than at a friend's house or an Internet café, where there
probably aren't the same controls that you have at home.

Part I

Real Threats to Your Children on the Internet

Who Owns the Internet?

Nobody owns the Internet. ARPA created it to be decentralized, so it doesn't rely
on a central computer or computers to operate. There is no company or government
entity that owns or manages the Internet.

There are, however, some standards organizations that oversee the management of Internet addresses, domain names, and the design of computer networks. Some of these organizations include the Internet Engineering Task Force (IETF) and the Internet Corporation for Assigned Names and Numbers (ICANN). The IETF is an international community of computer network designers, vendors, and researchers. These people work in groups on the technical design (architecture) of the Internet. ICANN is a nonprofit corporation that oversees "the technical coordination of the Domain Name System (DNS), which allows Internet addresses (for example, web pages and e-mail accounts) to be found by easy-to-remember names, instead of numbers."[3] ICANN is a bit like an organization that allocates street names where you can build a number of houses.

I Have a Mac. Aren't These Computers Safer?

The brand of computer does not matter. Whether you run Mac OS, Windows, Linux, or whatever, your kids are still vulnerable to pedophiles, pornography, spyware, and many other Internet threats.

What Does an Internet Service Provider (ISP) Do?

An ISP connects you to the Internet. To use an automotive analogy, an ISP provides a "driveway" or "onramp" to get you onto the Internet. In return for using the ISP's driveway, you pay them a fee, just like paying a toll to get onto a highway. In other words, your ISP connects your computer to the ISP's computers, which are already connected to the Internet. Your computer then uses their computers as a gateway to access the Internet.

Can My ISP See Everything I Do Online?

Yes. Your ISP can see every website you visit, all the graphics you download, and even read your e-mail. Is it legal for them to do this? Maybe, but that depends on the contract you agreed to when you signed up. Read the fine print.

If you use computer software that encrypts your e-mail and you visit websites using HTTPS (Secure Sockets Layer, or SSL), your ISP shouldn't be able to see anything. This is because the encryption software will hide the information. All your ISP will see on their end is that you visited a particular website, but they can't read the actual content. The same applies to e-mail. If you send an encrypted e-mail message to simon@keepyourkidssafe.com, for example, your ISP shouldn't be able to read the contents.

Many responsible ISPs keep logs of when people used their service. This can be used for billing purposes and may also be forwarded to law enforcement. This information can be particularly useful in tracking down hackers, pedophiles, and cyberstalkers.

Apart from monitoring your Internet use, ISPs can easily block you from accessing certain websites, receiving e-mail from certain people, and even block certain computer programs from working properly. A very small percentage of ISPs have family filtering services. These services are usually provided as add-ons and cost extra. You can find a list of family friendly ISPs at http://www.keepyourkidssafe.com.

Why don't the majority of ISPs block inappropriate websites then? Probably because many don't see themselves as being responsible for filtering the content you can access. Just like a telephone company doesn't block you from ringing certain numbers or saying particular words during a telephone call.

Part I

Real Threats to Your Children on the Internet

How Is the Internet Regulated?

Strictly speaking, the Internet is not regulated. The decentralized nature of the Internet makes it impossible to regulate. There are too many computers in different parts of the world for anyone to regulate it effectively. However, various nations, such as the USA, UK, and Australia, have sought to regulate how their citizens use the Internet and the personal information recorded by website owners.

Isn't My ISP Legally Liable for Inappropriate Content That Is Accessed Using Their Service?

This is a tricky question, and it's best left to the lawyers. Many ISPs probably see themselves in a similar light to a telephone company (carrier) in that they just provide the service. In this instance, you can say whatever you like over the telephone, and your telephone company isn't going to filter it out.

The flip side of the coin is that ISPs can easily monitor their service and prevent access to illegal content. When it comes to services such as newsgroups, ISPs may store illegal content on their own servers. This was the case in Buffalo, New York in the U.S., where a large ISP called BuffNET went before the State Supreme Court. They pleaded guilty to knowingly providing their customers access to child pornography.[4] Although the ISP was just fined $5,000, the negative publicity associated with the case was immeasurable.

The U.S. Federal Trade Commission introduced the Children's Online Privacy Protection Act of 1998. The legislation was passed by the U.S. Congress and was designed to prevent the owners of certain types of Internet websites from collecting information on children under the age of 13 years without verifiable parental consent. The FTC has successfully prosecuted a number of organizations, one of which resulted in a fine of U.S.$400,000.[5]

In Australia, the Broadcasting Services Amendment (Online Services) Act of 1999 attempts to regulate content that is physically located within Australia and the ability of Australians to access content (whether located in Australia or outside Australia). Content located in other parts of the world is obviously out of the jurisdiction of the Australian government. Unfortunately, the legislation does not apply to e-mail, chat services, or content that is accessed in real time, such as streaming audio and video.

In the UK, indecent images of children are covered in the Protection of Children Act of 1978 (as amended by Section 84 of the Criminal Justice and Public Order Act of 1994).[6] Not only does this law make it illegal to possess or distribute indecent images of children, it makes it illegal to actively seek out such images.[7] The U.S. also has similar anti-child-porn laws that apply to the Internet. Apart from child pornography there are other laws that are designed to protect you from inappropriate content. These include the Controlling the Assault of Non-Solicited Pornography & Marketing (CAN-SPAM) Act of 2003. You can find more information at http://www.ftc.gov.

Although governments can legislate against sending spam, it doesn't mean that spammers are going to take any notice. For example, when the CAN-SPAM Act became law, a U.S. security firm examined 1,000 spam e-mail messages and found that only three spam e-mail messages complied with the law.[8]

In particular, spammers can largely avoid prosecution by moving their operations and their websites offshore to countries that have weak child-protection laws. For example, even though the CAN-SPAM Act applies to spammers worldwide, it is difficult for the U.S. authorities to track down and prosecute perpetrators who reside overseas. Although more governments are beginning to introduce laws against spam and particularly pornography, there are things you can do to help protect your kids now. This book will show you everything you need to do.

Why the Internet Is Good for Your Children

The Internet is a massive, worldwide communications and information resource that your children can use to find information on just about any topic, play games, meet friends, take courses, and participate in countless other fun and educational activities.

Part I

Real Threats to Your Children on the Internet

To grasp how powerful the Internet is, imagine you are back at school and need to do some research on an important assignment. Where do you go to get the information you need? Your school library? The local library in your suburb or town? The encyclopedias at home? What if you can't find the book(s) you need—or someone else has borrowed them?

Now imagine having access to your school library, the local library, your encyclopedias at home, plus thousands of other libraries, books, encyclopedias, people you can interview, and other resources—all at your fingertips. And these resources never get borrowed or taken away by someone else. This is what the Internet gives your children.

The benefits of the Internet go far beyond assisting your children in doing a school assignment. The Internet gives your children the ability to literally travel the world and learn new things for themselves—about other places, cultures, and people; about science; about history; about the arts; and much more.

Not only is the Internet a valuable resource for your children, but it is also fast becoming a tool that your child must master in order to survive and thrive at school. Partly, this is because Internet proficiency is required for many college courses and jobs. For example, many college lecturers require students to submit their assignments electronically, rather than printing them out, and increasingly the resources and materials used in college courses are located on the Internet.

The majority of professional jobs also require people to use the Internet on a daily basis. In fact, you almost need Internet access to find a job nowadays—with more and more jobs being presented exclusively on websites devoted to job advertisements, such as Monster.com.

In summary, here are my top seven reasons why your children must have access to the Internet:

1. To gain access to a wealth of knowledge. Thousands of reference libraries and encyclopedias are available on the Internet.

   - **Encyclopedia Britannica**   http://www.britannica.com

   - **Wikipedia (free)**   http://www.wikipedia.org

   - **Merriam-Webster**   http://www.merriam-webster.com

   - **U.S. Library of Congress**   http://www.loc.gov

   - **New York Public Library**   http://www.nypl.org

2. To talk to experts in certain fields to gain access to information.

   ○ **Communicate**   http://www.bbc.co.uk/communicate/

   ○ **Ask Yahoo**   http://ask.yahoo.com/ask/

   ○ **Ask Jeeves Kids**   http://www.ajkids.com

   ○ **FirstGov for Kids**   http://www.kids.gov

3. To obtain up-to-the-minute news on current affairs.

   ○ **CNN**   http://www.cnn.com

   ○ **BBC**   http://www.bbc.co.uk

   ○ **ABC News**   http://abcnews.go.com

4. To keep in touch with family and friends inexpensively (for example, via e-mail).

   ○ **MSN Kids Passport**   http://kids.passport.net

   ○ **The #family_chat channel on IRC**

5. To play educational games online with people from all over the world.

   ○ **Disney Online**   http://disney.go.com/playhouse/today/index.html

   ○ **Nick Jr.**   http://www.nickjr.com

   ○ **Up To Ten**   http://www.uptoten.com

6. To learn about other cultures, places, and languages.

   ○ **Smithsonian**   http://www.smithsonianeducation.org/migrations/

   ○ **Children's stories from other cultures**   http://www.miscositas.com

7. To be judged by the quality of their ideas, not based on their age or appearance. There is that saying, "On the Internet, nobody knows you're a dog."[9]

   Now you know why your children need to use the Internet, but how do they use it? In the next section, I explain how, and describe the various components of the Internet that they use.

What Do Children Do on the Internet?

Children, like adults, typically use the Internet to communicate with friends, find and play games and music, find and read information (for example, based on their interests or for a school assignment), and purchase products. They use the following Internet applications and services to do these things:

- Web browsers
- Websites
- Search engines
- E-mail
- Mailing lists
- Usenet ("newsgroups")
- Message boards
- Chat rooms
- Internet Relay Chat (IRC)
- Instant messaging
- Audio and video conferencing
- Peer-to-peer (P2P) applications
- File Transfer Protocol (FTP) applications

Web Browsers

A web browser is a software program that allows you to view and access information that is stored on another computer, called a website. The majority of websites are free to access. However, some may require you to register your personal details, such as your name, e-mail address, postal address, and age. Some subscription sites may require you to pay a fee. Web browsers can also be used to talk or "talk," meaning type back and forth. This enables you to "chat" with people on the Internet

Are Macs More Secure Than Windows PCs?

More security flaws have been found in Windows-based PCs than Macs. In my opinion, the default security settings in Mac OS X are more secure than Windows XP. However, it could be argued that Mac OS X has not had the same level of scrutiny by hackers and security professionals as Windows XP. Therefore there could be many security flaws waiting to be discovered in OS X. Apart from security flaws, there are fewer viruses that infect Mac computers than Windows PCs.

Before you go out and purchase a Mac, you need to consider that they are generally more expensive than PCs and have a smaller range of software and peripherals available. However, there are exceptions to this rule. Macs are the predominant computer used in the advertising and publishing industries, so you may want to purchase a Mac if your kids are showing an interest in these areas.

via chat rooms and message boards. The most popular web browser is Microsoft Internet Explorer, which is included with many Microsoft Windows operating systems (see Figure 1-1). Other web browsers include AOL Netscape, Opera, and Mozilla. Although there are different brands, they all basically do the same thing—display websites.

Websites

A website is information in the form of text, graphics, audio, video, that is hosted on a computer. You can visit and view this information using a web browser. To visit a website, you must enter its unique address, called a Uniform Resource Locator (URL), in the navigation bar on your web browser (or you can click a URL or link existing on a web page). Typically, a web URL is prefixed with "http://". This tells the web browser how to access the information contained at the URL.

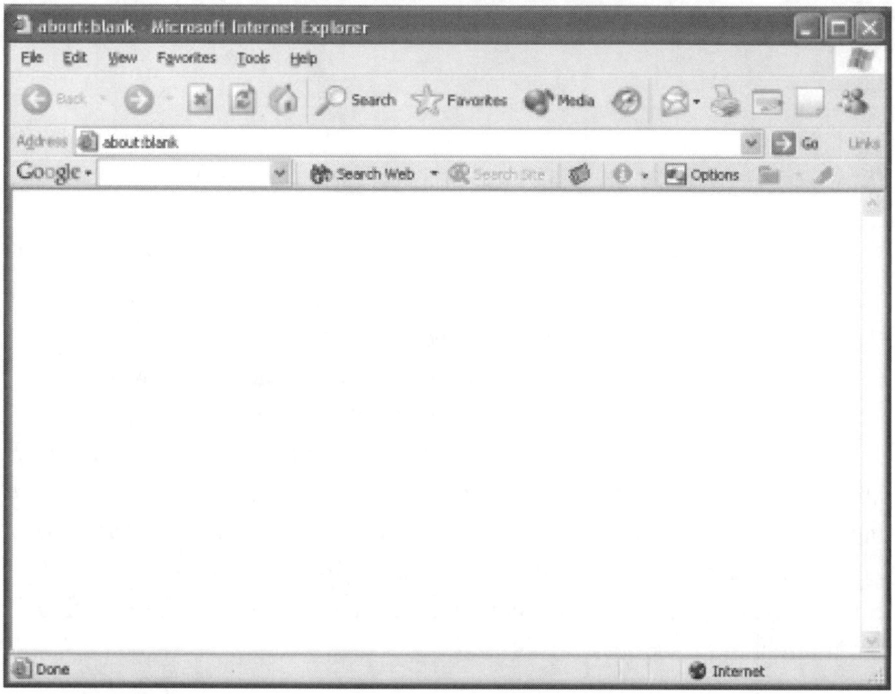

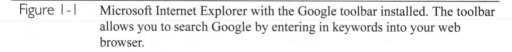

Figure 1-1   Microsoft Internet Explorer with the Google toolbar installed. The toolbar
allows you to search Google by entering in keywords into your web
browser.

The existence of "http://" means that the information does indeed represent a
website. Another prefix you can use is "ftp://", which stands for the File Transfer
Protocol (FTP). It indicates that the information at the given address is a file that
can be downloaded but not viewed by your web browser. An example of a URL
is http://www.example.com. It's important to note that you don't have to type
in "http://" every time you visit a website. You can just type in the address
into the toolbar. For example, www.example.com is the same as typing in
http://www.example.com.

- **www**   This is the name of the system or computer that hosts the website
  (often left as "www" to indicate that the website is part of the World Wide
  Web). Not all websites have "www" at the front. Some don't use it at all
  because it may not be necessary.

- ○ **example**   This is the name of the website (this could be the name of a person, organization, a brand name, or any word at all).

- ○ **.com**   This is the type of website (in this case, a commercial organization). Some other types are ".net" (for network organizations), ".org" (for nonprofit organizations), ".gov" (for government agencies), ".edu" (for U.S. educational institutions), ".info" (for information sites), and ".biz" (for business sites).

There is no enforcement of the naming standards for the majority of domain names. I could easily set up a fake nonprofit charity and register my .org domain name. However, some domain name registrars that handle names such as .gov and .edu have rules where you must provide supporting documentation. Apart from .com, there are a number of international domain names. For example, ".au" (for Australia), ".fr" (for France), ".de" (for Germany), ".jp" (for Japan), and ".uk" (for the United Kingdom).

Another example of a URL is http://www.whitehouse.gov, which breaks down as follows:

- ○ www is the name of the system.

- ○ whitehouse is the name of the website.

- ○ .gov stands for "government" in the U.S. only.

It's important to learn the difference between domain names because you may encounter websites masquerading as legitimate businesses, government agencies, or parodies. For example, www.whitehouse.gov is the official White House website, whereas www.whitehouse.net is a website parody. It may have a similar look and feel and may also incorporate links back to whitehouse.gov, but it's a fake.

Search Engines and Directories

There are millions of websites on the Internet. How do you know where they are? You use a search engine.

A search engine allows you to search a list of millions of sites to find those that match your search criteria (the keywords and any other criteria) for locating the information you want. You can access a search engine just as you would any other website, via your web browser. For example, as shown in Figure 1-2, if you

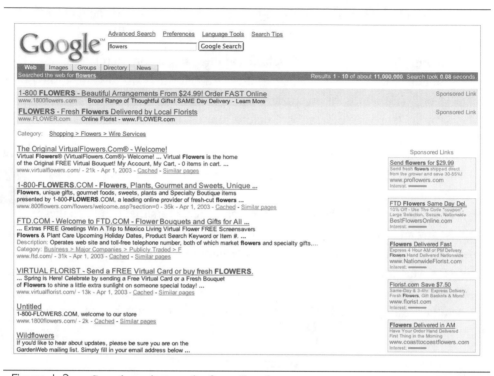

Figure 1-2   Search engine results from Google

wanted to order some flowers, you could type the word "flowers" in the search box and see what web pages the search engine generates.

Basically, there are two different types of search engine—those that use a directory and those that use keywords. Directories organize websites by subject; some also provide a description. A keyword-based search engine generates a list of websites according to words you type. Your search terms are matched to an index of words found on the web pages themselves. Yahoo! (http://www.yahoo.com) is a directory, whereas Google (http://www.google.com) is known for its keywords. One is not necessarily better than the other; they are just two different types. However, you might find one better than the other depending on the information you are trying to find. Incidentally, Yahoo! and Ask Jeeves have search engines specifically for children. You can access them at http://www.yahooligans.com and http://www.ajkids.com, respectively. The Google search engine, shown in Figure 1-3, is one of the most, if not the most, popular search engines on the Internet. It is very big and very fast. It has indexed more than 3 billion web pages and responds to more than 200 million search queries per day.[10]

Figure 1-3   The Google search engine

E-mail

E-mail is the computer version of postal mail. Each letter (e-mail message) has a unique address that identifies you. While e-mail addresses are traditionally written in lowercase, your program will also accept upper or mixed case. My e-mail address is simon@keepyourkidssafe.com.

"Simon" is the name of the person to whom the e-mail is addressed, and "keepyourkidssafe.com" is where I live on the Internet (also known as the domain name). As in the real world, more than one person can live at an address, so you could also have john.smith@keepyourkidssafe.com and jane.smith@keepyourkidssafe.com.

E-mail messages contain a subject and a message body and can also have file attachments. These file attachments are computer files sent with the e-mail. So if you wanted to send your resume to a recruitment company, you wouldn't type it in the message body; instead, you would write it in a word processing application such as Microsoft Word and attach the file to the e-mail as a file attachment. Not all file attachments are innocent documents; some contain computer viruses, and others could run malicious computer code on your computer, but we will get to that later. As shown in Figure 1-4, e-mail messages can be written in plain text or in Hypertext Markup Language (HTML). HTML is the same computer code or language that websites are written in. HTML enables you to include graphics, color, video, and audio in your e-mail messages. One drawback is that HTML e-mail messages can also take up more space on your computer. Another drawback is that some messages can contain malicious code.

Children with their own e-mail address are vulnerable to receiving "junk e-mail"—otherwise known as "spam." Although the overwhelming majority of spam messages are merely annoying, some spam can harm children, with many junk e-mails containing offensive words and disgusting images.

| tip | *E-mail addresses can be easily forged. I can send you an e-mail from simon@whitehouse.gov. When you receive it in your e-mail box, it looks like it came from the White House, but it didn't.* |

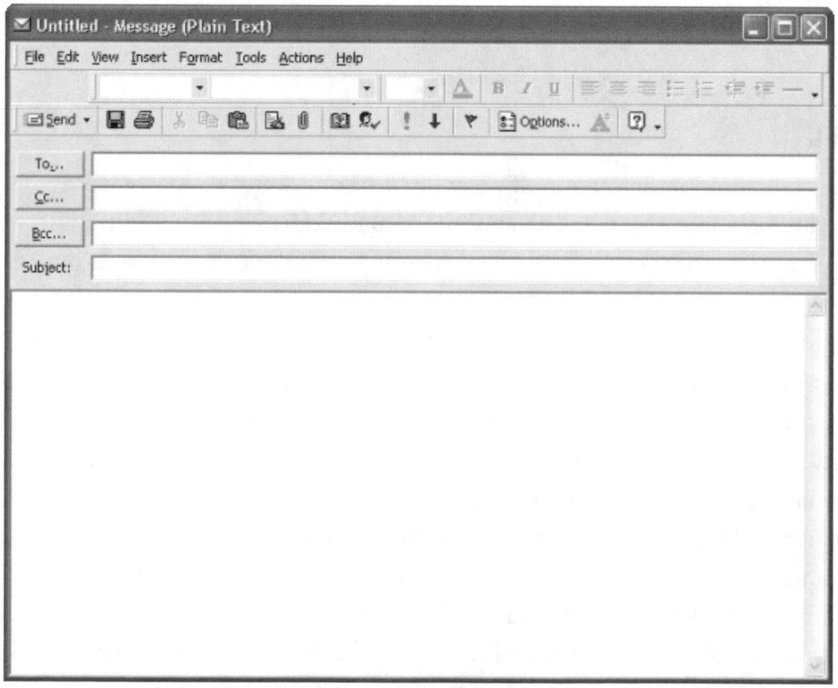

Figure 1-4   A blank e-mail message using Microsoft Outlook

You may be familiar with the web and e-mail, but children often use other Internet tools to communicate with each other as well. One of the most popular methods of communication is instant messaging.

Instant Messaging (IM)

Instant messaging (also known as IMing) is one of the most popular forms of text-based chat on the Internet. For those people who have used mobile phones, IM is like an Internet version of SMS (short message service), also known as "texting." IM is commonly used for conversations among close friends, but unlike SMS, your children can have multiple conversations at once. According to one report, AOL carries more than 2 billion messages per day, and Yahoo Instant Messenger has more than 19 million users in the U.S. alone.[11] Popular IM software programs include:

- AIM (AOL Instant Messenger)

- ICQ (pronounced "I seek you" or "I see queue")

- Microsoft Instant Messenger

- Yahoo Instant Messenger

note *You don't have to be an AOL subscriber to use AOL Instant Messenger.*

These programs allow you to type in real time to multiple people who are connected to the Internet anywhere in the world. For instance, your children could use IM to send messages to a family member living on the other side of the world. They could also use it to work on school assignments with other students. Most IM programs are used to chat one on one. However, they can easily be used to chat with multiple people at the same time.

Instant Messaging is still evolving. You can play games using IM against your friends and send instant messages to cell (mobile) phones or any other Internet connected device. In fact, some companies such as "Microsoft, Yahoo and AOL have done deals to put smaller versions of their software on mobile phones, PDAs and even gaming devices."[12]

Another popular tool children use to chat with other people on the Internet is Internet Relay Chat. Although IRC is not as popular as instant messaging software such as AIM, it's still used by children worldwide.

Internet Relay Chat (IRC)

Ever walk into a bar, cocktail party, dinner party, or a house with lots of people in it? You would probably find many groups of people talking about different topics. If you stand in the middle of the room, you can hear many conversations at once. If you go into another room, you may find more people talking about different topics. Internet Relay Chat (IRC) is the Internet version of a cocktail party.

IRC (pronounced "eye-are-see" or "erk") is accessed by computer software. The most popular program for personal computers (PCs) running the Microsoft Windows operating system is mIRC, (pronounced "em-eye-are-see" or "merk"). This is available at http://www.mirc.com. Figure 1-5 shows the mIRC interface. The most popular program for Macs is Ircle, available at http://www.ircle.com.

When you use IRC, you need to choose a name (also known as a "handle," "nick," or "alias"). This is the name you wish to be known by on IRC. It can be any name you wish. For example, you could be J Lo, Santa, or anything you can

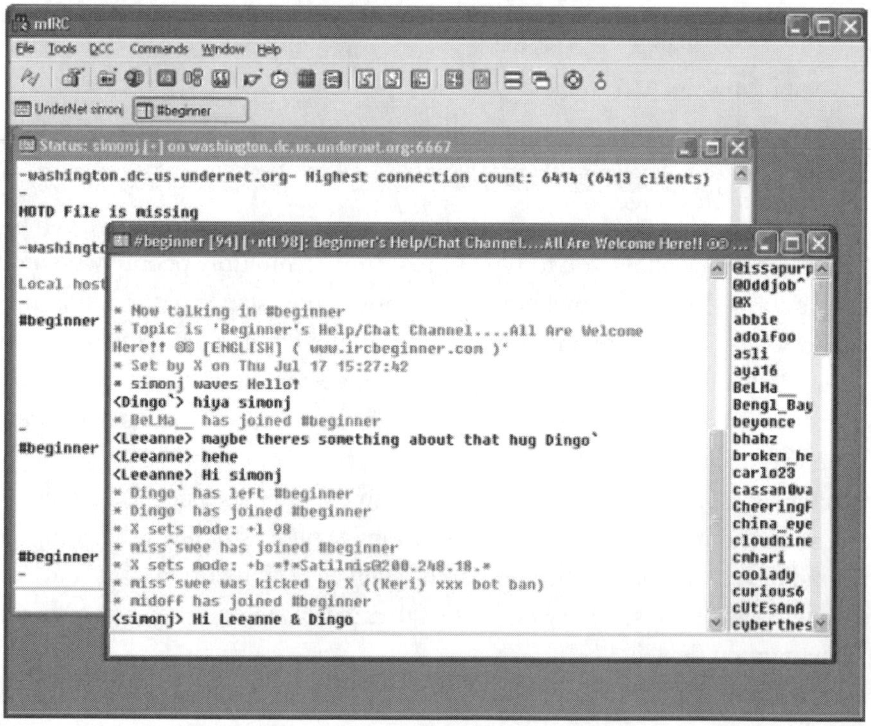

Figure 1-5   The mIRC chat program

possibly think of. However, some names may be already taken by people chatting on IRC, so you may have to select another one. While your nickname can't have spaces in it, some people use an underscore or a hyphen. This means that J Lo would become J-Lo or J_Lo.

When you first log in, you will notice that IRC is not very user friendly, but this depends largely on the software you use. If you are using mIRC, a pop-up box will list a number of channels that you can visit. These channels are rooms at your cocktail party. Each room has one or more people in it, and they are talking about different topics. Each channel has a name and begins with a pound sign (#). Some channels are moderated by people who enforce rules. For example, the channel called #Family_Chat has a number of rules, including but not limited to, no offensive language, no advertising, no private messaging without asking first, and no transfer of MP3 files. The majority of channels do not have any rules at all, so anything goes. It is important to note that on IRC, you should type in lowercase (uppercase is used for YELLING). When you enter a channel, you will see the name of the person and what they are saying. Here's an example:

<simon> hello

<jane> hi simon, how are you?

This log is displayed in a small box on your screen and enables you to read who said what and when. This is very useful because it enables you to go back through the conversation. IRC users can also use a number of actions, such as smiling, waving, and hugging people. This would be displayed on the channel as follows:

* simon waves goodbye to jane

<jane> bye simon

Simon and Jane could also chat in a virtual room by themselves. This gives them a lot more privacy because they can restrict who has access to their room. If they don't want to set up another channel (private room), they can send private messages to each other. These messages are not displayed in the main channel but rather on a separate box on the computer screen. This is how the majority of chat occurs on IRC.

IRC can also be used to transfer files between two or more computers. This is known as DCC (Direct Client-to-Client). Files that are transferred using this method bypass the IRC server and connect the parties directly. DCC is often used to transfer files that contain photographs of the people who are talking on the channel.

Why Do Children Use IRC?

Why do children use IRC? It's extremely fast, they can type in a public channel (room) to hundreds of people at once, or, if they prefer, in a private channel to one or more people. Public channels are available for everyone to access. Private channels are password-protected or you have to know the name of the channel to access it. For example, I can create a channel called "keepyourkidssafe." Unless you know the name of the channel, you can't enter it. However, in case you were to guess it, I could password-protect the channel. There are thousands of topics, and people are always chatting at any time of the day or night. You will always find someone to talk to on IRC.

When children don't just want to talk, but want to transfer files (such as pictures, documents, and music) to each other, they may use a peer-to-peer program.

Peer-to-Peer (P2P) Applications

Now imagine yourself at a dinner party, but this time nobody is talking. In fact, there are thousands of people at this dinner party, and all of them are walking around with handfuls of audio CDs. Some people are giving these CDs to their friends. Others are walking up to people they don't know and exchanging CDs with them. This is how file-swapping—otherwise known as "peer-to-peer" applications—work on the Internet. In technical terms, a person can save copies of music (for example, from a CD) into a file format such as MP3 on their computer and then use a peer-to-peer application to swap their music with someone else. Although the service does not store the actual song files on its system, it provides a means to obtain the songs.

Popular peer-to-peer applications include Kazaa, BearShare, Blubster, eDonkey, Gnutella, Grokster, iMesh, Limewire, Morpheus, Overnet, and WinMX. Some of the makers of these applications are being pursued in the courts for facilitating copyright infringement. At the time of writing, however, they are available for use by anyone.

You don't have to exchange your own songs to use any of these services. You can search for a song by using a keyword, and the program will display all the people who are currently connected who have that particular song. For example, you could search for "The Beatles" and get a list of their songs and albums that are available to download. If you wanted to download the song "She Loves You," all you would need to do is click it, select Download, and the application will automatically send the file to your computer. Once the download is complete, you could use a CD-ROM burner and save it to CD or just leave it on your computer.

By now you may be wondering how file-sharing companies make money if they give away their software for free. In one word, advertising. Think of free-to-air television vs. cable. Free-to-air television is paid for by advertisers, who place commercials throughout the program. The same thing applies here. The file-sharing companies give away their software for free because it's bundled with advertising. Quite often, the software that delivers the advertising is accused of spying on users and is labeled as "spyware."

File-sharing programs are very popular with children because: (a) they are free and (b) they allow children to get music for free. Unfortunately, as well as enabling your child to infringe someone's copyright, such applications can also lead to your child giving advertisers private information. (More about that in the next chapter.)

Apart from file-sharing programs, there are a number of other ways for your children to send and receive files. One of the oldest and most efficient is via File Transfer Protocol.

File Transfer Protocol (FTP) Applications

FTP applications are similar to a web browser in that they allow you to access information that is stored on another computer (known as an "FTP site" or "site"). However, FTP applications display lists of files instead of a graphical interface (see Figure 1-6).

Once connected to an FTP site, you can select one or more files and download them to your computer. Companies often use FTP sites to distribute their software. Some free or shareware games and utilities are also available on FTP sites. FTP is a very efficient means to download large amounts of information, especially when your Internet connection is unreliable. If you are in the middle of downloading something, the FTP application can restart the transfer from where it left off. If

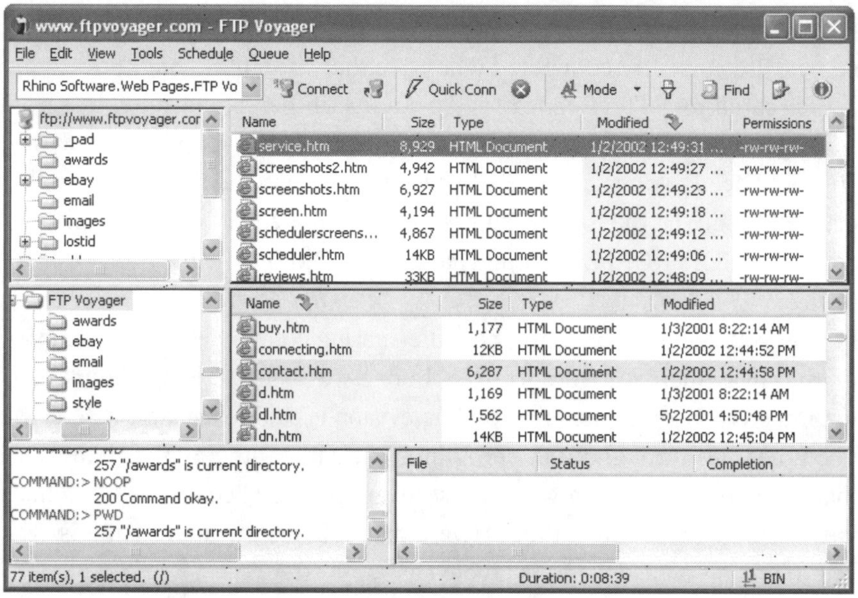

Figure 1-6   FTP Voyager

you were using a web browser to do this, you might have to transfer the file from the beginning.

A very popular FTP application is CuteFTP. Also, Microsoft has built FTP capability into Internet Explorer, which makes downloading FTP files almost seamless when used with Microsoft Windows. Other FTP applications include FTP Voyager, WS_FTP, and CoffeeCup Direct FTP (see Figure 1-7). It should be noted that Microsoft FTP has very limited features compared with the other products available in the marketplace.

Children are attracted to FTP because it's easy to use, does not require any third-party software, and provides a fast way to download games and other computer files.

Apart from talking one-on-one or to groups of friends, or exchanging files, your children might communicate with others on Usenet (also known as "newsgroups"), message boards, or chat rooms that are devoted to a specific hobby or interest. For example, if your child is a big baseball fan, they may talk to other baseball fans on Usenet, message boards, and chat rooms. Usenet, message boards, and chat rooms function differently. Let's consider Usenet first.

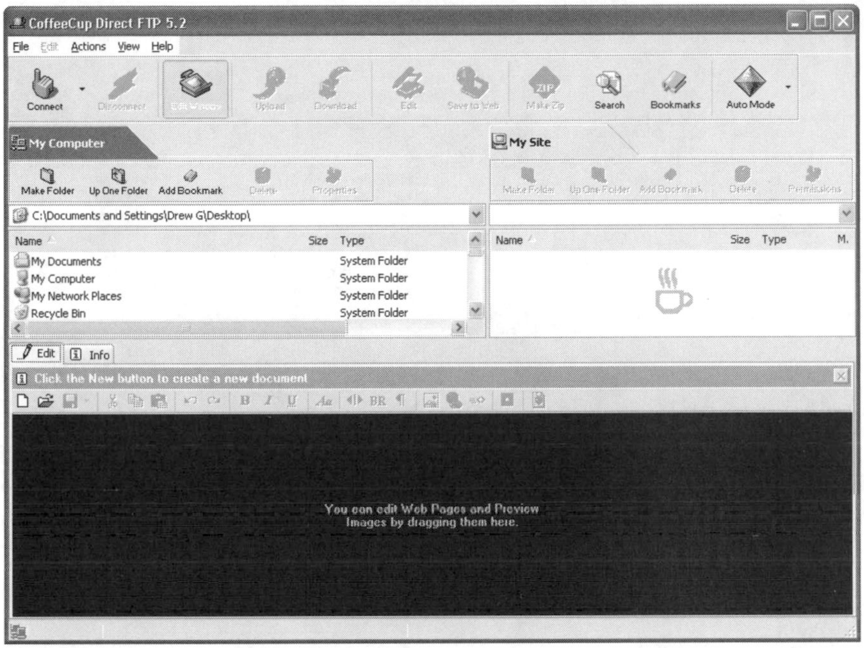

Figure 1-7   CoffeeCup Direct FTP

Usenet/Newsgroups

Usenet is like an assortment of notice boards where people can post messages by sending e-mail. Once the e-mail has been sent, everyone looking at that particular notice board can view it. Each of these notice boards—known as a "newsgroup"—is devoted to a specific topic (see Figure 1-8). Although newsgroups are not as popular as they once were, they are still used to distribute pornography and other inappropriate content.

Some newsgroups are moderated, meaning that a person reviews your message to see whether it is suitable to post. There are occasions where a computer program (called a bot or a robot) will look at the message instead of a person. The bot will look for profanity and other inappropriate content. If it's deemed to pass a predefined set of rules then it's allowed. Posting a message to a newsgroup is similar to sending an e-mail message. You have a subject and message body, as well as the name of the newsgroup to which you wish to post (see Figure 1-9).

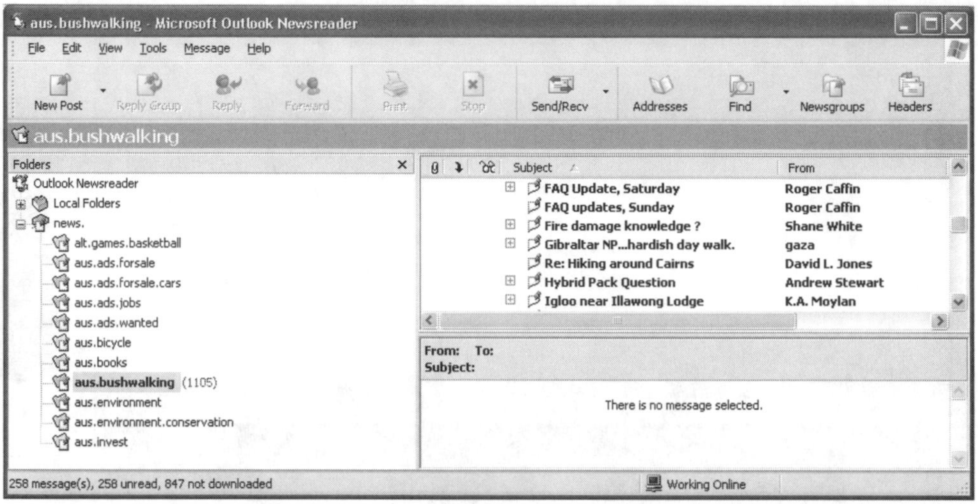

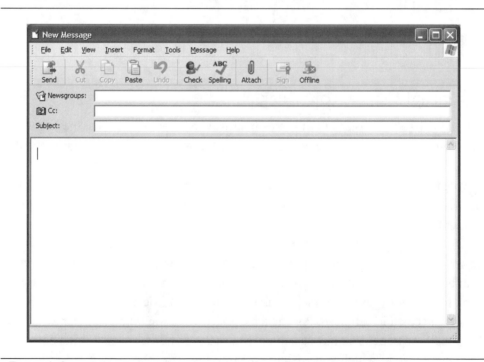

Figure 1-8   The Usenet group aus.bushwalking, as shown in Microsoft Outlook Newsreader

Figure 1-9   A blank newsgroup message using Microsoft Outlook

Usenet messages, also called "posts," can have files attached to them or encoded in the message body. This allows people to transfer files using Usenet rather than by FTP or by downloading them from a website.

A "newsreader" is required to read and post to newsgroups. Microsoft Outlook Newsreader is very popular, primarily because it's bundled with Windows. Other popular newsreaders include Free Agent for the PC and NewsWatcher for the Mac. You can also access newsgroups via websites that archive messages. The most popular site is http://groups.google.com.

Your newsreader software will connect to your ISP's Usenet server (also called a "news server"). When connected, it will download a list of available newsgroups for you to choose from.

Newsgroups are classified hierarchically by name and are words separated by dots (for example, rec.pets.dogs and rec.crafts.dollhouses).

When Usenet was first created, the top seven categories were as follows:

Usenet Name	Topics
Comp	Computer related
Misc	Miscellaneous
News	Usenet news
Rec	Recreational activities
Sci	Scientific issues
Soc	Social issues
Talk	Controversial social and cultural issues

Part I

Real Threats to Your Children on the Internet

The creation of an alt.* category (for "alternative") reduced the load on the top seven categories, and since then, there has been an explosion of different categories. There are currently more than 60,000 different newsgroups, many aimed at children with topics on everything from alt.tv.rugrats and alt.tv.teletubbies to talk.environment, rec.kites, and rec.bicycles.rides. Unfortunately, the alt newsgroups are home to the majority of pornography. However, they do contain a lot of legitimate newsgroups as well.

> **tip** | *If your filtering software allows you to restrict access to newsgroups, you should block access to alt.binaries.* *and alt.bainaries.**. This will block access to the majority of inappropriate content found on newsgroups.*

Newsgroups were the first kinds of notice boards on the Internet, and they existed long before websites. With the advent of the Web, websites began to feature their own notice boards, known as "message boards."

Message Boards

Message boards are similar to newsgroups, but they are operated from a website, so you don't need a newsreader, just a web browser to view them. Some message boards require you to register first, before you can post a message. Some may allow you to post anonymously or give you the ability to read the message board without registering your details. Unlike IRC, messages posted to message boards are not read in real time. There may be minutes, hours, days, or weeks before someone replies. Yahoo! Groups (http://groups.yahoo.com/) is an example of a message board (see Figure 1-10).

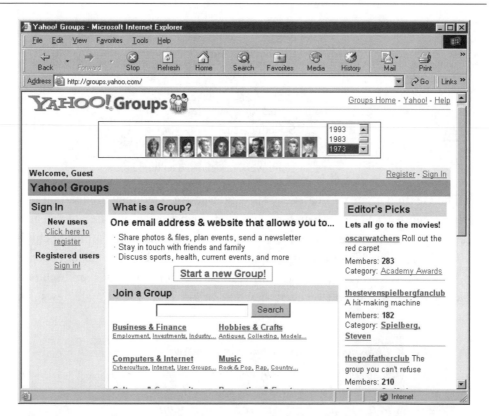

Reproduced with permission of Yahoo! Inc. © 2003 by Yahoo! Inc. YAHOO! and the YAHOO! logo are trademarks of Yahoo! Inc.

Figure 1-10   Yahoo! Groups allows people to share interests and ideas.

Children are likely to post messages on message boards (and websites) that are relevant to their interests. One example of this relates to a popular children's singing group/band that I won't name. A quick check of the boards associated with this band showed some of their fans revealing personal information. This included their full name, date of birth, the place where they went to school, and even when/where they will see the band perform. One girl revealed exactly where her tickets were in the audience. It took me less than three minutes to find this information.

Even without these intimate details, anyone can still find information on children by using their name or e-mail address. A quick search of websites such as groups.google.com will reveal every message your child has ever posted to a newsgroup.

Although children need to visit a message board to read the messages, another way of communicating with others with similar interests is to subscribe to a mailing list. In this case, messages are sent in an e-mail to everyone on the mailing list.

Mailing Lists

A mailing list is composed of a group of people who receive e-mail messages on a particular topic. There are three different types of mailing lists:

○ Announcement

○ Open discussion

○ Moderated discussion

Announcement lists are often used to send out product and service information to subscribers. For example, if you subscribe to the Microsoft Security Notification Service, you will receive e-mail messages about new security flaws in Microsoft products. You cannot reply to these bulletins, nor can you talk to other people who subscribe to the mailing list. Announcement lists are also known as "read-only lists."

Open discussion lists are exactly as the name suggests—anyone who subscribes to the list can send e-mail to the entire list. The content of the e-mail messages is discussed between the subscribers.

Moderated discussion lists are the same as open discussion lists, except that a person gets the e-mail message that you post, prior to it being distributed to the list. This person is known as a "moderator."

Again, children are likely to subscribe to mailing lists relevant to their interests. Examples range from their favorite singers, such as Britney Spears, to lists where preteens discuss issues affecting them today.

Finally, your children may visit websites that contain "chat rooms." Chat rooms allow them to talk to others in real time.

Website Chat Rooms

Unlike IRC, most website chat rooms only have one room with multiple people in them. Some chat rooms require you to register before you can enter the "room"; others just require you to enter your name or an alias. Chat rooms that are run from a website use your web browser and a computer programming language called Java or a third-party plug-in (software application), which you have to download in order to participate.

Children will be attracted to using chat rooms on websites that interest them. For example, many popular movies, pop stars, and other entertainers have websites, and many with chat rooms.

Most chat rooms are "text based," meaning that you chat by typing words. However, "voice chat," which enables people to talk using their voice, is now becoming more popular.

Voice Chat

Many computers have a sound card and microphone to enable you to record your speech and send it over the Internet to another person running the same application. This technology is known as "Voice Over IP," or VOIP. To the average user, it is known as "Internet phone."

Popular Internet phone programs include FWD (Free World Dialup), NetMeeting, ICQphone, Skype, and Net2Phone. Many of these programs have their own proprietary instant messaging capability as well as video conferencing, video mail, voice mail, file transfers, picture transfers, and real-time chat. Some of them also allow you to use your computer to make telephone calls anywhere in the world for free or at a reduced cost, compared with a traditional telephone call.

Free World Dialup is a great example of Internet telephone. It costs you nothing to call another user anywhere in the world. However, the person you are calling must have an Internet phone. This could be in the form of software on their computer or a physical VOIP phone that connects to your DSL modem. If you want to call a person who doesn't have an Internet phone, you can sign up with a PSTN service provider that acts as a bridge between your Internet phone and the regular telephone network. PSTN means "Public Switched Telephone Network" and is just another name for a telecommunications company. While the PSTN service provider will probably charge you for the service, it could work out a lot cheaper than using your existing telephone company. You can visit http://www.freeworlddialup.com for more information.

The main attraction of VOIP is the ability to speak to people on the other side of the world, without having to pay a cent in telephone charges. Although this technology has existed for a long time, it has only recently become popular, as faster Internet access has become available. Now if you have broadband Internet access, you can speak to someone using VOIP and receive e-mail with very little impact on your Internet connection.

As you can probably imagine, faster Internet access is also heralding greater use of videoconferencing—the combination of audio and video chat.

Videoconferencing (Audio and Video Chat)

Videoconferencing is one of the most popular methods of communication on the Internet. It enables you to hear and see another person on the other side of the world, using the Internet. This is accomplished by using your existing digital camera or web camera in conjunction with the microphone on your computer. Many users who use chat programs such as ICQ or Instant Messenger use these facilities to enhance their Internet experience. Popular audio and video chat programs include AOL Instant Messenger (AIM) and Microsoft NetMeeting.

Depending on your Internet connection, the quality of audio- and videoconferencing by these means can be excellent. On the other hand, if you are using a 56K modem, the quality of both the audio and video is likely to be poor.

Videoconferencing can consume large amounts of Internet bandwidth due to the large volume of information (traffic) transferred between the communicating parties. This may significantly increase your Internet bill if used frequently or for long periods of time. However, this depends on how you are charged by your ISP.

Not only can your children use videoconferencing to talk and see their friends in real time, but they can also converse with family members and friends overseas. Now you know why your children must have access to the Internet, and you have an idea of what your children are doing—or may in the future do—on the Internet. But what can you do to ensure that their experience of the Internet is a positive one—that they are only exposed to the positive, educational, inspiring side of the Internet, and not its "dark" side?

You can do a lot—read on.

Endnotes

1. ISC, 2004. "Internet Domain Survey, Jan 2004," Internet Software Consortium. http://www.isc.org/ops/ds/reports/2004-01/. March 2, 2004.

2. Zakon, Robert, 1997. "RFC2235," The Internet Society. http://www.faqs.org/rfcs/rfc2235.html. August 24, 2003.

3. ICANN, 1999. "ICANN Background Points," The Internet Corporation for Assigned Names and Numbers. http://www.icann.org/general/background.htm. August 24, 2003.

4. Office of New York State Attorney General Eliot Spitzer, 2001. "Breakthrough Cited In War Against Child Porn," Eliot Spitzer. http://www.oag.state.ny.us/press/2001/feb/feb16c_01.html. February 16, 2001.

5. FTC, 2004. "UMG Recordings, Inc. to Pay $400,000, Bonzi Software, Inc. To Pay $75,000 to Settle COPPA Civil Penalty Charges," FTC. http://www.ftc.gov/opa/2004/02/bonziumg.htm. February 18, 2004.

6. West Midlands Police, 2003. "Indecent Images of Children," West Midlands Police Paedophile Unit. http://www.west-midlands.police.uk/paedophile/images.shtml. August 24, 2003.

7. IWF, 2004. "UK Law Covering Remit," IWF. http://www.iwf.org.uk/hotline/uk_law.html. March 9, 2004.

8. Leyden, John, 2004. "CAN-SPAM means we can spam," The Register. http://www.theregister.co.uk/2004/01/09/ canspam_means_we_can_spam/. January 9, 2004.

9. Steiner, Peter, 1993. "On the Internet, nobody knows you're a dog." The New Yorker. http://www.unc.edu/depts/jomc/academics/dri/idog.html. July 5, 1993.

10. Google, 2004. "Company Overview," Google. http://www.google.com/press/overview.html. March 4, 2004.

11. Hardy, Ian, 2004. "Instant Messaging Grows Up," BBC. http://news.bbc.co.uk/2/hi/technology/3757297.stm. May 29, 2004.

12. Ibid.

Part I

Real Threats to Your Children on the Internet

CHAPTER 2

What Are the Threats to Your Children and How Serious Are They?

In this chapter, I explain what the threats are to your children. You will learn how the Internet exposes them to pedophiles, makes pornography available to them, and how companies violate their privacy. By the end of the chapter, you'll have a solid understanding of the real risks, so you can make an educated judgment and take action to keep your kids safe.

Pedophiles Are Using the Internet to Look for Kids

A pedophile is an adult who is obsessed with and has a sexual attraction to children. Pedophiles are increasingly using the Internet to organize and participate in rings that distribute and share child pornography, as well as to target and contact individual children. It is a global problem, with UNICEF estimating that 80 percent of pedophile-related investigations involve more than one country and 90 percent involve the Internet.[1] It is a growing problem, too. In the U.S., reports to the CyberTipline have increased 750 percent in the last five years alone! In the UK, the Greater Manchester police seized just 12 indecent images from Internet users in 1995, compared with 41,000 in 1999.[2] That's an increase of 3,416 percent in just four years. Of course, it might also be argued that the Greater Manchester police improved their investigative ability between 1995 and 1999! But, seriously, I think the increase has more to do with the explosion of Internet usage and, in particular, its use for criminal purposes. Police are also prosecuting more pedophiles than ever before. UK children's charity NCH reports that 35 people were cautioned or charged in 1988 compared to 549 people in 2001—a 1,500 percent increase. The numbers for 2002 will be significantly higher because the names of 6,500 people were handed over to the UK police from authorities in the U.S. The 6,500 names were a part of a larger database of subscribers who had purchased child pornography on a single website.[3]

It is estimated that around one million images of child pornography are in circulation on the Internet and that this number is expanding at some 200 a day. One estimate is that more than 27,000 people access child pornography sites every day.[4] According to the Internet Watch Foundation (IWF), more than 55 percent of child-abuse images on the Internet (that were reported in Britain last year) originated from the USA. There has also been a substantial increase in child pornography from Russia, from 5 percent in 1997 to 23 percent in 2003.[5]

Unfortunately, the number of websites that contain child pornography are also increasing. In 2002, the Internet Watch Foundation (IWF) reported a 64 percent increase in people reporting websites that contain images of child abuse. More than half of all illegal websites known to the IWF are hosted in the USA; however, the number in Russia has more than doubled (from 286 to 706).[6]

Pedophiles also use newsgroups (see Chapter 1 for a description of what newsgroups are) to discuss and exchange images of children. I found 12 newsgroups dedicated to providing pictures and video of young, naked children.

Not only are pedophiles using the Internet to view child pornography, but they are using it to target children. The following police operations and arrests demonstrate the enormous scale of the problem:

February 26, 2004   "Operation Odysseus" resulted in simultaneous police raids in more than 40 locations across ten countries, including Australia, Belgium, Canada, Germany, the Netherlands, Norway, Peru, Spain, Sweden, and Britain.[7] A spokesperson for Europol said, "Today's operation has exposed a complex and organised hierarchical structure that Internet networks of pedophiles and child molesters are using to protect themselves by hiding their identities and their atrocious activities."[8]

September 27, 2003   "Operation Marcy," spearheaded by German police, cracked what is believed to be one of the largest pedophile rings in the world. The Internet-based pedophile ring involved 26,500 people in 166 countries.[9] Raids in Germany involved 1,500 police officers across 502 premises. Police seized 745 computers, 35,500 CDs, 8,300 computer disks, and 5,800 videos.[10] Officials said that some of the 26,500 suspects are located in countries including the United States, Australia, and Switzerland.

December 17, 2002   "Operation Ore" resulted in the arrest of 1,300 people across the UK and the U.S. This operation was part of a larger FBI operation tracing 250,000 pedophiles worldwide via credit card details, which were used to download child pornography from the Internet.[11]

July 2, 2002   "Operation Twins" involved a raid of 50 premises in seven countries, all part of a worldwide pedophile network. Police stated that the prolific pedophile gang "exchanged photos and videos of violence committed against children…. The abuse was filmed and broadcast in 'real time' over the Internet." Europol stated that the "data reviewed during the investigation numbered hundreds and thousands of images, thousands of videos depicting hundreds of child victims, most of whom remain unidentified."[12]

There is other scary news: If your child falls victim to a pedophile or cyberstalker, chances are they won't tell you. A 2004 study of 1,566 students in grades 4 through to 8 in the U.S.[13] found the following:

- 57 percent of students said someone said hurtful or angry things to them online with 13 percent saying it happens "quite often."

- 53 percent of students admit saying mean or hurtful things to someone online while 7 percent admit to doing it "quite often."

- 35 percent of students have been threatened online with 5 percent saying it happens "quite often."

- 42 percent of students have been bullied online with 7 percent admitting it happens "quite often."

- 20 percent of students have received mean or threatening e-mails.

- 58 percent of students have not told their parents or another adult about someone being mean or hurtful to them online.

These results are very similar to an Australian study conducted in 2001.[14] It surveyed 238 students in grades 7 through 10 and found the following:

- 66 percent of the children regularly used the Internet to access a chat room.

- 27 percent of those who regularly used a chat room believed that a child predator had contacted them.

- 31 percent of those contacted were distressed about the incident.

- ○ 23 percent of those who had been distressed told nobody.

- ○ 36 percent of those who had been contacted told nobody.

- ○ 24 percent told a parent.

- ○ Nobody told the police.

Obviously, there is no real way to verify that child predators had contacted the kids in this survey. As such, it could simply be a case of kids hitting on other kids, but that's not the point.

Not all pedophile activity revolves around the Internet, but enough of it presents a serious risk to your child that it might be useful to know a little about the type of person you're up against. You can find more information on the book's website at http://www.keepyourkidssafe.com.

Who Are They?

There is no perfect profile of a pedophile. Pedophiles are as varied in terms of background, social status, and profession as are people in general.

In an FBI investigation in 1999, Special Agent Pete Gulotta found that among those arrested were military officers with high clearances, pediatricians, lawyers, school principals, and tech executives.[15] Interestingly, he found that they were almost all white males between the ages of 25 and 45.[16]

Unfortunately, in many incidents the pedophile is a family friend. In one investigation, UK police found images of a child on CD-ROM[17] and noticed the background of the Australian bush. They also discovered a magazine in the footage that led them to believe that the abuse took place in either Victoria or NSW. After contacting the Australian police, the investigation was broadcast on the police TV show *CrimeStoppers*.[18] In a stroke of luck, the victim's mother was watching the show and saw footage of her child. It turns out that the alleged pedophile was known to the family and had traveled extensively with the child throughout central Australia. The man now faces more than 80 charges in the Cairns Magistrates Court, ranging from indecent dealing with a child under 12 to making an objectionable computer game.[19]

Part I

Real Threats to Your Children on the Internet

Why Do They Prey on Children?

I am no psychiatrist, and I cannot comprehend why a person would (a) be sexually attracted to a child or (b) victimize a child to satisfy the predator's own selfish, criminal, and immoral desires. What I do know is that there is no length to which some of these predators will not go to gratify themselves—including traveling to third-world countries and "renting" child prostitutes (the most vulnerable and forsaken children on the planet) for their own pleasure.[20]

Incredibly, many pedophiles do not even consider themselves to be pedophiles or as doing anything wrong. A pedophile who was jailed as a part of Operation Ore in the UK and the USA described child pornography on the Internet as providing a resource for men with sexual fantasies of young girls.[21] He claimed that when he was in prison, he met over 100 other men who had been convicted with offenses against children, none of whom considered themselves to be pedophiles.[22] In the British trial of the pedophile ring, called the "Wonderland Club," the operators of the ring thought of themselves as simply providing "a market that made it worth someone else's while" to victimize children.[23]

Pornography and Inappropriate Content on the Internet

There are possibly hundreds of thousands of websites that contain content which you may feel is inappropriate. Such content can range from still pictures to movies that play on a computer screen. A sample of the types of websites that are freely available on the Internet include those that depict hate and abhorrent and horrific acts.

There is a saying that "ignorance is bliss." In the case of children being ignorant of inappropriate content, I am inclined to agree. Unfortunately, not enough children are ignorant of such material. An Australian study revealed that nearly 50 percent of children surveyed aged between 11 and 17 had experienced something on the Internet that they thought was offensive or disgusting.[24] Those surveyed said that they felt "sick," "yuck," "disgusted," "repulsed," and "upset."[25]

The Pornography Industry

It's important to differentiate between legal (adult) pornography and illegal child pornography. The adult pornography industry is almost impossible to measure. It has been reported as the third largest income producer for organized crime in the USA and as generating $8 to $10 billion dollars per year.[26] This statistical range originates from the U.S. Attorney General's Final Report on Pornography. However, this report was finalized in 1986, well before pornographic websites existed. With the explosion of amateur pornography on the Internet, you can only imagine what this figure is now. Some estimates are that the Internet pornography industry alone is currently earning U.S.$3 billion per year in revenue.[27]

The Target Market

In the U.S., teenage boys between the ages of 12 and 17 are the largest category of users of hardcore (adult) pornography.[28] In Australia, a survey[29] of 16- and 17-year-olds revealed how often teenagers search the Internet for sex sites (see Table 2-1).

Access to Pornography

Do you really know if your child is viewing pornography on the Internet? Before you say, "Oh no, my child wouldn't dare do such a thing," think again. A U.S. study revealed that 62 percent of parents are unaware that their children have accessed objectionable sites.[30]

Boys	Girls	Result
38%	2%	Have searched the Internet for sex sites
4%	0%	Search the Internet on a weekly basis
22%	0%	Search the Internet every two to three months

Table 2-1   Survey of Teenagers Accessing Sex Sites on the Internet

The Internet gives children quick and easy access to pornography. They need only enter keywords and phrases to generate thousands of websites containing pornographic images. In addition, more than 1,000 newsgroups—easily accessible to children—are dedicated to providing pornographic pictures and video.

Pushing Pornography

It's almost guaranteed that your children will be exposed to pornography, even if they don't go looking for it. A survey conducted by the Spam Recycling Center in the USA showed that 30 percent of spam was pornographic in nature.[31] A similar survey by the firm AC Neilsen.Consult showed that the majority of unsolicited e-mail messages contain pornography.[32]

In Chapter 5, I will explain how you can protect your children against spam. For now, just realize that pornography can find its way to your children; they don't have to go looking for it.

Committing Crimes: Bombs, Drugs, Theft, and Fake Identification

Not only can children readily find pornography, but they can also easily obtain information about committing crimes, such as making bombs, manufacturing drugs, and stealing money. These documents provide detailed information and instructions that your kids may want to explore even further.

In less than 60 seconds after typing in some keywords, I found several documents containing detailed instructions with titles such as the following:

○ How to make a basic pipe bomb

○ How to make a CO_2 bomb

○ How to make explosives from bleach

○ Amphetamines, Beginner's Guide

○ How to Make Cocaine

○ Beating Drug Metabolite Tests

○ The Marijuana Grower's Guide

○ Phoney degrees from a school/university of your choice

○ Counterfeiting and Bank Fraud

There are numerous instances of children and teenagers bringing weapons to school and making bombs. Although this is rare, it does happen, and it's important that you are aware that your kids have access to this information. The following police operations and arrests demonstrate the scale of the problem:

February 10, 2004   Four students in the ninth grade at Thomas Jefferson Junior High School were arrested after a boy brought a homemade bomb to school.[33] The 14-year-old boys had helped the suspect assemble the bomb at his home. It was later brought to school, where one component was added. The motive behind the bomb was an incident three weeks prior when a boy had bumped into the suspect in the school lunchroom and exchanged glances.

March 13, 2003   A 14-year-old student from Lawndale High School and his cousin from a nearby school were arrested for making threats to explode a pipe bomb on campus. Los Angeles County sheriff's investigators found a book containing the names of students and teachers who they wanted to target.[34]

June 29, 2000   Two 15-year-old boys and a 14-year-old girl were caught red-handed by security guards at their local school early in the morning. They had knapsacks containing burglary tools and a copy of an Internet publication on the chemicals needed to make a bomb.[35]

March 8, 2000   Police arrested three high school students after finding a live grenade in a school locker. Two were aged 14 and one aged 17. A search of one of the boys' homes found another grenade, pipe bombs, bomb-making supplies, and instructions downloaded from the Internet.[36]

Cyberbullying: How Bullies Harass Your Kids 24/7

"Cyberbullying" is a term used to describe harassment that takes place via an electronic medium. This can range from defamation on websites, to threats made via e-mail or mobile phone.

Unlike traditional bullying, where a child can escape by going home to the sanctuary of his bedroom, cyberbullying continues when the child is at home. Consequently, many adults are not aware of cyberbullying and its effect on their children.

One of the most famous examples of cyberbullying was on a Canadian child, Ghyslain Raza, nicknamed "The Star Wars Kid." Ghyslain made a home video of himself pretending to fight a battle with a pretend lightsaber. The video was leaked onto the Internet and made available through P2P file-sharing networks, where it was downloaded by more than 15 million people.[37] The video was subsequently edited with more than 106 different versions or parodies created, including *Benny Hill, The Matrix, Mortal Kombat, The Hulk,* and *The Lord of the Rings.*[38] Ghyslain was so affected by it that he dropped out of school and was admitted to a child psychiatric ward. His parents have filed a lawsuit against the families of his fellow classmates who published the video and are claiming U.S.$160,000 in damages.[39]

In the UK, a 15-year-old girl discovered that a website had been created to insult and threaten her. The site contained comments about her weight and even posted a date for her death.[40]

A large part of bullying and harassment among boys focuses on sex and sexual orientation, whereas girls are bullied about their appearance and clothes.[41] Research on primary school children reveals that 37 percent had been insulted or sworn at by using text messages on cell phones.[42]

You can detect the presence of cyberbullying by watching your kids' reaction when they receive an instant message on the computer or an SMS on their cell phone. Other signs may include a reluctance to go to school, a sudden drop in self-esteem, depression, or a reluctance to use the computer or a cell phone.

If your kids have fallen victim to cyberbullying, there are a number of things you can do about it:

○ If your kids receive inappropriate messages on their cell phone, you can contact the telephone company and report the sender.

○ If your children are being harassed by e-mail, you can report it to your ISP. They may have the technical expertise to tell if the e-mail address is legitimate or has been spoofed.

○ Talk to your kids' school principal and make them aware of the situation.

Cyberbullying is the twenty-first-century equivalent of schoolyard bullying. Watch out for the signs, and if you suspect your kids are falling victim, do something about it straight away.

Invasion of Privacy

The lack of regulation of the Internet combined with differing privacy laws throughout the world may compromise your children's privacy when using the Internet.

Through the Internet, advertisers form a profile of your children in three main ways:

○ When they sign up for free services on the Internet

○ When they enter contests and sweepstakes

○ When they click banner advertisements

Some advertisers combine this information with the data they receive from programs that contain "spyware" and/or "adware." But more on that later.

The old saying that "nothing is for free" is just as true on the Internet as it is in the real world. In many cases on the Internet, you sacrifice your privacy for the "privilege" of using apparently free computer software and services.

The Dangers of Free E-mail Services—The Devil Is in the Details

According to a survey by Symantec, 76 percent of children have one or more e-mail accounts.[43] If your child signs up for a free e-mail account, they typically must provide the free e-mail company with all their sensitive information. This includes your child's name, address, phone number, gender, date of birth, the language they speak, the industry they work in, and their interests. That information is stored in a database with your child's name on it. While you may make a decision to give this information to a legitimate free e-mail service such as Hotmail for the purposes of creating a free e-mail account, it's important that you educate your kids not to provide such information to anyone else.

Some sites such as Hotmail require that parents provide consent when kids under the age of 13 sign up for the service. This is maintained using a special Kids Passport. The passport allows you to "choose whether a participating Kids Passport Web site can collect, use, or disclose your child's personal information."[44] Hotmail also has a Kids Privacy Statement so you know precisely how your kids are protected. While the Kids Passport is an excellent service, you need to ensure that your kids don't sign up with another service which doesn't have these safeguards built in. You can read the Kids Privacy Statement at http://www.passport.net/consumer/kidsprivacypolicy.asp and find out more information about the Kids Passport at http://kids.passport.net.

| tip | *If you are looking for a safe website for your kids to access, make sure you check out the MSN Kidz Homepage at http://kids.msn.com.* |

If your kids sign up to a service and provide false information then they will be monitored like any other user of the service. For example, the privacy policy for Hotmail states that they record personal information such as name, address, phone number, gender, and date of birth. However, they also record the user's "IP address, browser type, domain names, access times, and referring Web site addresses."[45] This means that they know:

- ○ What ISP you use

- ○ What web browser you use to view websites

- ○ What type of computer you have and what operating system it runs

- ○ The exact page on the Internet where you visited, prior to their site

Of course, Hotmail is a member of Microsoft's family of websites (MSN), so every time you visit an MSN website, information is added to your profile. The MSN privacy policy states the following:

"MSN keeps track of the pages our customers visit within MSN…. This data is also used by MSN to deliver customized content and advertising to customers whose behaviour indicates that they are interested in a particular subject area."[46]

Privacy: The Hidden Cost of Free Software

You can download many free software applications from websites on the Internet. These can range from games and business applications to Internet software that automates boring tasks on the computer. How can people afford to write such software and give it away? One probable answer is that it contains "spyware" or "adware" and is therefore subsidized by advertisers.

Spyware: Your Computer Is Watching You

"Spyware" refers to computer programs that gather information about someone without their knowledge. This information is usually sent to companies that provide it to advertisers and other interested parties. The information gathered can include the following:

○ Personal information such as your name, address, and phone number

○ Software applications installed on your computer

○ Websites you visit and the details of forms you fill in on web pages

○ Banner advertisements you click

○ A list of all the files you download

○ Your ISP details, including your modem dial-up phone number, user ID, and Internet password

You can find a list of spyware and adware in the appendix.

Adware: Creating an Online Profile of Your Interests

There are many definitions of adware and spyware; so many that the industry is yet to agree on a definition. Adware is similar to spyware in that it installs itself on your computer, but it tells you (usually in very fine print at the bottom of a license agreement) that it is gathering and using this type of information for advertising, marketing, or other commercial purposes. While adware usually targets you with pop-up advertising based on your web browsing habits, it's spyware that records personal information. BonziBuddy is an example of adware that can be used by children.

Example: BonziBuddy

BonziBuddy is a talking purple gorilla by Bonzi Software. It helps you navigate the Internet, sends e-mail messages, tells jokes, and eats bananas.

In order to use this cute little gorilla, your child has to sign up with their personal details and run it on their computer. To install this cute little gorilla, the company behind it adds this:

"For a limited time, you may download your own BonziBUDDY—FREE! BonziBUDDY normally retails for $40.00, but for a limited time, we'd like to say 'Thanks!' just for visiting BONZI.COM!"[47]

If you read the fine print in the Bonzi privacy policy, you will see that your personal information is shared "with consultants and affiliates for internal business purposes." You will also see that the advertisers that receive your personal information will use it to target specific advertising at you when you visit other websites. The Bonzi.com privacy policy states that the company may use information about "your visits to our and other websites in order to provide advertisements about goods and services of interest to you."[48] Although the company does state in their privacy policy that they don't recommend that children post information to the site, they will still collect it anyway. This is because Bonzi.com "offers users the option to submit their birth date and/or age." How many children are going to give their date of birth when it's optional, and how many of the dates given are going to be real?

At some stage after contacting Bonzi Software to request a screen capture of their product (and explaining the contents of this book), their privacy policy suddenly changed. It used to read, "No information should be submitted to or posted on our sites by users under the age of 13. Individuals under the age of 13 are not allowed to become registered users of our sites. BONZI.COM requests that children under the age of 18 not submit or post information to our sites. If an individual between the ages of 13 and 17 does so, BONZI.COM may collect information (including personally identifying information). This information may be used for marketing and promotional purposes by BONZI.COM and may, with the user's permission, be shared with pre-screened third parties."[49]

The privacy policy now reads, "We operate our site and services in compliance with the Children's Online Privacy Protection Act and therefore we do not seek to collect any personally identifiable information from anyone under 13 years of age."[50] Under the title "Community and Public Access," the policy states, "Users under the age of 18 should be particularly careful not to provide any personally identifiable information while using chat rooms or message boards."

In February 2004, the U.S. Federal Trade Commission (FTC) settled a complaint against Bonzi Software. The FTC alleged that Bonzi Software violated the Children's Online Privacy Protection Act (COPPA) by collecting "personal information from children online without first obtaining parental consent."[51] The company agreed to pay civil penalties of U.S.$75,000. Although this is a great first step toward protecting our children, I believe that fines such as U.S.$75,000 are nothing to a large corporation. Executives will take notice when they receive a U.S.$400,000 fine, like the one given to UMG Recordings,[52] which runs a number of music sites, some of which are popular with children.

Other Implications of Spyware and Adware

Apart from the fact that "some company somewhere has a file containing everything on your child," there are other implications relating to spyware. Spyware has a rolling effect because you suddenly begin to be continuously targeted with advertising. This can be in the form of e-mail messages, physical letters, phone calls, and pop-up screens on your computer. Some parents find that the intensity of this form of advertising undermines their authority, putting them at odds with their children.[53]

Pedophiles, pornography, hackers, viruses, credit card fraud—immoral and criminal activity is rampant on the Internet. If you do not take preventative measures, your child may be exposed to any one or all of these dangers. In Chapter 3, I explain why and how children are such easy targets—and what you can do about it. For now, though, you may be wondering why, if the Internet is such a dangerous place, you should allow your children to use the Internet at all. The answer is that the Internet contains a great deal of "good stuff" as well—and not just stuff that your children enjoy, but stuff that they *need* for school, university, and their future careers. In fact, the Internet has become so integral to our lives that denying your child access to it will deny them important opportunities to learn and grow. The next chapter briefly explains what the Internet is and why your children need it.

Endnotes

1. Whittle, Sally, 2002. "Battling paedophilia." The Guardian.
http://www.guardian.co.uk/online/story/0,3605,658949,00.html.
August 23, 2003.

2. McAuliffe, Wendy, 2001. "Paedophile swoop nets 13-year-old."
ZDNet. http://news.zdnet.co.uk/story/0,,s2085330,00.html.
August 23, 2003.

3. NCH, 2003. "Report highlights rocketing figures for child
porn offences." NCH. http://www.nchafc.org.uk/news/
news3.asp?ReleaseID=223. March 2, 2004.

4. Tran, Mark, 1999. "The Guardian: Police swoop on internet child porn."
Guardian Newspapers Limited. http://www.guardian.co.uk/freespeech/
article/0,2763,212452,00.html. August 23, 2003.

5. Batty, David, 2004. "55% of UK child abuse content traced to U.S." The
Register. http://www.guardian.co.uk/online/story/0,3605,1175373,00.html.
March 22, 2004.

6. NCIS, 2003. "United Kingdom Threat Assessment of Serious and
Organised Crime 2003." http://www.ncis.co.uk/ukta/2003/threat09.asp.
August 23, 2003.

7. Thomasson, Emma, 2004. "Police bust global Internet Child Porn
networks." Yahoo! News. http://news.yahoo.com/news?tmpl=story&u=/
nm/20040226/wr_nm/crime_europol_porn_dc_3. February 26, 2004.

8. The Age, 2004. "Wollongong man caught in child porn sting." The Age.
http://www.theage.com.au/articles/2004/02/27/1077676937084.html.
February 27, 2004.

9. The Guardian, 2003. "German police crack child porn web ring." Guardian Newspapers Limited. http://www.guardian.co.uk/child/story/ 0,7369, 1050578,00.html. September 26, 2003.

10. The Guardian, 2003. "German police crack child porn web ring." Guardian Newspapers Limited. http://www.guardian.co.uk/child/story/0,7369, 1050578,00.html. September 26, 2003.

11. Staff and agencies, 2002. "Police held in paedophilia investigation." Guardian Newspapers Limited. http://society.guardian.co.uk/children/story/ 0,1074,861751,00.html. August 24, 2003.

12. CNN, 2002. "Web child porn raids across Europe." Cable News Network LP, LLLP. http://www.cnn.com/2002/WORLD/europe/ 07/02/europe.porn/ ?related. August 24, 2003.

13. i-SAFE America, 2004. "National i-SAFE Survey Finds Over Half of Students are Being Harassed Online." i-SAFE America. http://www.isafe.org/imgs/ pdf/outreach_press/internet_bullying.pdf. June 28, 2004.

14. NAPCAN, 2001. "A recent survey on children and the Internet in the ACT." NAPCAN Online Newsletter, No. 2, November 2001. p. 11.

15. Seminerio, Maria, 1999. "Pedophile profile: Young, white, wealthy." ZDNet. http://zdnet.com.com/2100-11-515731.html?legacy=zdnn. August 24, 2003.

16. Seminerio, Maria, 1999. "Pedophile profile: Young, white, wealthy." ZDNet. http://zdnet.com.com/2100-11-515731.html?legacy=zdnn. August 24, 2003.

17. AAP, 2003. "Man in court over tape." News Limited. http:// www.news.com.au/common/story_page/0,4057,6090150%255E2,00.html. August 24, 2003.

18. ABC News Online, 2003. "Alleged paedophile appears in court." Australian Broadcasting Corporation. http://www.abc.net.au/news/newsitems/ s877054.htm. August 24, 2003.

19. AAP, 2003. "Man in court over tape." News Limited. http://www.news.com.au/common/story_page/0,4057,6090150%255E2,00.html. August 24, 2003.

20. Marks, Kathy, 2003. "The skin trade." The Independent. http://news.independent.co.uk/world/asia_china/story.jsp?story=371680. August 24, 2003.

21. The Guardian, 2003. "I cannot admit what I am to myself." Guardian Newspapers Limited. http://www.guardian.co.uk/child/story/0,7369,880251,00.html. August 24, 2003.

22. The Guardian, 2003. "I cannot admit what I am to myself." Guardian Newspapers Limited. http://www.guardian.co.uk/child/story/0,7369,880251,00.html. August 24, 2003.

23. Bynoe, Robin, 2001. "Chatroom Danger." ZDNet. http://news.zdnet.co.uk/story/0,,s2085049,00.html. August 24, 2003.

24. ABA, 2001. "Keeping children safe on the Internet." Australian Broadcasting Authority. http://www.aba.gov.au/abanews/news_releases/2001/105nr01.htm. August 24, 2003.

25. Flood, M and C Hamilton. Youth and Pornography in Australia. The Australia Institute, February 2003. p. 13.

26. Holgate, Karen, 2000. "Pornography and Its Effect on Children: Photographs don't affect us?" ChildCare Action Project (CAP): Christian Analysis of American Culture. http://www.capalert.com/pornandkids.htm. August 24, 2003.

27. Friess, Steve, 2003. "A Plan to Stop Online Kiddie Porn." Wired. http://www.wired.com/news/culture/0,1284,57136,00.html. August 24, 2003.

28. Holgate, Karen, 2000. "Pornography and Its Effect on Children: Photographs don't affect us?" ChildCare Action Project (CAP): Christian Analysis of American Culture. http://www.capalert.com/pornandkids.htm. August 24, 2003.

29. Flood, M and C Hamilton. Youth and Pornography in Australia. The Australia Institute, February 2003. pp. 8.

30. Rice Hughes, Donna, 1999. "Keeping Children Safe From Internet Predators." U.S. Health, Education, Labor and Pensions Subcommittee on Children and Families. http://www.protectkids.com/donnaricehughes/powerpoints/SenateHearing2000.ppt. August 24, 2003.

31. Oxman, Ian, 2000. "Anti-Spammers Call for Boycott of New DMA Opt-Out Database." Spam Recycling Center. http:// www.spamrecycle.com/pressrelease2.htm#9. August 24, 2003.

32. NOIE, 2003. "Final Report of the NOIE review of the spam problem and how it can be countered." NOIE. http://www.noie.gov.au/ publications/NOIE/spam/final_report/SPAMreport.pdf. August 24, 2003.

33. Broughton, Ashley, 2004. "Four teens arrested after bomb brought to school." The Salt Lake Tribune. http://www.sltrib.com/2004/Feb/02122004/utah/138140.asp. February 12, 2004.

34. SignOnSandiego, 2003. "Attorney for boy arrested said he was bullied by classmates." Union-Tribune Publishing Co. http:// www.signonsandiego.com/news/state/20030402-0215-ca-bombplot.html. April 2, 2003.

35. Loesing, John, 2003. "Agoura High students charged in bomb conspiracy." The Acorn. http://www.theacorn.com/News/2000/0629/Schools/18.html. August 24, 2003.

36. Johnson, Tracy and Aliya Saperstein, 2000. "Police find grenade in Tacoma school." Seattle Post. http://seattlepi.nwsource.com/local/bomb08.shtml. August 24, 2003.

37. Jedimaster.Net. http://jedimaster.net. March 1, 2004.

38. Mitchell, Alanna, 2004. "Bullied by the click of a mouse." The Globe and Mail. http://www.globetechnology.com/servlet/ArticleNews/TPStory/LAC/20040124/CYBER24/TPTechnology/. January 24, 2004.

39. Wired, 2003. "Star Wars Kid Files Lawsuit." Wired. http://www.wired.com/news/culture/0,1284,59757,00.html. July 24, 2003.

40. BBC, 2003. "Cyber bullies target girl." BBC News. http://news.bbc.co.uk/1/hi/england/nottinghamshire/2933894.stm. May 24, 2003.

41. Free Press, 2003. "Cyber-bullies make it tough for kids to leave playground." http://www.freep.com/money/tech/mwend17_20031117.htm. November 17, 2003.

42. Coughlan, Sean, 2003. "Texting insults at primary school." BBC News. http://news.bbc.co.uk/2/hi/uk_news/education/2925663.stm. April 7, 2003.

43. Symantec, 2003. "Symantec Survey Revels More Than 80 Percent of Children Using Email Receive Inappropriate Spam Daily." http://www.symantec.com/press/2003/n030609a.html. August 24, 2003.

44. Whittle, Sally. 2002. "Battling paedophilia." The Guardian, http://www.guardian.co.uk/online/story/0,3605,658949,00.html. August 2003.

45. MSN, 2002. "MSN Statement of Privacy (last updated: October 2002)." MSN. http://privacy.ninemsn.com.au. August 24, 2003.

46. MSN, 2002. "MSN Statement of Privacy (last updated: October 2002)." MSN. http://privacy.ninemsn.com.au. August 24, 2003.

47. Bonzi.com Software, 2003. "Take a minute… and make a 'Best Friend' for life—FREE!" Bonzi.com Software. http://www.bonzi.com/BonziBUDDY/BonziBUDDYFREE.asp. August 24, 2003.

48. Bonzi.com Software, 2003. "Bonzi Software, Inc. Privacy and Protection Policy." Bonzi.com Software. http://www.bonzi.com/bonziportal/index.asp?l=home&t=privacy&nav=ft. August 24, 2003.

49. Bonzi.com Software, 2002. "Privacy Statement." Bonzi.com Software. http://www.bonzi.com/bonziportal/index.asp?l=home&t=privacy&nav=ft. November 2002.

50. Bonzi.com Software, 2003. "Privacy Statement." Bonzi.com Software. http://www.bonzi.com/bonziportal/ index.asp?l=home&t=privacy&nav=ft. August 24, 2003.

51. FTC, 2004. "Bonzi Software, Inc. to Pay $75,000 to Settle COPPA Civil Penalty Charges." FTC. http://www.ftc.gov/opa/2004/02/bonziumg.htm. February 18, 2004.

52. FTC, 2004. "United States of America v. UMG Recordings, Inc., a corporation, defendant." FTC. http://www.ftc.gov/os/caselist/ umgrecordings/umgrecordings.htm. February 18, 2004.

53. National School Boards Foundation. "Research and Guidelines for Children's Use of the Internet." NSBF. http://www.nsbf.org/safe-smart/ overview.htm. August 24, 2003.

CHAPTER 3

How to Avoid and Reduce the Risks to Your Kids on the Internet

You have three lines of defense to protect your kids from the threats I described in Chapter 2: education, monitoring, and computer software. The most important of these is education. It is imperative that you discuss the Internet with your children and advise them of what they may and may not do on it, and why. Chances are that your kids will access the Internet from a computer other than your own—and one that may not have the software defenses installed (explained later)—so it is critical that they are personally motivated to avoid the Internet's dangers.

Monitoring is about taking an active interest in what your kids do on the Internet—monitoring what they do, so you can help keep them safe and away from dangers.

Software programs (also called "tools" and "applications") will make it much easier for you to reduce your children's exposure to Internet threats. There are five kinds of software that I recommend you implement: website-filtering software, e-mail-filtering software, antivirus software, firewall software, and malicious software–detection software. This might sound like a lot, but you can purchase software suites that bundle some, if not all, of these programs together. I also recommend that you *remove* certain software you may or may not know exists on your computer. I explain how to remove software at the end of this chapter.

In Chapters 4 through 8, I include the results of comprehensive evaluations of the top brands in each of these software categories and my recommendations for which you should use. In this chapter, I will go through each of the major threats to children and explain which software tools you can use to combat these. But first, let's talk about education. Just what should you say to your child?

Educate Your Kids

Educating your kids is about explaining to them what dangers exist on the Internet, *why* they should avoid them, and *what* they can do to avoid them. It is *not* about giving them a list of things they can't do. Without giving them the "why," such an approach could backfire—they might try to do everything you've banned!

There is no "one size fits all" when it comes to educating kids about Internet safety. What might seem acceptable for a teenager isn't necessarily going to be acceptable for a preschooler. What is acceptable to one parent may not be acceptable to another.

Here are some points you could raise in a discussion with your kids. I have voiced them as you might to your children.

○ Just as you need to be careful around strangers in the real world, you shouldn't talk to strangers on the Internet. Everyone on the Internet is a stranger—even if they seem nice. That's because it's easy to pretend to be someone who you're not on the Internet. Sometimes older people pretend to be friendly and young like you, but they are really trying to trick you, find out who you are, and hurt you.

○ You should avoid anyone who says rude things to you, asks you for your real name, wants you to send them a photo, wants to speak with you on the phone, or asks to meet you in person. If someone asks for anything like that, don't talk to them, just log off and tell your parents or your teacher (etc.) straight away. In particular:

  ○ Never give anyone, or any website, personal information such as your name, address, phone number, or the name of your school.

  ○ With the exception of your parents, never give anyone your password.

  ○ Never have a face-to-face meeting with a person you have talked to on the Internet.

  ○ Never send or post photos of yourself or anyone else on the Internet.

  ○ Never turn on your camera or microphone and chat with a person who you do not know.

  ○ Never run or save any files or games from a person you do not know. These could really be computer viruses or software programs that could damage the computer.

  ○ Don't respond to message boards, chat requests, or websites that contain rude language.

  ○ Don't believe everything you read on the Internet. Lots of people put information on the Internet, but some people make mistakes and others deliberately make up stories and tell lies.

Please don't skip any of these points in discussions with your child. Also, don't presume that they already understand the risks. A survey of 1,369 children between the ages of 9 and 16 found that 33 percent were unaware of the dangers of meeting people face-to-face.[1]

Not only should you educate your children, but you should also take an active interest in what they do on the Internet. As you'll learn in the following section, by putting the computer in the family room and going on the Internet with your kids, you can be aware of what they like doing, and you can guide them toward safer activities.

Monitor What Your Kids Do on the Internet

Here are some simple measures you can take to be involved in your children's Internet use and, in so doing, reduce the likelihood of them being harmed:

○ Keep the computer in a room where you can easily monitor your child's Internet activities, not in their bedroom. A family room is ideal.

○ Monitor your child's activities closely, especially their conversations in chat rooms.

○ Spend some time exploring the Internet with your child. This will allow you to learn about their interests and the sites they regularly visit.

○ Spend time with your child in a chat room until they learn the ground rules.

○ Show your child the difference between advertising and educational content.

○ Establish rules for ordering goods and services online. Kids should not be ordering anything online without their parents being present. Website operators in the USA must comply with the COPAA legislation. This legislation enforces a number of requirements, one of which is that the website owner must obtain verifiable parental consent to record information about children under the age of 13 years. You can find more information at http://www.ftc.gov.

○ Establish a reasonable time limit for Internet access based on the activity your child is engaged in (playing games, doing homework, etc.).

Now let's talk about the major threats to your children and what you can do about them. We'll start off with inappropriate content on websites.

Stumbling Across Inappropriate Content on Websites

Kids are most likely to see inappropriate content on a website. They might stumble across such a website when they use a search engine to look for information.

Search engine results depend on the match between the words typed into the search box and the words hidden in the software code—called Hypertext Markup Language, or HTML—of a given website.

Unfortunately, many pornographic and other inappropriate websites use normal, everyday words hidden in their web pages so that search engines will direct people to them. For example, I performed a search on a major search engine using the words "free," "stories," "pictures," "dog," and "horse"—the kinds of words your child might use to find a website containing information about dogs or horses. To my disgust, among the legitimate results were a number of sites containing bestiality.

You can reduce the chances of your child coming across a website containing inappropriate content by installing content-filtering software on your computer and using family friendly search engines. You can find a list of family friendly sites at http://www.keepyourkidssafe.com. In Chapter 4, I list a number of programs I have evaluated and recommend.

Unfortunately, as I explain next, your children may also be exposed to inappropriate content in the e-mail they receive.

Inappropriate Content Can Be Sent to Your Kids via E-mail

A lot of unsolicited e-mail—called "spam"—contains pornographic subject headers and even pornographic images. Even if your kids don't give out their e-mail address, they are likely to receive spam. This is because spammers obtain e-mail addresses from a range of sources, including website guest books, newsgroup postings, greeting card sites, party invite sites, computer programs known as "spiders" or "e-mail harvesters" that search websites looking for e-mail addresses, and even by guessing people's e-mail addresses!

A recent survey of children[2] between the ages of 7 and 18 revealed the following:

○ 80 percent received inappropriate e-mail on a daily basis.

- ○ 47 percent received e-mails with links to X-rated websites.

- ○ 57 percent felt uncomfortable and offended when viewing inappropriate e-mail messages.

Children's distress at receiving inappropriate spam is not surprising when you consider the kinds of messages they might receive, which regularly include advertisements for Viagra, penis enlargers, and breast creams—all of which may be deemed inappropriate—and even hardcore porno sites. One spam message I received advertised a child pornography site containing a huge quantity of child pornographic videos and referred to children in explicit, demeaning language. After receiving the e-mail message I reported it to the CyberTipline.

Spam is a huge problem, made especially so because it's very difficult to locate and take action against the "spammers" who send it. This is because spammers use techniques to hide their identities. For example, they typically find and use incorrectly configured mail servers owned by other people—generally ISPs—to send out the spam, which also allows them to hide their true identities.

Spammers are also motivated by greed. A spammer interviewed in an MSNBC investigation[3] admitted to receiving between $10 and $12 for every person who responded to a spam e-mail they sent. The same investigation found that a spammer based in Argentina usually sent between 30 and 40 million spam messages per day. Even with a low response rate, this spammer would probably make a lot of money.

You can combat spam by using an e-mail-filtering product. In Chapter 5, I describe the e-mail-filtering programs I believe are most effective in protecting your children against spam. In addition, you can reduce the likelihood of receiving spam by not giving away your e-mail address, and reminding your kids to do the same. Here are some other points to keep in mind:

- ○ Do not post messages to newsgroups, message boards, or mailing lists if possible, and if you do, avoid including your e-mail address. Usenet is a haven for spammers who harvest e-mail addresses by reading the messages that people post.

- ○ If you post messages using a free e-mail address such as Hotmail or Yahoo!, don't give out your regular e-mail address because this will also be harvested by spammers.

- ○ If you have a website, do not place your e-mail address on any of the web pages, especially in plain text. Spammers use many programs that read web pages looking for e-mail addresses. If you want to have a personal website and need to publish your e-mail address, display it in an image rather than in plain text.

○ Do not enter your real e-mail address into your Instant Message or IRC software. Spammers use programs to connect to IRC and look for such addresses.

○ Do not provide your e-mail address to websites that you do not know and trust. If you feel the need to do so, read their privacy policy first and find out with whom they share information. If the site does not have a privacy policy, do not submit any details to them.

○ Do not fill in product registration cards with your regular e-mail address. This can lead to "acquaintance spam," whereby the person to whom you gave your e-mail address then passes it onto someone else. If you have to fill in a registration card for warranty purposes, use a disposable e-mail address such as one from Hotmail or Yahoo!

A less restrictive approach that I recommend for people over 18 years of age is to have two e-mail addresses: one for friends and family only, the other (perhaps a free e-mail address) for websites, online forms, and newsgroup postings.

AOL Screen Names

If you use AOL, you can create a number of screen names and use Parental Controls (AOL Keyword: Parental Controls) to give your kids an appropriate level of access. Should one screen name become bombarded with spam or inappropriate instant messages, you can delete your kids screen name and create another.

There are many places where you can obtain a free e-mail address, but beware of submitting personal information to these free e-mail companies. Eventually, you will probably receive spam on your free e-mail address, but you can easily obtain another free e-mail address without losing contact with friends and family. To safeguard your kids, though, I strongly recommend installing an e-mail filter.

You can report spam containing child pornography to CyberTipline (http://www
.cybertipline.com), who will forward the information to law enforcement for
investigation and review.

E-mails to CyberTipline

When you submit an e-mail message to the CyberTipline you will need to
make a copy of the e-mail headers (hidden information in an e-mail message).
You can do this using Microsoft Outlook by double clicking on the e-mail
message, clicking on View, then Options. All the information you need is in
the box marked Internet Headers, so all you need to do is copy and paste this
information into the online form on the CyberTipline website.

By using a software tool such as VisualRoute (http://www.visualware.com), or
a web-based tool such as whois at http://www.geektools.com, you can find out who
owns that IP address as well as their name, e-mail address, and telephone number. In
the case of VisualRoute, you can zoom in on their physical location using a map of
the world. Often, the IP address will belong to an ISP. Although you won't have the
address and details of the actual sender, you can at least contact the ISP and advise
them that someone is using their computers to send spam. They may, in turn, be able
to identify the spammer. However, the IP address may be spoofed (forged), so the
information you see may not actually be the entity responsible.

Apart from spammers, pedophiles can also communicate with your kids via
e-mail—if, for example, your child has mistakenly revealed their e-mail address on
a message board or on a chat program. They are more likely to communicate with
your kids via IRC, web chat, or instant messaging.

Before I discuss these particular risks, though, I'd like to address the problem
of pop-up advertising.

Pop-Up Advertising Can Display Anything to Your Kids

Pop-up advertising is one of the most annoying, intrusive forms of advertising on
the Internet. There are three common types of pop-up ads: Windows Messenger
pop-ups, web browser pop-ups, and pop-under ads.

Windows Messenger pop-ups occur when spammers send messages using the Windows Messenger Service (see Figure 3-1). The Windows Messenger Service is a program on your computer that was originally designed to enable system administrators to send messages to users on a network. Unfortunately, spammers started abusing this program and are now using it to send pop-up advertising directly to your desktop.

If you have a firewall, then this should automatically block these types of messages. You can disable the Windows Messenger Service in Windows XP by doing the following:

1. Click the "Start" button and select the Control Panel.

2. Click on Performance and Maintenance and then click on Administrative Tools. (If Performance and Maintenance isn't displayed, just click on Administrative Tools.)

3. Double click on Services.

4. Scroll down to the line that says Messenger and double-click on it.

5. Change the Startup type to Disabled.

6. Click on the "ok" button.

note | *The Windows Messenger Service is not the same as MSN Messenger or any other Instant Message service.*

The second type of advertising is the web browser pop-up ad. Pop-up ads can be displayed by the web sites you visit as well as by adware (advertising software) installed on your computer. If pop-ups are displayed on your computer every time

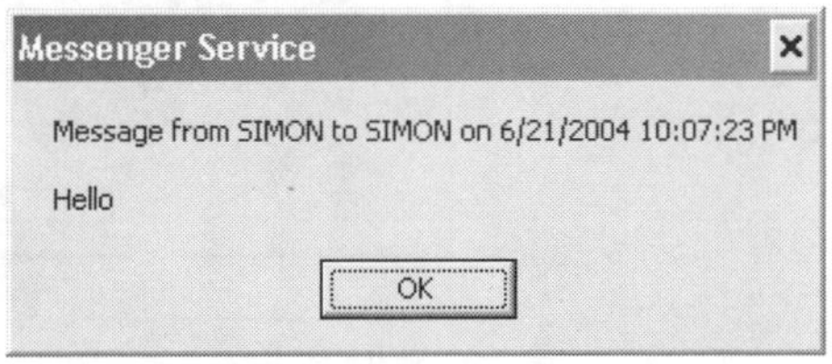

Figure 3-1   A pop-up box from the Windows Messenger Service

you visit a particular website, then it's probably the website that is causing the ads. If pop-ups occur every now and again, even when you are not browsing the web, then it's possible that you have adware installed on your computer. You can find out how to detect and clean adware in Chapter 8.

Last, pop-under windows are similar to pop-up ads, but they appear under the web browser window (as opposed to the top of the window). Pop-under ads appear only after the current web browser window has been closed or the web browser visits another website.

Pop-up ads and pop-under windows are easily blocked by most commercial firewall and filtering software. There are also free options available. One of the most popular and easy ways to block pop-ups is by using the Google Toolbar, which you can download for free at http://toolbar.google.com. However, if you are running Windows XP with Service Pack 2 (SP2) or greater, pop-up blocking is enabled by default. You can check if this has been turned on or off by

1. Clicking on the "Start" button and selecting Control Panel.

2. Clicking on the Security Center icon.

3. Clicking on the "Manage security center settings for Internet Options."

4. Clicking on the Privacy tab, as shown in Figure 3-2.

If you don't have the Security Center icon on your Control Panel, you need to install the latest Service Pack. You can find more information about this in Chapter 9.

Figure 3-2   Internet Explorer pop-up blocker in Windows XP

Newsgroups Can Expose Your Kids to Inappropriate Material

Newsgroups are like an assortment of notice boards where people can post messages by sending e-mail. As with searching using a search engine, kids can easily be exposed to inappropriate content due to innocently searching newsgroups for a topic that interests them.

For example, your child may search for a particular newsgroup using keywords such as "teen," "Britney Spears," "comics," "toys," "Barbie," high school," or "sports." When I tried this combination, however, among the results were newsgroups that contained pornographic material!

The majority of newsgroups are not regulated or "moderated" (monitored by someone). In fact, at the time of writing, fewer than 200 were actually moderated. This means that anyone can post anything without it being deleted. However, even the moderated newsgroups can contain pornography. Your ISP is the only entity that can control this particular content because it's physically located on their news server.

Fortunately, you can implement an Internet-filtering product to stop your kids from accessing all or certain newsgroups. Depending on the product, you can configure the software to allow your children access to specific groups, while blocking access to others. Some products will also filter the newsgroup messages themselves, blocking access to newsgroup posts that contain inappropriate words.

At the end of this chapter, I explain how to remove software that connects to Usenet from your computer. Unfortunately, removing these programs alone will not stop your children from using Usenet. This is because many computer operating systems such as Windows have Usenet newsreaders built in, such as the newsreader in Microsoft Outlook. In addition, Usenet can also be accessed by using a web browser as some websites provide a web interface to Usenet.

The best way to reduce the risks associated with using Usenet is to use a firewall in conjunction with filtering software. I discuss filters in Chapter 5 and firewalls in Chapter 6.

As well as being places where people can post indecent messages and attachments, newsgroups can also be used by predators to identify and stalk other users, such as kids. However, as I explain in the following section, predators are more likely to use IRC and website chat rooms for this purpose.

Part I

Real Threats to Your Children on the Internet

The Facts about Predators and Chat Rooms

Internet Relay Chat (IRC) is made up of a number of chat channels, which are accessed by computer software such as mIRC (pronounced *mirk*). Each chat channel is based on a particular topic and allows people to talk to each other simultaneously.

Many child predators use chat programs to find their victims. IRC is a very popular chat program; it allows people to lurk in chat channels, looking out for particular people as they enter and exit a channel.

Child predators often pose as boys or girls of a similar age to your child. They may also say that they are in the same state or go to the same school. They may even pose as your child's favorite singer or celebrity.

IRC is not regulated. It is nearly impossible to monitor all the chat channels and enforce any standard or law. IRC allows both anonymity and privacy, because you don't need to register to use it, and you can create your own chat channel and/or send private messages to people. IRC allows you to chat under any name you wish. If you want your name to be "Britney," you can log in with her name. You can also pretend to be a 10-year-old primary school student or an 18-year-old blonde female backpacker from Sweden!

Studies have shown that 53 percent of chat users have people talk to them about sex.[4] However, my research for this book indicates that the figure may be much higher. In each of the chat rooms I visited—none meant to be about sex—there was at least one person who tried to bring up sex.

To illustrate just how easy it is for a child to become victimized by a pedophile on IRC, consider my experience in November 2001 when I posed as a child logging onto IRC for the first time. Please note, you may find the following example upsetting.

Posing as a 10-Year-Old Girl

I pretended to be a 10-year-old girl and logged onto the #teenlounge channel. Given that young girls seem to be growing up faster than ever these days, I don't think that a 10-year-old girl logging onto a teen channel is that unusual.

It quickly became apparent that the #teenlounge channel is frequented by people other than teenagers. Within 60 seconds of logging on, eight males sent me private messages asking for my age, gender, and where I lived. Within 10 minutes, I was receiving private messages from 19 other people. Within 40 minutes, I was receiving private messages from 30 people. *All* of these people asked me—supposedly a 10-year-old girl—to have sex with them.

Three people sent me pictures of hardcore pornography and asked me what I thought of it. And, unsurprisingly, someone also asked me for the suburb in which I lived.

Frankly, I was sick to my stomach after conducting several experiments. It particularly concerns me how quickly and easily kids can be victimized on a seemingly innocuous IRC channel—remember, they only need receive one disturbing message for the damage to be done.

My wife and I are avid Internet users, but there is no way we will allow our children to use IRC. It is obvious to me that child predators use channels aimed at children and teenagers to make their advances. Although Internet-filtering software has improved, I don't think it has improved to the point of filtering out the majority of inappropriate content on IRC. So I think the best way to deal with the problem is to prevent your kids from using IRC in the first place. If your kids want to download IRC software (probably because their friends have it), explain why you don't want them to use it.

If you want to prevent your kids from using IRC, be sure to check whether IRC has already been installed on your computer. The most popular IRC client for Microsoft Windows is mIRC. If it is installed on your computer, you may see an icon, such as the one shown in Figure 3-3, on your desktop.

mIRC

Copyright © Tjerk Vonck & mIRC Co. Ltd. mIRC® is a trademark of mIRC Co. Ltd.

Figure 3-3   mIRC logo

Ircle is the most popular IRC client for Apple Mac users. It can be found in your File Menu. The icon shown in Figure 3-4 can identify the program.

Figure 3-4   Ircle desktop icon

I explain how you can remove IRC from your computer later in this chapter.

If you are concerned about your kids using IRC at a friend's place, I urge you to discuss the risks with the friend's parents.

Popular Chat Rooms Are Not Safe

Similar risks as those on IRC exist in website chat rooms. Although IRC is one of the most popular chat programs in the world, chat sites and instant messaging—including AOL, Yahoo! and MSN—are also widely used by kids. While there are moderated chat rooms, you can block access to these rooms by using Internet-filtering software.

In September 2003, MSN announced that it would shut down Internet chat rooms in 28 countries in order to provider "a safer online experience."[5] Geoff Sutton, European general manager of Microsoft MSN, said, "the straightforward truth of the matter is free, unmoderated chat isn't safe."[6] IRC and web chat rooms are not the only places where kids can be exposed to inappropriate content and overtures from pedophiles. Instant messaging carries similar risks.

What Are Your Kids Really Saying on Internet Chat Rooms?

When people chat or send messages using the Internet, they tend to use acronyms. In chat rooms it's very common for people to ask "ASL," which means "What is your age, gender and where do you live?" If you keep an eye on your kids when they use the Internet, it's important that you are aware of what these acronyms mean. For example, POS means "parent over shoulder"; in other words, don't say anything as my parents are watching me.

Table 3-1 contains a list of common acronyms that are used in Internet chat rooms:

Acronym	What It Means	Acronym	What It Means
A3	Anytime, anywhere, anyplace	LMAO	Laugh my ass off
AAMOF	As a matter of fact	LOL	Laugh out loud
ADN	Any day now	LTNS	Long time no see
AFAIK	As far as I know	LULAS	I love you like a sister
AFK	Away from keyboard	LUM	Love you man
AKA	Also known as	LUV	Love
AS	Another subject	LY	Love you
ASL	Age, sex, location	LYN	Lying
ASLP	Age, sex, location, picture	M8	Mate
ASAP	As soon as possible	M	Male
ATB	All the best	MOB	Mobile
ATK	At the keyboard	MOTD	Message of the day
ATM	At the moment	MMA	Meet me at
AWA	As well as	MMAMP	Meet me at my place
B	Be	MU	Miss you
B4	Before	MUSM	Miss you so much
BAK	Back at keyboard	MTE	My thoughts exactly
BBIAB	Be back in a bit	MYOB	Mind your own business
B/C	Because	NBD	No big deal
BC	Be cool	NRN	No reply necessary
BCNU	Be seeing you	NA	No access
BBL	Be back later	NC	No comment or not cool
BBS	Be back soon	NE	Any
BD	Big Deal	NE1	Anyone
BF	Boyfriend	NITING	Anything
BFN	Bye for now	NM	Not much
BFZ4EVR	Best friends forever	NP	No problem
BHL8	Be home late	NQA	No questions asked
BIF	Before I forget	NW	No way

Table 3-1   Commonly Used Acronyms in Internet Chat Rooms and Instant Messages

Acronym	What It Means	Acronym	What It Means
BL	Belly laughing	NWO	No way out
BN	Been	OTFL	On the floor laughing
BOL	Best of luck	OIC	Oh, I see
BOT	Back on the topic	OMG	Oh my god
BRB	Be right back	OT	Off topic
BRH	Be right here	OTOH	On the other hand
BRBGP	Be right back gotta pee	O4U	Only for you
BRT	Be right there	P911	My parents are coming
BTDT	Been there, done that	PITA	Pain in the ass
BTOBD	Be there or be dead	PCM	Please call me
BTW	By the way	PLS	Please
B4N	Bye for now	PLZ	Please
C	See	PPL	People
CU	See you	POS	Parent watching over shoulder
CU2	See you too	PRT	Party
CUB L8R	Call you back later	PRW	Parents are watching
CU@	See you at	QT	Cute
CYA	See you around or see ya	R	Are
CMI	Call me	RL	Real life
CMON	Come on	RLR	Earlier
CTN	Can't talk now	RMB	Ring my bell
CUB L8R	Call you back later	ROFL	Rolling on the floor laughing
CUL8R	See you later	ROTFLMAO	Rolling on the floor laughing my ass off
CYA	See you	ROTG	Rolling on the ground
CYO	See you online	RS	Real soon
DK	Don't know	RSN	Real soon now
DNR	Dinner	RTFM	Read the flaming manual

Table 3-1   Commonly Used Acronyms in Internet Chat Rooms and Instant Messages
(continued)

Acronym	What It Means	Acronym	What It Means
EG	Evil grin	RU	Are you
EOD	End of discussion	RUMF?	Are you male or female
EOS	End of story	RUOK	Are you ok
EZ	Easy	S	Smile
F	Female	SA	Sibling Alert
F?	Are we friends	SC	Stay cool
F2F	Face to face	SEC	Wait a second
F2T	Free to talk	SK8	Skate
FAQ	Frequently asked questions	SOHF	Sense of humor failure
FC	Fingers crossed	SOL	Smiling out loud
FCOL	For crying out loud	SOS	Same old stuff
FOFL	Falling on the floor laughing	SLM	See last mail
FITB	Fill in the blank	SLY	Still love you
FOAF	Friend of a friend	SPK	Speak
FS	For sale	SRY	Sorry
FTF	Face to face	STATS	Your sex and age
FUBAR	Fouled up beyond all repair	SWALK	Sent with a loving kiss
FWIW	For what it's worth	SWIM	See what I mean
FYEO	For your eyes only	SYS	See you soon
FYA	For your amusement	TA	Teacher Alert
GA	Go ahead	TBC	To be continued
GAC	Get a clue	TBYB	Try before you buy
GAL	Get a life	TC	Take care
GDW	Grin, duck, and weave	TCOY	Take care of yourself
GF	Girlfirend	THX	Thanks
GG	Good game	TIA	Thanks in advance
GJ	Good job	TMI	Too much information
GL	Good luck	TMIY	Take me I'm yours

Table 3-1   Commonly Used Acronyms in Internet Chat Rooms and Instant Messages *(continued)*

Acronym	What It Means	Acronym	What It Means
GMTA	Great minds think alike	THNQ	Thank you
GOL	Giggling out loud	TNX	Thanks
GR8	Great	TOY	Thinking of you
GTG	Got to go	TTFN	Ta ta for now
H	Hug	TTYL	Talk to you later
HB	Hug back	TUL	Tell you later
H8	Hate	TWF	That was fun
HAGN	Have a good night	TY	Thank you
HH	haha	U2	You too
HOAS	Hold on a second	U	You
HRU	How are you	UR	You are
HSIK	How should I know	U4E	Yours forever
HT4U	Hot for you	W8	Wait
HTH	Hope that helps	W/	With
H&K	Hugs and kisses	WB	Welcome back or write back
IAC	In any case	W/E	Whatever
IAD8	It's a date	W/O	Without
IC	I see	WOT	What
IDK	I don't know	WRT	With respect to
IIRC	If I recall correctly	WRU	Where are you
ILU	I love you	WT	Without thinking
ILU2	I love you too	WTF	What the heck
ILY	I love you	WTH	What the hell
IMO	In my opinion	WTG	Way to go
IMHO	In my humble opinion	WUF	Where are you from
IMNSHO	In my not so humble opinion	WUWH	Wish you were here
IMO	In my opinion	W4U	Waiting for you
IOW	In other words	W8	Wait
IRL	In real life	X	Kiss
ITILY	I think I love you	XO	Kisses and hugs
IUSS	If you say so	XLNT	Excellent

Table 3-1   Commonly Used Acronyms in Internet Chat Rooms and Instant Messages
(continued)

Acronym	What It Means	Acronym	What It Means
IYD	In your dreams	Y	Why
IYKWIM	If you know what I mean	YGBSM	You have got to be kidding me
JAM	Just a minute	YGM	You have got mail
JAS	Just a second	YIU	Yes I understand
J4F	Just for fun	YIWTGP	Yes I want to go private
JFK	Just for kicks	YR	You are
JK	Just kidding	YSWUS	Yeah sure whatever you say
JMO	Just my opinion	YW	You're welcome
K	Okay	ZZZ	Sleeping
KC	Keep cool	?	Huh
KHUF	Know how you feel	?4U	Question for you
KISS	Keep it simple stupid	1ON1	One on one
KIT	Keep in touch	2L8	Too late
KOTC	Kiss on the cheek	2MORO	Tomorrow
KOTL	Kiss on the lips	2NITE	Tonight
KWIM	Know what I mean	3 8 1	Three words, eight letters, one meaning - I love you
L8	Late	4	For
L8R	Later	4GM	Forgive me
LDR	Long distance relationship	4GVN	Forgiven
LJBF	Let's just be friends	4YEO	For your eyes only
		8	Ate

Table 3-1   Commonly Used Acronyms in Internet Chat Rooms and Instant Messages *(continued)*

Emoticons: What Your Kids Are Feeling

Emoticons (emotional icons or smileys) are computer characters that are used to express feelings. These are commonly found in e-mail messages or text based chat rooms such as mIRC. However, more graphical applications such as MSN Messenger tend to use pictures of a face to represent an emotion.

Emoticon	What It Means	Emoticon	What It Means
:-)	Smile	:-|	Disappointed
;-)	Wink	:-\	Undecided
;->	Sly wink	:-X	My lips are sealed
:-S	Confused	:O	Shocked
:-o	Surprised	: *	Kiss
:-(	Frown	:-P	Tongue hanging out
:(	Sad	O :-)	Angelic
:-<	Really sad	@}----'--	A long stemmed rose
:'-(	Crying	:OX	It's a secret

Table 3-2   Commonly Used Emoticons in Internet Chat Rooms and Instant Messages

Table 3-2 contains a list of emoticons that are used in Internet chat rooms.

Instant Messaging Gives Predators Access to Your Kids

Instant messaging (IM) is like an Internet version of SMS (Short Message Service) on your mobile phone. IM software allows you to talk in real time (shown in Figure 3-5) to people who are connected to the Internet anywhere in the world. Some child predators use instant messaging programs to find their victims. These programs include software such as AIM (AOL Instant Messenger), ICQ (shown in Figure 3-6), Yahoo! Instant Messenger, and MSN Messenger.

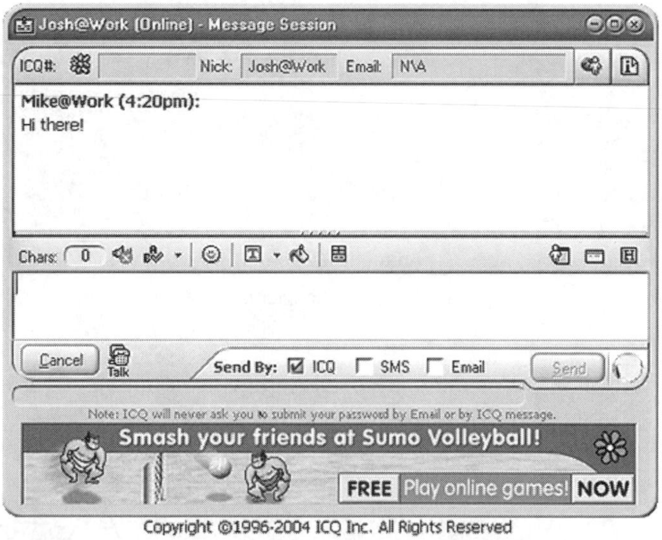

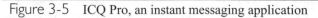

© ICQ Inc.

Figure 3-5   ICQ Pro, an instant messaging application

Just as child predators may pose as people on IRC, they can do the same thing using instant messaging. For example, if your child is a 9-year-old boy who is interested in playing computer games, the predator may pose as a 9-year-old boy who is also interested in playing computer games.

What makes instant messaging particularly dangerous is that predators can gain access to a lot of personal information about your child prior to talking with them. This is because many of these programs have directories of users that contain highly personal information.

A visit to the white pages at http://people.icq.com/whitepages/ search/1,,,00.html shows how easy it is for someone to use ICQ to find information. You can be as specific as searching for females with the name "Sarah" in a particular state or city. You can even search for children who attend a particular elementary school!

© ICQ Inc.

Figure 3-6   ICQ Pro's Instant Message window

A predator doesn't even need to register as an ICQ user in order to do this. He can just use his web browser to view the member's directory and obtain your child's physical address, e-mail address, phone number, and other personal details.

Instant messaging software is not regulated. Anyone can register with false information and create a fake profile. Your child may find someone listed in the white pages directory who appears to have very similar interests, but is really a predator who has deliberately created a profile to match that of your child.

I don't necessarily advise banning instant messaging—it can be very useful for kids doing homework and communicating with friends and family. When studying for exams or doing group assignments, your kids can quickly and easily talk to their friends about problems and swap information online.

Instead, to minimize the risks using instant messaging, I recommend the following:

○ Don't allow your kids to fill in *any* information in member directories or white pages.

○ Don't allow them to upload any photos of you or them using this software.

○ When subscribing to instant messaging, don't allow your children to fill in any fields that are not absolutely mandatory.

○ Don't allow your children to publish their information anywhere or make it available to other people.

○ Install parental controls in the instant messaging software. Some instant messaging software programs have controls that restrict who your child can talk to and even the chat room they enter. These controls are applied to multiple computers, so if your child goes to their friends house to log in, the same restrictions will apply.

○ Talk to your children about the risks of using instant messaging. In particular, explain that if they don't know the person who is sending them messages, they shouldn't talk to them.

○ Don't allow your kids to give out their instant messaging ID or ICQ number to anyone they don't know.

○ Don't allow your kids to include their instant messaging ID or ICQ number on e-mail messages or newsgroup postings.

○ Talk to your children about selecting an appropriate screen name, user id or e-mail address. Provocative names such as "sexychick" or "cutegrl" are likely to attract attention.

Many Internet-filtering products can record conversations conducted via instant messaging software, so you could also inform your children that you may monitor their conversations in order to dissuade them from breaking any of the preceding rules. However, this may backfire as your kids may go to their friend's place, school, or an Internet café to chat instead.

If you use Microsoft Windows, you can find out if any instant messaging programs are already installed on your computer by clicking the Start button and selecting Programs. If you see any of the following programs, they are likely to be installed on your computer:

- AIM (AOL Instant Messenger)
- ICQ
- MSN Messenger
- Yahoo! Messenger

I explain how to remove these software programs at the end of this chapter.

The white pages directory of an instant messaging program is not the only place where a predator could find out personal information about your child. Predators can also monitor your child's posts to message boards and mailing lists to build up a profile about them.

Privacy Risks from Message Boards and Mailing Lists

Message boards are similar to newsgroups, but they are operated from a website so you don't need a newsreader, just a web browser, to view them. A mailing list is also similar in that it allows people to communicate, but it does this by transmitting messages via e-mail. Messages posted to message boards are not generally read in real time. There may be minutes, hours, days, or weeks before someone replies, whereas messages posted to a mailing list arrive in the subscriber's e-mail box almost instantaneously.

Your child may post confidential or sensitive information—such as their name, age, where they live, and their interests—on a message board or to a mailing list, which could be used by a stalker to form a profile about your child. It is extremely easy for someone to search through a message board and find all the messages posted by a particular individual.

Also, your child may post information that tells a predator where they will be at a certain time. For example, your child may visit a message board that concerns their favorite singer or entertainer. They may post a message saying that they have front-row tickets to the entertainer's performance on a given night and may even describe what they plan to wear. This is exactly the kind of information a predator may use to identify and locate your child.

It is extremely important that you tell your kids not to reveal too much when they visit a message board. If you suspect that your child has already posted sensitive information, you should be able to delete the message from the bulletin board. If there is no delete button, contact the owner of the website and ask them to delete the message. Don't forget that in some countries, such as the U.S., the website owner must have verifiable parental consent in order to record personal information of children under 13 years old. You can find more information at http://www.ftc.gov/bcp/conline/pubs/buspubs/coppa.htm. If they are doing this without your consent, they are breaking the law and can be reported to the Federal Trade Commission at http://www.ftc.gov.

Blogs—What Are Your Kids Posting about Themselves?

A blog contains a summary of a person's life in a chronological order. It typically consists of a single web page or a number of web pages that are frequently updated in the same way as you would update a diary. You can read everything from personal thoughts, links to their favorite websites, news articles, pictures, and even video clips. Blogs allow visitors to contact the owner of the blog via e-mail or post a message in response to an article. While this allows people to contact your kids, you can disable these feature in the software itself. A number of specialist hosting sites, such as blogger.com, will host the blog for you, so you don't need any technical expertise. Many blog-hosting companies provide tools to enhance them. These may include a message board, calendar, and an easy-to-use online form to update the blog.

Blogs are very popular with both children and teens because their friends can interact with them in a world they create and control. While blogs can be a very positive experience for kids, they can also be misused. A blog can provide a predator with all the information he needs to profile your kids. It may contain their interests, what they are currently reading, who their friends are, and even a calendar of events they will be attending.

Meeting Sites—The Evolution of Internet Dating

When Internet dating first appeared, the gay and lesbian community predominantly used dating sites. This later evolved to include a large heterosexual demographic who were also looking for love, sex, or a partner to spend time with. The latest evolution has taken a step back from dating to just "meeting" or "hooking up."

A number of high profile web sites such as hotornot.com (4.3 million members),[7] facethejury.com (1.2 million members), and buddypic.com allow people to upload pictures of themselves as well as biographical information. Visitors can than rate their pictures on a scale of 1 to 10. If your ratings are high enough then you may be placed in the "Top Girls" or "Top Guys" category and made to feel like a celebrity. Of course, most of these sites are free and allow you to arrange to meet with other members.

Although some sites such as hotornot.com have policies restricting the age limits of their members to "persons 18 years or older,"[8] some don't. Unfortunately, there have been reports of high school students using these services. In one instance, two boys met with two high school girls.[9] One girl offered to "sneak them all into her house" where one couple "hooked-up on the floor" while the other couple "used the closet."

A quick two-minute search on facethejury.com found many teens that have signed up by selecting their age as 18, yet put their real age in their profile. In one case, a 16-year-old girl admitted in her profile that the picture she uploaded was taken when she was just 14! I couldn't find any mention of an age restriction on facethejury.com with the exception of a policy for individuals under the age of 13.

Buddypic.com was a completely different story. When I clicked on the list of "Newest Girls" that had signed up to the service, only two were 18 and 19, five were 15, one was 13, and the other was 14 years old. The BuddyPic Privacy Policy states "BuddyPic.com does not allow a child under the age of 13 to join the site."[10] Of course, how would they know?

While teenagers will be teenagers, they still need to be educated about the risks of meeting people on the Internet. There is simply no way to ensure that the person in the photo is the same person they are talking to online.

Mailing Lists Allow Predators to Lurk in the Background

Mailing lists carry the same risks to your children's privacy as do message boards. However, the risks are amplified because mailing lists send e-mail messages to everyone on the list. If your child posts sensitive information to the mailing list, it will be sent to everyone—and cannot be deleted! Your kids won't have access to see who subscribes to the mailing list because it is kept secret to avoid abuse by spammers.

Mailing lists can also be moderated in a similar way to newsgroups. If your child posts a message to a moderated newsgroup, a moderator will approve it first and then release it to the members of the mailing list. If your child posts a message to an unmoderated mailing list, it will be sent to the members of the mailing list without being reviewed by a moderator.

Mailing lists are also archived, whereas messages posted to message boards usually have a limited lifespan. For example, it took me less than 60 seconds to find a message I had posted to a computer security mailing list back in 1994—nearly ten years ago!

E-mail-filtering programs can block outgoing e-mail messages as well as incoming messages, so you might be able to prevent your children from sending messages containing sensitive information. In Chapter 5, I discuss e-mail-filtering programs in detail.

Let's now discuss how audio- and videoconferencing also pose threats to the privacy of your children.

Privacy Risks from Audio- and Videoconferencing

If your child uses audio and/or video chat, a predator can obtain much more information about them than is possible via text chat—what your child sounds and looks like, as well as details (sounds and images) of their background environment.

Combined with other information your child may have revealed, this allows a predator to build up a more complete picture of who your child is, what their interests are, and where they live. It's a scary thought.

Even scarier—there are many "Trojan horse" programs (I explain what these are in the section "Malicious Viruses, Worms, and Trojans") that can remotely activate the webcam and microphone on your computer, even when no one is using audio/video conferencing. A predator may send a Trojan horse program to your child by hiding it inside a game. When your child installs the game, the Trojan software installs itself silently in the background.

Personally, I don't see why a child would need to have a webcam, but if there is one on your computer, you can use an Internet-filtering program to limit its use. I explain Internet filters in Chapter 4. More importantly, though, you should talk to your child about why they shouldn't use a webcam when there is a danger that a stranger will see them.

So far we have discussed how, by using some of the features of the Internet, kids can come across inappropriate content or be targeted by predators. There are also other kinds of dangers that can jeopardize your children's enjoyment of the Internet. In the following section I explain how, by using peer-to-peer applications, your kids not only may see inappropriate material and endanger their privacy, but may also risk breaking the law themselves.

Legal Risks from Using Peer-to-Peer Applications

Peer-to-peer file-swapping programs allow anyone on the Internet to send and receive files. Although the majority of files swapped on peer-to-peer networks contain music, many contain still images or videos. Popular peer-to-peer applications include Kazaa, BearShare, Blubster, eDonkey, Gnutella, Grokster, iMesh, Limewire, Morpheus, Overnet, and WinMX.

It's probably safe to say that most peer-to-peer applications are used to transmit illegally copied audio in MP3 (compressed audio) format. You can find almost any song by any artist using such applications. In fact, peer-to-peer networks are not just used to traffic MP3 files, but files of any type. You may be asking yourself, "So what? Everyone I know copies songs, and the authorities know but they don't prosecute anyone because everyone does it." Well, prosecutions for individuals are increasing, and even kids are being targeted.

In April 2003, the RIAA (Recording Industry Association of America) began legal action against four students for sharing MP3 files on their university campus networks. Although the students had very large collections of illegally obtained MP3 files, this case is a warning to everyone who thinks they can safely swap music. The RIAA is seeking $150,000 for each copyrighted work (MP3 file) that was downloaded by the students.[11]

Even if your child doesn't have a large collection of MP3 files, the RIAA may still take you to court. In September 2003, the RIAA sued a 12-year-old girl from New York after she was caught sharing music over the Internet. Her mother paid U.S.$3,000 to settle the lawsuit, although the RIAA has indicated that future settlements will cost defendants a lot more. RIAA President Cary Sherman stated, "Yes, there are going to be some kids caught in this, but you'd be surprised at how many adults are engaged in this activity."[12]

Next to music files, one of the most popular content types to be transferred over these networks is pornography. Kids can easily download pornographic files by mistake. For instance, the results of a search on the music video files of a popular artist is likely to result in both legitimate videos as well as illegitimate—that is, pornographic—videos. Alternatively, your child may come across a pornographic file simply by looking for videos or files with the extension .mpeg, .mpg, .mov, .avi, or .qt and randomly picking one to download.

Also, because peer-to-peer file-swapping applications send files from one user's computer to another user's computer, there is no guarantee that the filename reflects what the file actually contains. However, some peer-to-peer applications are making an effort to ensure that the name of the file reflects its content. In the Kazaa file-sharing application, a file designated with a "gold icon" (shown in Figure 3-7) means that it has been digitally signed to ensure that the name actually reflects the content.

Figure 3-7   Kazaa gold icon

Apart from illegal MP3 files and pornography, peer-to-peer applications are used by pedophiles to transfer child pornography. According to Linda Koontz, director of Information Management Issues at the U.S. General Accounting Office (GAO), "The trafficking of child pornography through increasingly sophisticated electronic media, including Internet chat rooms, newsgroups, and peer-to-peer networks, has made these images more readily accessible."[13]

The privacy of your kids is also at risk when they use peer-to-peer applications. In order to use a free peer-to-peer program, you are typically required to accept the third-party software bundled with it. Such software is often referred to as "adware" or "spyware." Adware is software that causes advertisements to display on your desktop; spyware is software that tracks your Internet use and personal information, usually to direct advertising to you. These are explained in greater detail in the next section.

Children, in particular, are likely to download software that they don't even know about when installing a peer-to-peer program. This is the case for two reasons. First, they are likely to accept without reading the terms and conditions of obtaining the free peer-to-peer application (which includes the condition that they must install a number of third-party software programs which may include adware and spyware programs). Second, many adware and spyware programs download invisibly in the background. A more detailed list of third-party software, spyware, and adware can be found in Table A-1 in the appendix at the back of the book.

You can learn how to find and remove spyware and adware at the end of this chapter. If any of the pictures (icons) shown here appear on your desktop, then these programs are already installed on your computer. However, not all programs are indicated by desktop icons. Another way to look is (for Microsoft Windows users) to check for these programs by selecting the Start | Programs menu or (for Apple Mac users) to search for them in the File Menu.

BearShare   Blubster   eDonkey2000   Grokster   iMesh   Kazaa Media Desktop   Overnet   WinMX

Peer-to-peer file-sharing programs are not bad, per se. The main problem is that they can easily be misused for illegal means. In general, I suggest that you prevent your children from accessing these programs, at least the free versions, for the following reasons:

○ The parental controls on some file-swapping applications can be easily bypassed.

○ There is a large amount of inappropriate and illegal content on these networks, with no way to restrict access to it.

○ The majority of files I have seen on these networks breach the creators' and/or owners' copyright. To download them would be illegal.

If you wish to allow your children to use a file-swapping program, opt for the paid—rather than free—version that comes without the ads and includes security measures. Kazaa Plus (as opposed to the free version of Kazaa) costs U.S.$29.95 and, according to its makers, is ad free. Whether P2P file-sharing products are appropriate for your children is ultimately your decision.

I decided to test this claim by scanning Kazaa Plus v2.6.2 with three of the best malware detection products available: Ad-aware, Spybot, and PestPatrol. Both Ad-aware and Spybot did not detect any spyware or adware. However, PestPatrol detected SaveNow, TopSearch, WebHancer, Web P2P Installer, and XoloX. Additional details can be found in the appendix.

Apart from scanning Kazaa Plus with malware detection software, I also looked at the EULA (End User License Agreement). The Kazaa EULA states under section "4.5 SuperNode" that "Your copy of the Software may serve as a SuperNode..... When your computer is a SuperNode other peers will upload an index of files they are sharing to your computer and they will send search queries to your computer.

Your computer will reply to these requests and also forward the request to other SuperNodes … When you are a SuperNode your CPU and Internet connection is being used, but not more than 10% of the resources will be used." The SuperNode option is enabled by default. If you don't want other Kazaa users to use your CPU and Internet connection, you can turn off the SuperNode function by

1. Clicking on the Tools menu.

2. Selecting Options.

3. Clicking on Advanced.

4. Checking the box marked "Do not function as a SuperNode."

Apart from the Kazaa SuperNode function, the Altnet software, bundled with Kazaa, uses your computer's resources and records your interests. The Altnet End User Agreement states under section 3, "Permission to Utilize," that you "grant permission for Altnet and/or the Altnet Providers to utilize the disk space and bandwidth of your computer to share out files that you have downloaded using the Network." It then refers you to their privacy policy at http://www.altnet.com/ privacy.

The Altnet Privacy Policy reveals that Altnet collects information and uses it to display "content according to your interests and preferences" and sends "you information about us and promotional material from some of our partners." Altnet also "may retain your IP address and/or other machine-identifying information in order to … track downloading and uploading of files from your computer, to gather broad anonymous demographic information (such as the number of visitors from a geographic area), to enforce compliance with our End User's License Agreement …" The EULA also states that Altnet "may share your personally identifiable information with third parties."

The makers of Kazaa have built some security measures into their program to prevent users from coming across inappropriate content. For example, the family filter is designed to block content containing inappropriate material (see Figure 3-8). Kazaa also has integrated a virus scanner into their product called Bullguard, which scans files located in "My Shared Folder" for viruses.

So if you decide to allow your kids to use Kazaa Plus, be sure to turn on the family filters, block image files and instant messages, and ensure that your kids only swap content designated with a "gold icon." You should also disable the SuperNote function I mentioned before.

Figure 3-8   Kazaa Family Filter

As I noted earlier, my other big concern about peer-to-peer applications is that when you install them, you may have to install a range of adware and spyware as well. In the next section, I explain the problems these programs as well as another kind of software—malicious software or "malware"—pose to kids.

Privacy Risks from Adware, Spyware, and Malicious Software

As already indicated, adware and spyware programs are used by marketers to direct advertisements and promotions to people. Malware, on the other hand, has a much more harmful purpose: hackers and criminals typically use malware to do such things as steal people's credit card details and passwords, and to break into people's computers.

You or your kids might knowingly or unknowingly install spyware and/or adware that is included as part of an existing application, as part of a web browser plug-in, or is an application itself. Malware can be hidden in applications or inadvertently downloaded onto your computer by your children.

If you don't know whether you or your kids have downloaded some spyware or adware, or don't know what these programs do, then your family's privacy is at risk. Malware is even worse—it threatens the security of everything on your computer. Here is a list of things that popular spyware and adware can do on your computer:

- ○ Record all your personal information, such as name, age, gender, postal address, e-mail address, marital status, occupation, and the name of your ISP.

- ○ Record every website you visit.

- ○ Record keywords you type into a search engine.

- ○ Record information you fill in using online forms.

- ○ Form a profile on your personal interests.

- ○ Display targeted advertising to you when you visit websites.

- ○ Hijack legitimate advertising on websites and replace the ads with their own.

- ○ Add text and links on web pages to divert your attention elsewhere.

- ○ Display intrusive pop-up advertising on your computer.

- ○ Install third-party software on your computer without your knowledge.

- ○ Replace search engine results with other links.

- ○ Route your Internet purchases through third-party computers in order to siphon off commissions, which would have gone to the legitimate website.

- ○ Provide the resources of your computer (storage space and processing power) to other companies to use.

- ○ Use your Internet bandwidth to store and serve Internet content, thus costing you money in Internet fees.

Malicious software can do the following:

- ○ Use your modem to disconnect you from the Internet and then reconnect you via an expensive 1-900 number, all without your knowledge.

- ○ Record every key you press on the keyboard.

- ○ Capture your passwords.

- ○ Exploit security flaws in your computer and allow hackers to break in.

| note | *A list of applications and the third-party software, spyware, and adware within them can be found in the appendix at the back of this book.* |

You can combat third-party software, adware, and spyware by installing malware-detection software and then removing the programs it finds. Malware-detection software is like antivirus software, except it detects malicious software rather than viruses. Chapter 8 has additional information about malicious software detection.

Apart from finding and removing third-party software, adware, and spyware, you should tell your kids where these programs come from and how to avoid them.

For example, advise them to stay clear of free peer-to-peer applications that contain third-party software. Also, tell them to beware of downloading seemingly free software because this may contain third-party software, spyware, or adware.

The Claria Corporation produces a free software program, the Gator eWallet, that enables you to automatically fill in forms on websites with your personal details. According to The Claria Corporation's privacy statement,[14] the software enables the company to collect the following information about you:

- Some of the web pages viewed
- The amount of time spent at some websites
- Response to GAIN Ads (These are advertisements you click on.)
- Standard web log information (excluding IP Addresses) and system settings
- What software is on the personal computer
- First name, country, city, and five-digit ZIP code
- Non-personally identifiable information on web pages and forms
- Software usage characteristics and preferences

If the Gator eWallet is installed on your computer, you will see two eyes in the shape of an alligator at the bottom-right corner of your screen.

Your kids might also be tricked into installing third-party software, spyware, or adware by visiting a website where a pop-up box appears that claims they have to download a plug-in in order to view the contents of that website. For example, while I was visiting a website, the pop-up box shown in Figure 3-9 appeared.

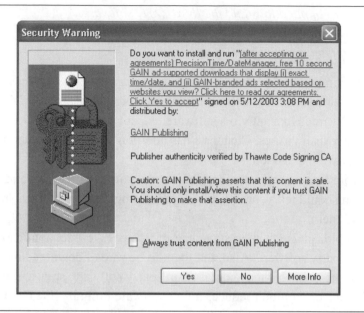

Figure 3-9   Internet Explorer pop-up box with Gator message

At first glance, it looked like I needed a plug-in to view the website, but when I read the text, I saw that it asked me to install the Precision Time and Date Manager. This program also belongs to Claria (The Gator Corporation). You need to educate your children to click No when this type of box appears. Otherwise, if they click Yes, the program will automatically download in the background.

Apart from accidentally downloading third-party software, spyware, or adware, kids can also be tricked into giving away personal information by filling in forms, such as contest forms.

Contests Put Your Privacy at Risk

Websites commonly use contests, sweepstakes, and website registrations to encourage people to reveal information about their identity, hobbies, and other personal preferences."[15] You may not be able to block access to all such websites, so your best strategy is to talk to your children about the risks of submitting personal information to websites and programs they download from the Internet.

Going "Fishing" Isn't What It Used to Be

Phishing (pronounced "fishing") or brand spoofing is where someone (the phisher) impersonates a legitimate organization (or brand) to obtain your personal or financial information. Phishers try to obtain personal information from you so they can steal your identity or defraud you. They commonly attempt to do this via e-mail, where it's relatively easy to impersonate a legitimate organization. However, there have been many elaborate phishing exercises where criminals have set up fake websites with similar domain names to legitimate companies ranging from ISPs to major banks. Popular phishing targets have been eBay, PayPal, and America Online. You can find more information on identity theft on the FTC website at http:// www.consumer.gov/idtheft/.

There are many phishing e-mails circulating on the Internet. I have been on the receiving end of many of them. In one case, I received an e-mail message from what appeared to be eBay. The e-mail read, "During our regular update and verification of the accounts, we could not verify your current information. Either your information has changed or it is incomplete. As a result, your access to bid or buy on eBay has been restricted." I was stunned. At the time I was in the middle of an auction! Then it occurred to me that nobody in their right mind would send me an e-mail asking for my user ID and password, so I decided to take a closer look at the e-mail.

> **tip** *You can report spam to the FTC by sending it to uce@ftc.gov or filling in a complaint form at http://www.ftc.gov.*

The e-mail message looked like it was from eBay. It displayed the eBay logo, TRUSTe logo, copyright information, the same colors, and even allowed me to log in using my eBay user ID and password. The links on the e-mail message all pointed back to the eBay website. But when I inspected the e-mail more closely, I noticed that the user ID and password were not being sent to the eBay website. The form made it look like I was logging onto eBay, but in fact I wasn't. It was a scam, a phishing exercise aimed at compromising my eBay account.

> **tip** *Do not click links or fill in forms contained in e-mail messages. If you must visit the website, type in the main website address into your web browser. Don't use the website address in the e-mail message unless you know for a fact that it is legitimate.*

What lessons can you take away from my phishing experience? Do not respond to e-mail messages asking you for personal information, even if they appear to be legitimate.

Another risk involves the use of the File Transfer Protocol (FTP). As I explain next, your kids may be tempted to download pirated music, games, and other software from illegal FTP sites.

Downloading Pirated Software

FTP sites are used to download files. They existed before the Web was even invented. Nowadays, many files are transferred using the Web; however, many underground (including pirated software sites, known as "warez" (pronounced where's) sites, and pornography sites) still use FTP because it is more efficient than the Web for transferring files. Kids are often tempted to use warez sites because they can obtain music, and particularly computer games and other kinds of software, for free. However, as well as it being illegal to download pirated software programs, these may contain backdoors, viruses, Trojan horses, and spyware, which may cause damage to your computer and compromise your confidential files.

How likely is it that your children will download pirated software from FTP sites or P2P file-sharing networks? That seems to depend on their age. A nationwide survey of 1,000 U.S. children was conducted in May 2004 for the Business Software Alliance (BSA).[16] Children were classified into two groups: tweens (between 8 and 12 years old) and teens (between 13 and 18 years old). The survey revealed that

- 3 percent of tweens and 33 percent of teens said they have illegally downloaded software.

- Tweens are less likely than teens to believe that it is okay to illegally download software (16 percent versus 38 percent).

- Tweens are less likely than teens to say that there are laws against illegally downloading software (40 percent versus 61 percent).

The results point to a severe lack of education among our children, in particular our younger children. When kids were asked why they thought downloading illegal software is okay,[17] they said:

- I do not have money to pay for software (51 percent).

- I wouldn't use the software if I had to pay for it (35 percent).

- Lots of people do it (33 percent).

- It doesn't hurt anybody when I do this (26 percent).

○ No one has ever told me not to do it (19 percent).

○ I won't get in trouble for doing it (15 percent).

○ My parents have said it is okay (8 percent).

What would your child say about downloading pirated software or music from the Internet? You can find out by downloading a free educational curriculum from The Business Software Alliance at http://www.playitcybersafe.com. While the educational curriculum is in the form of a test, you can run through it with your kids as a part of your discussion on Internet safety and family values. I'm sure you will find the results interesting.

Downloading pirated software carries huge penalties. In the U.S., a criminal prosecution by the government can result in a fine up to $250,000 and a maximum of five years in jail, and a civil action by the copyright owner can result in a fine of up to $150,000 for each program copied.[18]

Most Internet-filtering programs will enable you to prevent your children from accessing such sites. However, new warez sites are published every day, so if your children are dedicated to downloading pirated software, they will find them. The best way to deal with this is to use a combination of Internet-filtering software and talking with your child and explaining why it is not a good idea for them to download this software.

FTP programs are legitimate tools for quickly transferring files. I personally use FTP software in order to update my website. Unfortunately, it can also be used to transfer inappropriate or illegal content.

You can find out if an FTP program is already installed on your computer by looking for the icons (pictures) on your desktop. Microsoft Windows users will also find them in the Start | Programs menu. Apple Mac users will find them in the File Menu.

I explain how to remove FTP software at the end of this chapter. However, removing these programs alone will not stop your children from using FTP. This is because many computer operating systems, such as Windows, have FTP software built into them. The built-in Microsoft FTP software is complex to use, so it's unlikely that your children will even know it's there. The best way to remove this software is to use a firewall. More information on firewalls can be found in Chapter 6.

Malicious Viruses, Worms, and Trojans

A "virus" is a computer program that is malicious or destructive in nature. A virus "infects" your computer by attaching itself to a legitimate program to replicate itself. Viruses contain "payloads," which are a list of instructions that cause damage to your computer. The damage caused by payloads can range from the corruption or deletion of computer files to disclosing confidential information to another computer. At the time of writing, my virus scanner reported the existence of 65,332 known viruses and variants, Trojan horse programs, and other malicious software.[19]

A "worm" is similar to a virus in that it can cause damage, but unlike a virus, a worm replicates by itself. It doesn't rely on a computer file as a host. Worms replicate and infest computer networks by many different means. These include taking advantage of Internet connections, computer networks, instant messaging applications, and security flaws in computer software.

Similar to the ancient Trojan horse, today's electronic version is an application that looks innocent—appears to perform a legitimate function—but really has a destructive purpose. For example, a Trojan might seem to be an innocent computer game, but in the background it installs a back door for hackers to break into your computer.

In fact, viruses, worms, and Trojans can all be downloaded from the Internet in the guise of games, applications, zip files, and even plug-ins for your web browser.

Many new viruses and worms exploit security flaws in Internet applications such as Internet Explorer. Some can send themselves to your friends using chat programs such as Instant Messenger or e-mail programs such as Microsoft Outlook. Many new worms are built to live on the Internet, infecting machine after machine. In order for your computer to be infected by a worm, you may not have to download a file; you could be vulnerable by simply having an insecure Internet connection or by not being up to date with the latest security patches for your operating system.

It is not clear why some people persist in writing viruses. Presumably, some virus writers crave attention from their peers, others want a challenge, and some may want to expose insecure programming practices. Whatever the reason, virus writers and their viruses are getting "smarter," with the latest viruses propagating using other applications and causing more destruction than ever before.

Kids are easy targets for viruses, worms, and Trojan horses because they are more likely to click strange e-mails and download programs if they seem fun or cute.[20] Virus writers know this and deliberately make viruses attractive to children. The Pokemon virus, released in August 2000, was one such virus specifically aimed at children. This virus came in the form of an e-mail message that read as follows:

Subject: Pikachu Pokemon

Great Friend!

Pikachu from Pokemon Theme have some friendly words to say.

Visit Pikachu at http://www.pikachu.com

See you.

The virus was contained in a file attached to the e-mail message. The file featured a cute animation of the yellow rabbit-like Pokemon called Pikachu. When children clicked the file attachment, the virus was activated and began to destroy all the computer files in the Windows and system directories, the files used by the Microsoft Windows operating system to operate the computer. If a victim's virus scanner wasn't up to date then the only way they could recover from the virus attack was to reinstall the files from scratch.

In March 2004, a virus writer modified an existing worm to take advantage of the excitement surrounding the release of the film "Harry Potter and the Prisoner of Azkaban." The Harry Potter worm (also known as Netsky-P) masquerades as content such as:

○ Harry Potter 1-6 book.txt.exe

○ Harry Potter 5.mpg.exe

○ Harry Potter all e.book.doc.exe

○ Harry Potter e book.doc.exe

○ Harry Potter game.exe

○ Harry Potter.doc.exe

Your children may think these files are Harry Potter books, movies, or games, but they are actually copies of the virus. This particular virus can also disguise itself as other file names in order to target your children: Britney Spears full album.mp3.exe, Eminem Song text archive.doc.exe, American Idol.doc.exe, and Ringtones.mp3.exe.

While most viruses spread via e-mail, this particular virus also spreads by P2P file-sharing networks. Therefore, if your kids use popular file-sharing programs and perform a search using the keywords "harry potter", they may unintentionally download the virus and infect your computer.

A simple rule for your kids to follow is that if they don't know or trust the sender or the website, they shouldn't download the file. An even more prudent approach is for your kids to avoid downloading any file you are not expecting. This is because even a sender they trust may have had their e-mail address spoofed (forged), or may have unwittingly sent them a virus or worm. Also, if you follow the next few steps, you will be able to detect and prevent most viruses from destroying information on your computer:

1. Install antivirus software from a well-known vendor. Chapter 7 contains a list of programs I recommend.

2. Configure the software to update itself on a daily basis, preferably every 30 minutes while you are connected to the Internet. This will retrieve the latest virus signature files from the vendor and ensure that you are protected from the latest virus outbreak. If you or your kids rarely use the Internet, make it a habit of connecting once a week and downloading the latest updates. This will ensure you are protected from any new viruses your children may inadvertently download from the Internet or bring home on a floppy disk or CD.

3. Install all the security patches and fixes available from your software vendors (i.e., the makers of all the software you use). For example, if you are running Microsoft Windows, use the Windows Update feature to install the latest "critical" updates and service packs, as well as those that are not so critical, such as driver updates and operating system updates. You can do this by starting Internet Explorer and clicking Tools | Windows Update. If you have a fast (cable or ADSL) Internet connection, this process will take under an hour.

I believe that if you take these steps, 95 percent of viruses won't destroy your data because most new viruses are programmed in one of two ways:

○ **Using code from other viruses, which makes them easy for antivirus vendors to detect**   There is a high probability that your antivirus vendor will have programmed their software to detect and clean the virus before it infects your computer. If you configure your software to download the latest updates all the time, you should be able to recognize and clean the virus, and thereby avoid infection.

○ **To exploit security flaws (vulnerabilities) in software**   By the time virus writers get around to writing a virus that takes advantage of a security flaw, the application vendor has usually already written a program (patch) to fix the flaw. If you keep abreast of the latest security patches, a virus should not be able to infect your computer. This is because your software vendor has patched the security flaw that the virus takes advantage of.

Information on antivirus programs and how to configure them can be found in Chapter 7.

Throughout this chapter, I have mentioned that you can find and remove software programs from your computer that you don't want your children to use. In the following section, I explain how to remove these computer programs, except spyware, adware, and malware, which I cover in Chapter 8.

Removing Dangerous Software

Software can be very difficult to remove once it's installed on your computer. Most commercial software programs come with an uninstall program; however, malicious software isn't so generous, and you will most likely need specialized tools to remove it. So where do you start?

Finding Software Installed on Your Computer

In the same manner as checking into a hotel, most commercial software should "register" itself with your computer when it installs. You can find a list of installed programs by doing the following:

Windows 95/98 Users

1. Click Start and select Settings.

2. Click the Control Panel icon.

3. Double-click Add/Remove Programs.

Windows XP Users

1. Click Start and select Control Panel.

2. Double-click Add or Remove Programs.

Apple Mac Users (OS X)

1. From the Finder, select "File" and scroll to "Find."

2. Type in the name of the program you're seeking.

Finding Specific Files

You can find a file on your computer by doing the following:

Windows 95/98 Users

1. Click Start and select Find.

2. Click the Files and Folders icon.

3. Enter the name of the program in the box titled Name and put "*.*" after it (for example, morpheus*.*).

   This will find all the files on your computer with the name morpheus. You can then delete these particular files. Be very careful when doing this because you may accidentally delete something legitimate.

Windows XP Users

1. Click Start and select Search.

2. Follow the prompts.

Please note that there are many ways that files can be hidden on your computer. The techniques outlined in this chapter should enable you to find files that have not been intentionally hidden.

If your child is extremely advanced, they will have ways of hiding software programs. Fortunately, these programs won't work if you implement a firewall and filtering product, as discussed in the following chapters.

Removing Software

Here is the process for removing software from your computer, using mIRC as an example:

Windows 95/98 Users

1. Click Start and select Settings.

2. Click the Control Panel icon.

3. Double-click Add/Remove Programs.

4. Click mIRC in the list of programs.

5. Click the "remove" button.

6. Follow the prompts.

Windows XP Users

1. Click Start and select Control Panel.

2. Double-click Add or Remove Programs.

3. Click mIRC in the list of programs.

4. Click the "remove" button.

5. Follow the prompts.

Apple Mac OS X Users

There are a number of ways to uninstall programs in Mac OS X.

1. Use the uninstall program if it's provided.

2. Start the installation program and select "Uninstall" from the Easy Install menu.

3. Drag the icon into the trash.

You can find more information about uninstalling applications using Mac OS X at http://aroundcny.com/technofile/texts/mac031004.html.

So now you know how the various Internet applications endanger your kids, and you have discussed the risks with them. Your next step is to obtain the software tools you need to complete your defense. I have examined what I believe to be the top programs available in each category of software you need. Read on to work out which of these programs suit your needs and budget.

Endnotes

1. Batty, David, 2002. "Children unaware of Internet dangers." Guardian Newspapers Limited. http://society.guardian.co.uk/children/story/ 0,1074,757307,00.html. August 24, 2003.

2. Symantec, 2003. "Symantec Survey Revels More Than 80 Percent of Children Using Email Receive Inappropriate Spam Daily." http://www.symantec.com/press/2003/n030609a.html. August 24, 2003.

3. Sullivan, Bob, 2003. "Who profits from spam? Surprise." MSNBC. http://www.msnbc.com/news/940490.asp. August 24, 2003.

4. Batty, David, 2002. "Children unaware of Internet dangers." Guardian Newspapers Limited. http://society.guardian.co.uk/children/story/ 0,1074,757307,00.html. August 24, 2003.

5. Jenkins, Chris, 2003. "Yahoo sits tight on chat rooms." Australian IT. http://australianit.news.com.au/articles/0,7204,7360959%5E15318% 5E%5Enbv%5E15306,00.html. September 24, 2003.

6. Reuters, 2003. "Microsoft to Shut Down Chat Rooms." Wired. http:// www.wired.com/news/culture/0,1284,60567,00.html. September 23, 2003.

7. Denizet-Lewis, Benoit, 2004. "Friends, Friends With Benefits and the Benefits of the Local Mall." *The New York Times*. http://www.nytimes.com/ 2004/05/30/magazine/30NONDATING.html?ex=1087531200&en=96e718 d8877f1319&ei=5070&pagewanted=1. May 30, 2004.

8. Hot or Not. "Terms of Service." http://meetme.hotornot.com. June 17, 2004.

9. Denizet-Lewis, Benoit, 2004. "Friends, Friends With Benefits and the Benefits of the Local Mall." *The New York Times*. http://www.nytimes.com/ 2004/05/30/magazine/30NONDATING.html?ex=1087531200&en=96e718 d8877f1319&ei=5070&pagewanted=1. May 30, 2004.

10. BuddyPic.com, 2004. "Privacy Policy." http://www.buddypic.com/ privacypolicy.php. June 17, 2004.

11. Dean, Katie, 2003. "RIAA Hits Students Where It Hurts." Wired. http://www.wired.com/news/digiwood/0,1412,58351,00.html. August 24, 2003.

12. Bridis, Ted, 2003. "Girl, 12, settles piracy suit." News Limited. http://www.news.com.au/common/story_page/ 0,4057,7223447% 255E15306,00.html. September 10, 2003.

13. United States General Accounting Office, 2002. "Why GAO did this study in Combating child pornography." GAO. http://www.gao.gov/highlights/d03272high.pdf. August 24, 2003.

14. The GAIN Publishing Privacy Statement and End User License Agreement ("Terms and Conditions"). http://www.gainpublishing.com/help/app_privacy/app_ps_v51.html.

15. National School Boards Foundation. "Research and Guidelines for Children's Use of the Internet." NSBF. http://www.nsbf.org/safe-smart/overview.htm. August 24, 2003.

16. BSA, 2004. "New Survey Shows that Teens Are More Likely to Illegally Download Than Tweens." http://www.bsa.org/usa/press/newsreleases/New-Survey-Shows-that-Teens-Are-More-Likely-to-Illegally-Download.cfm. May 26, 2004.

17. BSA, 2004. "Majority of Youth Understand Copyright But Many Continue To Download Illegally." http://www.bsa.org/usa/press/newsreleases/Majority-of-Youth-Understand-Copyright.cfm. May 18, 2004.

18. BSAA, 2004. "Piracy and the law." BSAA. http://www.bsa.org/usa/antipiracy/Piracy-and-the-Law.cfm. March 19, 2004.

19. McAfee. "DAT 4248, Engine 4160." Network Associates. http://www.nai.com/us/downloads/updates/default.asp. February 19, 2003.

20. Meares, Richard, 2000. "Cuddly Pokemon Virus Targets Kids." TechTV Inc. http://www.techtv.com/news/internet/story/0,24195,7629,00.html. August 24, 2003.

PART II

The Best (Not Necessarily the Most Expensive) Software to Protect Your Kids

CHAPTER 4

Content-Filtering Software

In this chapter I explain what content-filtering software does and the results of my comprehensive evaluations of the top eight content-filtering products. You will see that, based on my evaluations, I recommend certain products. I have included my rationale for these recommendations as well as some pointers for you to keep in mind for selecting the best product for protecting your children.

To Filter or Not to Filter—That Is the Question!

Filtering access to websites is a controversial issue. While conducting research for this book, I found that most parents either used filtering software or planned to purchase it to protect their kids. However, I also found people who opposed the use of Internet-filtering software. They considered it more important to educate their children and trust them not to access inappropriate material.

In theory, I agree with the view that if you educate and trust your kids—and keep an eye on what they are doing on the Internet—then filtering should be unnecessary. After all, implementing filtering software may seem a little heavy handed and as undermining the trusting relationship you are trying to develop with your children.

However, all the trust in the world won't prevent your children from inadvertently accessing some inappropriate websites, and that's where content-filtering software is useful.

For example, your kids could be using a search engine to find out information about their favorite singer and then find that some of the search results lead them to a pornographic website. This happens because some pornographic websites use keywords that are common words for children to use. If you have ever performed a search using the word "Barbie" or "Britney," you will almost certainly come across pornographic websites and other inappropriate content. Other websites use domain names that are likely to be used by kids. For example, who would have thought that a website called boys.com would be a pornographic website?

Some search engines have recognized this problem and are trying to filter out inappropriate sites from their search results. However, this is nearly impossible because such websites can simply use normal keywords to ensure that they appear in a list of results.

If you are not concerned about your kids viewing something pornographic, then the possibility of them accidentally coming across such a site may not trouble you. It is also hard to say how likely it is that your kids will inadvertently come across inappropriate content. But if you are at all concerned about this possibility—as I am—then I recommend implementing content-filtering software.

Are Your Kids Protected at School?

I also believe that schools and libraries should use content-filtering software to protect kids. Again, you may be concerned about schools and libraries having too much control over what your children do on the Internet, but this concern must be balanced against the risk of your kids viewing inappropriate material.

This is a view shared by the U.S. Government, which, by means of the Children's Internet Protection Act (CIPA), requires schools and libraries that use federal e-rate subsidies to install a "technology protection measure" on their computers. A "technology protection measure" is defined as a specific technology that blocks or filters Internet access. By law, it must prevent anyone from viewing child pornography and minors from visual depictions that are harmful or obscene.

Assuming you have decided to implement content filtering, let's first consider a couple of filtering tools you already have at your disposal—and that cost you nothing.

note | *AOL users may want to use both the Parental Control and Internet Access Control features. You can use the Parental Control features to filter websites and also restrict the amount of time your kids spend on the Internet. The Internet Access Control features will help prevent your kids from using an external web browser (such as Internet Explorer) to access the Internet. For more information, go to Keyword: AOL Parental Controls.*

Use the Content Advisor in Your Web Browser

Some web browsers have a "Content Advisor" that can block inappropriate websites; this is a free tool you may be able to put into place right away. The Content Advisor works only for websites that have been labeled by a third party labeling system such as the Internet Content Rating Association (ICRA, http://www.icra.org). While labeling systems are good, they are not foolproof: some websites label themselves rather than getting ICRA to rate them.

| caution | *Turning the Content Advisor on doesn't mean you don't need an Internet-filtering program; it merely strengthens your defenses.* |

You can turn this feature on in Internet Explorer by doing the following:

1. Click Tools and then Internet Options. The Internet Options dialog box, shown in Figure 4-1, appears.

2. Click the Content tab in the Internet Options dialog box.

Figure 4-1   The Internet Options dialog box in Internet Explorer

3. Click the Enable button, shown in Figure 4-2. The Content Advisor
   dialog box appears.

Figure 4-2   The content tab allows you to enable the Content Advisor.

4. Adjust the settings in the
   Content Advisor dialog
   box to allow or deny
   certain levels of content,
   as shown in Figure 4-3.

Figure 4-3   The Ratings tab allows you to adjust the level
              of language, nudity, sex, and violence.

5. Click the General tab, shown in Figure 4-4.

Figure 4-4   The Content Advisor dialog box has a number of options that can be customized to meet your needs.

6. Click the Create Password button. This opens the Create Supervisor Password dialog box as shown in Figure 4-5.

7. Click on the OK button.

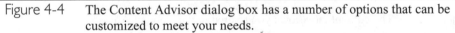

Figure 4-5   Setting a password ensures that your children cannot change the content settings in Internet Explorer.

Your settings have been saved. The password allows only you to alter the settings and prevents your children from tampering with them.

You Can Use Search Engine Filtering Too

Some search engines provide a filtering option whereby they filter out inappropriate content. However, this is not 100 percent foolproof and will not prevent your children from typing in an Internet address such as www.playboy.com into the web browser. What it will do is filter out some of the inappropriate results of Internet searches conducted using those search engines.

Unfortunately, search engine filters prevent legitimate websites from being displayed. A report by the Harvard Law School's Berkman Center for Internet & Society revealed that thousands of legitimate websites were not displayed in search engine results provided by Google.[1] These included the White House, IBM, and Mattel's website about its game of scrabble. Google questioned this study as some of the sites had a robots.txt file, which places limitations on what the crawler (robot) can actually index. A quick check using Google revealed that these sites are no longer blocked. In any case, you can use the filters on the major search engines by following the steps outlined in the following subsections.

AltaVista

The AltaVista site has a family filter that is controlled by setting a password. You can turn it on by doing the following:

1. Visit http://www.altavista.com/web/ffset.

2. Check the box labeled All.

3. Type in a password. Then type it in again to confirm it.

4. Click the button Save Your Settings.

That's it! From now on, any searches performed by AltaVista will be filtered.

> **note** *Should AltaVista change the URL at http://www.altavista.com/ web/ffset, you can access the menu by visiting the main website at http://www.altavista.com and clicking More >> from the Tools section and then clicking Family Friendly Filter.*

Google

The Internet-filtering option for Google.com is very easy to use. You can turn it on by following these instructions:

1. Visit http://www.google.com/preferences?hl=en.

2. Under SafeSearch Filtering, click the option Use Strict Filtering (see Figure 4-6).

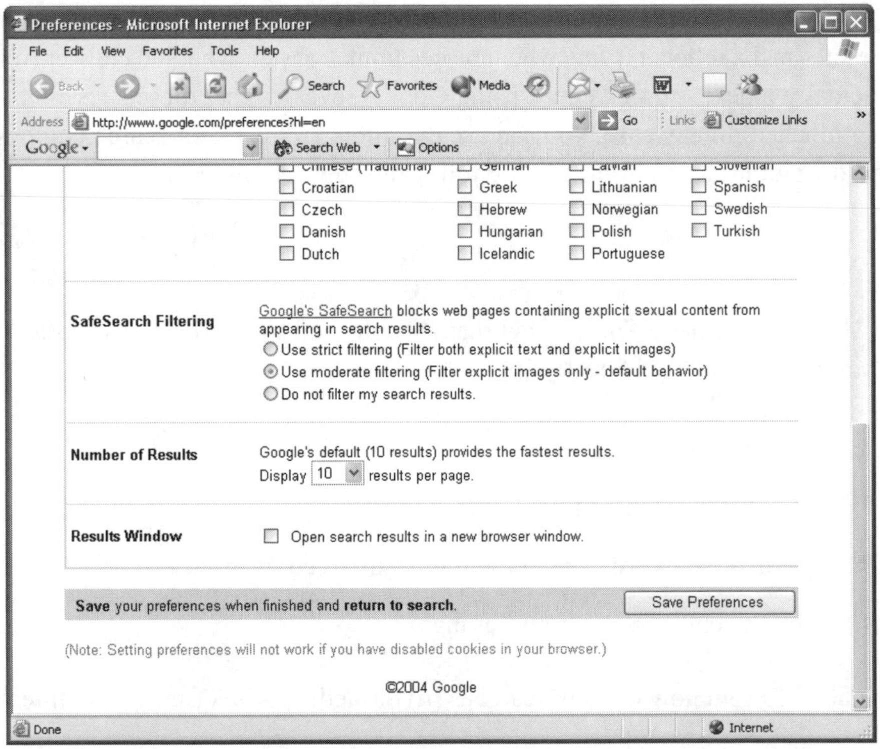

Figure 4-6   Google SafeSearch filtering blocks some web pages that contain inappropriate content.

3. Click the Save Preferences button.

That's it! From now on, any searches performed by Google will be filtered.

> note *Should Google change the URL at http://www.google.com/ preferences?hl=en, you can access the menu by visiting the main website at http://www.google.com and clicking Preferences.*

Lycos

The Lycos website has a similar filtering mechanism to that of Google. To turn it on, follow these steps:

1. Visit http://searchguard.lycos.com/.

2. Enter a password and a hint.

3. Click the Submit button.

> note *Should Lycos change the URL at http://searchguard.lycos.com, you can access the menu by visiting the main website at http://www.lycos.com and clicking More>> and then Parental Controls.*

AOL Users

Unlike the Internet, AOL is a closed, controlled community. Although AOL gives users access to the Internet, parents can restrict what their children see by implementing AOL's Internet-filtering feature, AOL Parental Controls, or opting to use KOL, a kids version of AOL.

Unlike traditional AOL, KOL is designed for kids aged between 6 and 12 years old. It provides games, music, moderated chat, cartoons, homework help, and a daily radio program for kids. KOL has Parental Controls built in, so you can still control what your kids have access to. You can find more information on the AOL website at http://www.aol.com/optimized/family.adp.

Part II

The Best Software to Protect Your Kids

AOL Parent Controls takes a "whitelist approach" by banning access to everything except certain sites. Although this is very effective, the downside is that your children will only have access to a snapshot of what is available on the Internet. This may be appropriate for young kids who are still learning about computers and use the Internet for basic games, but it may be too restrictive for teens.

For example, after creating an AOL profile for a young teenage girl (aged 13–15), I used the "AOL Teen Search" facility to perform a search on the phrase "women's health." Out of the six results displayed, only one was relevant to the topic. When I clicked the link, the website turned out to be owned by a pharmaceutical company that displayed some very basic advice before selling its product as the solution.

In another example using my teenage daughter's profile, I was able to access the CNN website but not the *LA Times* website.

Although it is a fairly simple matter for your kids to request your (a parent's) permission to access a given website, it may not always be practical.

If you have older kids, you can choose the AOL Parental Controls mature teen setting (aged 16–17). This allows your kids to access a wider range of sites, as well as giving them full access to e-mail, instant messaging, and chat.

If you use AOL, consider testing AOL Parental Controls. However, if after using it for some time, you consider it to be too restrictive for your kids, I suggest using regular content-filtering software that integrates with AOL. You can find a list of software that supports AOL in Table 4-7 later in this chapter.

Content-Filtering Software

You can purchase Internet-filtering software to prevent your children from visiting inappropriate websites and to prevent certain e-mails from being sent to them. Many products listed in this chapter filter websites reasonably well, but their e-mail-filtering capability is very poor. Chapter 5 provides information on e-mail-filtering software in detail.

Internet-filtering software will not give you 100 percent protection. The extent to which it will protect your children while they are online depends on the quality of the filtering software and how you configure it.

> **note** *In some cases, content-filtering software may block access to sites that are not inappropriate. This is known as a "false positive."*

How Content-Filtering Software Works

There are three main methods to filtering out inappropriate websites:

- Inclusion filtering
- Exclusion filtering
- Acceptability filtering

How Inclusion Filtering Works

The philosophy behind inclusion filtering is "guilty until proven innocent." That is, the program presumes everything is inappropriate unless you say otherwise.

Inclusion filtering allows you to select specific websites that your children can visit. Websites that are not in this list are blocked. In order to save you time, many software products come with a list of sites that are deemed appropriate for children, otherwise known as a "whitelist." The main disadvantage of this approach is that the lists of legitimate sites tend to be very small, and you will be blocking access to many other good information resources that are yet to be classified.

How Exclusion Filtering Works

The philosophy behind exclusion filtering is "innocent until proven guilty," meaning that the program allows your children to visit any website on the Internet, other than those listed in particular categories. These banned categories are known as "blacklists" or "blocking lists," which you can determine. The main disadvantage of this method is that sites that are yet to be classified are not blocked. This is due to the fact that vendors have to manually visit and classify websites, and the Internet is rapidly expanding with thousands of new websites being published each day.

How Acceptability Filtering Works

This method examines content and blocks it when it fails certain tests. Such tests could include detecting skin tone in graphics files or profanity found in chat room conversations. This method is prone to errors. For example, if you are blocking content based on the presence of skin tone, it is very difficult to distinguish a pornographic image from a legitimate image (for example, an image displayed for medical purposes). Also, some content filters in use today still block the word "breast," which could be used in searching for information on "breast cancer" and "breast feeding."

Results of My Tests of Content-Filtering Software

I tested eight content-filtering software products (listed in alphabetical order in Table 4-1) to determine which ones are the most and least effective in filtering out inappropriate content.

Keep in my mind that other content-filtering products are available that may be appropriate for your needs. You can still use the methodology I have used to evaluate the products listed in Table 4-1 to analyze a program I haven't looked at.

The next major section of this chapter provides the results of my evaluation of each product, and each of the critical features I believe are essential for an Internet-filtering program. After this, I include a discussion of each individual program.

Application Name	Version	Website Address
Privacy Service	4.0.1.24	http://www.mcafee.com
CyberPatrol	6.1.0.27	http://www.cyberpatrol.com
Cyber Sentinel	3.4.1.0	http://www.securitysoft.com
CYBERsitter	2003.4.1.30	http://www.cybersitter.com
Cyber Snoop	4.062	http://www.pearlsw.com
Net Nanny	5.0.600.11	http://www.netnanny.com
Optenet PC	8.0.2 build 242	http://www.optenet.com
We-Blocker	2.1.0 build 82	http://www.we-blocker.com

Table 4-1   The Content-Filtering Software Products I Tested

Table 4-2 shows the software used to test the Internet-filtering applications.

Application	Version	Application	Version
Internet Explorer	6.0.2800	Kazaa	2.6
Opera	7.23	BearShare	4.3.5
Netscape	7.1	eDonkey 2000	0.52
Outlook	2000	Overnet	0.52
Agent	1.93/32.576	Piolet	1.05
mIRC	6.12	Blubster	2.5
AOL IM	5.1	Grokster	2.6
ICQ	Pro 2003b	WinMX	3.31
MSN Messenger	6.1	IMesh	4.2 Build 137
Yahoo Messenger	5.6	Morpheus	4.0
Windows Messenger	4.7	LimeWire	3.8.3

Table 4-2   Software Used to Test the Content-Filtering Applications

Minimum System Requirements

If you have an old computer and are not sure that the filtering software will run on it, you must look at this issue closely. The last thing you need is to buy some software, only to find that your computer is not powerful enough to run it. However, if you have purchased a computer within the last two or three years, you shouldn't have any problems.

Some Internet-filtering applications consume a lot of memory and processing power, so understand that these are minimum requirements. Ideally, your computer should have more memory (in megabytes), processing power (the power of its central processing unit, or CPU), and hard disk space (in megabytes or gigabytes) than what I mention here. If not, you will find that the Internet-filtering application will slow down your computer considerably, and you may end up not being able to use the software at all.

Tables 4-3 to 4-6 provide the minimum hard disk, RAM, CPU, and operating system requirements for your computer in order to run content filtering software. Table 4-7 provides you with a list of web browsers that are supported.

	Privacy Service	CyberPatrol	Net Nanny	Cyber Sentinel	CYBERsitter	Optenet	Cyber Snoop	We-Blocker
3MB					Yes			
5MB								Yes
10MB	Yes			Yes		Yes		
20MB							Yes	
30MB		Yes						
50MB			Yes					

Table 4-3   Minimum Hard Disk Requirements for Internet-Filtering Applications

	Privacy Service	CyberPatrol	Net Nanny	Cyber Sentinel	CYBERsitter	Optenet	Cyber Snoop	We-Blocker
4MB							Yes	
32MB	Yes		Yes		Yes			
64MB		Yes		Yes		Yes		Yes

Table 4-4   Minimum RAM Requirements for Internet-Filtering Applications

	Privacy Service	CyberPatrol	Net Nanny	Cyber Sentinel	CYBERsitter	Optenet	Cyber Snoop	We-Blocker
486 at 66 MHz							Yes	
Pentium 100 MHz	Yes							
Pentium 120 MHz			Yes		Yes	Yes		
Pentium 166 MHz				Yes				
Pentium 200 MHz								Yes
Pentium II 233 MHz		Yes						

Table 4-5   Minimum CPU Requirements for Internet-Filtering Applications

	Privacy Service	CyberPatrol	Net Nanny	Cyber Sentinel	CYBERsitter	Optenet	Cyber Snoop	We-Blocker
Windows 95	No	No	No	No	Yes	No	Yes	Yes
Windows 98	Yes	Yes	Yes	Yes	Yes	Yes	Yes	Yes
Windows 98 Second Edition	Yes	Yes	Yes	Yes	Yes	Yes	Yes	Yes
Windows Me	Yes	Yes	Yes	Yes	Yes	Yes	Yes	Yes
Windows XP Home	Yes	Yes	Yes	Yes	Yes	Yes	Yes	Yes
Windows XP Professional	Yes	Yes	Yes	Yes	Yes	Yes	Yes	Yes
Windows 2000 Professional	Yes	Yes	Yes	Yes	Yes	Yes	Yes	Yes
Windows NT 4.0 Workstation	No	Yes	Yes	Yes	Yes	Yes	Yes	Yes

Table 4-6   Operating Systems That Support Content-Filtering Applications

	Privacy Service	CyberPatrol	Net Nanny	Cyber Sentinel	CYBERsitter	Optenet	Cyber Snoop	We-Blocker
AOL	Yes	Yes*		Yes	Yes		Yes**	Yes***
Internet Explorer 4.0 SP2		Yes		Yes	Yes	Yes	Yes	Yes
Internet Explorer 5.01 SP2			Yes					
Internet Explorer 5.5 SP2	Yes							
Netscape 6.0		Yes						
Netscape Navigator 4.08			Yes		Yes	Yes	Yes	
Netscape 3.02								Yes

* CyberPatrol 6.2 is compatible with AOL 9.

** Cyber Snoop has a sister product called "Cyber Snoop for AOL."

*** We-Blocker supports AOL version 6.0 and up.

Table 4-7   Minimum Web Browser Requirements for Internet-Filtering Applications

The More Types of Blocking, the Better

There are many ways to block inappropriate content. You can block certain keywords and websites that are known to contain inappropriate material, and you can also analyze the context and structure of the material. Although there is no "best" approach, a product that uses different techniques to block inappropriate content will decrease the likelihood of your children coming across anything untoward.

It is critical that your software has as many of the characteristics shown in Table 4-8 as possible.

Product	Blacklists	Keyword Analysis	Context Sensitive	Pattern Analysis
Privacy Service	Yes	Yes	Yes	No
CyberPatrol	Yes	Yes	Yes	Yes
Net Nanny	Yes	Yes	Yes	No
Cyber Sentinel	Yes	Yes	No	No
CYBERsitter	Yes	Yes	Yes	Yes
Optenet	Yes	No	No	Yes
Cyber Snoop	Yes	Yes	No	No
We-Blocker	Yes	Yes	No	No

Table 4-8   Blocking Characteristics for Internet-Filtering Applications

No product can categorize every website on the Internet. As previously discussed, some products use "blacklists" to block out inappropriate sites; others use keyword analysis to determine what content could be on the web page. Many companies have created their own "pattern analysis" criteria to determine sites that are inappropriate. These three characteristics combined can be a very powerful tool to block out a large proportion of content. If your product has all three, you are doing everything to make sure the content won't get through.

Do You Speak Another Language?

Not everyone in the world speaks English. More than one billion people in China and nearby countries speak Mandarin (also called Chinese, even though there are actually two main Chinese languages—Mandarin and Cantonese). Hindi, English, Spanish, and Russian are in the top five.[2] If English is your second language, you may prefer to use a filter in your native tongue. It's important to note that the filter itself doesn't block inappropriate content written in another language; it's the user interface (or computer program itself) that's written in another language. Table 4-9 details the languages supported by the content-filtering applications.

Filter	English	Italian	Spanish	Portuguese	French	German
Privacy Service	Yes	Yes*	Yes*	No	Yes*	Yes*
CyberPatrol	Yes	No	No	No	No	No
Net Nanny	Yes	No	No	No	No	No
Cyber Sentinel	Yes	No	No	No	No	No
CYBERsitter	Yes	No	No	No	No	No
Optenet	Yes	Yes	Yes	Yes	Yes	Yes
Cyber Snoop	Yes	No	No	No	No	No
We-Blocker	Yes	No	No	No	No	No

* The functionality may vary.

Table 4-9   Language Support for Internet-Filtering Applications

Filtering Different Types of Programs

Your kids can be exposed to Internet threats in any number of ways. If your content-filtering application does not block particular Internet applications, it will only be partially effective in protecting your children. For example, your child may not be able to use a web browser to accidentally view pornography, but might be able to get onto a chat program and talk to a pedophile. The applications listed in Table 4-10 through Table 4-13 are necessary for a full Internet experience, but they are also some of the most dangerous because they can expose your children to Internet threats. Table 4-14 tallies up the total number of content types blocked by the Internet-filtering applications.

Application	Privacy Service	CyberPatrol	Net Nanny	Cyber Sentinel	CYBERsitter	Optenet	Cyber Snoop	We-Blocker
Internet Explorer	Yes	Yes	Yes	Yes	Yes	Yes	Yes	Yes
Netscape	Yes	Yes	Yes	Yes	Yes	No	No	No
Opera	No**	Yes	No	No	Yes	No	No#	No
Outlook	Yes***	No	Yes	No	Yes	No	Yes	No
mIRC	Yes	No*	Yes	No	No	No	Yes	No

* CyberPatrol claims to filter chat based on keywords sent from the other person. You can specifically block the application from running in the first instance.

** The application blocked part of a web page that contained inappropriate content.

*** Outlook froze while trying to download e-mail containing inappropriate content.

\# The software caused the web browser to crash.

Table 4-10   Web Browsing, E-mail, and Chat Programs—Content Blocked by Internet-Filtering Applications

Application	Privacy Service	CyberPatrol	Net Nanny	Cyber Sentinel	CYBERsitter	Optenet	Cyber Snoop	We-Blocker
AOL	Yes	Yes*	No*	No	Yes*	No	No#	No
ICQ	Yes	Yes*	No*	No	Yes	No	Yes#	No
MSN Messenger	Yes	Yes*	No*	No	Yes*	No	Yes	No
Yahoo Messenger	Yes	Yes*	No*	No	Yes	No	Yes#	No
Windows Messenger	Yes	Yes*	No*	No	Yes*	No	Yes	No

* The program can also be blocked from connecting to the instant messaging service, thus preventing your children from using it.

\# The application did not block the program from connecting to the instant messaging service.

Table 4-11   Instant Messaging Programs—Content Blocked by Internet-Filtering Applications

Application	Privacy Service	CyberPatrol	Net Nanny	Cyber Sentinel	CYBERsitter	Optenet	Cyber Snoop	We-Blocker
Kazaa	No	No	No#	No*	Yes	No	N/A@	No
BearShare	No	No	No#	No*	No	No	No	No
eDonkey	No	No	No#	No*	No	No	No	No
Piolet	No	No	No#	No*	No	No	No%	No
Blubster	No	No	No#	No*	No	No	No%	No
Grokster	No	No	No#	No*	No	No	No	No
WinMX	No	No	No#	Yes	No	No	No	No
IMesh	No	No	No#	No*	No	No	No	No
Morpheus	No	No	No#	No*	No	No	No	No
Overnet	No	No	No	No*	No	No	No	No

* The file-sharing program was minimized, not shut down. Access to inappropriate content is still available when you click (maximize) the icon in the task bar.

\# The file-sharing program can be prevented from running in the first instance (rather than filtering the results or closing down the program).

@ The product could not be tested against this particular file-sharing program due to an incompatibility.

% The file sharing program was prevented from connecting to the peer-to-peer network and therefore was blocked.

Table 4-12   Peer-to-Peer File-Sharing Programs—Content Blocked by Internet-Filtering Applications

Application	Privacy Service	CyberPatrol	Net Nanny	Cyber Sentinel	CYBERsitter	Optenet	Cyber Snoop	We-Blocker
Outlook Newsreader	No	Yes*	Yes#	Yes	Yes	No	Yes	No
Free Agent	No	Yes*	Yes	Yes	Yes	No	Yes	No

* The filter was easily bypassed. However, you can specifically block the application from running in the first instance.

\# The content of the news post was not visible, but I could still connect to the news server, subscribe to newsgroups, and read the subject, name, and e-mail address of the message.

Table 4-13   Usenet Programs—Content Blocked by Internet-Filtering Applications

	Privacy Service	CyberPatrol	Net Nanny	Cyber Sentinel	CYBERsitter	Optenet	Cyber Snoop	We-Blocker
Total:	9	10	6	5	12	1	9	1

Table 4-14   Total Content Blocked by Internet-Filtering Applications

How to Stay Up to Date with the Latest Information

New websites are appearing on the Internet at a staggering rate. Many content filtering vendors keep track of new sites by employing teams of people to review and categorize sites. Your filtering software becomes aware of these new sites when it downloads an update file from the vendor's website.

When you purchase a product, it will typically come with a 12-month license that gives you the ability to receive regular updates. This means that for the term of your license, you can automatically or manually download updates (for example, to your blacklist). Some programs do not include updates at all because they require you to type in sites that you want to block.

If the program includes automatic updates, it should automatically update itself (you don't have to do anything); if it includes manual updates, you have to keep track of any revisions to the product. In general, I recommend getting a filtering program that comes with regular, automatic updates so you can be confident that your filtering is as current as possible. Table 4-15 shows the update features of the Internet-filtering applications.

	Privacy Service	CyberPatrol	Net Nanny	Cyber Sentinel	CYBERsitter	Optenet	Cyber Snoop	We-Blocker
Automatic updates	Yes	Yes	No	No	Yes	Yes	No	Yes
Update daily	No	Yes	Yes	No	No	N/A	No	No
Update weekly	No	Yes	Yes	No	Yes	N/A	No	No
Update hourly	No	No	No	No	No	N/A	No	No
Update monthly	No	No	Yes	No	No	N/A	No	No
Update at startup	No	No	No	No	No	N/A	No	Yes
Update at a specific time	No	No	No	No	No	N/A	No	No
Update manually	Yes	Yes	Yes	Yes	Yes	N/A	Yes	No

Table 4-15   Update Features of the Internet-Filtering Applications

Does Content Filtering Slow Everything Down?

One of the most common complaints I hear about computers in the home is that
they are too slow. Unfortunately, some Internet-filtering applications are not very
well written and consume a lot of computing resources, thus slowing down your
computer. This is compounded even more if you have an old computer because it
probably won't have the memory or processing power to cope with the filtering
software. Table 4-16 shows you the results of running various content-filtering
products on my computer. The computer is a relatively new and fast machine with
a Pentium 4-M 2.0 GHz processor and 256MB of RAM running Windows XP.

Impact on Computer Resources	Net Nanny	Cyber Sentinel	We-Blocker
Computer slows down slightly.			Yes
Internet slows down slightly.			Yes
Application stability—does the program interfere with other applications?	Caused the Opera, Outlook, and Agent newsreaders to crash	Caused the Opera web browser to crash	

Table 4-16   Performance of Internet-Filtering Applications

Very little impact was made on the computer's resources when using Privacy
Service, CyberPatrol, CYBERsitter, Optenet, and Cyber Snoop.

How Easy Is Filtering Software to Use?

Usability is the ease with which anyone can use the software program in
question. Although Internet-filtering programs are aimed at parents (without
any particular computer background), some of them are harder to understand
than others and seem to require the user to be highly computer literate. Needless
to say, these programs are less than ideal for the average user because there is
a high chance that a hard-to-use program will not be configured correctly or
used to its full potential. Table 4-17 details the usability level of the Internet-
filtering applications.

	Install	Uninstall	Configure	Use	Update
Privacy Service	Easy	Easy	Easy	Easy	Easy
CyberPatrol	Easy	Easy	Moderate	Easy	Easy
Net Nanny	Easy	Easy	Easy	Easy	Easy
Cyber Sentinel	Easy	Easy	Difficult	Easy	Easy
CYBERsitter	Easy	Easy	Easy	Easy	Easy
Optenet	Easy	Easy	Easy	Easy	Easy
Cyber Snoop	Easy	Easy	Moderate	Moderate	Easy
We-Blocker	Easy	Easy	Easy	Easy	Easy

Easy: A person with basic computer knowledge can perform this activity.

Moderate: A person with average computer knowledge can perform this activity.

Difficult: A person with expert computer knowledge can perform this activity.

Table 4-17   Usability Level of the Internet-Filtering Applications

Installing and Removing Filtering Software

Some filtering applications heavily modify your computer and may also require you to have expert knowledge to configure them. Others may automatically install the software for you. Table 4-18 details the installation features of the Internet-filtering applications, and Table 4-19 details the removal features.

	Privacy Service	CyberPatrol	Net Nanny	Cyber Sentinel	CYBERsitter	Optenet	Cyber Snoop	We-Blocker
Completely automatic	Yes	Yes				Yes		
Semiautomatic			Yes	Yes	Yes		Yes	Yes
Need to alter web browser	No	No	No	No	No	No	No	No
Need to reboot computer	Yes	Yes	Yes	Yes	No	Yes	No	No
Automatically downloads the latest updates after you install	No	No	No	No	No	N/A	No	No

Table 4-18   Installation Features of Internet-Filtering Applications

	Privacy Service	CyberPatrol	Net Nanny	Cyber Sentinel	CYBERsitter	Optenet	Cyber Snoop	We-Blocker
Completely automatic	Yes	Yes	Yes	Yes	Yes	Yes		
Semiautomatic							Yes	Yes
Need to reboot computer	Yes	Yes	Yes	Yes	No	Yes	Yes	No
Password protected	Yes	Yes	Yes	Yes	Yes	Yes	Yes	Yes

Table 4-19   Removal Features of Internet-Filtering Applications

What Kind of Documentation Can You Expect to Get?

Documentation explaining how to use a software program (including an index, frequently asked questions, and help page) is often the last thing that software developers write. It's often rushed, or not included at all, which can be very frustrating if you are struggling with how to configure or use a software program. Some vendors provide printed manuals, whereas others provide documentation on CD-ROM or on their website. Keep this in mind if you have a particular preference for the format of your documentation. Table 4-20 details the types of documentation available for the Internet-filtering applications.

	Printed Manual	Online Documentation	CD Documentation
Privacy Service	Yes	Yes	Yes
CyberPatrol	N/A	Yes	N/A
Net Nanny	Yes	Yes	Yes
Cyber Sentinel	N/A	Yes	N/A
CYBERsitter	N/A	Yes	N/A
Optenet	N/A	Yes	N/A
Cyber Snoop	Yes, for U.S.$9.95	Yes	N/A
We-Blocker	N/A	Yes	N/A

Table 4-20   Documentation Types Available for Internet-Filtering Applications

What Kind of Technical Support Can You Expect?

Technical support for a filtering product can be critical if the software you use is hard to use and/or comes with inadequate documentation. It is unlikely that your local computer store will offer or be able to provide technical support for the software you have purchased. The more avenues available for support—including telephone support, e-mail support, website forums, and so on—the quicker and more likely you are to solve any problems you might encounter with your software program. Consider also the costs for support—including the costs of contacting the vendor by telephone, which may require you to call interstate or overseas rather than a local telephone number. Table 4-21 details the technical support provided with the Internet-filtering applications.

	Website	E-mail	Telephone	Fax	Internet Groups
Privacy Service	Yes	No	U.S.$2.95 per minute, with the first two minutes free, 5 A.M.–11 P.M. Pacific Time, OR U.S.$39.00 per single incident, 6 A.M.–10 P.M. Pacific Time	No	Yes
CyberPatrol	Yes	Yes	U.S.$16.99 per incident OR GBP £9.99 per incident	Yes	No
Net Nanny	Yes	Yes, for registered customers in the U.S. and Canada for 30 days after purchase	U.S.$19.95 per incident	No	No
Cyber Sentinel	Yes	Yes	No	No	No
CYBERsitter	Yes	Yes	Yes, free for one year. Premium support costs $20 for two years for upgrades and free phone and e-mail support	No	No
Optenet	Yes	Yes	Spain only	No	No
Cyber Snoop	Yes	Yes	U.S.$35 per incident	Yes	No
We-Blocker	Yes	Yes	U.S.$20 for 15 minutes	Yes	No

Table 4-21   Technical Support Provided with Internet-Filtering Applications

Part II

The Best Software to Protect Your Kids

How Much Should You Expect to Pay for Filtering Software?

The price you see on the box of software you are considering buying may not reflect the full cost of the program, so when comparing prices, consider the following "tricks" that some vendors use when pricing their products.

Some companies offer their software products at a cheaper price than their competitors but require that you regularly upgrade it (and pay for each upgrade). So just as you get used to using the software application, in six months' time it no longer works effectively (because the company is no longer updating your blacklist for the version of software you have purchased, making your blacklist out of date), and you need to upgrade. What do you do? You have to pay more money for the upgrades. If only you knew about this before you purchased the software!

Many licenses are subscription based or limited to a short period of time, such as one year. After that year, your license expires, and you have to buy the product again.

The opposite of subscription-based licenses are perpetual licenses. This means that you effectively own the software. However, some vendors require that you "buy support" from them after the first year, which also increases the amount of money you ultimately have to pay. Table 4-22 details the costs involved with purchasing the Internet-filtering applications.

	Free Trial	Upfront Cost	Free Updates Included	Cost of Future "List Updates"	Cost of Future Product Updates
Privacy Service	30 days	U.S.$34.99	12 months	U.S.$34.99 for a 12-month subscription	Free with a valid subscription
CyberPatrol	14 days	U.S.$39	12 months	U.S.$39 to renew your subscription	U.S.$39 to renew your subscription
Net Nanny	15 days	U.S.$39.95	Unlimited	Unlimited	50% off the new version
Cyber Sentinel	N/A	U.S.$39.95	12 months	U.S.$39.95	U.S.$39.95
CYBERsitter	10 days	U.S.$39.95	Unlimited	Unlimited	U.S.$20 for two years

Table 4-22   Pricing of Internet-Filtering Applications

	Free Trial	Upfront Cost	Free Updates Included	Cost of Future "List Updates"	Cost of Future Product Updates
Optenet	7 days	EU$39	12 months	EU$39 to renew your subscription	U.S.$39 to renew your subscription
Cyber Snoop	7 days	U.S.$49.95	12 months	U.S.$39.95 for 12 months**	U.S.$39.95 for 12 months**
We-Blocker	Free	U.S.$19.95*	Free	Free	Free

* The program is free to use; however, it displays pop-up advertising every 75 clicks, and your children can easily remove the software from your computer. If you register for U.S.$19.95, the program will be password protected and you will not see any pop-up advertising.

** This price is based on the Cyber Snoop 4.0 upgrade license.

Table 4-22   Pricing of Internet-Filtering Applications *(continued)*

General Features You'll Find with Filtering Products

As detailed in Tables 4-23 and 4-24, some of the features you'll find in the content-filtering applications are "bells and whistles" or "nice to have" (B), others are absolutely mandatory (M), and some, although not mandatory, are essential if you want records you can pass on to law enforcement (P). In other words, they may be the difference in the police catching a child predator.

Feature	B/M/P	Privacy Service	CyberPatrol	Net Nanny	Cyber Sentinel	CYBERsitter	Optenet	Cyber Snoop	We-Blocker
Multiple users	M	Yes	Yes	Yes	Yes	No	Yes	Yes	Yes
Multiple access levels	M	Yes	Yes	Yes	Yes	No	Yes	Yes	Yes
Block using time of day	B	Yes	Yes	Yes	Yes	Yes	Yes	Yes	No

Table 4-23   Features of Internet-Filtering Applications

Feature	B/M/P	Privacy Service	CyberPatrol	Net Nanny	Cyber Sentinel	CYBERsitter	Optenet	Cyber Snoop	We-Blocker
Block using day of week	B	Yes	Yes	Yes	Yes	Yes	Yes	Yes	No
Number of hours per week	B	Yes	Yes	Yes	No	Yes	Yes	No	No
Add to blacklist/ blocking list?	M	Yes	Yes	Yes	No	Yes	Yes	Yes	Yes
Add sites not to filter?	M	Yes	Yes	Yes	No	Yes	Yes	Yes	No*
Add to keyword list?	M	N/A	Yes	Yes	Yes	Yes	No	Yes	Yes
Add keywords not to filter?	M	N/A	Yes	Yes	Yes	No	No	No	Yes

* The product has this feature, but it did not work when tested.

Table 4-23   Features of Internet-Filtering Applications *(continued)*

Feature	B/M/P	Privacy Service	CyberPatrol	Net Nanny	Cyber Sentinel	CYBERsitter	Optenet	Cyber Snoop	We-Blocker
Logs attempts to banned sites?	P	Yes	No	Yes	Yes	Yes	Yes	Yes	Yes
Logs access to permitted sites?	P	No	No	No	No	Yes	Yes	Yes	Yes
Logs chat conversations?	P	No	No	Yes	No	Yes	No	No	No
Logs instant messages?	P	No	No	No	Yes	Yes	No	Yes#	No
Logs keyboard strokes?	P	No	No	No	No	No	No	No	No

Table 4-24   Logging Features of Internet-Filtering Applications

Feature	B/M/P	Privacy Service	CyberPatrol	Net Nanny	Cyber Sentinel	CYBERsitter	Optenet	Cyber Snoop	We-Blocker
Tells you the site is blocked	M	Yes	Yes	Yes	Yes	No	Yes	Yes	Yes
Prints all the log files?	P	No	No	Yes	Yes	Yes	Yes	Yes	Yes*

* The product does not have a print feature; however, you can export the log files and print them using a word processor.

\# The program logs instant messages that contain profanity.

Table 4-24   Logging Features of Internet-Filtering Applications *(continued)*

My Verdict on the Content-Filtering Products I Tested

There are many Internet-filtering products on the market. They all have strengths and weaknesses and will have varying appeal depending on your needs. I must emphasize that the main job of Internet-filtering software is to block inappropriate access to websites. With that in mind, here are my thoughts on the Internet-filtering products reviewed in this chapter.

First Place: CYBERsitter

CYBERsitter is very easy to use and has unlimited updates. While it doesn't have as many features as its competitors, it blocks a lot of inappropriate websites. The interface uses plain English, so you don't have to be a rocket scientist to understand it. One excellent feature of CYBERsitter is its ability to prevent your children from changing the settings on the computer. This makes it extremely difficult for computer-literate children to tamper with the settings. It also blocks various types of hacker programs your children might download that may alter the settings.

Honorable Mention: Net Nanny

Net Nanny was one of the "pioneers" of Internet filtering; the first version of the product appeared back in 1995. It's one of the best products for recording what your kids are up to on the Internet. Net Nanny can provide detailed logs of chat conversations and websites that have been accessed and blocked.

Honorable Mention: Optenet

If you need a product that filters inappropriate websites and doesn't have all the bells and whistles, Optenet is the one for you. Optenet contains user profiles, so you can assign an appropriate level of access for your kids. It also automatically updates itself in the background, so you always have the latest updates.

> **tip**   *Try before you buy. Many vendors have evaluation versions on their website for you to download. Evaluation versions are free and typically last between 14 and 30 days.*

Content-Filtering Products in Detail

In the rest of this chapter, I evaluate CyberPatrol, Cyber Sentinel, CYBERsitter, Cyber Snoop, Net Nanny 5, Optenet, Privacy Service, and We-Blocker.

CyberPatrol

Overall Rating

Product: 3.5 out of 5
Support: 3.5 out of 5

Version Tested

6.1.0.27
CyberLIST Category List: 623
CyberPATTERNS – Blocks: 623
CyberPATTERNS – Exceptions: 613
Hard Allows Site List: 622

Installation Process

Downloading the software from the Internet is a very easy two-step process. You only need to visit the CyberPatrol website at http://www.cyberpatrol.com and click the Trial button. It takes less than ten minutes to download and install CyberPatrol on your computer.

Pros

- ○ Completely automated installation. You don't need to download, save, or configure anything (see the upcoming section titled "Filtering").

- ○ Uses context-sensitive filtering. This allows you to search for words on the Internet such as "breast cancer" without the search being blocked because it contains the word "breast."

○ Has an extensive list of features to enable you to customize your filtering to the way your family uses the Internet.

○ Settings are password protected to prevent your children from bypassing the filtering.

○ Uninstall program is password protected to prevent your children from removing the product.

Cons

○ The software asks you to disable your antivirus and firewall software when it's being installed. This is very dangerous and exposes your computer to hackers while the installation is taking place. See if you can install the product without disabling anything. If you run into problems, you can always install the program again.

○ Does not automatically download the latest updates after the installation process is completed.

○ Most security programs operate on a concept that anything that isn't explicitly allowed is denied. For example, unless you tell your content-filtering software that you want to access the Web using Microsoft Internet Explorer, it will not allow Internet Explorer to connect to the Internet. Unfortunately, CyberPatrol doesn't allow you to block everything and then individually select applications that you want to allow. Also, it does not have an extensive list of profanity to block. If you want to use this feature, you will have to type in your own profanity to block.

○ Incorrectly classifies a number of Internet censorship websites (see "Filtering").

○ The software automatically blocks web usage from 11 P.M. to 7 A.M. by default. Unless you go into the settings and change this yourself, you might be wondering why you can't browse the Web after the children have gone to bed!

Filtering

A two-minute search for pornography using a search engine found three websites that were not blocked by CyberPatrol. All three sites contained explicit pornography. Having said that, it does block a very impressive, substantial amount of websites.

However, CyberPatrol was a little disappointing when it came to filtering newsgroups and chat programs. The default settings did not block access to a number of newsgroups that contained pornographic images. The default settings also didn't block chat conversations in programs such as mIRC.

The company incorrectly classifies websites that are critical of its products as "hacking" or "hate speech." These have included popular anticensorship sites such as http://peacefire.org to articles in online computer magazines. In order to view these sites, you will need to manually type in the URLs (web addresses) into the allowed list.

Support

When I used the free technical support via the online form, it stated that the turnaround time would be anywhere from one to three days. When I contacted the support team via e-mail, it took less than 24 hours for them to respond. If you need help immediately, you can always try the support sections of the CyberPatrol website. A number of resources are listed there that may answer your problem, including a list of top questions and "quick start" guides.

Cyber Sentinel

Overall Rating

Product: 2.5 out of 5
Support: 2.5 out of 5

Version Tested

3.4.1.0

Installation Process

The evaluation version is 19.2MB in size and took under 12 minutes to download using a fast Internet connection. For technical people reading this book, I used a 256K ADSL connection. In the U.S., this type of connection is referred to as DSL. Unlike other products, the evaluation version was not available on the website; I had to specifically ask for it. Nonetheless, the response was very fast, and the company provided me with a link to download it.

The installation was fast and required me to reboot the computer when it finished.

Pros

○ Takes screen captures of inappropriate websites and violations of policy. If anything untoward happens to your kids, these images could be used as evidence in an investigation.

○ Displays an "acceptable usage policy" upon the computer starting up. This reminds your kids about the dangers of Internet use.

Cons

○ Does not work with the Opera web browser (see the upcoming section titled "Filtering").

○ Does not shut down peer-to-peer file-sharing applications such as BearShare and Morpheus, thus exposing your children to inappropriate content.

○ Does not properly filter content in mIRC chat rooms and instant messages.

○ Does not properly filter inappropriate e-mail messages in Microsoft Outlook.

Filtering

Cyber Sentinel did not work properly with the Opera web browser. When inappropriate content was displayed in the browser window, Cyber Sentinel displayed more than 68 "access denied" messages and crashed the Opera web browser. When the web browser was restarted, Cyber Sentinel didn't block the content in the browser window. If your child was using the Opera web browser, they would have been exposed to inappropriate content.

Chat programs such as mIRC and e-mail messages in Microsoft Outlook were not filtered at all. Users can send and receive inappropriate content without any filtering.

The majority of peer-to-peer programs were minimized instead of shut down when inappropriate content was displayed on the screen. Just one click on the icon on the taskbar brought the application back (maximized it). Access to inappropriate content on the peer-to-peer network was not prevented.

Support

The website support area contains a very basic "quick start" and help manual. Unfortunately, the Top 10 FAQ page has been "coming soon" for more than 12 months. The online help manual found on the website contains instructions on

Part II

The Best Software to Protect Your Kids

how to install and configure the product. It includes screen captures so you can relate to what is being displayed on the screen. You can also contact technical support by filling in an online form in the support section of the website.

CYBERsitter

Overall Rating

Product: 4 out of 5
Support: 4 out of 5

Version Tested

2003.4.1.30

Installation Process

CYBERsitter is a great product. It blocks a substantial amount of inappropriate content and is very easy to use and configure. The evaluation version is 1.78MB and downloaded in less than two minutes. It did not require a reboot of the computer and took less than one minute to install.

Pros

○ Scans your computer for objectionable material before the software itself installs. This could include previous Internet searches for pornography and files that have been saved on your computer.

○ Allows you to block all instant messages, file sharing, FTP sites, and other means of obtaining inappropriate content.

○ Allows you to block specific ports. Each program uses a unique number (port) to connect to the Internet. This feature can be used to block specific applications that are unknown or new Internet applications that are developed in the future.

○ Can provide automated, daily reports on inappropriate usage. The reports can be automatically generated and sent via e-mail to any address on the Internet. For example, if your kids arrive home from school early and you are at work, you could receive an e-mail to say they tried to access a chat room or download some inappropriate content.

○ Contains many antitampering features that prevent unauthorized changes to the computer and its settings. This includes preventing your children from accessing the network settings to changing the inner workings of your computer (accessing the registry).

○ Notified me that some adware and spyware was installed and asked if I wanted them to be removed.

○ Can only be uninstalled from the password-protected CYBERsitter console. This prevents children from removing the software from the control panel on your computer.

Cons

○ Is not compatible with Norton Internet Security and Norton Personal Firewall. Unfortunately, there is no solution or workaround. If you have Norton Internet Security or Personal Firewall, CYBERsitter will not work properly.

○ The Block All File Sharing button blocks only one out of ten file-sharing programs.

○ The Block All Instant Messengers button does not block ICQ or Yahoo!

○ Updates itself automatically once per week rather than at user-defined intervals.

○ Does not block IRC as an option; however, the software can block specific ports. In theory, file-sharing, chat, and instant messaging programs can be blocked using this functionality.

Filtering

CYBERsitter filtering is excellent. I spent a considerable amount of time attempting to bypass the filters and found only part of one inappropriate (pornographic) website that was not filtered. This is an excellent result; 99.9 percent of the inappropriate websites I tried to access were blocked.

Support

The support for CYBERsitter is excellent. The CYBERsitter website has a list of frequently asked questions as well as a step-by-step guide for new users. I contacted the support via e-mail and received a response the following day.

CYBERsitter has a "premium subscription service" for U.S.$20 for two years. You receive free program upgrades, priority seven-day-a-week e-mail support and priority toll-free telephone technical support (U.S. only).

Cyber Snoop

Overall Rating

Product: 3 out of 5

Support: 3.5 out of 5

Version Tested

4.062

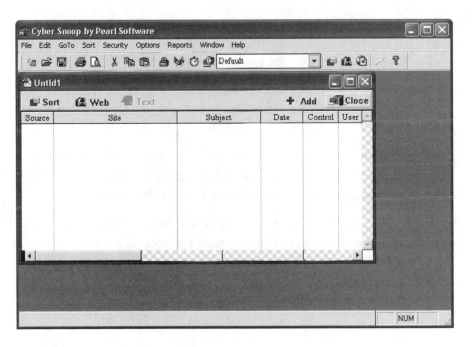

Installation Process

The evaluation version is a massive 19.4MB. Although the Cyber Snoop website said that the download would take less than six minutes, it took approximately 13 minutes using an ADSL connection. This was due to Cyber Snoop's slow website.

The installation process took one minute; however, when it ended, Cyber Snoop didn't start. I was left wondering if it had actually installed. I then found the program icon, clicked it, and the program prompted me to configure it. This process took another three minutes.

Cyber Snoop doesn't like being installed if you already have certain types of spyware or firewalls installed. If you choose to use Cyber Snoop, make sure you check the support pages. The last thing you need is to buy this software and then discover it doesn't work with your firewall! I had to remove Cyber Snoop, remove two lots of spyware, reboot three times, and then reinstall Cyber Snoop.

Pros

○ Found some spyware on the computer when first installed.

○ Blocks Java chat applets located on web pages. This prevents your kids from accessing chat rooms that use Java applets, which download automatically when you visit a website.

○ Many reports are available on Internet usage. You can obtain reports on your children's Internet usage, including the top websites, newsgroups, e-mail messages, file transfers, and chat rooms they visit.

○ Filters Internet newsgroups very effectively. Newsgroup postings are similar to e-mail in that they can contain inappropriate content in the form of message body text and file attachments. It's important that the filtering software prevents your children from accessing both the newsgroup itself as well as the messages within it.

Cons

○ The interface may be difficult to use for first-time Internet users. The main screen displays the contents of log files and leaves the configuration to a series of menu and submenus. This leads to clutter and "information overload" because too much information is being displayed on the screen at once.

○ The software does not come with a predefined blacklist. You have to program it with every web address you want to block, and this can be a long and tiresome process. Plus, if you forget to blacklist a site, it'll be accessible to your kids.

○ It contains a very short list of keywords to block, and you are on your own to add in additional words to block.

○ If you already have spyware on your computer or run certain types of firewall software, you may have trouble getting this program to run at all!

Filtering

The company has a "not recommended starter list" that is supplied to customers. This is essentially a blacklist; however, they did not respond to my request to obtain a copy to evaluate.

For example, Cyber Snoop doesn't block websites on topics such as breast cancer, but some pages on testicular cancer are blocked. When I investigated further, it seemed that Cyber Snoop blocked the pages because the word "penis" appeared in the text.

If you set up the software to ban everything with the exception of a few Internet sites, you wind up getting many error messages on the screen. This is due to the fact that the site you permit may obtain graphics or content from another site. Therefore, for every graphic located elsewhere, you receive a message. Although you can turn off the warning message, this may lead to certain websites not being displayed properly. This isn't exactly a fault in the software; it's just something I wanted to highlight when using the software in a particular configuration.

Cyber Snoop has great difficulty working when file-sharing programs such as Kazaa, eDonkey, and Grokster are installed. This is due to the spyware and adware that is bundled with these file-sharing programs. The end result is Cyber Snoop not working at all and the file-sharing programs crashing constantly (although that's not necessarily a bad thing!).

Instant messages sent and received by a number of popular programs such as MSN and ICQ are also filtered. Although some of the profanity is not displayed on the screen, Cyber Snoop displays a warning box anyway. This may cause the user to think they are doing something wrong, when in fact they are receiving profanity but don't actually know about it (because it has been blocked).

Support

If it weren't for the support part of the website, I wouldn't have been able to run the program in the first place. The installation instructions informed me that Cyber Snoop conflicts with certain types of spyware and adware. After I removed the spyware, the program worked without any problems.

Cyber Snoop has an online user guide, tutorials, and a list of frequently asked questions. Telephone support is free within 30 days of purchasing the product. After 30 days, it's U.S.$35 per incident. Support via e-mail and fax is free.

Net Nanny 5

Overall Rating

Product: 3 out of 5
Support: 3 out of 5

Version Tested

5.0.600.11
Update status – permitted and restricted websites: 2/15/2004
Words and phrases: 12/5/2003
NN file-trading programs: 12/5/2003
NN games: 2/15/2004
NN instant messages: 12/5/2003

Net Nanny 5 Settings

File   Edit   Help

System Settings

Activity Consequences

List Updates

Activity Logs

Web Sites

Content Filtering

Newsgroups

User Settings

Activity Logs

Activity Summary | User Account Summary | Activity Details | Chat IRC

Summary Date Range
From: 03-09-04   To: 03-09-04

User Sessions

Name	Sessions	Date
Anybody	1	09-03-04
Anybody	1	09-03-04
Totals	2	

Violations

Name	Web ...	File Tr...	Inst M...	Games	IRC C...	News...	Filtering	Time ...
Anybody	0	0	0	0	0	0	0	0
Totals	0	0	0	0	0	0	0	0

Log Files

Current size of logs:	0	Bytes
Available disk space:	38154	MB
Space remaining:	30137	MB

Email notification: Disabled

Most recent list update on: 03-09-04

Date & Time tampering: None

Settings...   Delete All   Export...   Print...   Tell me more

Apply   Close

Copyright © 2002-2004 BioNet Systems, LLC.

Installation Process

It took approximately 17 minutes to download the huge 19.7MB file from the Net Nanny website. The entire installation process took less than four minutes and included a reboot of the computer.

Pros

○ Fantastic logging capability. Net Nanny can record websites, file transfers, instant messages, online games, IRC chat, and access to newsgroups. This information is summarized in the "activity summary" section. It's ideal for a family with multiple children because it gives you a snapshot of who is accessing what.

○ Many in-depth features for computer experts. For example, it comes with a fully searchable database of websites, keywords, and Internet applications. This enables you to see if a particular website is being blocked and what category it's listed under.

○ Easy-to-use interface.

Cons

○ Does not properly block inappropriate websites viewed using the Opera web browser.

○ Automatic updates are turned off by default, which prevents Net Nanny from automatically updating itself. If your software isn't getting updated, your children are not protected against inappropriate websites. If you are installing Net Nanny, after the installation you need to click the List Update button, click Daily, and then click the Apply button. This will cause Net Nanny to check the vendor's website on a daily basis and install any updates.

Filtering

Unfortunately, Net Nanny permitted access to a few inappropriate websites when I conducted the test. It took only seconds for inappropriate content to be displayed on the screen after a keyword search using a major search engine. However, this isn't entirely unexpected because new sites are popping up all the time, and with search engine rankings constantly changing, it can prove very difficult to classify new websites.

Some pornographic websites that were blocked by Net Nanny using Internet Explorer were not properly blocked when I used Opera as the web browser. On a number of occasions, the content would start to be displayed, Net Nanny would display a violation pop-up screen, and then the web browser would crash. Upon restarting the browser, the inappropriate content would be displayed.

Newsgroups were also not blocked properly. Although the content of the message was filtered, the Outlook newsreader could still connect to the news server, subscribe to a newsgroup, and view the message's subject and the poster's name and e-mail address. Net Nanny also caused both the Agent and Outlook newsreaders to crash.

The logging features are extremely good, with logging of IRC chat sessions, websites, and even inappropriate programs that have been executed on the computer. Good logs are very important in content-filtering software. They serve two main purposes:

○ They tell you exactly what your children are doing on the Internet. If your children are spending a substantial amount of time in a chat room, you may want to keep an eye on things to ensure they're okay. This would be a good time to talk to them about their Internet use just to be on the safe side.

○ They provide evidence for law enforcement. Log files can record conversations and give vital clues to law enforcement as to the identity of the individual or the location of inappropriate content.

Logging has educational benefits as well. The more Internet applications that are logged, the more coverage you have in monitoring your kids' activities. For example, if you can see in the logs that your kids are trying to download or run a file-sharing program such as Morpheus, you can talk to them about the dangers of peer-to-peer file sharing. Most importantly, you can get to the root of the problem. In this case, it could be that the kids at school are listening to new music and your kids want to join in.

Support

Net Nanny provides e-mail support with a turnaround time of two working days. There is also a large list of FAQs (frequently asked questions) on the Net Nanny website. Telephone support is available in the U.S. for U.S.$19.95 per incident.

Optenet

Overall Rating

Product: 3.5 out of 5
Support: 2 out of 5

Version Tested

8.0.2 build 242

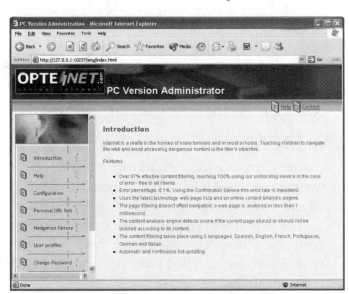

Installation Process

The evaluation version is 6.4MB and took 11 minutes to download using ADSL. The installation was under 60 seconds, which is very fast indeed. After the installation was finished, I had to reboot the computer.

Pros

○ Extremely effective web filtering.

○ Updates happen automatically; you always have the latest information.

○ Contains user profiles so the filter behaves differently depending on who is using the computer.

○ You can modify the list of allowed or blocked web pages.

○ The uninstall program is password protected so your children cannot easily remove the software from your computer.

Cons

○ Does not filter file-sharing, chat, newsgroups, or any third-party applications.

○ Conflicts with spyware and adware installed on your computer. You will have to remove the spyware and adware before Optenet will work.

Filtering

Optenet filters access to websites only. It does this extremely well. Every inappropriate website that I tried was correctly blocked. Optenet claims that they have "97% effectiveness" and from what I've seen, I believe it.

The only minor complaint about Optenet is the fact that it didn't tell me that it conflicted with spyware and adware. I had to remove perfectnav and newdotnet for the web browser to work. I found this out only after my web browser shut itself off every time I visited a website.

Support

Support for Optenet doesn't jump out at you when you visit their website, but it is available. You can call or fill in an online form. There are no discussion forums or user manuals available online; however, the product does include a good help feature. To the average PC user, this may seem a little poor; however, the product installs itself and is pretty much self-explanatory. I received a response in 24 hours after e-mailing the technical support staff.

Privacy Service

Overall Rating

Product: 3.5 out of 5

Support: 4 out of 5

Version Tested

4.0.1.24

Installation Process

The installation process took less than ten minutes to download and install the evaluation version from the McAfee website. The configuration of the software was almost completely automated, with the software requiring a username and password for administration purposes.

Pros

- ○ Filters a large number of inappropriate websites.

- ○ Filters chat from instant messaging programs.

- ○ You can create individual users with appropriate restrictions.

Cons

- ○ Does not properly filter peer-to-peer file-sharing programs such as Kazaa, Morpheus, BearShare, and WinMX. It also failed to filter inappropriate content from newsgroups. Messages posted to newsgroups can contain inappropriate content in the message body as well as file attachments. It's important that the filtering software prevents your children from accessing both the newsgroup itself as well as the messages within it. Blocking access to the newsgroup itself prevents your kids from viewing a list of message subjects that have been posted.

- ○ The logs provide very little detail about what was blocked and why it was blocked in the first instance.

- ○ You cannot block or allow pages based on keywords.

Filtering

Privacy Service filters a surprisingly large number of inappropriate websites. When I tested the content-filtering products, I was able to bypass the filtering mechanisms in a few minutes by proactively searching for inappropriate content.

It took me approximately ten minutes to get Privacy Service to display inappropriate content on the screen. Although ten minutes seems like a short period of time, it's actually quite an achievement because I was deliberately trying to access inappropriate content.

If you visit a page containing inappropriate content, the web browser displays the message, "The Web page you requested has been blocked by McAfee Privacy Service." Unfortunately, it doesn't properly block inappropriate content in other web browsers such as Opera.

Unlike many other programs, Privacy Service also filters instant messages by blocking profanity. Unfortunately, it doesn't prevent inappropriate material from being accessed by peer-to-peer file-sharing programs.

Support

The online help at http://www.mcafeehelp.com categorizes problems into topics such as installation, configuration, and errors. Each category has a number of questions and answers. Unfortunately, the online help does not provide any screen captures or graphics to relate to. This could be due to the simple operation of the program and because it doesn't have many options to configure.

One fantastic feature that differentiates McAfee from its competitors is that you can chat online to a technician online for free. Just visit http://www.mcafeehelp.com, select Privacy Service, select the category (such as Configuration), and then scroll down and click Contact a Live Technician.

We-Blocker

Overall Rating

Product: 3 out of 5
Support: 2.5 out of 5

Version Tested

2.1.0 build 82

Installation Process

The evaluation version is 2.47MB and took less than seven minutes to download using an ADSL connection. The installation process took less than 30 seconds. The default installation settings are questionable. Although they block access to "Pornography," "Adult Subjects," and the "User Defined Category," they permit access to sites that contain "Violence/Criminal Activity," "Drugs and Alcohol," "Hate/Persecution," "Gambling," and "Weaponry."

Pros

○ Filters a lot of inappropriate websites.

○ Inappropriate keywords can be given a numerical rating. If the words are found with others and the total numerical rating is over a certain threshold, then the site is blocked. This prevents blocking of pages that may contain one inappropriate word.

○ If you have more than one computer at home and you want to link them together using a network, you can use We-Blocker as a filter for all the computers. However, you only need to install We-Blocker on one computer and then tell the other computers to use it to access the Internet. This is known as a "proxy server" because the computer with We-blocker installed acts a proxy (traffic cop) and filters information to and from the Internet. This will save you time and money because you don't have to install and maintain We-Blocker on every computer.

○ When the computer started, We-Blocker asked if it could download the latest updates.

Cons

○ Does not filter access using another web browser such as Netscape or Opera. This means your children can bypass the filter and access inappropriate websites.

○ Does not block chat software such as mIRC.

○ Does not filter content accessed by file sharing applications such as BearShare, Morpheus, and WinMX.

Filtering

There are basically two ways to install We-Blocker. The first is to ban every website and only allow specific websites that you type in. The second way is to configure We-Blocker to use its blacklist and ban certain categories. This is the configuration I used for the evaluation. Although the software blocked a lot of inappropriate websites, I noticed that it also blocked access to sites that contained topics such as gay rights. Is gay rights an "adult subject" and therefore banned? How do you define an adult? If the rights of gay men and women are an adult subject and are blocked, why does the software allow you to access the website of the Ku Klux Klan?

Part II

The Best Software to Protect Your Kids

Rather than use a pop-up box to tell you that the site you accessed contains inappropriate content, We-Blocker displays a page on its own website that says, "The site you have requested has been blocked, and will not be displayed."

When We-Blocker is uninstalled from your computer, it doesn't put back settings in your web browser, such as any web proxies you may use. A web proxy is basically a computer at your ISP that is used as a gateway to display websites. If your ISP uses a web proxy and your web browser doesn't point to it, you may loose your ability to access websites. If you don't know what a web proxy is and have never changed any settings in your web browser, don't worry too much about this, because it probably doesn't affect you. If you want to access your proxy settings and you have Internet Explorer 6.0, then start Internet Explorer and follow these steps:

1. Click the Tools menu and select Internet Options.

2. Click the Connections tab.

3. Click the LAN Settings button.

You will then see the proxy server settings. If the proxy server button is unchecked, you have nothing to worry about. You can find more information on the We-Blocker website at http://www.we-blocker.com.

Support

The We-Blocker website has detailed instructions on installing, configuring, and troubleshooting the software. There is also a list of frequently asked questions (FAQs) on how to use the product. Unfortunately, there are no screen captures in the FAQs to enable you to relate what you are reading to what you see on the screen. Also, the FAQs are in small print, which may prove difficult for some people to read.

Telephone support for general issues is available by calling a U.S. telephone number and paying U.S.$20 for 15 minutes. Recovering your password costs U.S.$10, and if you need help to uninstall the product, it will cost you U.S.$20.

Endnotes

1. McCullagh, Declan, 2003. "Report criticizes Google's porn filters." CNET News.com. http://news.com.com/2100-1032-996417.html?tag=fd_top. August 24, 2003.

2. About.com, 2003. "What is the most popular language in the world?" About, Inc. http://geography.about.com/library/faq/blqzlanguage.htm. August 24, 2003.

Part II

The Best Software to Protect Your Kids

CHAPTER 5

Using Filtering Software to Keep Out the Junk Mail

What Is E-mail-Filtering Software?

There are many commercially available e-mail-filtering products in the marketplace. Some of the most popular ones include MailWasher Pro, SpamKiller, and SpamNet. All these programs use different techniques to determine if an e-mail message is unsolicited (that is, you have not, and would not ordinarily have, requested it) or contains misleading, inappropriate, or offensive content.

How Does E-mail Filtering Work?

E-mail-filtering programs use the following six main methods to filter e-mail messages:

- Blacklists and whitelists
- Real-time blackhole lists
- Keyword filtering
- Bayesian filtering
- Rule-based filtering
- Fingerprinting

Blacklists and Whitelists

A blacklist is a list of e-mail addresses known to be used to send spam. An e-mail-filtering program that uses blacklists compares an incoming e-mail address with those in its blacklist and, if it is listed, deletes the e-mail or flags it for deletion. The main problem with blacklists is that spammers keep changing their e-mail addresses. This is yet another reason why you need to set your software to download the latest updates from the vendor's website.

Most blacklists are compiled and maintained by volunteers who submit this information to a large database. Some e-mail filtering vendors also maintain blacklists that they integrate into their anti-spam products. For example, subscribers to the SpamNet product who receive spam can highlight the message and click the "block" button. Blocking a message sends the details of the spam e-mail to the software vendor, which in turn protects other SpamNet users.

A whitelist is a list of e-mail addresses that you compile as being e-mail addresses that are allowed to send you and your children e-mail messages. An e-mail-filtering program that uses whitelists allows you to compile a list of permitted e-mail addresses and automatically deletes or flags for deletion all e-mails that originate from e-mail addresses that are not on your whitelist. Although whitelists are relatively safe, they can filter out e-mail messages from people you want to hear from. For example, if you don't know the e-mail address of a relative and they send you an e-mail, it could get trapped in the filter.

Real-time Blackhole Lists

Real-time blackhole lists (RBLs) are lists of insecure e-mail servers that can be used to send spam. Mail servers are computers on the Internet that handle e-mail, much like a post office. Mail servers are set up so that only local users can send and receive e-mail. For example, your ISP has an e-mail server that you can use, but I couldn't. Unfortunately, some mail servers allow anyone in the world to send e-mail through them. This means that they are open to abuse by spammers.

Most blackhole lists are compiled and maintained by volunteers who submit this information to a large database. Such databases are compiled by the Open Relay Database (www.ordb.org) and SpamCop (www.spamcop.net). As with blacklists and whitelists, e-mail-filtering programs that use RBLs delete or flag for deletion e-mails that derive from a mail server listed in their RBL.

A major problem with using RBLs is that these lists can quickly become out of date. For example, a mail server may only temporarily be insecure and used by someone to send spam. Although the ISP may subsequently secure the mail server, the RBL may not be updated to reflect that. Consequently, all the e-mail from a given e-mail server—many of it legitimate—could be rejected. Another problem with RBLs is that some overzealous users may report ISPs that have secure mail servers. Although some RBLs have a checking mechanism to determine whether the claim is true, some don't, and therefore legitimate e-mail messages could be rejected.

Keyword Filtering

Keyword filtering examines the content of an e-mail message for words that are commonly associated with spam. E-mail-filtering programs typically delete or highlight e-mails containing profanity or words that are often found in spam, such as "XXX," "porn," "sex," "free," and so on. The main problem with keyword filtering is that spammers change the spelling of words in order to bypass the filters. For example, porn could be "p0rn" and sex could become "s3x."

Bayesian Filtering

The Bayesian filtering method is based on a theorem named after the Reverend Thomas Bayes. Bayes' theorem uses mathematics to determine probability. If you apply it on the context of e-mail filtering, the idea is that certain characteristics and words are found more often in spam than in legitimate e-mail. An e-mail-filtering program analyzes an e-mail message and calculates the probability that it is or is not spam. E-mail messages containing words such as "Viagra" and misspelled versions such as "V1agra" have an extremely high probability of being spam.[1]

Rule-based Filtering

Rule-based filtering software allows a user to apply a set of rules to differentiate between spam and legitimate e-mail messages. For example, a user could determine that spam has the following features:

- The characters < and > in the From Address field

- Strange characters such as @> in the From Address field

- JavaScript that automatically executes when the e-mail message is viewed

- Embedded HTML in the message body

- Certain types of files attached to the e-mail message

Users need to take care in applying rules such as these, though. Although there are no legitimate reasons why someone would send e-mail without a proper from address, many people use HTML or JavaScript to make their e-mail messages look more appealing. Consequently, these rules may delete legitimate e-mail messages.

> **tip** *You can get around this problem by adding the e-mail addresses of your friends to a whitelist or friends list. Your e-mail-filtering program will process your e-mail using your friends list first. This way, important e-mail messages will get through, and the spam will be processed accordingly.*

Using Fingerprints to Identify Spam

Much like police use fingerprints to record the identities of criminals, a similar technology can be applied to spam. E-mail-filtering programs use fingerprinting to record a fingerprint for each known spam message, and they store these fingerprints in a database. Each incoming e-mail message is also given a fingerprint, and this is checked against the database of "spam fingerprints." If there is a match, the incoming e-mail is spam and is deleted or highlighted for deletion. In my opinion, fingerprinting is one of the most accurate ways of detecting spam, but it is only as good as the reliability of the fingerprints contained in the database. For example, if a spam message has been changed even slightly (for example, it contains one extra character), its fingerprint and the fingerprint in the database will be different. As you can imagine, the more of these techniques a given program uses, the more effective it is likely to be.

Brands of E-mail-Filtering Software

Although many different e-mail-filtering software programs claim to remove spam, some of these products are difficult to use and don't offer the level of protection required to effectively combat spam.

I have tested what I believe to be the top five e-mail-filtering products (listed in alphabetical order in Table 5-1) to determine their effectiveness in filtering out spam.

Application Name	Version	Website Address
MailWasher Pro	3.4.00	http://www.firetrust.com
Norton AntiSpam	2004.1.0.147	http://www.symantec.com
SpamKiller	2004 v5.0.72	http://www.mcafee.com
SpamNet	2.4	http://www.cloudmark.com
SpamTrap	N/A	http://www.messagecare.com

Table 5-1   E-mail-Filtering Applications

Types of E-mail-Filtering Software

The following are the four distinct types of spam-filtering products available in the marketplace:

○ **Independent applications**   Computer programs that run by themselves and are not attached to, or a part of, any other program.

○ **Plug-ins**   Computer programs that add functionality to the e-mail software you already have on your computer.

○ **Services**   A third party that monitors your e-mail for spam.

○ **Challenge and response systems**   These systems act as a gateway and respond to the sender of the e-mail before it's delivered to your mailbox.

> | tip | *Your ISP may offer an e-mail filtering service for free or at an extra cost. It's worthwhile contacting them to find out.*

Each of these four types has advantages and disadvantages, as detailed in the following subsections.

Independent Applications

These computer programs run independently from your e-mail software program (for example, Outlook). This means they can support virtually any type of e-mail software because they don't rely on them to run.

You typically need to load an independent program prior to running your e-mail software. A major benefit of loading these filtering programs first is that you can double-check whether the program has correctly identified all the spam and—depending on how the program works—specify new e-mails as spam for future reference.

The downside is that your child might run your e-mail software before the filtering program, in which case the spam will not be filtered at all. If this is a risk, you might be better off having a program that automatically loads and deletes spam before your child can run your e-mail program. Although you can set some programs to load automatically, they might not finish processing your e-mail in time. Unfortunately, there are no easy answers! Examples of independent applications are MailWasher Pro and SpamKiller.

Plug-Ins

Plug-ins are programs that integrate themselves into your e-mail software. You can install them just as you would any other product; however, you don't run them as a separate program. For example, the SpamNet product is basically a button on Microsoft Outlook, as shown in Figure 5-1. Because these programs become a part of your e-mail software, you do not need to load them before checking your e-mail. One drawback of plug-ins is that you have to wait for the e-mail to be downloaded onto your computer. This can be a hassle if you receive lots of spam or access the Internet via an old dial-up modem.

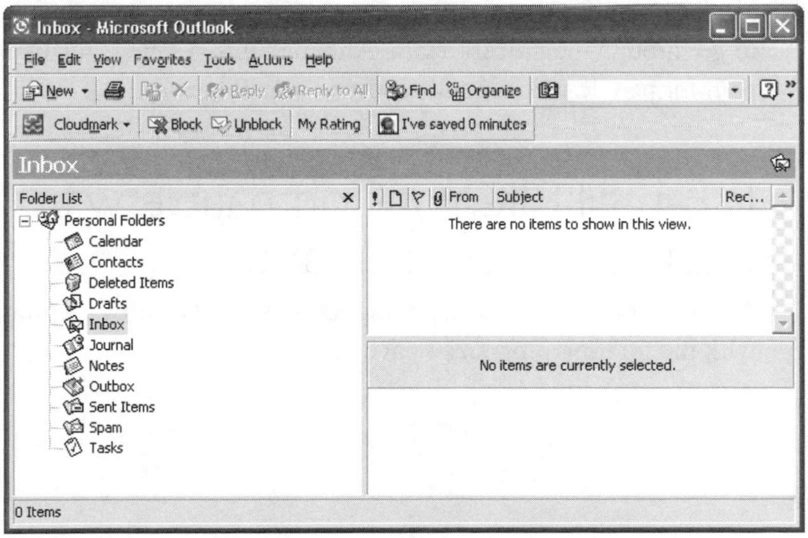

Figure 5-1   Microsoft Outlook with SpamNet installed

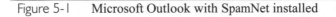

Application Service Providers

An Application Service Provider (ASP) is a company that delivers software—usually via the Internet—to customers on a subscription basis. Some ASPs offer e-mail-filtering services. In most cases, the service does not require any additional software to be installed on your computer; however, you must modify your e-mail software settings to change the way you retrieve your e-mail. An ASP spam-filtering service retrieves the e-mail for you, filters it, and then passes the e-mail onto your e-mail software, which stores it on your computer. An example of an ASP is SpamTrap by messagecare Pty Ltd.

Challenge and Response Systems

A challenge and response system works on the premise that computers cannot easily translate a simple picture into text. For example, we as humans can see a picture and read the numbers 12345 contained in it, whereas computers cannot do this…yet.

Challenge and response systems verify the sender before their e-mail message is delivered to your mailbox. They do this by sending a challenge in the form of an e-mail message to the sender. The sender must type in the contents of a picture into the e-mail and send it back (the response). If the information is correct, the sender is validated and can send e-mail messages to the recipient without having to go through the process again. Although this system is relatively secure, it's a pain for people who want to send you e-mail messages.

Is E-mail Filtering Compatible with My Existing E-mail Program?

Table 5-2 provides a list of popular e-mail clients (software programs) that work with the filtering programs I have reviewed.

E-mail Client	AntiSpam	MailWasher Pro	SpamKiller	SpamNet	SpamTrap
Outlook 2000	Yes	Yes	Yes	Yes	Yes
Outlook 2002	Yes	Yes	Yes	Yes	Yes
Outlook 2003	Yes	Yes	Yes	Yes	Yes
Outlook XP	Yes	Yes	Yes	Yes	Yes
Outlook Express 5	No	Yes	No	Yes	Yes
Outlook Express 6	Yes	Yes	Yes	Yes	Yes
Netscape 7.1	No	Yes	No	No	Yes
Pegasus Mail v4.12	No	Yes	No	No	Yes

Table 5-2   E-mail-Filtering Software Compatible with E-mail Clients

Minimum System Requirements

In general, e-mail-filtering applications can run on most computers (as seen in Table 5-3 through Table 5-6) because they don't consume a lot of memory or processing power. This doesn't mean that you should ignore the minimum requirements, however. It just means that you need a smaller amount of spare memory to run these programs than you would if you were installing a firewall or Internet-filtering product.

Minimum Disk Requirements	AntiSpam	MailWasher Pro	SpamKiller	SpamNet	SpamTrap
4MB		Yes			
8MB			Yes		
70MB	Yes for Windows 98, 98SE, Me, 2000				
150MB				Yes*	Yes*

* The minimum requirements are based on running Outlook 2003.

Table 5-3   Minimum Hard Disk Requirements for E-mail-Filtering Software

Minimum RAM Requirements	AntiSpam	MailWasher Pro	SpamKiller	SpamNet	SpamTrap
4MB		Yes			
32MB	Yes for Windows 98, 98SE, Me				
64MB	Yes for Windows 2000				
128MB	Yes for Windows XP		Yes*	Yes*	Yes*

* The minimum requirements are based on running Outlook 2003.

Table 5-4   Minimum RAM Requirements for E-mail-Filtering Software

The minimum requirements for SpamTrap are based on the minimum requirements for running Outlook 2003. This is because SpamTrap is a service that does not require additional software to be installed on your computer. If you have purchased a computer within the last year, you can skip the minimum requirements because your computer should meet or exceed them.

Minimum CPU Requirements	AntiSpam	MailWasher Pro	SpamKiller	SpamNet	SpamTrap
Pentium 120 MHz		Yes			
Pentium 150 MHz	Yes for Windows 98, 98SE, ME, 2000				
Pentium 233 MHz			Yes*	Yes*	Yes*
Pentium 300 MHz	Yes for Windows XP				

* The minimum requirements are based on running Outlook 2003.

Table 5-5   Minimum CPU Requirements for E-mail-Filtering Software

Operating System	AntiSpam	MailWasher Pro	SpamKiller	SpamNet	SpamTrap
Windows 95		Yes			Yes
Windows 98	Yes	Yes	Yes	Yes	Yes
Windows 98 2E	Yes	Yes	Yes	Yes	Yes
Windows Me	Yes	Yes	Yes	Yes	Yes
Windows XP Home	Yes	Yes	Yes	Yes	Yes
Windows XP Pro	Yes	Yes	Yes	Yes	Yes
Windows 2000 Pro	Yes	Yes	Yes	Yes	Yes
Windows NT 4.0 Workstation		Yes		Yes	Yes

Table 5-6   Minimum Operating System Requirements for E-mail-Filtering Software

Blocking Characteristics

If your e-mail-filtering application (see Table 5-7) does not use multiple techniques to block spam, it may only be partially effective in protecting your children from spam. Ideally, your software should use as many of the methods described earlier as possible. On the other hand, it's better for a program to use one or two highly effective methods, rather than multiple less-effective methods.

Product	Blacklists and Whitelists	RBL	Keyword Filtering	Bayesian Filtering	Rule-based Filtering	Fingerprinting
AntiSpam	Yes	No	Yes	Yes	No	No
MailWasher Pro	Yes	Yes	Yes*	Yes	Yes*	Yes
SpamKiller	Yes	No	Yes	Yes	Yes	No
SpamNet	No	No	No	No	No	Yes
SpamTrap	No	No	No	Yes	No	Yes

* The product supports this feature, but you have to add the specific details. (For example, you might need to add a list of keywords to block.)

Table 5-7   Blocking Characteristics for E-mail-Filtering Software

How Easy Is It to Use?

Usability is the ease with which you can use the software program in question. Many e-mail-filtering programs were originally built for people with a background in computing, which meant that the average non-computer-literate parent would have difficulty using them. This has changed, however, with more e-mail-filtering products being designed for the home user market, as you can see in Table 5-8, which rates the usability level of e-mail-filtering software.

	AntiSpam	MailWasher Pro	SpamKiller	SpamNet	SpamTrap
Install	Easy	Easy	Easy	Easy	Moderate
Uninstall	Easy	Easy	Easy	Easy	Moderate
Configure	Easy	Moderate	Easy	Easy	Moderate
Use	Easy	Easy	Easy	Easy	Easy
Update	Easy	Easy	Easy	Easy	Easy

Easy: A person with basic computer knowledge can perform this activity.
Moderate: A person with average computer knowledge can perform this activity.

Table 5-8   Usability Level of E-mail-Filtering Software

What to Look for in an E-mail-Filtering Program

Table 5-9 details the features I value in an e-mail-filtering program. This isn't a list of "must have" features, because the features you'll need depend on how you intend to use the software.

Testing with Live Spam

It is very difficult to accurately measure the effectiveness of an e-mail-filtering product. This is due to the changing nature of spam. Once a technique has been identified to "flag" an e-mail message as spam, the spammers will often change the way they send e-mail in order to bypass the filter.

E-mail Filtering Features	AntiSpam	MailWasher Pro	SpamKiller	SpamNet	SpamTrap
Modify blacklist?	Yes	Yes	Yes	No	No
Modify whitelist?	Yes	Yes	Yes	Yes	No
Add keywords to filter?	No	Yes	Yes	No	No
Add keywords not to filter?	No	Yes	Yes	No	No
Deletes spam from the ISP's e-mail server?	No	Yes	No	No	Yes
Quarantines spam for review later?	Yes	No	Yes	Yes	Yes
Controls who can access quarantined spam?	No	N/A	Yes	No	Yes
Supports Hotmail.	Only with Outlook XP/2004	Yes	Yes	No	No
Supports Yahoo!	No	Yes	No	No	No
Supports AOL/Netscape.	No	Yes	No	No	No
Supports IMAP.	No	Yes	No	Yes	No
Supports SSL.	No	Yes	N/A	N/A	No

Table 5-9   Features Supported in E-mail-Filtering Software

In order to give you some indication of the effectiveness of each product, I tested them all against 50 of the spam e-mail messages I received on separate days (see Table 5-10).

It's important to note that the spam processed by each product was different. It would be close to impossible to test the same spam e-mail messages against each product because the software must download each e-mail message in order to process it.

Application	Spam Detected	Spam Not Detected	Effectiveness
AntiSpam	42	8	84%
MailWasher Pro	42	8	84%
SpamKiller	50	0	100%
SpamNet	44	6	88%
SpamTrap	45	5	90%

Table 5-10   Spam Detected by E-mail-Filtering Software

Installation and Removal

Some e-mail-filtering applications heavily modify your computer and may also require you to have expert knowledge to configure them. Others may automatically install the software for you. Table 5-11 shows how easy it is to install and remove e-mail filtering products. Of particular importance is the program's ability to automatically download the latest updates from the vendor's website. This ensures that you have the latest version of the product.

	AntiSpam	MailWasher Pro	SpamKiller	SpamNet	SpamTrap
			Installation		
Completely automatic?	Yes	Yes	Yes	Yes	No
Need to alter e-mail software?	No	No	No	No	Yes
Need to reboot computer?	Yes	No	Yes	No	No
Automatically downloads the latest updates after you install the product?	Yes	N/A	Yes	N/A	N/A

Table 5-11   Installation and Removal Features of E-mail-Filtering Software

	AntiSpam	MailWasher Pro	SpamKiller	SpamNet	SpamTrap
			Removal		
Completely automatic?	Yes	Yes	Yes	Yes	No
Need to alter e-mail software?	No	No	No	No	Yes
Requires a password?	No	No	No	No	No
Need to reboot computer?	Yes	No	Yes	No	No

Table 5-11   Installation and Removal Features of E-mail-Filtering Software *(continued)*

Documentation

E-mail-filtering software should operate in such a way that you don't even know it's there. Unfortunately, this isn't a reality just yet, as many programs require a lot of interaction with the user. If you are a novice user or even an Internet-literate computer user, you should pay particular attention to the level of documentation available. It may save you from some late nights hunched over the computer! Table 5-12 details the type of documentation available for the e-mail-filtering software. (N/A indicates you download the product from the Internet—it doesn't come with a CD-ROM or printed manual. SpamTrap is a service and doesn't require you to download anything.)

	AntiSpam	MailWasher Pro	SpamKiller	SpamNet	SpamTrap
Printed manual	Yes	N/A	Yes	N/A	N/A
Internet	Yes	Yes	Yes	Yes	Yes
Included on CD-ROM	Yes	N/A	Yes	N/A	N/A

Table 5-12   Documentation Available for E-mail-Filtering Software

Technical Support

Technical support can be critical if the software you choose is hard to use. Table 5-13 details the type of technical support available for the e-mail-filtering software.

	AntiSpam	MailWasher Pro	SpamKiller	SpamNet	SpamTrap
Website	Yes	Yes	Yes	Yes	Yes
E-mail	No	Yes, free	No	Yes, via an online form	Yes
Telephone	U.S.$29.95 per incident. 6:00 A.M. to 5:00 P.M. PT, Monday through Friday	No	U.S.$2.95 per minute, with the first two minutes free, 5 A.M. to 11 P.M. PT, or U.S.$39.00 per single incident, 6 A.M. to 10 P.M. PT	No	No
Fax	No	No	No	No	No
User groups	No	Yes, free	Yes	Yes	No

Table 5-13   Technical Support Available for E-mail-Filtering Software

Price

The pricing for e-mail-filtering software is different from other software products such as firewalls and antivirus software. Often, the lower-priced software (even free software) works more effectively than the more expensive software!

What's more, companies such as SpamTrap have removed the need for software altogether, so you don't have the hassle of installing software and keeping up to date. Table 5-14 details costs involved with the various e-mail-filtering software products.

Application	Free Trial	Upfront Cost	Cost of Future Product Updates
AntiSpam	15 days	U.S.$39.95	$29.95
MailWasher Pro	30 days	U.S.$37.00	Unlimited
SpamKiller	30 days	U.S.$49.99 box or U.S.$39.99 download	$34.95 annual subscription
SpamNet	30 days	U.S.$3.99 per month (U.S.$47.88 per year)	Unlimited
SpamTrap	30 days	AU$33 for 12 months	Unlimited

Table 5-14   Pricing of E-mail-Filtering Software

| note | *MailWasher Pro has a sister product called MailWasher that's free for personal use. MailWasher supports one e-mail account (address) and has fewer features. MailWasher Pro supports virtually unlimited e-mail accounts (addresses). Because most families have multiple e-mail addresses, MailWasher Pro may be more suitable.* |

My Verdict

There is no "best" e-mail-filtering software, because what suits me probably won't suit you. I don't need to have most of the features an average family might require. As such, my recommendation is based on a family with young children and parents who want to install the filter and not spend time configuring it and manually sorting through spam.

With this in mind, here are my recommendations.

First Place: SpamKiller

Families with young children need a product that sits in the background and automatically deletes spam from multiple mailboxes. When your children use the Internet and click their e-mail program, their e-mail has already been filtered. When I tested SpamKiller against 50 spam e-mail messages, it correctly identified 100 percent of the test e-mails as spam.

SpamKiller was obviously developed with the family in mind. It's easy to use, automatically downloads updates, and is password protected. You can't ask for a more family-friendly filter. In addition, the maker, McAfee, has many avenues for technical support should a problem arise.

Second Place: MailWasher Pro

MailWasher Pro is very fast because it doesn't have to download your e-mail in order to remove spam. It's also a bargain, as it costs a lot less than its competitors. If MailWasher Pro operated in the background and processed e-mail without human intervention, it would have taken first place.

Part II

The Best Software to Protect Your Kids

However, there is a philosophical issue here. If you don't object to your children viewing spam (which could contain inappropriate content), you may want to give them control over the filtering. This would be an ideal situation for a family with teenagers, because you can get them to do the filtering for you.

If you don't have children and are reading this book for the advice on protecting your home computer or your small business, MailWasher Pro may be the program for you.

Third Place: SpamNet

Although SpamNet is easy to use, unlike MailWasher, it requires you to download all your e-mail, including the spam. This can take time, especially over a dial-up Internet connection. Onc advantage that SpamNet has over Norton AntiSpam and SpamTrap is that it has a large subscriber base that submits spam e-mails to be blocked. This enables SpamNet to build a large database of known spam, as opposed to using techniques that could lead to legitimate e-mails being blocked.

Content-Filtering Products in Detail

I have evaluated each of the five e-mail-filtering products discussed in this chapter. For each product you will see an illustration, which will give you an indication as to the look and feel of the product. Depending on how much e-mail you receive, you may spend quite a lot of time using your e-mail filtering software. As such, it's important that you take the time to look closely at the user interface so you can get a feel for how easy the program is to operate.

AntiSpam

Overall Rating

Product: 3.5 out of 5
Support: 3.5 out of 5

Version Tested

2004.1.0.147

```
Norton AntiSpam                                              [ _ ][ □ ][ X ]
  LiveUpdate    Options                                          Help &
                                                                Support ▾

Norton AntiSpam          AntiSpam Status: OK ✔
    Status & Settings ◀   AntiSpam Features                      Details
           Statistics                                    The items marked in
                          ✔ AntiSpam          On         red need your
                                                         attention.
                          ✔ Allowed List      0
                                                         To learn more and
                          ✔ Blocked List      0          take the necessary
                                                         action, click an item
                          Ad Blocking Features           to the left.

                          ✔ Ad Blocking       On

                          ✔ Popup Blocking    On

                          Norton AntiSpam Subscription Status

                          ✔ Renewal Date      11/03/2005

  symantec.                              Norton AntiSpam 2004
```

Installation Process

The installation process took three minutes. After it was finished, the software updated itself to the latest version. The LiveUpdate program downloaded 1.4MB of updates in less than a minute.

When you start AntiSpam for the first time, it asks if you want to import all the people in your e-mail address book into your friends' list. This saves you a lot of time, which would be otherwise spent typing of all your friends' e-mail addresses into your e-mail-filtering software.

Pros

○ Adds two buttons to e-mail programs such as Microsoft Outlook and Eudora to make it easier to use. In Microsoft Outlook, the buttons are located on a separate line between your inbox and the buttons that already exist.

○   Moves spam out of your inbox and into a separate spam folder that is automatically created for you.

○   Easy to maintain blacklists and whitelists.

○   Easy-to-use interface.

Cons

○   Does not prevent the user from viewing quarantine spam. The spam folder is just like any other folder in Microsoft Outlook. There are no restrictions on who can view the contents of each folder, so your kids can read all the spam that has been filtered (quarantined). Although you can get around this problem by adding a rule to automatically delete anything in the spam folder, you run the risk of deleting legitimate e-mail messages.

○   The configuration is very limited (see the following section, "Filtering").

○   The uninstall program is not password protected.

Filtering

AntiSpam filtered a surprising amount of spam e-mail from my e-mail box. The program allows you to easily mark e-mails in your inbox as spam so you don't receive them again.

Unfortunately, AntiSpam isn't very family friendly. It won't prevent your children from viewing the contents of spam because it places known spam in a folder in Outlook for anyone to view. Although it's possible to add rules to a product such as Microsoft Outlook to delete messages contained in the spam folder, it's a bit of a hassle for most users.

The configuration options for AntiSpam are limited. AntiSpam allows filtering based on keywords found in the From, Recipient, or Subject line, the body text, or the entire e-mail message. Unfortunately, there is no way to configure the software to filter e-mail messages based on the e-mail headers or the location of the mail server. These techniques can drastically cut down the amount of spam you receive.

Support

The Symantec website provides a limited amount of online technical support. Its knowledge base contained only seven articles on AntiSpam. I suspect this is because AntiSpam is very easy to use, and there are not many options to configure.

The user manual provides screen captures of the program to guide you through the process of installation and configuration. It's very easy to read and provides a glossary of Internet terms. The manual was available both on the CD and on the Symantec website. It's 2.9MB in size, in PDF format, and took less than three minutes to download.

MailWasher Pro

Overall Rating

Product: 4 out of 5
Support: 4 out of 5

Version Tested

3.4.00

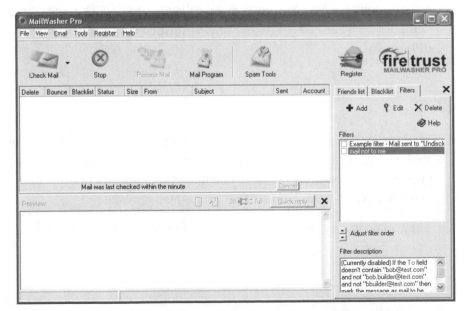

Installation Process

MailWasher Pro was very quick to download. The file is 3MB in size and took less than two minutes to download. The entire installation process took less than one minute. The whole process was extremely fast.

When you start MailWasher Pro for the first time, the software displays a "quick start" guide that shows you how to import the details of all your e-mail addresses. This saves you a lot of time, which would be otherwise spent typing in details from your e-mail software.

Pros

○ Uses RBLs to identify e-mail servers that have been used by spammers.

○ Easy-to-use interface.

○ Supports bouncing of e-mail messages. Bouncing e-mail messages back to spammers can trick them into thinking your e-mail address is invalid. This can cause spammers to remove your e-mail address from their database.

○ Easy-to-maintain blacklists and whitelists.

○ Uses its own database of known spam, called FirstAlert! The database is compiled by Mailwasher Pro users and is verified by the staff at Firetrust (the vendor).

Cons

○ Mailwasher Pro runs by itself. It does not integrate itself with any e-mail applications. Instead, it runs in parallel with your e-mail software, checking your mailbox every few minutes. You must manually process your spam using MailWasher Pro before using your e-mail application.

○ Time taken to read through spam (see the following section, "Filtering").

Filtering

MailWasher Pro has excellent e-mail filtering because it combines RBLs with heuristics to detect possible spam. Heuristics are special techniques used to identify spam. For example, it's common for the word "Viagra" to be used in spam. If the e-mail filter finds the word "Viagra" in the body of an e-mail message, it may identify the e-mail as possibly containing spam. Although RBLs can lead to legitimate e-mail messages being tagged as spam, this doesn't happen very often.

The user interface on MailWasher Pro is very easy to use, even for the novice computer user. Everything you need to process and manage your e-mail can be found on the one screen and is easily accessible by a click of the mouse.

The main issue with using MailWasher Pro is changing the way you check your e-mail messages. Normally you would connect to the Internet, open Microsoft Outlook, and download your e-mail. With MailWasher Pro, here's what you do:

1. Connect to the Internet.

2. Start MailWasher Pro.

3. Click the Check E-mail button.

4. Select the spam you want to delete.

5. Click the Process button, which deletes the spam from your e-mail box.

6. Close MailWasher Pro.

7. Start Microsoft Outlook.

Although this may seem like a lengthy process to go through every time you check your e-mail, there are some real advantages in doing this.

First, you don't download your e-mail; MailWasher Pro checks it using the ISP's mail server. This saves you time because you don't have to wait for your e-mail to download. It also saves you money because you don't pay your ISP for the spam you download. Second, it takes less time to process mail using MailWasher Pro than using Outlook by itself. If you use Outlook, you have to go manually through all your e-mail messages, one by one, determining what is and isn't spam.

Support

The support for MailWasher Pro is excellent. There is a large list of FAQs (frequently asked questions) on the Firetrust website in addition to help files and a user forum. The FAQs are written in plain English and are categorized in a logical order. Support is also available by e-mail, and the vendor claims to answer questions within 24 hours. My query was answered in three hours and 21 minutes from when I sent the e-mail. Although I can't imagine you would have a problem that hasn't already been answered by their FAQ list, an online forum is available to use for support and to discuss issues with other MailWasher users.

SpamKiller

Overall Rating

Product: 4 out of 5
Support: 4.5 out of 5

Version Tested

2004 v5.0.72

Installation Process

The installation process took less than three minutes, including rebooting the computer and automatically updating the software to the latest version.

Pros

○ Easy to use and "family friendly."

○ Supports multiple user accounts (e-mail addresses).

○ Provides detailed statistics on spam.

○ Has a number of built-in "global filters" that separate out the spam.

○ Provides two different methods for filtering spam (see the following section, "Filtering").

Cons

○ Not tightly integrated with Microsoft Outlook (see "Filtering").

○ Marked a legitimate e-mail messages as spam during my testing (see "Filtering").

○ Does not prompt you for a password to uninstall the product.

Filtering

SpamKiller automatically detects your settings and imports them from Microsoft Outlook (Hotmail addresses are also supported). It then starts filtering spam straight away, deleting spam from your ISP and placing it in the "blocked e-mail" folder (in SpamKiller) for your review. SpamKiller can also be configured to add the word "spam" (or another keyword of your choice) to the subject header of an e-mail and then leave it in your inbox. This enables you to identify spam and process it using your own rules in Microsoft Outlook.

The only major issue with SpamKiller is how it loosely integrates with Microsoft Outlook. In order to read blocked e-mail, you need to start a separate window rather than use Microsoft Outlook itself. This "going back and forth" between two windows can be both frustrating and time consuming.

One minor problem I had with SpamKiller occurred when testing it on live e-mail. In addition to 50 spam messages, I also included some additional, legitimate e-mail messages to see if the product would mark any as spam. One message was marked as spam and deleted from my mail server (but stored for review by SpamKiller). Fortunately, I was able to retrieve the e-mail using the "rescue message" feature.

SpamKiller uses global filters (rules) to detect spam. One of the rules was set to mark messages as spam if they contained the phrase "received this message in error." It is very common for legal disclaimers in corporate e-mail messages to state, "if you have received this message in error, please contact XYZ." Consequently, I would strongly advise anyone using SpamKiller to review the rules it uses to filter e-mail messages and remove any that might quarantine legitimate e-mail messages. Be sure to also review any new updates that SpamKiller downloads. You can change the rules by going into the SpamKiller settings and selecting the Global Filters option.

Apart from changing the rules, I would recommend that you use the "friends" feature, which allows you to choose e-mail addresses that are exempt from filtering. This will ensure that e-mail from your friends will not be marked as spam.

Support

SpamKiller has extensive documentation, which you can access by clicking the Help button found in the top-right corner of the screen. The hardcopy user manual is very detailed but does not display any screen captures, so you can't relate to what you are seeing on the screen.

McAfee users in the U.S. can access the telephone support for U.S.$2.95 per minute (with the first two minutes free) from 5 A.M. to 11 P.M. Pacific Time. Alternatively, a single incident charge is U.S.$39.00, available from 6 A.M. to 10 P.M. Pacific Time.

Many Asia/Pacific countries (Australia, New Zealand, China, Hong Kong) have free telephone technical support for one year from the date of registration. In Australia, telephone support is via a toll-free 1-800 number.

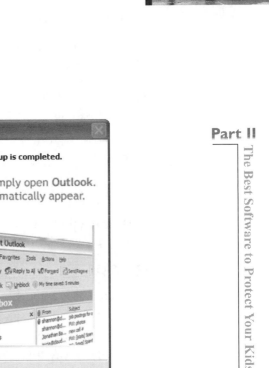

SpamNet

Overall Rating

Product: 4 out of 5

Support: 3.5 out of 5

Version Tested

2.4

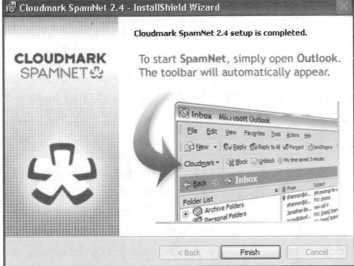

Installation Process

The installation file is 2.8MB and took less than two minutes to download using a 256K ADSL connection. Installation took approximately 45 seconds. Configuring the product wasn't necessary because it automatically modified Outlook and was working straight away.

Pros

○ Very easy to set up and use.

○ Integrates directly into Microsoft Outlook.

○ Has a large community of people identifying new spam (see the following section, "Filtering").

○ Uses fingerprinting to identify known spam, thus reducing the probability that it will quarantine legitimate e-mail.

Cons

○ Does not work with e-mail programs other than Microsoft Outlook.

○ Does not prevent your kids from viewing quarantined spam.

Filtering

SpamNet integrates with Microsoft Outlook and installs a number of buttons above your inbox. It also adds a spam folder to your inbox where it places known spam. When you check your e-mail, SpamNet identifies known spam and moves it into the spam folder, away from your inbox. SpamNet can also be configured to move spam to the "deleted items" folder so it effectively gets deleted without any human intervention.

What makes SpamNet stand out from its competitors is its community of users, called SpamFighters, who have signed up for the service. Each person can submit new spam to SpamNet for analysis. This ultimately means that SpamNet may recognize significantly more spam than its competitors.

One minor issue I had with SpamNet was its icons disappearing from Outlook. A quick search of the knowledge base on the support site answered the question. Apparently, Microsoft Outlook had started another instance of itself on my computer and caused the SpamNet icons to disappear. The issue was fixed by following the instructions in the knowledge base.

Support

The online support for SpamNet is excellent and has obviously been thought through carefully. There are four sets of FAQs (frequently asked questions) on different topics as well as a knowledge base and community forum.

SpamTrap

Overall Rating

Product: 3 out of 5
Support: 3.5 out of 5

Version Tested

N/A

Installation Process

The SpamTrap website provides you with step-by-step instructions on how to change your e-mail software to use their service. This took me a few minutes because I had to really concentrate on what they wanted me to change in my e-mail software.

Pros

○ Does not require you to install additional software on your computer.

○ Does not download the spam it detects to your computer, thus saving you ISP bandwidth costs.

Cons

○ A number of a security issues divulge your password (see the following section, "Filtering").

○ A number of legitimate e-mail messages were marked as spam during my testing.

Filtering

SpamTrap filters spam behind the scenes so you don't actually see it in action. You can log into their website and view a list of trapped spam that was heading for your e-mail account. You can also release a trapped e-mail and view statistics on how many spam e-mail messages have been caught.

While testing the service, I noticed that two e-mail messages were incorrectly identified as spam. The first was a Security Bulletin from Hewlett-Packard (HPSBUX0208-209), and the second was an e-mail message from Jobnet, a recruitment website. Unfortunately, SpamTrap did not tell me why the messages were flagged as spam. The SpamTrap website states that if a legitimate e-mail is blocked, you can either release the e-mail by clicking the "resend" button or forward the e-mail message to the support team for investigation. However, if you send the e-mail to the support team, they will need to read it in order to see why it was blocked.

Security and privacy could be a concern to some people using this service because you have to divulge your password to use SpamTrap. The terms and conditions state, "…when you log in to view your e-mail retained in our trap file, your password is routed through our server to your ISP's server. Our system and our staff will not access, cache or retain details of your password."[2] Although SpamTrap claims that it doesn't store your password, you still send it to their computers, which use it to log into your ISP on your behalf. When someone asks for you to divulge your password, it should send off alarm bells in your head. In 99.9% of the cases, there is no valid reason for someone to ask you for your password. However, in this instance, SpamTrap uses your password to process your e-mail.

If someone hacks into the SpamTrap service or intercepts your password, they can impersonate you on the Internet. If you use the Internet to send e-mail messages to a few friends, you might not be so concerned about someone reading your e-mail or posting messages in your name. However, if you use online banking or if you have registered your credit card details on a website, it's possible that someone could use your e-mail address to access this information. I'm not going to go into detail about how to do this—this book isn't an instruction manual for stealing a person's identity.

The second security problem is when you log into the service to check your spam; you do so via a web browser. The SpamTrap website does not use SSL (Secure Sockets Layer), which is the standard for security on the Web. In basic terms, SSL protects confidential information that is sent to and from a website. It's widely used by banks, online shopping, and other e-commerce sites. When you log into SpamTrap using the Web, your e-mail address and password are sent in plain text over the Internet. Although e-mail is traditionally insecure (your e-mail password is normally sent over the Internet in plain text), it's possible for someone sitting between you and SpamTrap to obtain your e-mail password.

Many hackers target e-commerce sites because many customers use the same user ID and password to dial up their ISP, purchase goods, and download their e-mail. This makes SpamTrap an attractive target, particularly when there is only a password protecting their customers' information. This isn't necessarily a fatal flaw in the product because POP3 e-mail passwords are sent in plain text over the Internet anyway. POP3 (which stands for Post Office Protocol 3) is a computer protocol that allows people to download e-mail to their computers.

SpamTrap could use an SSL certificate to significantly increase their level of security. This would scramble the information sent between you and SpamTrap so that a third party couldn't read it.

Support

SpamTrap provides a very brief list of FAQs (frequently asked questions) as well as an e-mail form for users to submit questions. The customer support staff responded to my online support request in less than two hours. Although this was during business hours, it's still very impressive.

Endnotes

1. Graham, Paul, 2003. "So far so good." Paul Graham. http://store.yahoo.com/paulgraham/sofar.html. August 24, 2003.

2. messagecare, 2003. "Terms and Conditions." messagecare Pty Ltd. http://www.spamtrap.net.au/tandc.php. August 24, 2003.

CHAPTER 6

Internet Firewall Software

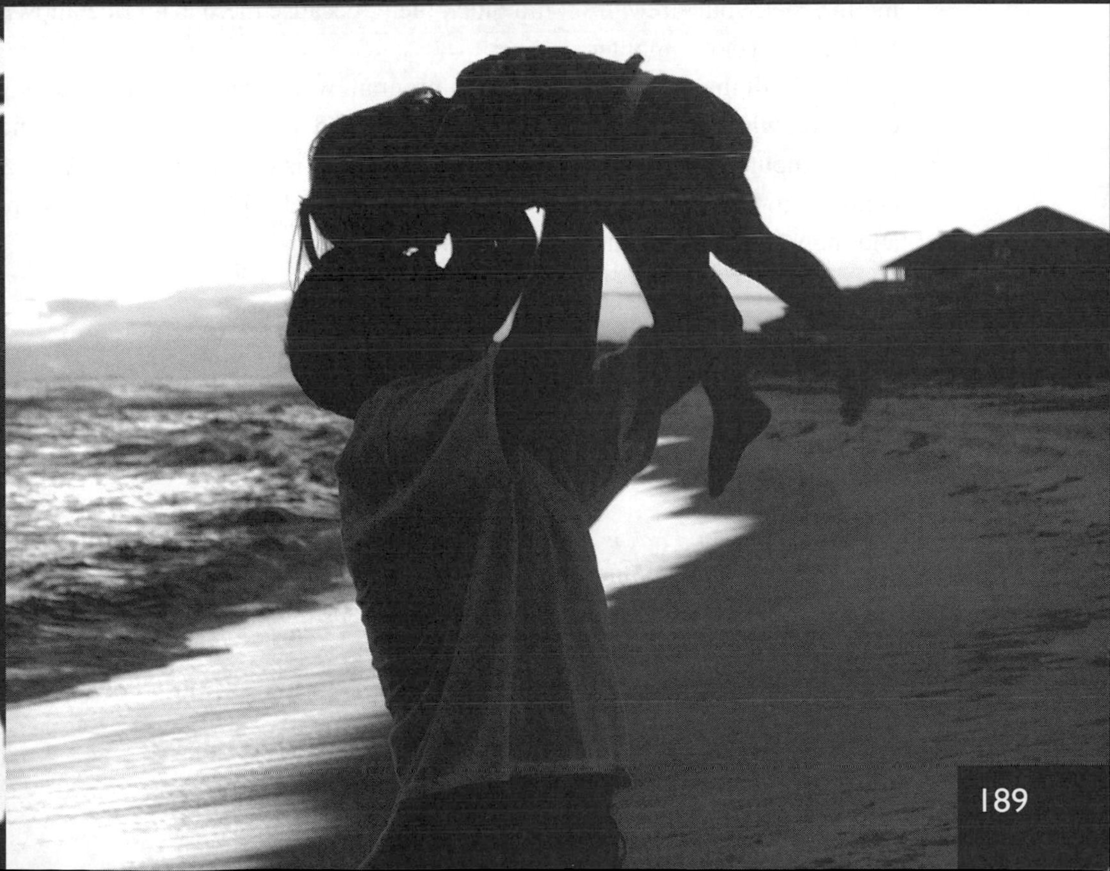

Hundreds of Internet firewall applications are available. The majority of them require you to have detailed technical knowledge of the Internet in order to install and configure them. However, a number of organizations have seized this opportunity and have developed firewalls that are easy to operate.

How a Firewall Works

A firewall is a bit like the traffic police; it directs and can stop traffic coming into your computer *from* the Internet and out of your computer *to* the Internet. In fact, a firewall is designed to allow you to determine what traffic is allowed to flow between your computer and the Internet by enabling you to establish rules for the flow of information.

For example, you want to visit a website, so the firewall will ask you if you want to add a rule to allow you to browse websites. You want to read e-mail using Microsoft Outlook, and your firewall will ask you if this is okay. This is a great feature because you only need to respond to these questions once, and the firewall will remember your answers. Now if a hacker tries to get into your hard disk from the Internet, your firewall should block them, because there is no rule allowing the hacker into your computer.

That's all that a firewall really is: a program with a set of rules that tells your computer what is allowed and what is not allowed to send information to and from your computer. As discussed previously, a firewall is essential for preventing your children from using or downloading dangerous Internet applications (such as Trojans) and inappropriate content. It is an invaluable tool.

Brands of Internet Firewall Software

There are many different types of firewalls. If your computer runs Windows XP with Service Pack 2 (SP2) or later, then you already have a firewall installed on your computer.

> **tip** | *A Service Pack is a computer program that fixes a number of security flaws in your computer. You can find more information on installing security patches in Chapter 9.*

You can turn on the Windows XP firewall by following these instructions:

1. Click on the Start button.

2. Click on Control Panel.

3. Click on the Security Center icon.

4. Click on the Windows Firewall icon.

5. Click on the On button.

If you don't see a Security Center icon in the Control Panel, then you don't have Service Pack 2 (or later) installed and you need to follow the instructions in Chapter 9.

By now you are probably asking the question: "If I already have the Windows XP firewall, then why do I need another firewall as well?" The Windows firewall is good in that it blocks access to your computer, but it doesn't have the features or offer the same level of protection as many of the commercial firewall products. Don't get me wrong; the Windows XP firewall significantly increases the level of security to your computer, but this should be regarded as a foundation to build upon.

Based on my research, I've listed the top five Internet firewall software applications for home use, in alphabetical order, in Table 6-1.

I like these firewalls because they cater to the home user and perform very well. Also, the companies that own these firewall products are well established and invest a lot of money in continually improving their products.

Application Name	Version	Website Address
Kerio Personal Firewall	4.0.11	http://www.kerio.com
McAfee Personal Firewall Plus	2004 v5.0.1.5	http://www.mcafee.com
Norton Personal Firewall	2004	http://www.symantec.com
Outpost Firewall Pro	2.1	http://www.agnitum.com
ZoneAlarm Pro	5.0.590.015	http://www.zonelabs.com http://www.zonelabs.com.au/

Table 6-1 Brands of Internet Firewall Software

My ISP Provides a Firewall Service; Do I Still Need Firewall Software?

Yes. Many ISPs block Internet users from accessing your computer. This is either done by installing third-party software on your computer or restricting access on the ISP's computers. However, I would still install firewall software on your computer for the following reasons:

○ You control who has access to your information.

○ It's very unlikely that your ISP will allow you to see how their firewall is configured, so you are not in a position to assess the real risk.

○ Your firewall software is customized to your computer and the programs that you want your children to use. This will be different from your ISP's settings.

○ Your ISP's firewall can't restrict what programs your children run on your computer.

○ It is more secure for you to use your own firewall software than to rely on a third party to configure their firewall with some general settings.

Even if your ISP offers an additional service in which you pay a fee to download and install firewall software, I would still recommend being very cautious. If it were my child, I wouldn't take the risk.

What to Look for in a Firewall

There is no "best" firewall. One that suits me may not suit you. For home use, the best choice is usually based on the following criteria:

○ Which one can I run on my home computer without slowing it down?

○ Which one can I easily set up and run?

○ Which one takes almost no effort to maintain?

○ Which one will automatically update itself?

The answer to the first question depends on the minimum requirements for the software and how powerful your computer is. In the following few pages, I provide a comparison of products based on their minimum system requirements and a number of other characteristics. Before setting out a comparison based on these other characteristics, I explain what these are and why they are important. After this, I look at the pros and cons of each firewall, along with their features and pricing. I also provide tips on how you can save real money on computer software. This is a must-read for families on a tight budget.

Minimum System Requirements

Firewall applications consume a lot of memory and processing power. This is because they are working in the background, scrutinizing everything coming in and out of the computer. Your computer should have 64MB of memory (RAM) at a minimum. To operate a firewall without slowing down your computer, I recommend 128MB of RAM. Don't forget that you will also have antivirus software and other applications running at the same time. Therefore, 128MB of RAM should enable you to access the Internet faster because your computer shouldn't slow down. Tables 6-2 and 6-3 provide the minimum hard disk, RAM, and CPU requirements for your computer in order to run firewall software. Table 6-4 provides you with a list of web browsers that are supported.

	Kerio	McAfee	Norton	Outpost Firewall Pro	ZoneAlarm Pro
Hard Disk Space					
8MB		Yes			
10MB	Yes				Yes
20MB				Yes	
25MB					
35MB			Windows Me, 2000 Pro and XP		
RAM					
32MB		Yes		Yes	
48MB			Windows Me		Windows 98SE, Me
64MB	Yes		Windows 2000 Pro		Windows 2000 Pro
128MB			Windows XP		Windows XP

Table 6-2   Minimum CPU Requirements and Operating System

	Kerio	McAfee	Norton	Outpost Firewall Pro	ZoneAlarm Pro
CPU					
Pentium 133 MHz	Yes	Yes	Windows 2000		
Pentium 150 MHz			Windows Me		
Pentium 200 MHz				Yes	
Pentium 233 MHz					Yes
Pentium 300 MHz			Windows XP		
Operating System Compatibility					
Windows 95				Yes	
Windows 98				Yes	
Windows 98 SE	Yes	Yes		Yes	Yes
Windows Me	Yes	Yes	Yes	Yes	Yes
Windows XP Home	Yes	Yes	Yes	Yes	Yes
Windows XP Pro	Yes	Yes	Yes	Yes	Yes
Windows 2000 Pro	Yes	Yes	Yes	Yes	Yes
Windows NT 4.0 Workstation				Yes	

Table 6-3   Minimum CPU Requirements and Operating System

	Kerio	McAfee	Norton	Outpost Firewall Pro	ZoneAlarm Pro
CD-ROM		Yes	Yes		
Internet Explorer 5.01			Yes		
Internet Explorer 5.5		Yes			

Table 6-4   Minimum Web Browser and CD Requirements

Keeping Track of Programs That Try to Access the Internet

Your computer has many programs installed on it. Some of them can connect to the Internet for a variety of purposes, but typically they do so in order to check if there is an update available from their vendor's website. So how do you know which programs are connecting to the Internet?

Application control enables your firewall to become aware of programs on your computer that try to access the Internet. Such programs include legitimate software such as web browsers as well as malicious programs such as Trojan horses and back doors that might infect your computer.

Application control enables you to control what applications your children can use to access the Internet by only allowing them to use "authorized programs" and preventing them from using programs you have disallowed.

Application Scanning Finds All the Programs on Your Computer

Part II

Your firewall needs to know the name and the location on your computer (directory) for every program you use to access the Internet. Instead of having to type this in manually, the firewall can scan your computer for programs and then ask you to select the ones that you use. (You will recall from Chapter 1 that there are different Internet applications for accessing e-mail, the World Wide Web, ICQ, and so on.) This process is known as *application scanning*. It can save you both time and frustration because you don't have to manually configure your firewall.

Password Protection

Password protection means that you need to submit a password before you can change the configuration of the firewall. This prevents your children (or anyone else) from changing the firewall rules and installing software on your computer that might expose them to inappropriate content.

Alert Assistant

The Alert Assistant feature alerts you when something unusual happens—such as a hacker trying to break into your computer. The major benefit of this feature is that even if you have configured the firewall to allow certain risky activities, the

The Best Software to Protect Your Kids

software will prompt you when such an activity takes place. For example, you may have mistakenly configured the firewall so that a hacker has a means of breaking into your computer. If a hacker does try to break in, the Alert Assistant will let you know of the attempt and give you a chance to stop the hacker.

JavaScript and ActiveX Filtering

JavaScript and ActiveX are computer programs that run on web pages. These programs are downloaded and automatically run on your computer when you view a website. JavaScript and ActiveX run in sandbox (secure environment) on your PC and therefore can't damage it. However, there have been many security vulnerabilities in the way companies implement JavaScript and ActiveX. These vulnerabilities are often exploited by malicious JavaScript and ActiveX controls. If your firewall supports filtering these scripts, you can prevent them from being downloaded by your web browser. If you do this, however, some websites might not operate properly.

These controls can be used by malicious websites for anything from reading files to running programs on your computer without your knowledge. Should a new vulnerability (security flaw) be discovered in a program that uses JavaScript and ActiveX, you should be able to prevent these scripts from running on your computer.

Persistent, Session, and Third-party Cookie Filtering

A *cookie* is a file on your computer that is created when you visit a website. Cookies are not all bad; however, they do store information in order to track visitors to a particular website. Three types of cookies are session, persistent, and third party.

Session cookies are commonly found on websites that sell products. They are usually deleted when your web browser is closed or once your order is processed.

Persistent cookies are like session cookies; however, they have an expiration date and are not deleted when your web browser is closed.

Third-party cookies are commonly used by advertisers. For example, if your kids visit website A, they may see a banner advertisement. If website A displays advertising from a third party (website B), the advertiser may also send them a cookie. Both the banner and the cookie have come from website B, even though your kids visited website A. Advertisers use cookies across multiple websites so they can track what pages your kids visit. This enables them to create a profile of their interests and target them with specific advertising.

Cookie management assists you in protecting the privacy of your kids. To some extent, proper management of cookies can prevent them from being tracked and profiled by advertisers. Unfortunately, some cookie management products treat all cookies the same. As such, when you visit a website, the website being visited may not work properly. Depending on how cookies are used, you may experience problems such as having to enter your user id and password constantly and items going missing from your shopping cart. In my experience, here are the best actions to take to protect the privacy of your kids and still access websites you trust:

○   Block all third-party cookies.

○   Allow session and persistent cookies for websites you trust.

○   Block session and persistent cookies for all other websites.

Allowing cookies from sites you trust still allows you to shop online, but it blocks third-party advertising. Although traditionally it's not the job of a firewall to block cookies, it's a great function that home firewalls offer.

| tip | *You can use malware-detection software such as PestPatrol (reviewed in Chapter 8) to detect and remove cookies that are known to have come from advertisers. This way, you don't have to distinguish between the different types of cookies or add your favorite websites to your firewall software.* |

Filtering Out E-mail Attachments, Pop-ups, Banners, and Other Forms of Advertising

E-mail attachments are files that are sent along with e-mail messages. They can contain everything from photos and documents to audio and video. Attachment filtering scrutinizes these files. File attachments can contain viruses and other malicious software that can cause damage to your computer. In addition, these files could also contain inappropriate content and sensitive information. Although this feature is usually found in antivirus or spam-filtering software, many firewalls are also adding this functionality.

Pop-ups are additional web browser screens open on your computer when you visit a website. Some websites open up many additional web browser screens when you visit. This is usually done to increase advertising on the website and thus earn the website owner more money from advertisers. Banner advertisements are small graphics on the website. The more advanced version of banner advertising uses animation. This is where an animated graphic is placed over the website itself.

Pop-ups cause screen clutter as well as slow down your computer. They can also be very annoying. The website owner may or may not have control over the banners and animation that is displayed on their website. This is due to advertising agreements with third parties. If enabled, your software can block out annoying advertising, which saves you time and money because you don't have to pay for downloading the ads!

Intrusion Detection System (IDS)

An intrusion detection system, or IDS, recognizes common types of attacks on computer systems. It does this by looking for known patterns in information sent to and from your computer. An IDS will tell you if your computer becomes the subject of a "hacker attack." You can then make an informed decision about what to do if your computer becomes subject to an attack. For example, you may want to disconnect from the Internet. An IDS can provide a visual alert to tell you—via an onscreen display—if a hacker or worm is trying to break into your computer. You can also configure an IDS to trigger a sound that your computer generates (an audible alert) when there is suspicious activity. The advantage of an audible alert is that it will let you know about a possible attack while you are away from your computer.

Real-time Traffic Analysis Tells You What Is Going On

Real-time traffic analysis provides you with a report on Internet access in real time—that is, you can see from moment to moment what applications (such as your e-mail application or your web browser) are accessing the Internet. This is beneficial because you will not only be able to monitor what applications you are using to access the Internet but also what systems (or hackers) are connecting to your computer from the Internet.

A Firewall Rule-Base Check Makes Sure Everything Is Set Up Properly

A firewall rule-base check is a process that checks your firewall to ensure that it is configured correctly. This process checks the configuration to ensure that there are no security holes in your firewall.

Automatic Updates Keep Your Software Up to Date

If your firewall software has an automatic update feature, you will receive updates to your software, ensuring it remains current and receives additional features and fixes to any problems with the software that may be identified. By receiving updates automatically, you do not need to worry about checking the vendor's website for new updates or spend time downloading and installing any new updates yourself.

| tip | *Set your firewall software to automatically download and install updates as often as possible. That way, you can just set it once and forget it's even there.* |

Hacker Tracking

Hacker tracking is a process that tracks the source of Internet traffic sent to your computer. If your computer is being hacked into, you may be able to obtain the details of where the attack is coming from. This information can be very useful if you need to contact the police about a hacker attack and they need to investigate the attack.

This is *not* an essential feature—basically because competent hackers do not use their own computers to attack others. Instead, they break into computers owned by other people and use them to launch an attack.

Color-Coded Firewall Alerts Tell You the Level of Severity of an Attack

Depending on the firewall software you use, each attack might be listed as one line on your screen or as multiple lines. Each attack has a different risk associated with it. Color-coded alerts are an easy way for you to quickly sort out the more serious security alerts from the less dangerous ones.

> | tip | *When you first install a firewall, you may be concerned about the number of attacks you receive on your computer. Don't worry, because this is quite normal. Looking through firewall alerts can be quite time consuming, so you may want to set the firewall to ignore the less severe ones and only notify you of the more dangerous attacks.*

What to Do in an Emergency

An emergency button is a button you can press that immediately stops Internet access to and from your computer. For instance, if a hacker breaks into your computer, you can use the emergency button to instantly disable all Internet traffic on the firewall and stop the hacker in their tracks.

An External Security Scan Gives You a Hacker's View of Your Computer

Some firewall vendors offer to perform an "external security scan" on your computer. This involves the vendor performing a general assessment of the security of your computer and notifying you of any vulnerabilities that could give a hacker an entry into your computer. An external security scan gives you a hacker's view of your computer from the Internet and allows you to fix any security flaws it has.

> | tip | *Your modem could have a built-in firewall. This is often the case with fast ADSL Internet connections. Check with your vendor or ISP, and if you have a firewall built into your modem, turn it on. This doesn't mean you don't need a firewall for your computer; it just provides another layer of defense. A built-in firewall will not protect you from Trojans or spyware running on your computer. However, it will protect you from hackers trying to break in from the Internet.*

The Features You Need in a Firewall

There are many different types of firewalls. Some operate the same; some operate entirely differently. However, it's important to note that the requirements for a home user are entirely different from a corporate user.

The most important attribute of a firewall for home users is how easy it is for you to set it up correctly and prevent your children from modifying the settings. This is *absolutely critical* because it is your firewall that prevents inappropriate applications, such as chat and file-sharing programs, from running on your computer.

The bottom line is that your children will probably try to download computer programs from websites or get them from their friends. Correctly configured, however, your firewall will prevent them from doing so. Why? The firewall will stop them from connecting to the Internet. If a chat program can't connect to the Internet, your children can't use it to talk to anyone. If a file-sharing application can't connect to the Internet, it can't download any files to your computer. This is why the configuration of your firewall is so vital. Table 6-5 through Table 6-8 detail the setup and filtering features for each firewall product that I evaluated.

	Kerio	McAfee	Norton	Outpost Firewall Pro	ZoneAlarm Pro
Application control	Yes	Yes	Yes	Yes	Yes
Application scanning	No	Yes	Yes	Yes	Yes
Password protection	Yes	No	Yes	Yes	Yes
Firewall Rule Wizard	No	Yes	Yes	Yes	Yes
Alert Assistant/Help	Yes	Yes	Yes	Yes	Yes

Table 6-5   Setup Features

	Kerio	McAfee	Norton	Outpost Firewall Pro	ZoneAlarm Pro
JavaScript	Yes	No	Yes	Yes	Yes
ActiveX	Yes	No	Yes	Yes	Yes
Persistent cookies	Yes	No	No	No	Yes
Session cookies	Yes	No	No	No	Yes
Third-party cookies	Yes	No	No	No	Yes
All cookies	Yes	No	Yes	Yes	Yes
E-mail attachments	No	No	Yes	Yes	Yes
Pop-up advertising	Yes	No	Yes	Yes	Yes
Banner advertising	Yes	No	Yes	Yes	Yes
Animation advertising	No	No	Yes	Yes	Yes

Table 6-6   Filtering Features

	Kerio	McAfee	Norton	Outpost Firewall Pro	ZoneAlarm Pro
Logging					
Intrusion detection system	Yes	Yes	Yes	Yes	Yes
Onscreen visual alerts	Yes	Yes	Yes	Yes	Yes
Audible alerts	No	Yes	No	No	No
Real-time traffic analysis	Yes	Yes	Yes	Yes	Yes

Table 6-7   Logging, Maintenance, and "Nice to Have" Features

	Kerio	McAfee	Norton	Outpost Firewall Pro	ZoneAlarm Pro
Maintenance					
Firewall rule-base check	No	Yes	No	No	No
Automatic updates	Yes	Yes	Yes	Yes	Yes
Nice to Have					
Hacker tracking	No	Yes	Yes	No	Yes
Color-coded alerts	No	Yes	No	No	Yes
Emergency button	Yes	No	Yes	Yes	Yes
External security scan	No	No	Yes	Yes	No

Table 6-7   Logging, Maintenance, and "Nice to Have" Features *(continued)*

Why Price Is Important

Firewall companies charge you for updates in the same way that Internet filtering and antivirus companies do. Updates to your firewall are not optional, in my opinion. New vulnerabilities (security flaws) are published in software every day, including

	Kerio	McAfee	Norton	Outpost Firewall Pro	ZoneAlarm Pro
Installation					
Completely automatic	Yes			Yes	
Semiautomatic		Yes	Yes		Yes
Manual process					
Installation tutorial	No	Yes	Yes	Yes	Yes
Need to reboot computer	Yes	No	Yes, twice	Yes	Yes

Table 6-8   Installation and Removal Features

	Kerio	McAfee	Norton	Outpost Firewall Pro	ZoneAlarm Pro
Automatically downloads the latest updates after you install	No	Yes	Yes	No	No
Removal					
Completely automatic	Yes	Yes	Yes	Yes	Yes
Semiautomatic					
Requires a password	No	No	No	No	Yes
Need to reboot computer	Yes	Yes	Yes	Yes	Yes

Table 6-8   Installation and Removal Features *(continued)*

firewall software. It is therefore vital that you install not only the latest security patches but also upgrades to your firewall software. A firewall vendor isn't necessarily going to promote the fact that their fantastic, whiz-bang firewall software has a major security hole in it. What they will do is release a new version and quietly fix the flaw. It's up to you to keep it up to date. Table 6-9 shows the upfront and ongoing costs of firewall software.

Application	Free Trial Days	Upfront Cost	Free Updates Included	Cost of Future Product Updates
Kerio	N/A	Free for home and personal use	Unlimited	Unlimited
McAfee	30 days	U.S.$49.99 in a box or U.S.$39.99 to download	One year	U.S.$39.95 annual subscription
Norton	15 days	U.S.$49.95	One year	U.S.$29.95
Outpost Firewall Pro	30 days	U.S.$49.95	One year	U.S.$19.95 for one year
ZoneAlarm Pro	30 days	U.S.$49.95 for one year or U.S.$69.90 for two years	One year or two years	U.S.$19.95 for one year or U.S.$39.90 for two years

Table 6-9   Pricing in U.S. Dollars

My Verdict on the Best Firewall Product to Use

As you have seen, many different Internet firewall products are available in the marketplace today. Here's my view on which ones are the best.

 ## First Place: ZoneAlarm Pro

In my opinion, ZoneAlarm Pro is the best personal firewall for home users. Here are the top five reasons why I'd choose ZoneAlarm Pro:

- It's very easy to use; once you install it, you'll probably forget it's there.

- A lot of support and tutorials are available, so you shouldn't have any problems installing it or finding out how to do something.

- It has many features that protect your information and privacy.

- It blocks annoying advertising while still allowing you to view a web page properly.

- It password-protects your configuration and setup so your children will not be able to remove it.

ZoneAlarm Pro outperforms all the firewall products evaluated by a long shot. Its manufacturer, ZoneLabs, has obviously designed the firewall from scratch, aiming at the home-user market, and it really shows.

| tip | *ZoneAlarm Pro has a sister product called ZoneAlarm. ZoneAlarm doesn't have any of the features found in ZoneAlarm Pro, with the exception of the firewall. However, ZoneAlarm is worth considering because it's free for personal use. You can view a list of free products on the Keep Your Kids Safe website at http://www.keepyourkidssafe.com* |

Second Place: McAfee Personal Firewall Plus

Personal Firewall Plus is easy to install and configure. McAfee provides many different ways to obtain technical support before you need to spend more money by using their paid telephone support. For example, you can read through their knowledge base of solutions or talk with other users on their forums. Best of all, you can chat with a McAfee technical support on the Internet for free.

Third Place: Norton Personal Firewall

Norton Personal Firewall and McAfee Personal Firewall Plus are very similar in terms of functionality, although Norton has slightly more advanced Internet filtering. Unfortunately, their technical support isn't as good as McAfee. There are no forums or online chat, and their telephone support is very expensive.

Honorable Mention: Outpost Firewall Pro

If you have a working knowledge of computers and the Internet, you can't ignore Outpost Firewall Pro. It's extremely customizable and will enable you to lock down your PC and home network so they are "watertight."

Internet Security Suites

Both Symantec and Network Associates have bundled together their most popular home-security products into competing suites. These suites are sold at a lesser cost than buying the individual components and appear to provide a good value for your money. Table 6-10 provides a comparison of these two Internet security suites.

	Norton Internet Security 2004	McAfee Internet Security 2004
Antivirus software	Yes	Yes
Firewall software	Yes	Yes
Content filtering	Yes	Yes
Spam filter	Yes	Yes
Intrusion detection	Yes	Yes
Ad blocking	Yes	Yes
Cookie filtering	Yes	Yes
Secure deletion of files	No	Yes
Strong encryption of files	No	Yes
Web usage cleaner	No	Yes

Table 6-10   Comparison of Internet Security Suites

Problems with Internet Security Suites

Both McAfee and Symantec started in the antivirus industry. Both companies have acquired technology such as their firewall products from buying other, smaller companies. This technology has been re-branded and upgraded to become a suite of security products.

On face value, Internet security suites look as if they have everything you need. However, based on the research in this book, more effective and cheaper products are available in the marketplace, and you are better off with them. However, you must make sure you get the right product for the right reasons. Just as you wouldn't go out of your way to purchase the cheapest baby seat for your car, you shouldn't base this decision solely on price either.

How You Can Save $$$

Although Internet security suites may seem very attractive to budget-conscious people, there are a number of other alternatives that can save you money and get you better software to keep your children safe. Here are my top six tips for getting the best value for your money:

○ *Buy online and download the software from the Internet.* In most cases, you will save up to U.S.$10 per product, and you don't have to pay for postage. Just make sure you back up the software you download. Some vendors give you an option to order a backup CD (which they post to you) at an extra cost. Other vendors offer an extended download service whereby you can download the product again for up to 12 months. This is also useful if your computer crashes and you have to rebuild/reformat it.

○ *Be on the lookout for software bundles because you can save money when you buy a few products together.* Some software companies bundle other vendors' software with their products. For example, if you order the ZoneAlarm Pro firewall from the Zone Labs website, you can purchase PestPatrol for U.S.$19.95 (saving you U.S.$10).

○ *Buy more support and updates up front.* Some vendors give you a discount if you purchase two or more years of support when you initially buy the product. Although you might spend a little extra here, you will save a lot of money when it comes time to renew the product in 12 months.

○ *Use shopping carts on Internet websites wisely.* Some vendors try to sell you additional software at a discount, just before you enter your purchasing details. Use this to your advantage by going as far into the shopping cart as possible (without committing to buy anything) and see what they offer.

○ *If you like two particular products from the same vendor, have a look on their website for a special deal or a software bundle.* You can save up to 20 percent off the total cost of the software. For example, McAfee offers a Webessentials software bundle that contains VirusScan and Personal Firewall Plus for U.S.$69.90 (downloaded from the Internet). If you were to purchase these two products separately, they would cost U.S.$89.98. Buying the Webessentials package would save you U.S.$20!

○ *Take advantage of competitive upgrades.* If your virus scanner is outdated and you need to purchase a new subscription, you should seriously think about moving to a different vendor. As I type this paragraph, McAfee is currently offering a U.S.$20 competitive rebate. You will need to search through the vendor's website in order to find the terms and conditions, but a U.S.$20 discount is definitely worth it.

You can find a list of other moneysaving tips on the book's website at http://www.keepyourkidssafe.com. Make sure you check it out before you buy anything!

Firewall Products in Detail

I have evaluated five firewall products in detail: Kerio Personal Firewall, McAfee Personal Firewall Plus, Norton Personal Firewall, Outpost Firewall Pro, and ZoneAlarm Pro. Here are my findings.

Kerio Personal Firewall

Overall Rating

Product: 3 out of 5
Support: 3 out of 5

Version Tested

4.0.11

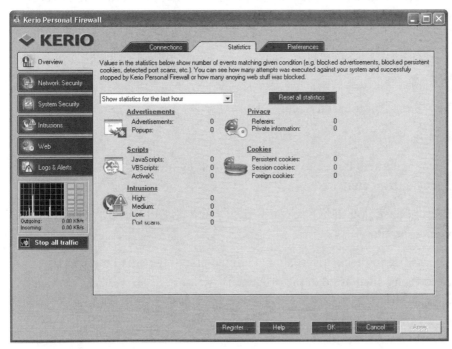

Installation Process

Kerio Personal Firewall is 4.96MB and took me less than three minute to download from the Kerio website. Installation was lightning fast—a few clicks, and in the blink of an eye it was done.

Pros

○ Excellent real-time statistics on software that is running on your computer.

○ Allows you to save the firewall configuration, which can be very handy if your computer crashes and you need to reinstall the software.

○ Contains built-in protection against modem hijacking software (see the upcoming section titled "Firewall").

○ Uses a complex algorithm (MD5) to validate the authenticity of programs that access the Internet. This ensures you are protected from malicious software impersonating legitimate programs that have permission to access the Internet.

Cons

○ Very technical user interface.

○ Limited online help.

○ There is no help button to assist you in making a decision in how to respond to an alert.

○ Does not ask you for a password when you uninstall the software from your computer.

○ The ability to block advertising is limited due to the small number of advertising sites listed in the product.

Firewall

The firewall has been written for Internet-savvy users. Unfortunately, the user interface isn't as friendly as it could be. It displays technical terms such as TCP, UDP, remote point, and trusted zones. As such, first-time Internet users may have difficulty using the product.

One brilliant feature I believe will become mainstream is the built-in modem-hijacking protection. This protects against programs that hijack your dial-up Internet connection (without you knowing) and dial an expensive 1-900 number on your telephone. If you use an ADSL modem or have a broadband connection, you are not at risk.

Hijacking software is known as a "dialer" or "porn dialer" because it's often used to provide access to pornographic websites. To some people, this may sound far fetched, but it happens all the time, and people don't know about it until they see their phone bill; by then, it's far too late.

Support

The user manual is over 30 pages and is available on the Kerio website. There is also a set of frequently asked questions as well as links to external forums and discussion groups pertaining to the firewall. Telephone support is not available; however, e-mail support is, which is quite good for a free product!

McAfee Personal Firewall Plus

Overall Rating

Product: 3.5 out of 5
Support: 4 out of 5

Version Tested

2004 v5.0.1.5

Installation Process

The installation was very easy. It took six minutes to download the evaluation version from the McAfee website and another three minutes to configure the software and reboot the computer. The configuration was extremely automated; however, you can also customize the software to meet your individual requirements.

Pros

- Shows you all the programs running on your computer and accessing the Internet.

- Automatically allows programs on your computer to communicate with the Internet based on your security settings.

- Provides a setup assistant to guide you through configuring the firewall to suit your own requirements.

Cons

- Does not block cookies, advertisements, and scripts.

- The security settings are quite technical in some areas (see the upcoming section titled "Firewall").

- Automatically reports attacks on your computer to hackerwatch.org (see "Firewall").

Firewall

The McAfee Personal Firewall performs very well and has many of the advanced features that make your life easier. These include remembering what applications access the Internet and providing detailed information on security violations.

McAfee Personal Firewall has an alert system of red, green, and blue alerts that informs you about possible security threats. The color system provides the level of severity, with red being the highest. One feature that could be overlooked by home users is that the software automatically reports attacks on your computer (called "inbound events") to the hackerwatch.org website using a unique identification number to identify you. The hackerwatch.org website provides high-level information on threats that try to break into your computer. These threats could be crackers or the latest worm or computer virus. Although the user manual states that your e-mail address is kept confidential, I personally feel comfortable with my computer sending this kind of information to a third party. You can turn this off by clicking the Settings button, selecting the Event Log Settings tab, and unchecking the box that says "Automatically report events to Hackerwatch.org."

One very minor issue with Personal Firewall Plus is that some areas of the program, such as the firewall/security settings, are quite technical. For example, "Accept ICMP Pings" may not mean anything to the home user. The online help doesn't provide much insight into what this actually means. It states "ICMP traffic is used mainly for performing traces and pings. Pinging is frequently used to perform a quick test before attempting to initiate communications."

Support

The user manual is over 30 pages and is written for a computer-literate audience. Although it has a few screenshots so you can relate what you are reading to what you actually see on the screen, it could do with a few more. The manual has a little too much jargon, with phrases such as "source IP address is spoofed" that don't mean anything to the end user. The online documentation on the McAfee website is excellent. It contains a list of frequently asked questions that are grouped by subjects such as error messages, install, and registration. If the online documentation doesn't answer your question, you can chat live with McAfee's technical support staff for free!

Norton Personal Firewall

Overall Rating

Product: 3.5 out of 5
Support: 3.5 out of 5

Version Tested

2004

Installation Process

The installation process took six minutes. The computer had to reboot twice, once after installing the firewall software and another after LiveUpdate downloaded the latest updates (3.9MB) from the Internet. Norton Personal Firewall automatically creates rules to allow MSN Messenger to communicate with the Internet.

Pros

○ Has an "Ad Trashcan" where you can configure your firewall to block specific types of advertisements.

○ Blocks a large number of advertisers and advertising methods.

○ Recognizes different networks and applies the relevant security settings.

○ Has a very-easy-to-use interface.

○ Real-time statistics are extremely detailed.

Cons

○ The default security settings are insecure (see the upcoming section titled "Firewall").

○ Does not ask for a password when you uninstall it from your computer.

Firewall

Norton Personal Firewall has a "Private Information" area that allows you to enter sensitive information you don't want transmitted on the Internet. This feature includes several categories of information, such as your bank account details, credit card number, pin number, address details, and social security number. This "feature" is a great concept but a very bad idea. What if a new Trojan horse or a worm exploits a new security flaw and steals this information? Entering in sensitive information such as your bank details into a computer is almost asking for trouble.

The "Automatic Program Control" feature is also very insecure. If you use this feature, the program changes the security settings for programs that "Symantec has identified as safe." I don't believe that peer-to-peer and instant messaging programs are safe for children to use. Because this feature is turned on by default, the firewall will allow such programs. The "Automatic Program Control" feature should be turned off and left off.

One major flaw with Norton Personal Firewall is that it doesn't ask you for the password when you uninstall the software from your computer. This means that your children can remove the firewall and run their own programs, rendering the firewall useless.

Support

The user manual that comes with Norton Personal Firewall is fantastic. It is well written and one of the best I've seen.

Telephone support is a whopping U.S.$29.95 per incident. If you want help to remove a virus, it will cost you between U.S.$39.95 and U.S.$69.95 per incident. A few calls to the technical support line could cost you more than you paid for the product.

Outpost Firewall Pro

Overall Rating

Product: 3.5 out of 5

Support: 3.5 out of 5

Version Tested

2.1.292.3816 (307)

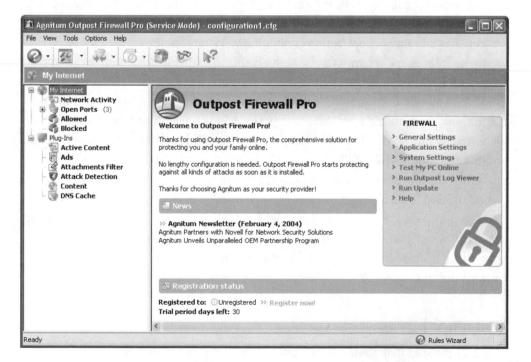

Installation Process

The software is 5.9MB in size and downloaded in less than four minutes using an ADSL modem. This quick download can be attributed to the Agnitum website, which was very fast. The installation itself took approximately two minutes because I allowed the firewall to configure itself and then reboot the computer.

Pros

- ○ Supports different languages, including Italian, Spanish, and Russian.

- ○ Provides multiple ways to configure your firewall (see the upcoming section titled "Firewall").

- ○ Provides extremely detailed logging of applications.

- ○ Displays Internet activity in real time.

- ○ Displays the number of open ports running on the computer.

- ○ Contains an extensive list of advertising companies (in order to block ads).

- ○ Filters scripts and cookies contained in e-mail messages.

Cons

- ○ The user interface can be overwhelming to the average home user.

- ○ The auto-configured rules find and automatically allow file-sharing applications (and any other programs they find) access to the Internet.

- ○ Ad blocking may cause web pages to be displayed incorrectly.

- ○ Allows anyone to uninstall the program even when password protected (see "Firewall").

Part II

The Best Software to Protect Your Kids

Firewall

Outpost Firewall Pro has many configurable features. An IT/Internet expert would feel at ease with this product; however, a home user would be quite daunted. For example, the firewall shows a list of "open ports" (programs that are listening to the Internet) but doesn't provide any detail as to what an open port is.

The online help is difficult to use; for example, clicking a question mark activates the help function and also changes the cursor (the pointy mouse thing) to a question mark. After this, you then have to click the item you need help with. The "standard" help key, F1, displays the documentation rather than providing help on the item you require.

Outpost Firewall Pro has the ability to password-protect the configuration settings. This prevents your children from changing the firewall. Unfortunately, it doesn't prevent your children from uninstalling the product.

The firewall has a number of good features that other products lack, such as the ability to configure the firewall to operate according to different policies. For example, you may want to prevent all programs from connecting to the Internet unless you specifically allow them. Alternatively, you may want to make the rules up as you go along.

Support

A lot of support is available for Outpost Firewall Pro, ranging from frequently asked questions, online forums, and live chat (unofficial) to websites that have been created by Outpost Firewall enthusiasts.

During the evaluation process, I connected to the live chat facility and nobody was in the chat room. It seems that Agnitum (the makers of Outpost Pro) does not provide any full-time resources to manning the chat room.

ZoneAlarm Pro

Overall Rating

Product: 4.5 out of 5
Support: 3.5 out of 5

Version Tested

5.0.590.015

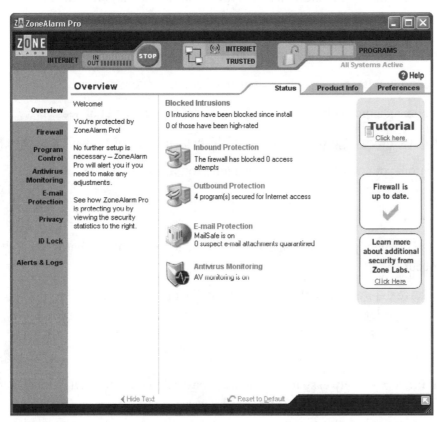

Installation Process

ZoneAlarm Pro is 5.6MB and took me less than three minutes to download.

The installation process was very easy. Everything was explained in detail, and the application went as far as to provide a tutorial so that the whole thing went smoothly.

Pros

○ Automatically blocks more than 48 types of unsafe e-mail attachments.

○ Blocks JavaScript and ActiveX scripts that run on websites.

○ Blocks third-party, session, and persistent cookies.

○ Blocks annoying pop-up advertisements that clutter your screen.

○ Recognizes home networks and applies an appropriate level of security.

○ Provides a web page with "plain English" explanations of firewall alerts.

○ Monitors your antivirus software and tells you if it's up to date.

Cons

○ Does not allow you to set a specific time/date for automatic updates to occur.

○ You have to pay for telephone support and it's only available in North America.

Firewall

ZoneAlarm Pro is extremely easy to use and has many unique features. Of particular note is the ability to control cookies (files used by websites to keep track of visitors). For example, you can block third-party cookies that usually reside in advertisements on websites, but allow cookies for the websites you visit. This type of blocking is great for protecting your privacy. The ability to block JavaScript and ActiveX controls is also excellent.

Support

A substantial amount of technical support is available on the ZoneLabs website. This consists of a bulletin board where users can talk to one another as well as a set of frequently asked questions. Also, a large amount of online documentation comes with the product. Toll-free premium telephone support is U.S.$2.95 per minute, 8 A.M. to 5 P.M., Monday to Friday, which is billed to your credit card. Alternatively, you can use a 1-900 number that is applied to your telephone bill.

CHAPTER 7

Antivirus Software

In this chapter, I explain the results of my evaluation of what I believe to be the top antivirus software programs available today. I begin with a discussion of what antivirus software is and why you need it, before moving on to a summary of the key differences between the products I evaluated. I then explain the pros and cons of each program in detail.

A "virus" is a computer program that is malicious or destructive in nature. A virus "infects" your computer by attaching itself to a legitimate program (file) to replicate itself. Viruses contain instructions that cause damage to your computer. This can range from the corruption or deletion of computer files to disclosing confidential information to another computer. A "worm" is similar to a virus in that it is malicious; however, unlike viruses, worms replicate themselves and infest computer networks. This eventually leads to the consumption of all the available computing resources and results in computer networks slowing down and crashing.

What Is Antivirus Software and Why Do You Need It?

An antivirus software program looks for and destroys known computer viruses and worms. It identifies a virus by looking for a fingerprint that identifies that virus. Just as you and I have a unique fingerprint that identifies us, a virus has a unique digital fingerprint that identifies it. In computer virus terminology, this fingerprint is called a "signature."

In addition to identifying known computer viruses using a signature, antivirus software can also look out for unusual behavior. For example, a program that reads your address book and sends out e-mail messages could be seen as hostile. This method of identifying viruses can lead to a previously undiscovered virus or a different version (strain) of an existing virus.

The two main types of antivirus programs are online scanners and programs you must install on your own computer. An online scanner is a computer program that you download directly from the antivirus vendor. Unlike a traditional virus scanner, which remains on your computer all the time, an online scanner is only active when you visit the antivirus vendor's website, download the scanner, and commence scanning your computer. Trend Micro produced the first online scanner in May 1997. It's still free and available for anyone to use. Other companies caught onto the idea, and in 1999, McAfee (Network Associates) launched its VirusScan Online, with Symantec following suit in 2000 with its Security Check service. A few years later, McAfee created a free virus-scanning service called FreeScan, and Computer Associates followed suit in late 2003 with eTrust Antivirus. Table 7-1 details the differences between the products.

You can find more information at the following websites:

- **Trend Micro**   http://housecall.trendmicro.com

- **McAfee FreeScan**   http://www.mcafee.com

- **Symantec Security Check**   http://www.symantec.com/securitycheck

- **eTrust AntiVirus Web Scanner**   http://www3.ca.com/virusinfo/virusscan.aspx

You may be asking yourself why you should pay for a software product when you can just use a free online virus scanner? The answer is that an online scanner doesn't stay on your computer and actively look for viruses. If your children bring home CDs or disks from school, an online scanner won't work because you won't be connected to the Internet. Unfortunately, virus writers are creating new viruses, such as the Klez virus, that disable online scanners and render them useless.

Product	Cost	Scans for Viruses	Cleans Viruses	Scans Inside Compressed Files
Trend Micro HouseCall	Free	Yes	Yes	Yes
McAfee FreeScan	Free	Yes	No	Yes
Symantec Security Check	Free	Yes	No	No
eTrust AntiVirus Web Scanner	Free	Yes	Yes	Yes

Table 7-1   Comparison of Online Scanners

Antivirus software also comes as part of a Security Suite of programs. Many vendors bundle together their own brand of firewall, antivirus, and privacy-protection products and sell them at a discount. Although saving money on computer software seems attractive, you need to assess exactly what you are getting. You can find more information on Internet Security Suites in Chapter 6.

Which Antivirus Software Is the Best?

There is no "best" antivirus software. Many vendors claim that their software detects the "most" viruses, but this cannot be easily proven.

A good, independent source of analysis is the *Virus Bulletin,* a magazine that tests antivirus software against viruses that are known to be causing incidents worldwide. The viruses selected in the testing process are located on a list called the Wild List, which is made up of submissions from more than 70 antivirus professionals. Table 7-2 summarizes the results of tests conducted by the *Virus Bulletin.* It shows the number of times an antivirus company has failed independent tests between June 2002 and February 2004. Failing means that the product did not detect all the viruses in the Wild List. This doesn't necessarily mean that the product cannot provide adequate protection, because there are a number of reasons why a product could fail. You can find more information and read the reviews on the *Virus Bulletin* website at http://www.virusbtn.com/vb100/.

	June 2002	November 2002	February 2003	June 2003	November 2003	February 2004
	Windows XP	Windows 2000 Advanced Server	Windows NT	Windows XP Pro	Windows 2003 Server	Windows NT
Kaspersky	Fail	Pass	Pass	Fail	Pass	Pass
McAfee	Pass	Pass	Pass	Pass	Pass	Pass
Norton	Pass	Pass	Pass	Pass	Pass	Pass
Trend	Fail	Pass	Pass	Pass	Pass	Pass
EZ Antivirus	Pass	Pass	Pass	Pass	Fail	Pass

Table 7-2   *Virus Bulletin* Testing Results

However, as with firewalls and Internet filtering programs, you have other considerations to think about with antivirus programs, namely the following:

- ○ Which program can you run on your home computer without slowing it down?

- ○ Which program can you set up and run the easiest?

- ○ Which program takes the least ongoing effort to maintain?

- ○ Which vendor will not charge you more money for updates in 12 months' time?

As with all software products, the answer to the first question depends on the minimum requirements for the software and how powerful your computer is. In the following sections, I summarize the differences between the programs I evaluated in terms of minimum requirements, how the programs update, virus definition file size, price, technical support, and general features.

Table 7-3 gives details about the top five antivirus programs in question, in alphabetical order.

Minimum System Requirements

Antivirus software can consume both memory and processing power. This increases when you scan files in real time and configure the software to scan web pages and e-mail messages. As a minimum, your computer should have more memory and processing (CPU) power than what is mentioned here. Otherwise, you will find that the antivirus software will slow down your computer.

Antivirus Program	Version	URL
eTrust EZ Antivirus	2005 v6.2.0.28	http://www.my-etrust.com
Kaspersky Anti-Virus Personal	4.5.0.94	http://www.kaspersky.com
McAfee VirusScan	2004 v8.0	http://www.mcafeeathome.com
Norton AntiVirus	2004	http://www.symantec.com
Trend PC-cillin Internet Security	2004	http://www.antivirus.com

Table 7-3   Antivirus Scanners

	Kaspersky	McAfee	Norton	Trend	EZ Antivirus
9MB	All versions				All versions
35MB	Windows 98, Me, 2000, XP				
85MB			Windows 2000 Pro, XP Home, XP Pro		
100MB				Windows 98, 98SE, Me, 2000, XP	
125MB			Windows 98/98SE, Me		

Table 7-4   Hard Disk Requirements

If you start sweating at the mention of RAM, CPU, and hard disk space because you have no idea what they are, don't worry! Generally speaking, if you purchased your computer within the last three years, you should have no problems. If your computer is older than three years, you may need to upgrade it. If you run Windows XP and don't know how much RAM or what CPU you have, you can find out by clicking on the Start button, selecting My Computer and then selecting View System Information.

When upgrading your computer, it's better to get more memory (RAM) and CPU (processing) than anything else. Although some programs ask for a minimum of 256MB of RAM, you would be better off buying 512MB of RAM. Computer programs are constantly consuming memory, so an extra $50 to $100 spent now could save you from having to upgrade in another year or two. Tables 7-4 through Table 7-7 provide the minimum hard disk, RAM, and CPU requirements for your computer in order to run antivirus software. Table 7-8 provides you with a list of web browsers that are supported.

	Kaspersky	McAfee	Norton	Trend	EZ Antivirus
32MB		Windows 98, Me, 2000, XP	Windows 98, 98SE, Me		Windows 95, 98, Me
64MB	All versions		Windows 2000 Pro	Windows 98, 98SE, Me, 2000	Windows NT Workstation
128MB			Windows XP Home, XP Pro	Windows XP Home, XP Pro	Windows 2000, XP Home, XP Pro

Table 7-5   RAM Requirements for Antivirus Software

	Kaspersky	McAfee	Norton	Trend	EZ Antivirus
Pentium 133 MHz		Windows 98, Me, 2000, XP	Windows 98/98SE, Windows Me, 2000 Pro		Windows 95, 98, Me, NT, 2000, XP
Pentium II 233 MHz				Windows 98, 98SE, Me	
Pentium II 300 MHz	All versions		Windows XP Home, XP Pro	Windows 2000, XP Home, XP Pro	

Table 7-6   CPU Requirements for Antivirus Software

	Kaspersky	McAfee	Norton	Trend	EZ Antivirus
Windows 95					Yes
Windows 98	Yes	Yes	Yes	Yes	Yes
Windows 98 SE	Yes	Yes	Yes	Yes	Yes
Windows Me	Yes	Yes	Yes	Yes	Yes
Windows XP Home	Yes	Yes	Yes	Yes	Yes
Windows XP Pro	Yes	Yes	Yes	Yes	Yes
Windows 2000 Pro	Yes	Yes	Yes	Yes	Yes
Windows NT 4.0 Workstation	Yes				Yes

Table 7-7   Operating Systems Supported

	Kaspersky	McAfee	Norton	Trend	EZ Antivirus
Internet Explorer 4.01 SP2	Yes				
Internet Explorer 5.0		Yes			
Internet Explorer 5.1 SP2			Yes		
Internet Explorer 5.5 SP2				Yes	
Netscape Communicator 7.0				Yes	

Table 7-8   Web Browser and CD-ROM Supported

Part II

The Best Software to Protect Your Kids

Automatic Updates Are Critical—Update as Often as Possible

As with Internet filtering software and firewalls, an automatic update feature means that your software will automatically connect to the vendor website and receive updates. These updates are also known as "virus definition files" or "DAT files." With respect to antivirus software, updates mean *virus signatures*—the ability to detect and prevent the latest viruses. Because viruses are being created and spread all the time, the automatic updating feature is critical. Also, the *automatic* part of automatic updates is particularly important in relation to antivirus software. You are unlikely to have the time to check your antivirus software vendor's website all the time. To put it bluntly, if your antivirus program can't detect and prevent the very latest viruses, it is next to useless. Depending on the antivirus program, you can configure it to automatically update at regular intervals, when you connect to the Internet, or upon a virus outbreak.

Should You Update When Your Computer Connects to the Internet?   Some antivirus software programs update when they see that you are connected to the Internet. This is a great feature, but you need to be connected to the Internet long enough for the updates to download onto your computer. In addition, if you are connected to the Internet via a 56K modem, Internet access may appear slow until the download is completed. Norton AntiVirus uses LiveUpdate to check for an Internet connection every five minutes until one is found and then checks for updates every four hours. McAfee Auto Update checks every 24 hours from the time you installed your product.

What about the Update upon a Virus Outbreak Option?   This option allows the antivirus vendor to give you the latest patch when there is a virus outbreak. Although this may seem like a good idea in theory, you may get the virus before you have the opportunity to download the patch.

Should You Update at Regular Time Intervals?   Some antivirus software programs connect to the vendor at regular time intervals and download the latest patches.

Is the Auto Inquiry Option a Good Idea?   This option is similar to updating at regular time intervals, but in this case the patches are not downloaded. The software just tells you that they are available so that you can go and download them manually. This is a good option for the paranoid computer user who doesn't want strange files being downloaded to their computer. But, in reality, it's just more work for you.

Virus Definition Files

When your antivirus software downloads the latest updates from the Internet, it basically downloads and installs a file from the manufacturer's website. This file is called a "virus definition file" and is known as an "update." Some updates can be quite large and take considerable time to download. This may cost you money in Internet charges, as well as slow down your Internet access until the download is complete. If you use a 56K modem to connect to the Internet, you will definitely notice the slower Internet speed when your antivirus software is updating itself.

Table 7-9 compares the size of the virus definition files from each vendor. Definition files can be downloaded either automatically using antivirus software or manually via the vendor website.

Part II

The Best Software to Protect Your Kids

	Kaspersky	McAfee	Norton	Trend	EZ Antivirus
Size	3.21MB	5.51MB	4.47MB	3.6MB	1.12MB
Version	avp0401	4320/4324	20040217-017	767	5238
Date	Jan 2004 #	Feb 17, 2004	Feb 6, 2004	Feb 17, 2004	Feb 17, 2004
Average Download Speed	26.3 Kbps	28.0 Kbps	28.1 Kbps	27.5 Kbps	20.9 Kbps
Time *	2 minutes, 4 seconds	3 minutes, 21 seconds	2 minutes, 42 seconds	2 minutes, 14 seconds	54 seconds

* Based on the average download speed.

\# Kaspersky has daily, weekly, and monthly updates, the largest being monthly. The monthly update (the largest one) was used in this comparison. The average download speed was tested using a 256 Kbps ADSL connection.

Table 7-9   Comparison of Virus Definition File Sizes and Download Speeds

The amount of time to download a file can vary significantly. It can depend on the quality of the phone line, your distance from your telephone exchange, the quality of your ISP, and where the file is located. As such, the download speed provided is an estimate only.

Price: What Are the Hidden Costs?

One of the most common mistakes people make when purchasing antivirus software is to make their purchasing decisions based on the retail price. This might seem strange until you realize that ongoing costs are associated with antivirus products. Although one product might be cheaper to purchase up front, you may have to pay extra for support. Other products may be more expensive to purchase up front, but they are cheaper when it comes time to renew your annual subscription.

At the time of writing, Table 7-10 gives details of what you'll pay for each product.

It's common practice among antivirus vendors to give you a one-year free subscription when you buy the product. This subscription allows you to download updates from the vendor's website over the course of that year. Remember that if you can't download these updates, your antivirus software is useless.

	Kaspersky	McAfee	Norton	Trend	EZ Antivirus
United States (U.S.$)					
Boxed Version	$49.95 (excluding shipping)	$59.99 ***	$58.90 **	N/A	N/A
Internet Download	$49.95	$49.99	$49.95	$49.95	$29.95
Australia (AU$) (inc. GST)					
Boxed Version	$75.24	$89.95	$99.95	$99.95	N/A
Internet Download	N/A	$74.95	$90.85 *	$89.95	N/A

* The file you download from the Internet is 24.83MB.

** The boxed version must be ordered from the Symantec website and includes a U.S.$8.95 shipping charge to the "lower 48" states in the U.S.

*** The boxed version must be ordered from the McAfee website. The price does not include shipping.

Table 7-10   Pricing

At the end of the year, many antivirus vendors have a new product that you can upgrade to, or you can take out a subscription for virus definition files for another year.

Annual Cost (Virus Definition Subscription)   Antivirus software is only as good as the last virus definitions it contains because your software will expire one year after you purchase it, and you will need to renew. Table 7-11 compares the annual costs of antivirus upgrades.

You will know when your antivirus software is due for renewal because it will display a message on your computer screen or just stop downloading the latest updates.

	Kaspersky	McAfee	Norton	Trend	EZ Antivirus
United States (U.S.$)	$34.96 (30% off the retail price.)	$34.95 **	$29.95 *	$24.97 (50% off the retail price.)	$19.95
Australia (AU$)	$52.69	$59.95 **	$63.60 *	$59.95	N/A

* The upgrade cost for Norton AntiVirus 2004 using the Symantec online store

** The cost to renew your subscription via the McAfee website

Table 7-11   Annual Cost of Antivirus Upgrades

Do You Get Technical Support with Your Virus Scanner Software?

If your virus scanner stops working or updating, then your system is vulnerable to attack. This means that information stored on your computer, such as your children's assignments as well as your resume, accounting, and household budget, may be erased. Here are two key questions you should ask yourself:

○ Is technical support available in my country?

○ Do I have to pay more money to speak to someone on the telephone?

If you have to call overseas for technical support and/or pay for technical support, this could add up to a lot of money. Table 7-12 compares the technical support provided by the antivirus vendors.

Part II

The Best Software to Protect Your Kids

	Kaspersky	McAfee	Norton	Trend	EZ Antivirus
Website Knowledge Base	Yes	Yes	Yes	Yes	Yes
Online Chat with Technician	No	Yes (free)	No	No	No
E-mail	Yes (free)	1 year free (24/7)	Yes, via an online form	Yes	Yes, via an online form
Telephone	Yes. Free with a current subscription	1 year free (24/7). Afterward, it's U.S.$2.95 per minute, first 2 minutes free, or U.S.$39.00 per single incident	U.S.$29.95 per incident, 6:00 A.M. to 5:00 P.M. Pacific Time, Monday through Friday	Toll free U.S. 1-800 number. 5 A.M. to 5 P.M. Pacific Time, Monday through Friday	U.S.$49.95 for one support issue, U.S.$99.95 for three support issues, and U.S.$149.95 for five support issues
Internet Message Boards/Forums	Yes	Yes	No	No	No
Internet Software Manuals	Yes	Yes	Yes	Yes	Yes

Table 7-12   Technical Support Comparison

Features: What Do You Really Need?

It's critical that your software scans e-mail and files you download from the Internet and looks for malicious scripts in JavaScript and ActiveX. This will block all the avenues for viruses to infect your computer. If you or your children use Instant Messaging, the software should also scan files that are sent by these programs. If your children have a tendency to get into your computer and change things, you will find that password-protecting your antivirus software is extremely useful. Tables 7-13 through Table 7-15 show the setup, security, and scanning features found in antivirus software.

	Kaspersky	McAfee	Norton	Trend	EZ Antivirus
Configuration Wizard	Yes	Yes	Yes	Yes	Yes
Automatic Update after Install	No	Yes	Yes	Yes	Yes
Automatic Scan after Install	No	No	No	Yes	Yes

Table 7-13   Setup Features Included in Antivirus Software

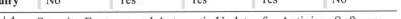

	Kaspersky	McAfee	Norton	Trend	EZ Antivirus
Security Features					
Password Protected Configuration	Yes	No	Yes	Yes	Yes
Password Protected Uninstall	No	No	No	No	No
Automatic Updates					
Upon Connecting to the Internet	No	No	No	Yes	Yes
Upon a Virus Outbreak	No	No	No	Yes	No
Automatically	Yes	Yes	Yes	Yes	Yes
Auto Inquiry	No	Yes	Yes	Yes	No

Table 7-14   Security Features and Automatic Updates for Antivirus Software

	Kaspersky	McAfee	Norton	Trend	EZ Antivirus
Scans Incoming E-mail	Yes *	Yes	Yes	Yes	Yes *
Scans Outgoing E-mail	Yes *	Yes	Yes	Yes	Yes *
Scans Internet Downloads	Yes *	Yes	Yes	Yes	Yes *
Scans JavaScript and ActiveX	No	Yes *	Yes	No	No
Scans Yahoo! IM	No *	v4.1 +	v5.0 +	No *	No *
Scans AOL IM	No *	v2.1 +	v4.7 +	No *	No *
Scans MSN Messenger	No *	v6.0 +	v4.6 +	No *	No *
Scans Windows Messenger	No *	No *	v4.7 +	No *	No *
My Computer Integration	Yes	Yes	Yes	Yes	Yes

+ The software version number is a minimum requirement.

* The product uses its real-time scanner to detect viruses when a file is saved to the computer or when an e-mail attachment is opened.

Table 7-15   Scanning Capability

My Verdict

I recommend the following products in order of preference: McAfee, Norton, EZ Antivirus, Trend, Kaspersky. McAfee has the best technical support—there are a number of avenues you can easily explore before calling them or forking out more money.

First Place: McAfee VirusScan

VirusScan is easy to use and automatically updates itself in the background. McAfee's online knowledge base provides detailed answers to frequently asked questions and its online forums allow you to discuss the software with other users. If you don't like wading through questions and answers, you can chat online with their technicians for free.

Honorable Mention: eTrust EZ Antivirus

If you are computer literate, or an experienced Internet user, and don't mind downloading antivirus software from the Internet, I recommend EZ Antivirus over all the other products reviewed. Although it doesn't come with all the bells and whistles of some of the other products, it does the job quite well. EZ Antivirus is easy to install, updates itself in the background, and has both e-mail and online support if you need it. The price is also very attractive—nearly half of what the others cost!

Honorable Mention: Norton AntiVirus

Norton AntiVirus is very similar to McAfee; however, Norton's paid telephone support is quite expensive. Norton doesn't have anywhere near the resources (chat, forums, etc.) that McAfee has, so if you need support, go with McAfee.

Antivirus Products in Detail

Now let's look at each of the antivirus products in detail. For each product, you will see an illustration, which will give you an indication as to the look and feel of the product. Take the time to look closely at the user interface so you can get a feel for how easy the program is to operate. However, when you are looking at a particular product, the most important factors to consider are the features. Think about buying a car; you wouldn't pick "the red one" without looking under the hood and making sure it has a motor.

Please note that my observations and evaluations are based on my own experiences and won't necessarily apply when you use the product. For example, a number of factors influence how fast you can access the Internet. These can range from how fast you connect to your ISP, to how many people are currently downloading files from the vendor's website. The factors that influence the type and level of support range from the number of staff answering the phone at a particular time, to their peak and off-peak periods during which their call volume varies.

Kaspersky Anti-Virus Personal

Overall Rating

Product: 2 out of 5

Support: 2 out of 5

Version Tested

4.5.0.94

Part II

The Best Software to Protect Your Kids

Kaspersky Anti-Virus Control Centre

Tasks | Components | Settings | Quarantine

Name	Status
Start Kaspersky Anti-... Always	▶ Running
Update anti-virus bases Daily at 7:30 PM	✔ Done
Start Kaspersky Anti-Viru... Daily at 8:00 PM	

Statistics: Start Kaspersky Anti-...

Wednesday, 10 Marc...   Kaspersky Anti-Virus ...
Anti-virus bases were l..   83627

Scanned:

Sectors	6
Files	1100
Archives	5
Packed files	12
Last object	C:\Documents and ...

Found:

Known viruses	0
Virus bodies	0
Disinfected	0
Deleted	0
Renamed	0
Quarantined	0
Warnings	0
Suspicious	0
Corrupted	0
I/O Errors	0

OK   Cancel   Apply   Help

Installation Process

Kaspersky Anti-Virus Personal is usually downloaded from the Internet rather than purchased in a box at your local computer store. This is because the Kaspersky retail channel is not as big as its competitors, such as McAfee and Symantec.

The software is 12.9MB in size and took more than eight minutes to download using a fast ADSL modem. Although the file is huge, the download speed from the Kaspersky website was very fast, so the time wasn't a huge factor. If you are using a 56K modem, downloading this file will take you a long time. You could save yourself a lot of time by purchasing the product from a computer retailer; however, you still may have to download a few updates to ensure that you have the latest version.

During the installation process, the software asks you for the location of a key file, rather than a serial number. A key file is basically a file attachment that is sent to you via e-mail when you purchase the product from the Kaspersky website. You have to save this file on your computer in order to use the software. Although this could be a more secure way of protecting software, it's a hassle for users to remember where they saved that file on their hard disk. The installation process took less than four minutes, including a reboot of the computer.

Pros

- Automatically schedules a scan of the complete system and automatic updates.

- You can set the product to update the virus signatures on an hourly basis.

Cons

- The user interface is very cluttered and difficult to use as it has buttons everywhere. Computer novices or first-time antivirus users may experience difficulty using this product.

- Allows the user to uninstall the antivirus software without entering a password.

Antivirus

Checking for the latest signature updates can result in up to three pop-up windows on your screen: the Kaspersky AV Updater software, the wizard that guides you through the process, and the antivirus software itself. All these screens can be quite overwhelming.

When ordering the product via the Internet, you can opt for a "CD on demand." This means that Kaspersky Labs will send you a backup copy of your software on CD-ROM for an additional U.S.$6.95. This could be invaluable if your PC crashes.

Support

Telephone

Kaspersky Labs' partners provide technical support worldwide, except in Russia, where you can call Kaspersky Labs directly.

If your local Kaspersky partner doesn't have adequate support, your alternative is to call Kaspersky Labs in Moscow directly; something I won't be doing in a hurry due to the cost.

Website

The helpdesk section of the Kaspersky website was painfully slow, even when accessed by a high-speed 256K Internet connection. When I visited, it took nearly 30 seconds for one page to load!

Kaspersky has a number of options when it comes to support. Although its website has a list of frequently asked questions (FAQs), these presume you have a reasonably detailed knowledge of how computers work. For example, the answer to the question, "How to delete the Klez virus?" says that you need to "re-boot your PC in Safe Mode." It doesn't say *how* to do it, but that you *need* to do it.

The support section on the Kaspersky website has a database of questions that are categorized according to the Kaspersky product you are using. This allows you to skip answers to questions that are not relevant to you. The database further categorizes questions into the following types:

○ General questions

○ Installation, deinstallation

○ License, license period, key files

○ Updates

○ Usage

○ Virus disinfecting

User Manual

The user manual is available for users to download from the Kaspersky website in PDF format. This requires you to install Adobe Acrobat Reader. The manual is 3.4MB in size and takes approximately two minutes to download using a 256K Internet connection.

The manual is 198 pages in length, is extremely detailed, and reads like it has been written for computer-literate users. There are a number of screen captures to help you relate to what you see on your computer screen, although computer novices may find it difficult to understand them.

McAfee VirusScan

Overall Rating

Product: 4 out of 5
Support: 4.5 out of 5

Version Tested

2004 v8.0

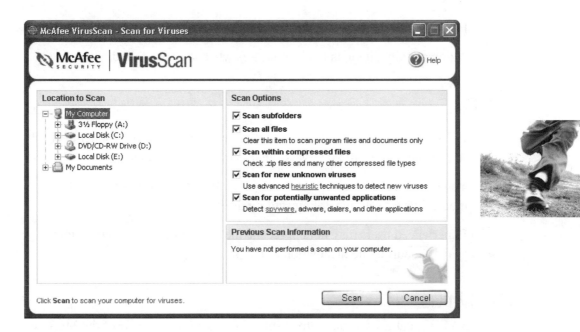

Installation Process

The installation process took just over three minutes and was very quick and easy. VirusScan displayed two progress bars, so I could see exactly how long I had to go until it finished. After the installation was complete, the computer rebooted and VirusScan automatically downloaded the latest updates.

Pros

○ Secure default settings. VirusScan scans all files and updates itself regularly.

○ Very easy to install and configure.

○ A wide range of options for downloading the latest updates.

○ New features to identify and prevent worms and scripts from damaging your computer.

○ Includes spyware and adware detection.

○ Automatically attempts to clean viruses when they are found.

Cons

○ Unlike previous versions of VirusScan, you cannot set the product to check for updates at specific intervals, such as every 30 minutes.

○ You cannot password-protect the software to prevent your children from modifying the settings or uninstalling the product.

○ Experienced users may not appreciate the lack of configuration options available during the installation of the product.

Antivirus

VirusScan is available as a stand-alone software program or as part of the McAfee Internet Security package, which in addition to VirusScan includes SecurityCenter, Personal Firewall Plus, Privacy Service, and SpamKiller (each discussed in the chapters on their respective topics). McAfee SecurityCenter enables you to manage your antivirus, firewall, and filtering software from one location. Whether as a stand-alone program or as part of McAfee Internet Security, the VirusScan user interface is extremely easy to use.

VirusScan can alert you to the latest virus outbreaks, but you shouldn't need these if your VirusScan is up to date. You can turn off the alerts to avoid those little boxes popping up on your desktop with news about the latest viruses.

I was simply amazed with the improvements made to VirusScan since the previous version. With its new user interface and features to prevent worms and malicious scripts, existing VirusScan users should definitely upgrade.

Support

Telephone

Users receive free technical support by telephone and e-mail for the first year. This is provided 24/7 in English only. Non-English support is available from 9 A.M. to 9 P.M., seven days a week.

A number of options are available if you live inside the U.S. These include pay-per-minute (U.S.$2.95, with the first two minutes free), available from 5 A.M to 11 P.M, Pacific, and pay-per-incident (U.S.$39), available from 6 A.M to 10 P.M. Pacific.

Website

The website (http://www.mcafeehelp.com/) has a step-by-step guide for online help. If you can't resolve the issue you're having, you can chat live with a support technician. When I requested help, I got straight through to a technician in less than five seconds! I asked the technical support staff some basic questions, and their answers were correct. Although the website has some good information on it, I was very impressed with the online chat with a support technician. Apart from online chat, http://forums.mcafeehelp.com provides a bulletin board style of questions and answers for the product. A lot of detailed information can be found here, including best practices and news on the latest viruses.

User Manual

The user manual has also improved over the previous version of VirusScan. There are a number of screen captures, which help you to relate what you see on your screen with what you are reading. Although the manual doesn't have many pages, I can't imagine anyone using it, because VirusScan is so easy to use.

Norton AntiVirus

Overall Rating

Product: 4 out of 5
Support: 3 out of 5

Version Tested

2004

Installation Process

The installation for Norton AntiVirus was extremely easy and took ten minutes, including a reboot of the computer. Before the computer rebooted, the software updated itself to the latest version by downloading 2.1MB of files from the Internet.

Pros

- ○ Extremely easy to use.
- ○ Easy-to-read and well-written user manual.
- ○ Scans for viruses located in Instant Message attachments.

Cons

○ When you remove the product, LiveReg and LiveUpdate are left on the computer. This clogs up the computer with unnecessary software.

○ Blocks a small number of spyware and adware.

○ Requires activation based on a key (similar to how you activate Microsoft products).

○ You cannot password-protect the software to prevent your children from uninstalling the product.

○ Technical support is extra and, depending on the incident, can cost you a lot of money.

Antivirus

My only real criticism of Norton AntiVirus 2004 is the use of password protection. Although you can set a password to protect access to your configuration of Norton AntiVirus—effectively preventing your children from changing how it works—the product doesn't ask you for a password when you uninstall it. This means that your children can delete Norton AntiVirus from your computer. This is probably a minor point, though, because your children are unlikely to do so—especially if you've told them why an antivirus program is so important!

Support

Telephone

When I installed Norton AntiVirus 2004 on my machine, I experienced a problem whereby the computer would restart and display a black screen, just before the login screen. I couldn't log in or type anything! I rebooted my computer in "Safe Mode" and removed the program. For the benefit of technically minded people, I also removed Registry keys, deleted temporary files, scanned for DLLs, defragmented the hard disk, changed the startup priority, and even downloaded two programs on the Symantec website that claimed to remove the remnants of prior versions of Norton AntiVirus. Two hours later, I gave up and called their support line.

I had to wait five minutes to get through to technical support. After speaking to two people, I spent one hour and 20 minutes on the telephone with the technician. This didn't cost me anything because it was an installation problem. Unfortunately, we couldn't find out exactly what the problem was, so I had to spend the next day reinstalling Windows XP and all my software.

As you can imagine, I was very annoyed and wanted the last two days of my life back, but I was impressed by the fact that Symantec called me back the following morning. They wanted to know if everything was okay and if there was anything they could do. Now this is what I call customer service! I still have no idea why Norton AntiVirus wouldn't install in the first place, but it works fine now.

The installation process took ten minutes using the CD-ROM version. In order to reduce the installation time, I did not opt for Norton AntiVirus to scan my computer because I already knew that it was virus free. After installing the product, I had to reboot my computer. When it restarted, Norton AntiVirus prompted me to download the latest updates from their website. Although this process took less than a minute, I had to reboot my computer again.

Website

Symantec's website has an online tutorial as well as a knowledge base with a number of "hot topics." Symantec has substantially improved its knowledge base over the past 12 months. The results are now sorted by relevance to ensure greater accuracy.

One particular knowledge base entry you may find useful is how to password-protect the Options menu. This will prevent your kids from changing the settings inside Norton AntiVirus. Unfortunately, it doesn't prevent them from uninstalling the product. You can read the document by searching on the words "password protect" without the quotes or by entering the document ID 2002082212235406.

User Manual

The user manual is easy to understand. It includes a number of screen captures as well as the technical support details of Symantec worldwide.

Trend PC-cillin

Overall Rating

Product: 3.5 out of 5
Support: 4 out of 5

Version Tested

2004

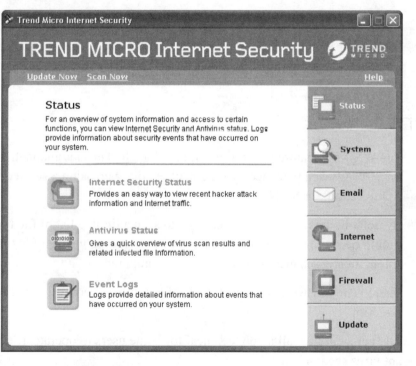

Installation Process

PC-cillin took me just three minutes to install. The registration process was simple, and the program also scanned my computer to detect any viruses before the installation process was complete. The only minor problem was that the product did not tell me when the installation process was complete—just a little icon appeared at the bottom of the screen.

After the installation completed, PC-cillin prompted me to download the latest updates. This process took approximately five minutes, after which I had to reboot the computer.

Pros

○ Extremely easy-to-use interface.

○ Can disable Internet access at a click of a button.

○ Scans your PC for viruses before installation to make sure you are starting from a clean system.

Cons

○ The WebMail feature is not turned on by default. This automatically scans for viruses when you check your e-mail via the Web using a service such as AOL, Yahoo!, or MSN.

○ By default, the real-time scanner is set to scan a limited list of file types. It should be set to scan *all* file types. If a virus is hiding inside a file that isn't automatically scanned, it can infect your computer.

○ There is no password to protect the configuration or removal of the program.

○ The personal firewall is too technical for home users to operate. (See the antivirus section below.)

○ The "site filter" doesn't come with a blacklist, meaning you have to manually type in the websites (URLs) you wish to block.

Antivirus

Trend Micro has built PC-cillin specifically for the home user, and it really shows. The product is easy to use with an uncluttered, basic user interface. By default, the product is configured to check the Trend Micro website for new updates every three hours. You can also configure the program to automatically update itself and not bother to tell you. This "set and forget" feature is very useful, because you really don't want to be bothered by your antivirus product when you are in the middle of doing something else.

As noted earlier, the "site filter" doesn't come with a blacklist and only enables you to prevent children from accessing websites that you manually select as being inappropriate for your kids to view. In addition, site filter doesn't come with any of the other Internet filtering features I recommend (see Chapter 4 on content filtering for more information). The site filter is turned off by default, and I suggest that you leave it off and use another content-filtering product instead.

PC-cillin also comes with a very, very basic personal firewall. Unfortunately, it is more like a commercial firewall than one designed for home users. Rather than enabling you to control what Internet applications—such as newsgroups and FTP—are allowed, you have to understand how ports, services, and protocols work before you can configure the firewall to allow or block such applications.

If you're not familiar with ports, services, and protocols, I suggest you leave the firewall off and use a different one instead (see the chapter on firewalls). However, if you are fairly technically literate, and especially if you use your laptop for business as well as home use, PC-cillin could be exactly what you need. PC-cillin supports wireless connections (Wi-Fi), and you can reconfigure your firewall should you walk into an area where you want to use the Internet.

Support

Telephone

Telephone support in the U.S. is via a toll free 1-800 number and is available Monday through Friday from 5 A.M. to 5 P.M. Pacific Time. Telephone support for PC-cillin users in Australia is via a local call 1300 number. Unlike other antivirus companies, telephone support is free.

Website

The support section on the Trend Micro website is tailored specifically to each of the company's products. The Trend Knowledge Base provides access to information that is relevant to PC-cillin and doesn't require you to sort through unrelated web pages. Trend Micro also provides a list of Top Solutions Per Product so you can find the most common questions and answers quickly. Also, there is a list of contact details for Trend Micro offices worldwide.

User Manual

The PC-cillin user manual gives you "plain English" explanations of the product and its features. In addition, it educates you about safer computing and explains how it protects your PC, in language you can understand. Unfortunately, the user manual does not contain any screen captures (graphics), so you can't relate what you are reading to what you see on the screen.

eTrust EZ Antivirus

Overall Rating

Product: 4 out of 5
Support: 3.5 out of 5

Version Tested

2005 v6.2.0.28

Installation Process

EZ Antivirus is 4.2MB and took 2 minutes and 24 seconds to download. The installation process took seven minutes, which included rebooting the computer. This was lightning fast compared to the other antivirus software programs.

Pros

- ○ Very easy to use.

- ○ Automatically updates itself from the EZ Antivirus website on installation.

- ○ Updates can be scheduled to download on certain days or every 24 hours.

- ○ Users can protect the software configuration by using a password.

Cons

- ○ The user interface is a little outdated and could be simplified. Antivirus software should operate in the background without the user having to know how the computer works. As such, it's not necessary to display a list of files, directories, and disk drives on your computer.

- ○ Expensive telephone support.

Antivirus

EZ Antivirus belongs to an elite club of "old-school" antivirus software programs that have stood the test of time. Australians will recognize it as Vet from Cybec (a company that was purchased by Computer Associates in 1999). Vet was written in 1989, just after the stoned virus first appeared. In the same year, McAfee was founded and Symantec had its IPO and subsequently acquired Norton AntiVirus a year later. Those older computer users who are used to seeing files and folders on the screen will feel right at home with the user interface. To scan a floppy disk, you just click the disk and then click Go. The whole process is very simple.

Support

The EZ Antivirus website offers many resources for users, including the following:

- ○ Getting Started tutorials
- ○ Online manuals
- ○ Top ten frequently asked questions
- ○ Knowledge base

If you are thinking of purchasing EZ Antivirus, be sure to check out the Getting Started video clip. It's a small video you can download from the Internet and play using Windows Media Player. The video shows a computer screen and gives you step-by-step instructions on how to update EZ Antivirus and scan your computer for viruses. You can access the video at http://www.my-etrust.com/tutorials.sammy.cfm.

Although EZ Antivirus has great website support, their telephone support is expensive. If you need telephone support on a regular basis, you will be charged U.S.$49.95 per issue. This can get to be quite expensive, especially for new users who are not comfortable downloading and installing software from the Internet. However, if you are comfortable purchasing software online and don't need the support, then EZ Antivirus is a bargain.

CHAPTER 8

Malicious Software Detection

A growing number of applications on the market today claim to eradicate spyware, and adware, and protect you from things such as keyboard (keystroke) loggers, hacking tools, Trojans, worms, and many other malicious software (also known as "malware").

You may ask, "Why doesn't my antivirus product detect this?" This is because these programs are not viruses! Yes, they can do damage, but they are not technically viruses; therefore, antivirus companies don't detect them. Unfortunately, many people don't realize that antivirus software isn't enough until it's too late.

Malicious Software

"Malware" is an umbrella term to encompass all types of malicious software. However, I have referred to malware in this book as malicious software other than viruses, worms, and Trojan horses. Strictly speaking, this is known as "nonviral malicious software."

Nonviral malicious software doesn't replicate like a virus or a worm. It's typically downloaded by accident, installed on your computer with another software package, or installed on your computer by hackers.

There are many different types of nonviral malicious software, including keystroke loggers, remote administration tools, spyware, adware, hacker tools, and DDOS (Distributed Denial of Service) agents.

Keystroke loggers record everything you type on your keyboard and are commonly used to capture passwords and credit card details.

Remote administration tools are programs that give someone the ability to take over your computer. This person can be physically located anywhere in the world; however, they can do anything that you can do at the keyboard.

Spyware refers to computer programs that gather information about someone without their knowledge. Information that is gathered can include personal information such as your name, address, and phone number.

Adware is similar to spyware, but it tells you (usually in very fine print at the bottom of a license agreement) that it is gathering and using this type of information for advertising, marketing, or other commercial purposes.

Hacker tools are programs that hackers use to break into computers. These include, but are not limited to, password crackers, sniffers, and scanners. Password crackers try to determine passwords, either by guessing (known as "brute force") or exploiting security flaws in computer software. Sniffers are programs that capture information sent between you and the Internet. Scanners (also known as "probes") are used to check if programs are running on a particular computer. Hackers then use this information to determine what security flaws are present on the computer.

DDOS (Distributed Denial of Service) agents (also known as "zombies") are programs that are installed onto your computer by hackers. These programs allow hackers to use your computer as part of a collective, global network of computers that can be used to attack other computers. For example, if a hacker wanted to cause a particular website to become inaccessible to the public, they could tell their armies of computers, all over the world, to flood it with useless information. This would consume all the available computing resources on the website and cause it to become unavailable.

How Malware Detection Works

Malware detection works in exactly the same manner as antivirus software. The computer program looks for a fingerprint that uniquely identifies malicious software. Once it finds the malicious software, it will ask you what to do with it, such as destroy it, view it, or keep it.

Software Brands Tested

Although a lot of malware-detection software is currently on the market, the majority of it is not worth mentioning. This is due to the fact that the market is in its embryonic stage, and a lot of people think they can make a quick dollar by creating software that removes spyware. To make matters worse, a number of vendors are being accused of blatantly copying other vendors' software. For example, the makers of Ad-aware posted a message on their website stating that Spy Cleaner and BPS Spyware/Adware Remover "have been cobbled together from stolen content, coding and design from our software and that of SBSD [Spybot Search & Destroy]."[1]

> tip | *Do not download malware-detection software from a website operated by a third party, other than those that the vendors link to themselves. Visit the vendor's website first and follow the instructions. This will ensure that you have original software, not a copy or a hacked version.*

Apart from vendors copying each other's software, a number of websites have been created on the Internet that mislead people into thinking they are downloading popular malware-detection software such as Spybot and Ad-aware.

While performing research for this book, I came across a website that appeared to make Ad-aware available for download. The words "Ad-aware" appeared in their domain name, and the website had a large screen capture of the Ad-aware product in the middle of their homepage. When I clicked the download button, a pop-up box appeared asking me if I wanted to install "Access to content" by SysWebSoft S.R.L. This wasn't Ad-aware, but a dialer program in disguise. I immediately wrote to Lavasoft (the makers of Ad-aware), and the site was quickly closed down.

It's obvious that the malware-detection industry is going to go through a shakeup in the next few years. In the meantime, it's extremely difficult for the average person to know which vendor to trust. Based on my experience, I've listed the top three software applications for home use, in alphabetical order, in Table 8-1.

Ad-aware is a free product. Its sister products Ad-aware Plus and Ad-aware Professional (which are not free) have more features, but they don't necessarily detect more spyware and adware. This is the reason why I tested Ad-aware and not the Ad-aware Plus and Professional versions.

Application Name	Version	Website Address
Ad-aware	6.0 Build 183	http://www.lavasoft.de
PestPatrol	v5 (1.0.0.21)	http://www.pestpatrol.com http://www.pestpatrol.com.au
Spybot Search & Destroy	1.2	http://www.spybot.info

Table 8-1   Malicious Software–Detection Programs

What Features Will Stop Malicious Software from Getting to You?

Although there are many types of malicious software, I have only listed some of the most dangerous for the purpose of this review. Table 8-2 shows the categories of malicious software these products can remove, and Table 8-3 details their major features.

	Ad-aware	PestPatrol	Spybot
Adware and spyware	Yes	Yes	Yes
Trojans and worms	Yes	Yes	Yes
Keystroke loggers	No	Yes	Yes
Hacker exploit code	No	Yes	No
Cracking tools	No	Yes	No
Denial of Service tools	No	Yes	No
Remote administration Trojans	Yes	Yes	No
Password-capture programs	No	Yes	No
Pirated software key generators	No	Yes	No
Internet dialers	Yes	Yes	Yes

Table 8-2   Categories of Malicious Software That Can Be Removed

	Ad-aware	PestPatrol	Spybot
	Scanning		
Scans for active processes	No*	Yes	No
Scans for registry changes	Yes	Yes	Yes
Scans inside archive (zip) files	Yes	Yes	No
Can ignore specific files	Yes	Yes	Yes
Remains in memory to detect new infections	No*	Yes	No

Table 8-3   A Feature Comparison of Malicious Software–Detection Products

	Ad-aware	PestPatrol	Spybot
Assessment and Cleaning			
Provides detailed information on spyware that has been found	No	Yes	Yes
Provides a website database of spyware	No	Yes	Yes
Quarantines spyware for recovery	Yes	Yes	Yes
Updates			
Manual	Yes	Yes	Yes
Automatically	No*	Yes	No

* The feature is available in the Plus and Professional editions.

Table 8-3   A Feature Comparison of Malicious Software–Detection Products
(continued)

How These Products Perform

In order to see how effective the products are in removing spyware and adware, I installed ten file-sharing applications on a new computer running Windows XP. Table 8-4 shows the spyware and adware that was found.

Spyware & Adware	Detection Programs		
	Ad-aware	PestPatrol*	Spybot
Avatar Resources	Yes		
BargainBuddy		Yes	
Brilliant Digital		Yes	
BroadCastPC	Yes	Yes	
Claria (Gator/Gain)	Yes	Yes	Yes
CommonName		Yes	Yes
Cydoor	Yes	Yes	Yes
DownloadWare		Yes	
eBates MoneyMaker		Yes	Yes

Table 8-4   Spyware and Adware Detected

Spyware & Adware	Detection Programs		
eUniverse_KeenValue (KeenValue.PerfectNav)	Yes	Yes	Yes
EUniverse.IncrediFind BHO		Yes	
eZula TopText	Yes	Yes	Yes
Flashtalk		Yes	
I-Lookup.GWS		Yes	
IPInsight		Yes	
MapQuest Toolbar		Yes	
MySearch		Yes	Yes
MyWay.MyBar		Yes	Yes
n-Case (180Solutions)	Yes	Yes	Yes
New.net	Yes	Yes	Yes
Radlight		Yes	
RVP		Yes	Yes
Shield-BLSS	Yes		
Shopathome (SahAgent)	Yes	Yes	Yes
TopMoxie	Yes		
TrojanDownloader.Win32.VB.ah		Yes	
VX2.h.ABetterInternet		Yes	Yes
Web P2P Installer		Yes	
Webhancer	Yes	Yes	Yes
WhenU.SaveNow	Yes	Yes	Yes
WhenU.WeatherCast	Yes	Yes	Yes
WurldMedia	Yes	Yes	Yes
XoloX		Yes	
Total (Out of 33):	**15**	**30**	**17**

*PestPatrol 4.3.0.8 was used to perform this analysis.

Table 8-4   Spyware and Adware Detected *(continued)*

Table 8-4 shows that PestPatrol detected more individual spyware and adware applications than any other program. It's very important to note that a single instance of spyware does not necessarily mean one file on your computer. One spyware program can be composed of many files, directories, and changes to the internal settings (registry) of the computer. Each program has a unique "signature," just like a fingerprint. This signature is used by malware detection software to detect the presence of the program on your computer. Table 8-5 shows the number of signatures detected by each product.

Program	Spyware/Adware Signatures
Ad-aware	19,085
PestPatrol	81,107
Spybot	12,171

Table 8-5   Malicious Software Detected By Each Project

You can see that there is a significant difference between these products. This is mainly due to the thoroughness of PestPatrol and the fact that it identifies file-swapping applications as being pests. File-swapping applications have a large number of files; therefore, the PestPatrol figure is huge compared to the others. The bottom line is that PestPatrol removes more file-sharing programs, along with their associated spyware and adware, than any other product I tested.

Additional Information

There is no widely accepted naming convention for spyware and adware. As such, malware-detection software has different names for the same spyware. For example, Ad-aware identifies a particular program as 180Solutions, yet PestPatrol and Spybot call it n-Case. There is no right and wrong; you just need to be aware of the different terminology for the purpose of making a comparison.

Support

Support is extremely important with any product. Luckily, these programs are very easy to use; in particular, Ad-aware should be congratulated on a fantastic user interface. Table 8-6 shows the different types of support available from Ad-aware, PestPatrol, and Spybot.

	Ad-aware	**PestPatrol**	**Spybot**
Knowledge base of malicious software	No	Yes	Yes
E-mail technical support	Yes	Yes	No
Telephone technical support	No	No	No
Online helpdesk	No	Yes	No
Online message boards/forums	Yes	No	Yes
Online tutorials	No	Yes	Yes
Online frequently asked questions (FAQs)	Yes	Yes	Yes

Table 8-6   Technical Support

Price

Your decision as to which product you choose can often come down to price. At the time of writing, Table 8-7 details what you'll pay for using the software for personal use.

	Ad-aware	**PestPatrol**	**Spybot**
Price	Free	U.S.$39.95 (includes one year of upgrades and technical support)	Free/donation

Table 8-7   Pricing

My Verdict

Comparing two free products against a commercial product such as PestPatrol is like comparing apples to oranges. PestPatrol detects more malicious software and has more features than both products combined. No other product in the marketplace comes close to PestPatrol. But, of course, you don't get all these benefits for nothing! So, here's my ranking.

First Place: PestPatrol

Second Place: Ad-aware

Third Place: Spybot Search & Destroy

PestPatrol just doesn't cover spyware and adware. It detects Trojans (which many antivirus software products don't), keystroke loggers, and Denial of Service tools, and it has a fantastic cookie management component. It's a great program and costs less than most antivirus products.

PestPatrol also offers a free online version called PestScan at http:// www .pestscan.com. PestScan will scan your computer for malware. If you want to remove the malware, you need to purchase PestPatrol.

Are Those Antivirus Software Claims for Real?

The makers of some antivirus products, such as McAfee VirusScan and Norton AntiVirus, now claim that their antivirus programs detect spyware and adware. I was initially skeptical about the ability of a virus scanner to scan for malware because a virus is a completely different type of program than spyware, although both can compromise your security and privacy. Consequently, I decided to test VirusScan and Norton AntiVirus against the file-sharing programs mentioned earlier. As indicated in Table 8-8, my results suggest that these virus scanners are still unable to identify the same number of programs that the leading malware-detection programs can locate.

Program	Files Detected
Norton AntiVirus	38
McAfee VirusScan	38
Ad-aware	242
PestPatrol	13,081
Spybot Search & Destroy	82

Table 8-8   Files Detected by Antivirus and Malware-Detection Software

Table 8-8 shows that both Norton AntiVirus and McAfee VirusScan detected significantly fewer programs than any other product tested. As you can see here, McAfee VirusScan showed a list of 38 potentially unwanted programs, and Norton AntiVirus showed a list of 38 files that are "at risk":

There is very little difference in the detection capabilities of McAfee VirusScan and Norton AntiVirus when it comes to spyware and adware. However, although Norton and McAfee's antivirus products do a great job at detecting and cleaning viruses, you are better off using Ad-aware or Spybot Search & Destroy to detect malware. However, all four of these programs have a very long way to catch up to PestPatrol, which detected significantly more spyware and adware than any other program.

Malicious Software–Detection Products in More Detail

Here are the results of my evaluations of each of the three products. I have included a screen capture of each product so you can see how easy they are to use.

Ad-aware

Overall Rating

Product: 3.5 out of 5

Support: 4 out of 5

Version Tested

6.0. Build 183. Reference Number: 01R256 09.02.2004

Installation Process

You can download Ad-aware from a number of sites on the Internet. The file is very small (1.67MB) and took me less than one minute to download. It literally took six mouse clicks and less than 20 seconds to install on my computer. This is faster than any program I have ever installed! Once Ad-aware was installed, it took 16 seconds for it to download the latest updates.

Pros

○ The user interface is easy to navigate.

○ Easy to update (just click Check for Updates Now).

○ Allows you to quarantine spyware and adware.

Cons

○ The scanning results provide very little information on what the spyware actually does (see the following section).

○ No telephone support.

Evaluating Ad-aware

One great feature of Ad-aware is the ability to quarantine spyware and adware. Many spyware and adware programs are bundled with commercial software. In some cases, when you remove these components, the commercial software stops functioning. If this happens to you, make sure you use the quarantine feature and restore the spyware and adware so you can gain back the functionality of the program. Presumably you would then remove the commercial program and find something else to take its place.

Ad-aware provides a quick-and-easy method of checking your system for common spyware and adware. Should you detect spyware on your system, Ad-aware won't necessarily tell you exactly what it does. For example, when Ad-aware finds a cookie, the description reads, "This cookie is known to collect information used either for targeted advertising, or tracking users across a particular website, such as page views or ad click-thrus." The description doesn't help the user to determine if the cookie is legitimate or part of an advertising campaign. Although you can erase all your cookies to be on the safe side, it may mean that you have to enter your user ID and password into certain websites that would otherwise remember you.

Support for Ad-aware

Ad-aware has e-mail support, online forums, and a set of frequently asked questions to help users. It also has a detailed help file that comes with the product. Ad-aware is so easy to use, I can't imagine anyone having problems with it.

PestPatrol

Overall Rating

Product: 4.5 out of 5
Support: 4.5 out of 5

Version Tested

v5 (1.0.0.21)

PestPatrol - Protecting your computer from hidden threats...

Pest **Patrol**™

Welcome   Scan   Advanced Settings

Active Protection

Active Protection: Protecting your computer

Updates
   Your last update was on:

License
   Evaluation Version. Your trial will expire in 30 days.

[Register and Enter License Key]   [Buy Now]

The Authority In Spyware Protection

Resources & Tools

View Our Product Tour

Contact Support

Search our online pest database

Glossary

Visit www.PestPatrol.com

Sign up for PestPatrol's newsletter

(Help)   (About)

© 2004 PestPatrol, Inc.

Installation Process

The installation file was 4.2MB, and it took fewer than three minutes to download using a 256k ADSL connection. After installing PestPatrol, I noticed that "Active Protection" had been turned off by default. I was able to quickly fix this by clicking on "Advanced Settings" and then clicking on "Active Protection."

PestPatrol version 5 is a significant improvement over the previous version. The two most noticeable changes are the complete redesign of the user interface and an automatic update feature, which enables the program to automatically update itself rather than running a separate updater program.

Pros

○ Extremely easy to use and configure.

○ Can automatically download and install the latest updates.

○ Remains active (in memory) looking for malicious software.

Cons

○ Prolonged use can slow down the computer slightly.

○ No telephone support.

PestPatrol is an excellent product. It's easy to use and detects more malicious software than any other product in the marketplace. One great feature of PestPatrol is that it also detects cookies that are a threat to your privacy. This is done in real time while you browse a website. It happens when the website sends you a file (cookie) containing information. The cookie is intercepted by PestPatrol and compared to its database of malware. If the cookie is a threat, it's blocked. Cookies that are not a threat to your privacy are not blocked (for example, those used to automatically log you into a website). It's this "intelligence" that separates PestPatrol from other programs that block cookies or claim to protect your privacy.

One concern I have with PestPatrol is that it doesn't provide a lot of information on what the "pest" actually does. For example, after I installed the P2P file-sharing program Kazaa Plus, PestPatrol detected that I had Xolox (among other things) installed on my computer. When I checked the PestPatrol website it said, "In an organization, can degrade network performance and consume vast amounts of storage. May create security issues as outsiders are granted access to internal files. Often bundled with Adware or Spyware."[2] Unfortunately, there was no information that would help me to understand what the program actually does or if it's a security risk. In case you are wondering, Xolox is a P2P client that enables people to connect to and search P2P networks. The company, XoloX B.V, can be found at http://www.xolox.nl.

Support for Pest Patrol

The online support for PestPatrol is excellent. There are a number of frequently asked questions, how-to documents, and an online support desk. The support area of the website also has documentation relating to running PestPatrol with popular firewall products, antivirus products, and other spyware-detection products. The only area where PestPatrol falls short is that they don't handle support questions on the phone. This could be an issue for beginners; however, there is a lot of information online, including a helpdesk that aims to answer problems within 24 hours.

Spybot Search & Destroy

Overall Rating

Product: 3 out of 5
Support: 3 out of 5

Version Tested

1.2

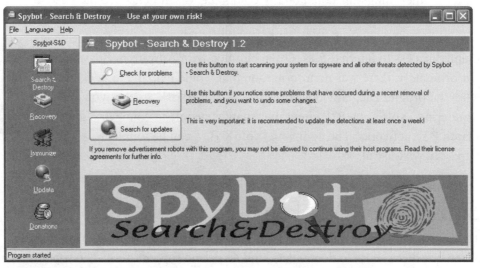

© 2000–2004 Patrick M. Kolla

Installation Process

The installation file is 3.49MB and took me less than three minutes to download. It took nine seconds to install this product on my computer. After the installation was completed, it took one minute to download all the updates from the Internet.

Pros

- Available in multiple languages.

- Displays detailed information on spyware found on your computer.

- Has an additional feature that finds hidden spyware and adware components.

- Removes "usage tracks" from many applications.

- It's free. The vendor will accept a donation, but it's not required.

Cons

○ User interface is cluttered and difficult to navigate.

○ No telephone support.

Evaluating Spybot Search & Destroy

One look at the Spybot website and you will see that a lot of effort has gone into tracking down third-party software including spyware and adware. Spybot posts regular updates on their website with the latest malicious code.

One particular feature that stands out is Spybot's ability to display Browser Helper Objects (BHOs) and installed ActiveX components. These components are often used by spyware to hide themselves deep within your computer. Now you can see what is in these locations and remove the programs if necessary.

Spybot has a less-than-ideal graphical user interface. First-time users may find it hard to use, because it doesn't follow conventional design rules. For example, a number of drop-down menus and buttons appear at the bottom of the screen instead of the top. If you are having trouble using Spybot, I recommend you try Ad-aware or PestPatrol.

Support for Spybot Search & Destroy

Support for Spybot relies heavily on a set of frequently asked questions and a website forum. Unfortunately, it doesn't have telephone support. Novice computer users may find Spybot frustrating to use because the user interface is cluttered, with buttons everywhere.

The documentation is written for a computer-literate audience and could be improved; however, I strongly suggest you use the online forums if you are in need of support. It's likely that the problem you are experiencing has already been answered. Many people use the Spybot forums to talk about spyware and adware, so finding someone to help you shouldn't be a problem.

Endnotes

1. Lavasoft, 2003. "Warning! 'bps Spyware Remover,' You may have been deceived!" Lavasoft. http://www.lavasoftsupport.com/index.php?act=ST&f=9&t=3912. February 13, 2003.

2. PestPatrol, 2004. "Xolox." http://www.pestpatrol.com/pestinfo/x/xolox.asp. 21. June 2004.

CHAPTER 9

Putting Your Defense into Place

Now that you know about the threats to your children that exist on the Internet, you understand the need for education and appropriate software tools to combat these threats. As you've learned in the preceding chapters, these tools include content- and e-mail-filtering software to block inappropriate content, firewalls to defend against hacker attacks, antivirus software to detect and prevent viruses and worms, and malware-detection programs to find and remove spyware and adware. You also have learned more details about which products suit you best.

Patching the Security Holes in Your Computer

Most hackers, viruses, and worms find their way into your computer by exploiting security flaws (vulnerabilities) in your software. In most cases, the security flaws have already been identified and fixed by the vendor. For example, Microsoft distributes patches for their software using Windows Update and publishes them on the Microsoft Security website (see Figure 9-1).

Your computer can be set up to automatically download the latest security patches and will even install them for you. If your computer is set up in this

Figure 9-1   The Microsoft Security website

manner you are essentially protected against a virus or a worm that tries to exploit security flaws and infect your computer from the Internet. That doesn't mean you don't need antivirus software, however; it just means that the virus or worm might not be able to get into your computer in the first instance.

There are a number of ways you can download the latest security patches depending on what operating system you run. If you run Windows XP then you should

1. Start Internet Explorer.

2. Click on the Tools menu.

3. Click on Windows Update (shown in Figure 9-2) and follow the instructions.

Installing the latest security patches will take quite some time. If you have a fast broadband Internet connection you shouldn't have any problems. Once this process has completed you can relax because all the hard work has been done. Now it's a matter of telling your computer to update itself automatically.

Figure 9-2   Windows Update installs the latest security patches to protect your computer.

Setting Your Computer to Update Itself

If you want to set your computer to download the latest updates automatically, you have a couple of options. For example, if you are running Windows XP with Service Pack 2 installed, you can do the following:

1. Click on the Start button.

2. Click on Control Panel.

3. Click on the Security Center icon.

4. Click on the Automatic Updates icon under Manage Security settings.

5. Ensure that the button labeled Automatic is selected (see Figure 9-3).

6. Click on the OK button.

If you have Windows XP, but the Security Center icon isn't in your control panel, you can

1. Click on the Start button.

2. Click on Control Panel.

3. Click on Performance and Maintenance.

4. Click on the System icon.

5. Select the Automatic Updates tab.

6. Select the most convenient option to download and install the updates.

Figure 9-3   Automatic Updates enable your PC to download and install the latest patches from Microsoft.

The settings indicated above tell your computer to automatically download the latest updates, and after they are finished downloading, the settings then display a message asking you if your computer can install them.

How to Create an Effective Defense

What do you do now? What is your first step, and how do you pull all the elements together to create an effective defense?

Here is my recommended approach:

1. Install the latest security patches for your computer.

2. Install the software we've discussed on your computer, choosing the brand that meets your budget and needs:

   ○ Internet firewall

   ○ Content-filtering software

   ○ E-mail-filtering software

   ○ Antivirus software

   ○ Malware-detection software

3. Sit down and discuss the Internet and its risks with your kids.

4. Move that computer out of your child's bedroom or the spare room and into your family room. Go on the Internet with your kids—learn about what they like doing and teach them safe Internet practices. Also, monitor what your kids do on the Internet. Take an interest in what they are doing, and every once in awhile take a look for yourself or ask them—in an interested, rather than inquisitive way—what they are looking at. Of course, this depends on the age of your kids. You may decide to allow your children under the age of 12 to use the Internet only while being supervised by a parent. If you have teenagers, you may decide to show an interest each time they use the computer.

Part II

The Best Software to Protect Your Kids

> **tip** *Instead of watching over your kids' shoulders (which they'll probably resent), ask them what they like to do on the Net and have them show you a favorite site.*

5. Stay alert to news about Internet threats and measures that you can take to further protect your children. This book describes the threats and defenses I am aware of at the time of writing. Both the threats and the

appropriate defenses are likely to change over time, and you need to keep up to date with these to keep your children safe. For example, you can visit this book's website at http://www.keepyourkidssafe.com to stay up to date.

> **note** *When you install each of the software programs, make sure you configure them to download the latest updates as often as possible. This could be every 24 hours or as soon as you connect to the Internet. If you rarely use the Internet, or use it in short bursts, then ensure that you're on long enough for the software to automatically download the updates.*

After you install the software, turn on the "Content Advisor" in your web browser and use the free filtering options on popular search engines such as Google. (See Chapter 4 for step-by-step instructions for turning it on.)

What Do You Do If Your Kids Are Subject to an Internet Threat?

Unfortunately, despite everything you do to protect your children, they may still fall victim to an Internet threat. This might come about, for example, if they use a friend's computer that does not have Internet filtering software, a firewall, antivirus, or malware-detection software installed. Or, a new threat may emerge that you are not quick enough to combat. Following are my suggestions for how to respond.

If You Suspect Your Child Has Been Talking to a Child Predator

If you suspect, but can't prove, that a pedophile has spoken with your child, here's what you should do:

○ Relax. You don't want to make your child feel as though they have done something wrong.

○ Talk to your child about your suspicions.

○ *Listen* to what your child has to say.

- ○ Review any log files that are on your computer. If you don't know how to do this, then ask a friend, relative, or trusted, knowledgeable person.

- ○ Call the CyberTipline or visit http://www.cybertipline.com.

| note | *You can find more information on how to read log files by using online help, reading user manuals, or contacting technical support.* |

If Your Child Has Spoken with a Child Predator

If you know your child has been talking to a predator, here's what you should do:

- ○ Again, relax.

- ○ Praise your child for telling you.

- ○ Call the police.

- ○ Call the CyberTipline or visit http://www.cybertipline.com.

Even if the predator did nothing physically to your child—for example, they merely made some suggestive remarks—call the police and get them to investigate the matter. The predator may be a wanted pedophile. By calling the police, you might be giving them the information they need to find a suspect and thereby help other children who would otherwise fall victim to this person.

If you have log files that show your child has been chatting to a predator, these should help any investigation into the incident. If you don't have log files, the police may still be able to recover some information from your computer.

| note | *If you have discovered that your child may have been the victim of a predator, don't touch the computer.* |

Leaving the computer turned on preserves information that is still in the memory of the computer—information that could otherwise be lost if you turn the computer off. It's safe to disconnect it from the Internet, but leave the computer running.

If You Have Seen Child Pornography

If you have visited a website, received an e-mail, or come across an image or images you think could be interpreted as child pornography, immediately call the police and report it to the CyberTipline at http://www.cybertipline.com. In some

Part II

The Best Software to Protect Your Kids

countries, such as the U.S., Australia, and Britain, it is against the law to even view or possess such content.

Importantly, even if you delete it, the child pornographic image may still be stored somewhere on your computer. Call the police and have them investigate the matter. The last thing you need is an image of child pornography, secretly stored somewhere on your computer, for someone to find. Should it ever be discovered, you could be arrested. For example, Pete Townsend (guitarist and co-founder of the English rock band The Who) was arrested on suspicion of possessing indecent images of children. He claimed that he visited a number of sites but never downloaded the images.[1] Regardless of whether or not Pete Townsend is guilty of a crime, the lesson is clear: Call the police and do not touch your computer the moment a suspicious image appears.

At the end of the day, child pornography on your computer is a permanent record of a crime being committed against a child. For the sake of all our children, please report it.

If Your Child Has Viewed Pornography

To my knowledge there have been no controlled studies on the impact of pornography on kids. This is because such studies would violate ethical standards and possibly the law. While I certainly don't approve of kids being exposed to pornography, I doubt that the occasional pornographic image will have a significant impact on them. However, there have been some very rare and extreme cases where children have committed violent crimes, apparently as a result of exposure to pornography.

If your child has seen pornography, it's not going to be the end of the world. However, it's likely that they will have questions to ask you. You need to address these questions in an environment that makes them feel comfortable. Even if your child doesn't have any questions, they need to know what is right and what is wrong. Talk to them about their feelings, attitudes, and reinforce that what they have seen is not appropriate for them to see and may even be illegal.

If your child is traumatized or doesn't want to talk about it, you should take them to counseling straight away. A number of counseling services and resources are available. Speak to your school counselor, kids help line, or even the police.

If Your Child Has Downloaded a Virus, Worm, or Trojan

If you have antivirus software installed on your computer and it is up to date, you should be fine. Antivirus software looks for viruses in the background and is usually set to clean them by default. If your antivirus software has displayed a message on the screen, either it's informing you as a courtesy or it's asking you what to do. In this instance, you just need to follow the prompts to clean the virus or tell the antivirus software to delete the file if it can't be cleaned.

| caution | *If you don't have antivirus software installed on your computer, you need to turn the computer off, read Chapter 8 on antivirus software, and go and buy some today.* |

If you don't know if your antivirus software is working or if it's up to date, then update it anyway. Connect to the Internet, start your antivirus software, and then click the automatic update button. The software should update itself automatically. If not, read the manual or contact the antivirus company's technical support.

If you have a virus, you must take action right now. Don't delay, because the next time you use your computer, a virus or worm could have already infected it. You should not use your computer until you have an up-to-date virus scanner installed.

A Note about the Police

Most of the police units I have encountered lack the staff, time, resources, and, in some cases, the technical abilities, to investigate all Internet-related cases that come across their desk. For example, Operation Ore in the UK reported 250,000 suspected Internet pedophiles. It took six months to identify just 10 percent of them.

In most cases, the police won't be able to deal with viruses, worms, Trojans, complaints about children downloading pornography, and other "minor" concerns. However, they take child pornography very seriously—and rightly so. So don't hesitate to contact them if you come across a case of child pornography. Specialist agencies in the following countries handle child pornography:

- **USA**   CyberTipline at http://www.cybertipline.com

- **UK**   Internet Watch Foundation (IWF) at http://www.iwf.org.uk

- **Australia**   The Australian Federal Police (AFP) at http://www.afp.gov.au

Part II

The Best Software to Protect Your Kids

There are also a number of victim advocacy agencies that pass on information to law enforcement officers. The United States Internet Crimes Task Force (USICT) is one such agency. To date they have closed more than 50,000 websites and chat rooms containing child pornography. If you experience anything from e-commerce fraud, cyber bullying, to spam e-mail, you can file a report on the USICT website at http://www.usict.org. On very rare occasions, the police might not be able to take action against a suspected predator. This could be due to insufficient information about the individual concerned. For example, if the predator lives in a country that does not have a relationship with the police force or government in your country, it is unlikely that you will be able to prosecute the individual. However, remember that there is nothing stopping your police force from referring the matter to the police in the country in which the predator resides!

Ernie Allen, president of the U.S. National Center for Missing and Exploited Children (NCMEC), says that it's very common for Internet-related cases to branch out into other states and/or countries. "The Exploited Child Unit maintains a database of law enforcement officers around the world who investigate child sexual exploitation cases. If a detective in Michigan finds his investigation spreading to an offender in England, the ECU will provide contact information for trained investigators in the UK."

Conclusion

Thank you for taking the time to read this book. You now have information and tools you can use to help keep your children safe from predators, cyberstalkers, inappropriate content, viruses, malware, and other Internet threats.

The Internet and the threats that exist on the Internet are only likely to grow. It is your responsibility to educate your children about the dangers of the Internet. Although I have filled a lot of pages with software evaluations, I can't stress enough that education is the key, not computer software and certainly not "banning the Internet" altogether. Internet filters, virus scanners, and firewalls reduce the risk, but they don't eliminate it. There will always be ways around computer software; it's not 100 percent foolproof, and you shouldn't rely on it as a baby-sitter.

By the same token, the sky is not falling. The Internet isn't a bad place, and the people who use it aren't all bad either. Unfortunately, with the Internet still in its infancy and without any one body regulating its use, it is still a wild, undiscovered, and unregulated frontier. If your kids are going to interact on this frontier, they need to be educated. You're not going to be with your kids 24 hours a day, and the best thing you can do is educate them and implement some software solutions to minimize the risk of exposure.

I truly hope this book helps you to protect your kids. Feel free to pass it on to other parents, friends, and families who could benefit. The more educated we become, the more we can win this battle. Please also visit the website for this book at http://www.keepyourkidssafe.com. It contains hints, tips, free software, and the latest methods available to keep your kids safe on the Internet. Feel free to send me an e-mail at simon@keepyourkidssafe.com. I'd really appreciate your feedback.

Endnotes

1. Associated Press, 2003. "Pete Townsend Released After Being Arrested on Suspicion of Possessing Child Porn." Fox News Channel. http://www.foxnews.com/story/0,2933,75380,00.html. August 24, 2003.

Part II

The Best Software to Protect Your Kids

APPENDIX

Spyware and Adware

When you install peer-to-peer file-sharing software, it often asks you to read through a license agreement or click "I accept" to acknowledge that third-party software will also be installed. This is typically how spyware and adware gets onto your computer.

Kids are typically attracted to these file-sharing programs because they are free and allow them to download the latest music. Of course, most kids wouldn't understand the pages and pages of legalese that license agreements are often written in. Popular peer-to-peer applications include BearShare, Blubster, eDonkey, Gnutella, Grokster, iMesh, Kazaa, Limewire, Morpheus, Overnet, and WinMX.

Table A-1 shows common peer-to-peer file-swapping applications and some of the third-party software, including spyware or adware, housed within them.

The information in this table was compiled by scanning file-sharing software with malware-detection software such as Ad-aware, PestPatrol, and Spybot Search and Destroy.

A number of malware-detection programs reported finding third-party programs, including spyware and adware, installed on my computer but didn't provide any information on what the programs actually did. The programs included Avatar Resources, Flashtalk, MapQuest Toolbar, MySearch, MyWay.MyBar, RVP, Shield-BLSS, TrojanDownloader.Win32.VB.ah, Web P2P Installer, WhenU .WeatherCast, VX2.h.AbetterInternet, and Xolox. Unfortunately, there is no way for me to check what these programs actually do without obtaining the source code (the program's instructions) from the vendors. Consequently, I've had to rely on a variety of resources, including news reports, databases, and websites that specialize in reporting information about third-party software, adware, and spyware. As such, I cannot guarantee the accuracy of this information.

After completing my research, Sharman Networks, owners and distributors of Kazaa, informed me that "CommonName, DownloadWare, IncrediFindBHO, I-Lookup, MyWay.MyBar and Xolox are not included in the Kazaa software." They also added that "BrilliantDigital is not adware, it is the mechanism to obtain guaranteed, legal, licensed and quality content," and that Web P2P Installer is not spyware or adware, but "the technology Sharman uses to install the Kazaa Media Desktop and distribute anti-virus definition files."

	Kazaa	Piolet	eDonkey	Grokster	IMesh	Bearshare	Blubster	Overnet	Limewire	Morpheus
Avatar Resources				Yes						
BargainBuddy		Yes								
BroadCastPC										Yes
BrilliantDigital	Yes			Yes						
Claria (Gator/Gain)	Yes			Yes	Yes					
CommonName	Yes									
Cydoor	Yes			Yes	Yes		Yes			
Downloadware	Yes			Yes	Yes		Yes			
eBates Moneymaker				Yes			Yes		Yes	Yes
eUniverse.Incredi Find BHO	Yes									
eUniverse_KeenValue	Yes									
EzuLa (TopText)			Yes					Yes		
Flashtalk							Yes			
I-Lookup.GWS	Yes									
IPInsight			Yes		Yes			Yes		
MapQuest Toolbar				Yes						
MySearch	Yes			Yes			Yes			
MyWay.MyBar	Yes			Yes	Yes		Yes			Yes

Table A-1   Third-party Software, Spyware, and Adware Included in P2P File-Sharing Programs

Part II

The Best Software to Protect Your Kids

	Kazaa	Piolet	eDonkey	Grokster	IMesh	Bearshare	Blubster	Overnet	Limewire	Morpheus
n-case (180Solutions)								Yes		
New.Net			Yes		Yes			Yes		
Radlight			Yes		Yes			Yes		
RVP										Yes
Shopathome (SahAgent)					Yes					
Shield-BLSS			Yes							
TopMoxie				Yes			Yes			Yes
TrojanDownloader .Win32.VB.ah				Yes						
Web P2P Installer	Yes			Yes						
Webhancer			Yes		Yes			Yes		
WhenU.SaveNow or SaveNow		Yes		Yes		Yes		Yes	Yes	Yes
WhenU.Weather Cast						Yes				
WurldMedia				Yes						
VX2.h.ABetter-Internet							Yes			
Xolox	Yes			Yes		Yes			Yes	Yes
Total (Out of 33)	**12**	**3**	**6**	**15**	**9**	**3**	**8**	**7**	**3**	**7**

Table A-1   Third-party Software, Spyware, and Adware Included in P2P File-Sharing Programs *(continued)*

BargainBuddy

BargainBuddy is offered by eXact Advertising, LLC. It displays advertising based on the websites you visit and the keywords you enter into your web browser. When your computer starts up, the software automatically downloads advertising and updates to the BargainBuddy program in the background.[1]

The BargainBuddy End User License Agreement states that it "does not collect personally identifiable information from you and does not store any personally identifiable information that records your browsing behavior."[2]

If you find BargainBuddy on your computer and no longer want to receive pop-up advertising, I suggest you remove it.

BroadCastPC

BroadCastPC displays advertising in the form of video on your computer. The advertisements are targeted to your web-browsing habits and are displayed on your computer regardless of whether or not you are connected to the Internet.[3] The BroadCastPC End User License Agreement states, "BroadCastPC anonymously categorizes the interests of its users, based on Web browsing usage, in order to deliver Desktop Video that is more appealing to its users' preferences."

The BroadCastPC website states, "BroadCastPC is not adware, and it is not spyware. We offer an exciting and trusted application that utilizes a small portion of your available disk space."[4] In one sense, I'd agree that BroadCastPC isn't spyware in that it doesn't appear to record any personal information. However, the fact that it displays advertising, in the form of video footage, would classify it, in my opinion, as adware.

BrilliantDigital

BrilliantDigital Entertainment, Inc. is the organization behind the b3d projector. This software allows you to view animation, movies, and other Internet content on your computer.

There were a small number of security concerns with old versions of the b3d projector. Consequently, you may come across a number of outdated websites that incorrectly allege that it's adware or spyware.

However, there are currently no known privacy or security issues with the current version of the b3d projector. Although it's known to be included with a number of file-sharing programs, if you find it on your computer, you shouldn't have anything to worry about.

Claria (Gator/GAIN)

The Claria Corporation (formerly known as the Gator Corporation) distributes free software such as Dashbar, DateManager, eWallet, PrecisionTime, SearchScout, and WeatherScope. GAIN (Gator Advertising Information Network) provides advertising for these applications, which are described in Table A-2.

At face value, this free software may perform a useful function; however, the software also displays advertisements on your computer based on your interests. In addition, when a user performs a search using popular search engines, the program displays the results from competing firms or websites.[5] Some people may argue that this gives them a choice and lets them know about competitive products. However, this practice may favor large companies that can afford to buy up advertising space and target their competitors' websites. Just imagine if you ran a business and when your customers visited your website, your competitor's advertisement popped up over the top of your website!

Product Name	What It Does
Dashbar	Dashbar provides a search box on your web browser and allows you to search for information using keywords.
DateManager	DateManager provides you with a calendar and appointment reminders.
eWallet	eWallet remembers your passwords and personal information so it can fill in online forms for you automatically.
PrecisionTime	PrecisionTime makes sure your computer's clock is correct.
SearchScout	SearchScout is Claria's search engine.
WeatherScope	WeatherScope provides a weather forecast.

Table A-2   Software from the Claria Corporation

Some web publishers have sued Claria (Gator)[6] claiming that its free software does the following:

○ Misleads website visitors into thinking that the ads have been delivered by the publisher.

○ Obscures ads that have been sold by the publisher.

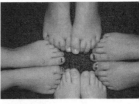

You can find more information about how Claria's advertising works by visiting http://cyber.law.harvard.edu/people/edelman/ads/gator/.

In recent times, a number of websites have used a technique known as a "drive-by download" to coax users into downloading Claria's software. In this case, the user browses a website and a box appears asking them to accept the file. To uneducated Internet users, the pop-up box may look like a plug-in that's necessary to view the website properly. However, this is not the case; it's actually a program that is trying to install itself on your computer.[7] Unfortunately, many users have clicked on the Yes button and have inadvertently installed the software onto their computer. This is clearly demonstrated by a recent survey of more than 34,000 users, which found that 75 percent couldn't recall installing software. You can see an example of the pop-up box in Figure A-1.

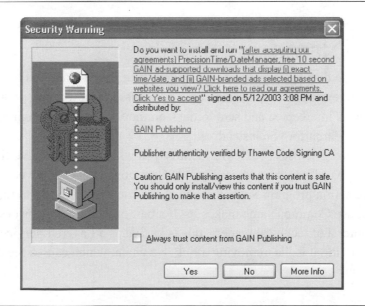

Figure A-1   Internet Explorer pop-up box with Gator message

The Gator Terms and Conditions[8] states that it obtains the following:

○ Some of the web pages viewed

○ The amount of time spent at some websites

○ Response to GAIN ads

○ Standard web log information (excluding IP addresses) and system settings

○ What software is on the personal computer

○ First name, country, and five-digit ZIP code

○ Non-personally identifiable information on web pages and forms

○ Software usage characteristics and preferences

I don't feel comfortable knowing that personal information and the web-browsing habits of my family are being recorded in order to target us with advertising. If you or your kids have installed some Claria software on your computer and you are also concerned about what information is being passed to Claria, then consider removing the software. You can find more information about Claria at http://www.pcpitstop.com/gator/.

CommonName

CommonName displays pop-up advertising on your desktop and redirects Internet searches.[9] For example, if you search on a particular keyword using your web browser, this is intercepted and sent to the CommonName search engine, which performs the search for you instead.

The product also uses cookies to identify you when you open advertising or enter a keyword into the address bar.[10] If CommonName is removed by the malware-detection program Spybot, it can cause you to lose access to the Internet. This is because CommonName makes itself a part of the innermost workings of your computer. For technical readers, this is known as a Layered Service Provider (LSP). Removing it is like removing a link in a chain, which causes the entire chain to break.

If you remove CommonName from your computer and find that your Internet access doesn't work, don't panic. You need to reboot your computer, run Spybot again, and scan your entire computer. Spybot should display a pop-up window stating that it has fixed the problem.[11]

Cydoor

Cydoor is integrated into peer-to-peer file-sharing products and requests that you "register" when the product is being set up. As a part of this process, it asks you for information, including your e-mail address, postal code, country, occupation, gender, age, marital status, education, and interests.[12] The product also monitors advertising metrics such as banners that you click on and what ads you were shown.[13]

The Cydoor Privacy Policy states, "Please be aware that Cydoor advertisers or Websites that have links in software on our network may utilize demographic information about you."[14] It doesn't say how it "may utilize" this demographic information.

The privacy policy also states that Cydoor "does not cover the information practices of those Websites linked from software on the Cydoor Network." Although it lists the names of its advertising partners, there are no links to their websites, privacy policies, or information on how they handle your personal details.[15]

Downloadware

Downloadware installs a number of other software programs, including Network Essentials, which scans your computer for file-sharing applications and reports on what is present.[16] The product also installs Casino Games and software known as KFH, which displays pop-up ads for casinos. The product also comes with MediaLoads or ClipGenie, which displays pictures in the background. In addition, it installs an e-mail program called WinEME; the purpose of this program is unknown.

Downloadware is also known to install three programs called MovieNetworks, Popcorn.net, and Real-Tens. These programs are known to add an entry into your Dialup Networking. If you use a dial-up modem to connect to the Internet and accidentally click the icon, the program will disconnect you from your ISP and dial a 1-900 phone number. This 1-900 telephone number charges approximately U.S.$25.00 to your telephone bill.[17] After your dial-up modem connects to the service (and charges your phone bill), it displays a user agreement asking you to accept certain terms and conditions for viewing adult movies.[18] If you accept the terms and conditions and click the Connect button, the service will automatically generate a user ID and password for you. This gives you access to "the world of extreme broadband videos" that the company describes as "grotesque and disturbing."

Even if you're not located in the U.S., you still can still access this "service" because the company has telephone numbers in countries including Australia, Canada, Germany, Sweden, and Switzerland.[19]

eBates MoneyMaker

The eBates website states that eBates obtains "sales commissions" from its partners and provides these to you in the form of a check when you make purchases from merchants affiliated with eBates.

The program is automatically included with certain peer-to-peer file-sharing software and displays advertising on your computer based on your interests.[20]

The eBates Terms and Conditions consist of many pages of tiny text. If you agree to these terms, you will find that, among other things, you have authorized eBates to do the following:

○ Disclose "to third parties information you have provided, or information that ebates has obtained about your ebates account or shopping behavior."[21]

○ "Disable, uninstall, or delete any application or software [that] might, in ebates' opinion, nullify its function and put you at risk of loosing the cash-back savings."

I don't feel comfortable knowing that a company is tracking the shopping habits of my family, obtaining commissions from our purchases, and sending information about us to third parties. I also believe that it's dangerous to allow a third party to automatically remove software from my computer.

It would be interesting to know if eBates would consider automatically removing malware-detection products; after all, malware-detection products remove eBates from your computer and "put you at risk" of missing out on their "cash-back savings."

eUniverse.IncrediFind BHO and eUniverse_KeenValue

KeenValue generates pop-up advertising on your computer based on the websites you visit. If you use a web browser such as Netscape to search for keywords, the program redirects your searches to its own "search engine" at incredifind.com. The program also adds a search box to your web browser, which allows you to search for sites using its own "search engine" at sirsearch.com. [22]

Apart from redirecting your searches, the program also diverts error pages to its own site.[23] For example, if you were browsing the web and came across a document that was no longer on a website, this program would replace the error message with its own page.

The KeenValue Privacy Policy states that it collects information on the following items:

○ Websites/pages you view

○ Your response to displayed advertisements

○ Standard web log information including IP address and system settings[24]

It also states that KeenValue "does not collect personally identifiable information." However, if you continue to read the rest of the policy, you will see that it has a number of measures to uniquely identify you and your computer when it's connected to the Internet.

Under the heading "Use of Cookies and Web Beacons," the privacy policy states that the company uses "cookies to collect and store information" and that the cookies "permit us to identify the user by recalling the user's email address and other information that the user has voluntarily provided. Cookies are also used to identify our software on your computer…." Under the next paragraph, titled "How

We Use Your Information," the company states that the information it collects "is associated with a particular personal computer through a randomly generated Anonymous ID number" and is used to do the following:

○ Generate advertisements that meet your personal interests

○ Generate ads and other contextual information that reflect your web-surfing habits

Although a "randomly generated Anonymous ID number" may sound safe, the company can still identify you by means of the unique number it assigns to you. Apart from this "Anonymous ID number," the company can also use information such as your IP address to uniquely identify you. This is because an IP address is a unique number that identifies your computer on the Internet. However, depending on your ISP, the IP address could change each time you connect to the Internet.

If you find KeenValue installed on your computer, I'd recommend that you remove it.

eZula

The "TopText" application integrates into Internet Explorer and superimposes yellow links on web pages that you view.[25] These links reference competitors' websites. For example, when I visited antivirus vendor Symantec, a link for McAfee AntiVirus appeared at the top of the Symantec web page.[26] Of course, these links do not appear normally and are not authorized by the website owner. Consequently, it may be difficult for your kids to distinguish between a link created by TopText and an actual, authorized link to content on the website.

The privacy policy on the eZula website states, "the eZula application collects information about its activity, such as the keywords that the application was activated on. When you react to the highlights then eZula will also collect a standard web log that may include more information about the action such as IP address, time etc." This "aggregated data" may be shared with "its advertisers, business partners, investors or otherwise as required by law."

eZula claims that it doesn't collect any "personal identifiable information" [sic].[27] However, it does say, "there are third-party sites or applications, which may collect personally identifiable information about you at that same time, with no connection to eZula. Although eZula's application may contain links to these sites, the information practices of the third-party sites or application are not covered by this privacy statement." These "third-party applications" could be the peer-to-peer file-sharing software that includes eZula, although this could also apply to other software contained within eZula itself. eZula doesn't list the names of these third parties as a part of the privacy statement. As a matter of common courtesy, eZula could at least display a list or even links to these websites.

Putting aside the privacy implications, if you don't want yellow links to appear on some of the web pages you view, then you may find that eZula doesn't add any real value to your Internet experience. Consequently, I suggest you remove it.

I-Lookup.GWS

I-Lookup displays pop-up advertising on your computer with some ads containing pornography. When I-Lookup is installed, it changes your home page and search sidebar in your web browser to use its own search engine.

Not a lot of information is known about I-Lookup. However, it has been reported that the product tracks your web browsing habits and reports them to a server (computer connected to the Internet). If your web browser security settings are low and you visit certain websites, the software may automatically download and install itself on your computer without your knowledge.[28] This is known as a "drive-by download." One particular pornographic website (whose name is too explicit to mention in this book) attempts to force your computer to download I-Lookup when you visit the site.

There is no privacy policy or Terms and Conditions document on the vendor's website, so it's hard to know what information is recorded and how it's used. The fact that I-Lookup has been reported to display pornographic pop-up ads on people's computers could be reason enough for you to remove it altogether.

IPInsight

The IPInsight website states that it records "Line Speed, Geography, Gender/Age estimates, User ID, and IP address information" in order to create a database of physical locations of IP addresses. This physical map of the Internet is then sold to advertising companies who want to target specific geographic areas with advertising.[29] According to IPInsight, this enables advertisers to determine "income groups, urban versus rural, the likelihood of children in the home, etc, all of which helps target advertising."[30]

The IPInsight Privacy Policy states that there "is no way for IPInsight to determine with any degree of confidence whether a child is using a computer at a given time." However, if "IPInsight becomes aware that it has inadvertently received personally-identifiable information from a user under the age of thirteen, IPInsight will delete such past data and/or information from our records and will cease to collect any new data from that computer, including any non-personally identifiable data."[31]

Although it's good that IPInsight acknowledges that children might be using their service, how many parents actually know that the software is even installed on their computer? Out of those parents who are aware that IPInsight is installed, how many are going to notify the company that their kids are using their computer?

If you don't want to assist advertising companies to target specific geographic areas with advertising then I can't see any reason why you should have IPInsight installed on your computer. You can remove it by using malware-detection software.

n-CASE (180Solutions)

180Solutions, Inc. is the organization behind n-CASE, which delivers targeted advertising based on the websites you visit, the order in which you visit web pages, and the keywords you enter into online forms. The program also displays targeted advertising on your computer, even when your web browser is closed.[32] n-CASE is also alleged to redirect your web browser to websites that are controlled by 180Solutions.[33]

I found the n-CASE Privacy Policy hard to understand. For example, the policy states that 180Solutions doesn't collect demographic information, but says that demographic information is linked to an anonymouse user ID: "180Solutions does not collect demographic information from you. This demographic information is linked to an anonymous user ID assigned to the n-CASE software installed on your computer, and is not connected or linked to PII about you. This demographic information may include, but is not limited to, your age, gender, geographic region and interests."[34] The definition of PII includes "demographic information such as date of birth, gender, geographic area and interests when such information is linked to other personal information that identifies you."

I find it confusing that demographic information is somehow linked to an anonymous user ID but is not "collected" by 180Solutions.

If you can make any sense of this, you are better informed than I. If in doubt, I suggest erring on the side of caution and removing n-CASE from your computer.

New.net

A number of malware-detection programs incorrectly identify New.net as spyware, adware, or other words to that effect. A report by PricewaterhouseCoopers LLP clearly states that the software "does not capture Personally Identifiable Information (PII) of its Users."[35]

New.net is basically a plug-in that gives the user access to subdomains that are hosted by New.net. Unlike top-level domain names such as .com and .net that anyone can view, the names sold by New.net can only be viewed by people using certain ISPs or by people who download and install the New.net plug-in.[36]

For example, if a user types in http://www.pie.shop into their web browser, this is intercepted by the New.net plug-in and translated into http://www.pie.shop.new.net. Without the plug-in, the user wouldn't be able to access anything by typing in http://www.pie.shop because the .shop domain name is not a domain name that has been approved by ICANN, and therefore doesn't exist in the ICANN-governed namespace. However, the user could access www.pie.shop.new.net because the .new.net domain name is an ICANN-approved domain name.

> note | *ICANN stands for the Internet Corporation for Assigned Names and Numbers and is the organization responsible for managing and coordinating the domain name system.*

The New.net Software Use Privacy Policy states that the software transmits "limited non-personally identifiable information, such as your IP address, type of browser and operating system, unique software ID, version of the New.net Software, internal software status indicators (including error codes to determine if the Software has encountered any internal errors), a tag that identifies any New.net distribution partner from whom you may have downloaded or installed the Software, and keyword and error search queries entered in your browser (applicable to New.net

Part II

The Best Software to Protect Your Kids

Domains only) and Internet search queries entered in the Internet Search Toolbar." It also states that the information "may be used in aggregate form to, among other things, determine the total number of distributed and active copies of the Software, prepare utilization reports for our partners or affiliates (collectively, 'Partners'), diagnose and fix compatibility problems or other bugs in our Software, and perform statistical analyses to enable New.net to build higher quality, more useful online services."[37]

Apart from incorrectly identifying New.net as spyware or adware, some malware-detection products incorrectly try to remove New.net and cause damage to your computer in the process. If you would like to remove New.net from your computer, you need to follow the instructions at http://www.newdotnet.com.

If you have New.net installed on your computer, it's likely that it came bundled with third-party software such as peer-to-peer file-sharing software. If you remove New.net, the software that it came with may stop working. However, some software allows you to opt out or deselect the third-party software that's bundled with it, so you might have some luck reinstalling it.

In my opinion, New.net isn't a threat to your privacy or the security of your computer, but I don't necessarily recommend its use. Here is why: ICANN manages the Internet and decides what domain names are available for use. For example, ICANN allows top-level domain names such as .com and .net. However, ICANN may provide other top-level domains in the future, such as .shop. If ICANN allows a .shop domain, this is going to clash with the .shop domain offered by New.net. For example, if .shop is approved, most people using the Internet could go to www.pie.shop and view one site, whereas people with the New.net plug-in could go to www.pie.shop and view a completely different site.

I'm not the first (and am probably not the last) person to raise these concerns. The Internet Architecture Board and ICANN have already discussed this issue at great length. You can find a technical discussion about this issue at http://www.rfc-editor.org/rfc/rfc2826.txt. You can also read a very interesting letter from New.net to ICANN at http://www.icann.org/correspondence/schecter-letter-to-icann-16jul01.htm and the response from ICANN at http://www.icann.org/correspondence/levee-letter-to-schecter-23jul01.htm.

If you have New.net installed on your computer, and are worried about the potential for confusion if ICANN approves certain new top-level domains, I recommend that you uninstall it.

Radlight

Radlight is a company based in the Slovak Republic and produces a media player with the same name. The media player is free to use; however, it contains advertising.

In May 2002, Radlight was programmed to disable the malware-filtering software Ad-aware.[38] The manufacturer of Ad-aware was forced to update the program to prevent it from being disabled. Consequently, a number of software sites removed Radlight from their download sections—only to be put back online after the Ad-aware-disabling code was removed.[39]

If you have Radlight installed on your computer and are experiencing pop-up advertising that you don't want, I suggest you remove it using malware-detection software.

Shopathome (SahAgent)

The Belcaro Group, Inc. makes ShopAtHomeSelect, also known as Golden Retriever or sahbundle. The Privacy Commitment on the ShopAtHomeSelect website states that the software obtains a commission from your online purchases and gives "as much of this commission to you, as a ShopAtHomeSelect.com member, in the form of real cash [sic]."[40] In order to be a ShopAtHomeSelect.com member, you have to register and give your name, date of birth, street address, e-mail address, your interests, gender, and occupation.

The ShopAtHomeSelect privacy policy states that Belcaro records "certain information online and offline deriving from your navigation of ShopAtHomeSelect.com and our Affiliate Merchants, including but not limited to the number and type of offers you have responded to and completed, so that we can make future relevant and personalized offers to you."[41] The company also uses your personal information for its own "internal mailing and database purposes." ShopAtHomeSelect is bundled with peer-to-peer file-sharing software (so unless you read the entire license agreement, you may not even know it's there).[42]

If you have ShopAtHomeSelect installed on your computer, I'd recommend that you remove it. In my experience, it's difficult to obtain much money from affiliate commission schemes like this. This is because these schemes are usually dependent on the end user allowing cookies on their system and following particular web addresses in order to record the transaction. Even if you manage to get through these hurdles, you are relying on the vendor to track the money owed to you. Apart from all this, the commissions are so small, unless you spend a substantial amount of money online, it's probably not going to be worth all your time and effort.

Webhancer

Webhancer is "a leading provider of next-generation web site customer intelligence solutions." This is a fancy way of saying that it uses a program called the Customer Companion to gather information about the websites you visit.[43]

Although Webhancer claims that its "Customer Companion is never installed on a user's computer without explicit permission," the software installs itself silently in the background when you install peer-to-peer software. In this instance, it's up to the peer-to-peer file-sharing company that includes Webhancer in their product to inform you that the software is present. This is usually included as a part of the license agreement or displayed on the screen when you click on "I accept" to install the program.

If you wish to remove Webhancer from your computer, follow the uninstall instructions at http://www.webhancer.com/support/index.asp?s=34. Removing Webhancer by deleting the files from your system could result in a loss of Internet access, so it's very important that you follow these instructions.

WhenU.SaveNow or SaveNow

WhenU describes itself as "a global Desktop Advertising Network (DAN)."[44] Its SaveNow software displays an average of "two to three ads per user per day." The advertising is based on "several factors, including: URLs associated with Web pages visited by the user, search terms typed by the user into search engines, HTML content of the Web pages viewed by the user and the local zip code of the user."

The software runs continuously (even when the program it came with isn't running) and downloads new advertising.[45] Although the WhenU.com website says that it doesn't "transmit URLs visited by the user to WhenU.com or any third-party server,"[46] it records a list of websites in an encrypted file on your computer at SaveNow\savenow.db[47] and uses this list to target you with advertising. You can read a list of frequently asked questions on the WhenU.com website at http://www.pestpatrol.com/pestinfo/s/savenow.asp.

If you don't want pop-up advertising to be displayed on your computer then I recommend that you uninstall it.

WurldMedia

WurldMedia, Inc. owns a product called BuyersPort. The software "offers customers cash rewards or the opportunity to donate their accrued rewards to a select group of reputable charities simply by shopping online with BuyersPort's featured merchants."[48]

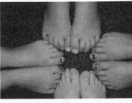

The BuyersPort software is commonly found when you install the Morpheus file-sharing program. It was originally designed to provide Morpheus users with rewards for shopping at participating merchants. The software uses a unique ID to track your computer and monitor websites that you visit.[49] Some people have accused the software of being predatory because it redirects your online purchases through a third party in order to obtain a commission from items you buy.[50]

The BuyersPort website states that the Morpheus Shopping Club has closed. As such, there is no need for you to have the BuyersPort software on your computer. You can uninstall it using malware-detection software, or you can download the uninstall program from http://morpheusshop.buyersport.com/info/info.html.

Part II

The Best Software to Protect Your Kids

Endnotes

1. PestPatrol, Inc., 2004. "BargainBuddy." PestPatrol, Inc. http://www.pestpatrol.com/pestinfo/b/bargainbuddy.asp. March 1, 2004.

2. eXact Advertising, LLC, 2004. "BargainBuddy End User License Agreement." eXact Advertising, LLC. http://www.exactadvertising.com/bargains/eula.htm. May 3, 2004.

3. Symantec, 2003. "Adware.Broadcastpc." Symantec Corporation. http://sarc.com/avcenter/venc/data/adware.broadcastpc.html. March 1, 2004.

4. BroadcastPC.com, 2004. "Not Adware or Spyware." BroadcastPC.com. http://www.broadcastpc.tv/using.html. May 3, 2004.

5. Olsen, Stefanie, 2003. "Search engines get 'Gatored.'" CNET News.com. http://news.com.com/2100-1023-980572.html. August 24, 2003.

6. Morrissey, Brian, 2002. "IAR Bits and Bytes." Internet Advertising Report. http://www.internetnews.com/IAR/article.php/10789_1503401. August 24, 2003.

7. Olsen, Stefanie, 2002. "Web surfers brace for pop-up downloads." CNET News.com. http://news.com.com/2100-1023-877568.html. August 25, 2003.

8. The Gator Corporation, 2003. "Gator Terms and Conditions." The Gator Corporation. http://www.gainpublishing.com/ help/privacystatement-hd_ 4.html?HDID=DM_PTE=4.0. March 1, 2004.

9. Spyware-guide. http://www.spywareguide.com/product_show.php?id=429.

10. PestPatrol, Inc., 2003. "CommonName." PestPatrol, Inc. http:// www.pestpatrol.com/PestInfo/C/CommonName.asp. March 1, 2004.

11. Borland, John, 2003. "Spike in 'spyware' accelerates arms race." CNET News.com. http://news.com.com/2009-1023-985524.html. August 24, 2003.

12. PestPatrol, Inc., 2004. "Cydoor." PestPatrol, Inc. http://www.pestpatrol.com/ pestinfo/c/cydoor.asp. March 1, 2004.

13. Cexx.org, 2003. "Advertising Spyware: CyDoor CD_Load.exe and CD_Clint.dll." Cexx.org. http://www.cexx.org/cydoor.htm. August 24, 2003.

14. Cydoor Technologies, 2003. "Cydoor Privacy." Cydoor Technologies. http://www.cydoor.com/Cydoor/Company/CompanyPrivacy.htm. August 24, 2003.

15. Cydoor Technologies, 2004. "Cydoor Privacy." Cydoor Technologies. http://www.cydoor.com/Cydoor/Company/CompanyPrivacy.htm. April 30, 2004.

16. PestPatrol, Inc., 2004. "Downloadware." PestPatrol, Inc. http:// www.pestpatrol.com/pestinfo/d/downloadware.asp. March 1, 2004.

17. Radlight, 2003. "Adware and Under-Wear—The Definitive Guide." SitePoint. http://www.sitepoint.com/article/888/6. August 24, 2003.

18. Mediacharger, 2004. "User Agreement." Mediacharger. http://mediacharger.com/terms.html. May 1, 2004.

19. MediaCharger, 2003. "How does MediaCharger work?" Vitalix, Inc. http://mediacharger.com/demo.html. August 24, 2003.

20. Mediacharger, 2004. "In which countries is MediaCharger available?" Mediacharger. http://mediacharger.com/international.html. May 1, 2004.

21. PestPatrol, Inc., 2004. "eBates MoneyMaker." PestPatrol, Inc. http://www.pestpatrol.com/pestinfo/e/ebates_moneymaker.asp. March 1, 2004.

22. eBates, 2004. "Terms and Conditions." eBates. http://www.ebates.com/terms_conditions.jsp. May 1, 2004.

23. PestPatrol, Inc., 2004. "EUniverse." PestPatrol, Inc., http://www.pestpatrol.com/pestinfo/e/euniverse.asp. March 1, 2004.

24. KeenValue.com, 2004. "License Agreement and Privacy Policy." Keenvalue.com. http://www.keenvalue.com/privacy.htm. May 2, 2004.

25. Olsen, Stefanie and Gwendolyn Mariano, 2001. "Peer-to-peer exchanges court advertisers." CNET News.com. http://news.com.com/ 2100-1023-271020.html. August 24, 2003.

26. Evangelista, Benny, 2001. "Mystery links. New Web advertising tool gets results, draws criticism." *San Francisco Chronicle*. http://www.sfgate.com/cgi-bin/article.cgi?file=/chronicle/archive/2001/07/30/BU231339.DTL&type=tech. August 24, 2003.

27. eZula, Inc., 2004. "TopText I-Lookup—Privacy Policy Statement." eZula, Inc. http://www.ezula.com/TopText/Privacy.asp. May 2, 2004.

28. PestPatrol, Inc., 2004. "I-Lookup." PestPatrol, Inc. http://www.pestpatrol.com/pestinfo/i/i-lookup.asp. March 1, 2004.

29. IPInsight, 2003. http://www.ipinsight.com/consumer.asp.

Part II

The Best Software to Protect Your Kids

30. IP Insight, 2002. "Consumer Policies." IP Insight. http://web.archive.org/ web/20021017122157/http://ipinsight.com/ consumer.asp. May 2, 2004.

31. IP Insight, 2003. "Children's Privacy Statement for Ipinsight." IPInsight. http://web.archive.org/web/20030603175610/http://www.ipinsight.com/ consumer.asp. May 2, 2004.

32. PestPatrol, Inc., 2004. "NCase." PestPatrol, Inc., http://www.pestpatrol.com/ pestinfo/n/ncase.asp. March 1, 2004.

33. Network Associates, Inc., 2004. "Adware-180Solutions." Network Associates, Inc. http://us.mcafee.com/virusInfo/ default.asp?id= description&virus_k=100696. May 2, 2004.

34. 180Solutions, Inc., 2004. "n-CASE Privacy Policy." 180Solutions. http://www.n-case.com/ncaseprivacy.html. May 2, 2004.

35. New.net, 2003. "User Privacy and Technical Compatibility Practices and Policies." PricewaterhouseCoopers. http://www.new.net/PWC_NewNet_ Software_Privacy_Attest_Report.pdf. May 2, 2004.

36. New.net, 2003. "Is the plug-in required to resolve New.net domains?" New.net. http://www.new.net/help_faq.tp#p2. August 25, 2003.

37. New.net, 2004. "Software Use Privacy Policy." New.net http://www.new.net/ policies_software_privacy.tp. May 2, 2004.

38. PestPatrol, Inc., 2004. "Radlight." PestPatrol, Inc. http://www.pestpatrol.com/ pestinfo/r/radlight.asp. March 1, 2004.

39. Borland, John, 2002. "In the trenches of techno-rebellion." CNet News.com. http://news.com.com/2009-1023_3-937861.html. June 25, 2002.

40. Spywareinfo.com, 2002. "Spyware Weekly Newsletter." http:// www.spywareinfo.com/newsletter/archives/may-2002/05022002.html. May 2, 2004.

41. Belcaro Group, Inc., 2004. "ShopAtHomeSelect.com Privacy Commitment." Belcaro Group Inc. http://www.shopathomeselect.com/privacy.asp. May 2, 2004.

42. PestPatrol, Inc., 2004. "SAHAgent." PestPatrol, Inc. http://www.pestpatrol.com/pestinfo/s/sahagent.asp. March 1, 2004.

43. Belcaro Group, Inc., 2004. "ShopAtHomeSelect.com Privacy Commitment." Belcaro Group Inc. http://www.shopathomeselect.com/privacy.asp. May 2, 2004.

44. Gibbs, Mark, 2004. "The cost of spyware." Network World. http://www.nwfusion.com/columnists/2004/0426backspin.html. April 26, 2004.

45. PestPatrol, Inc., 2004. "Webhancer." PestPatrol, Inc. http://www.pestpatrol.com/pestinfo/w/webhancer.asp. March 1, 2004.

46. WhenU.com, Inc., 2004. "Corporate Backgrounder." WhenU.com, Inc. http://www.whenu.com/backgrounder.html. May 2, 2004.

47. Borland, John. 2001. "Spyware piggybacks on Napster rivals." CNET News.com. http://news.com.com/2100-1023-257592.html?legacy=cnet. May 14, 2001.

48. WhenU.com. "About SaveNow." WhenU.com, Inc. http://www.whenu.com/about_savenow.html. March 1, 2004.

49. WurldMedia, Inc., 2004. "Benefits of BuyersPort Networks." WurldMedia, Inc. http://www.wurldmedia.com/bpbenefits.html. May 2, 2004.

50. PestPatrol, Inc., 2003. "WurldMedia." http://www.safersite.com/PestInfo/w/wurldmedia.asp. August 25, 2003.

Part II

The Best Software to Protect Your Kids

Index

References to figures and illustrations are in italics.

INTERNATIONAL CONTACT INFORMATION

AUSTRALIA
McGraw-Hill Book Company
Australia Pty. Ltd.
TEL +61-2-9900-1800
FAX +61-2-9878-8881
http://www.mcgraw-hill.com.au
books-it_sydney@mcgraw-hill.com

CANADA
McGraw-Hill Ryerson Ltd.
TEL +905-430-5000
FAX +905-430-5020
http://www.mcgraw-hill.ca

**GREECE, MIDDLE EAST, & AFRICA
(Excluding South Africa)**
McGraw-Hill Hellas
TEL +30-210-6560-990
TEL +30-210-6560-993
TEL +30-210-6560-994
FAX +30-210-6545-525

MEXICO (Also serving Latin America)
McGraw-Hill Interamericana Editores
S.A. de C.V.
TEL +525-1500-5108
FAX +525-117-1589
http://www.mcgraw-hill.com.mx
carlos_ruiz@mcgraw-hill.com

SINGAPORE (Serving Asia)
McGraw-Hill Book Company
TEL +65-6863-1580
FAX +65-6862-3354
http://www.mcgraw-hill.com.sg
mghasia@mcgraw-hill.com

SOUTH AFRICA
McGraw-Hill South Africa
TEL +27-11-622-7512
FAX +27-11-622-9045
robyn_swanepoel@mcgraw-hill.com

SPAIN
McGraw-Hill/
Interamericana de España, S.A.U.
TEL +34-91-180-3000
FAX +34-91-372-8513
http://www.mcgraw-hill.es
professional@mcgraw-hill.es

**UNITED KINGDOM, NORTHERN,
EASTERN, & CENTRAL EUROPE**
McGraw-Hill Education Europe
TEL +44-1-628-502500
FAX +44-1-628-770224
http://www.mcgraw-hill.co.uk
emea_queries@mcgraw-hill.com

ALL OTHER INQUIRIES Contact:
McGraw-Hill/Osborne
TEL +1-510-420-7700
FAX +1-510-420-7703
http://www.osborne.com
omg_international@mcgraw-hill.com